# Catalan
# Mini Dictionary

ENGLISH-CATALAN
CATALAN-ENGLISH

FLUO
EDITIONS

# Catalan mini dictionary

© 2015-2019 by Fluo Editions

Main editor: J. N. Zaff
Assistant editor: Natalia Baena Cruces
Cover and typesetting: Fluo Editions

ISBN-13: 978-1-07-538583-4
ISBN-10: 1-07-538583-0

First edition: July 2019

Fluo Editions
Granada, Spain
efluo.net

The ink used in this book is chlorine-free, and our acid-free interior paper stock is supplied by a Forest Stewardship Council-certified provider.

# Table of Contents

## Abbreviations

| | |
|---|---|
| *n* | noun |
| *v* | verb |
| *adj* | adjective |
| *adv* | adverb |
| *art* | article |
| *pron* | pronoun |
| *conj* | conjunction |
| *interj* | interjection |
| *prep* | preposition |
| *part* | particle |
| *num* | numeral |
| *det* | determiner |
| *phr* | phrase |
| | |
| *inf* | infinitive |
| *sp* | simple past |
| *pp* | past participle |
| *m* | masculine |
| *f* | feminine |
| *n* | neuter |
| *pl* | plural |
| *abbr* | abbreviation |

# English-Catalan

**abandon** /əˈbæn.dn̩, əˈbæn.dən/ •
  *v* abandonar, deixar ~**ment** •
  *n* abandó *m*
**ability** /əˈbɪl.ə.ti/ • *n* habilitat *f*,
  capacitat *f*
**able** /ˈeɪ.bl̩/ • *adj* capaç;
  competent
**abnormal** /æbˈnɔɪ.ml̩/ • *adj*
  anormal
**aboli|sh** /əˈbɒlɪʃ, əˈbɑl.ɪʃ/ • *v*
  abolir, suprimir ~**tion** • *n*
  abolició *f*
**abort** /əˈbɔːt, əˈbɔɪt/ • *n*
  avortament *m* • *v* avortar
  ~**ion** • *n* avort *m*, avortament
  *m*
**about** /əˈbaʊt, əˈbʌʊt/ • *prep* a
  punt de; sobre; de

**above** /əˈbʌv/ • *adv* dalt • *prep*
  damunt
**abroad** /əˈbrɔːd, əˈbrɔd/ • *adv* a
  l'estranger • *n* estranger *m*
**absen|t** /ˈæb.sn̩t/ • *adj* absent •
  *v* absentar ~**ce** • *n* absència *f*
**absolute** /ˈæb.səˌluːt, ˈæb.səˌlut/ •
  *adj* absolut ~**ly** • *adv*
  absolutament
**absorb** /əbˈzɔːb, æbˈsɔɪb/ • *v*
  absorbir ~**ent** • *adj* absorbent
  • *n* absorbent *m*
**abstract** /ˈæb.strækt, æbˈstɪækt/ •
  *adj* abstracte • *n* resum *m*;
  xifra *f*; abstracció *f* ~**ion** • *n*
  abstracció *f*
**absurd** /əbˈsɜːd, æbˈsɜɪd/ • *adj*
  absurd
**abundan|t** /əˈbʌn.dn̩t/ • *adj*
  abundant ~**ce** • *n* abundància
  *f*
**abus|e** /əˈbjuːs, əˈbjus/ • *n* abús
  *m* • *v* abusar; violar ~**ive** • *adj*
  abusiu

A

**academ|y** /əˈkæd.ə.mi/ • n
acadèmia f **~ic** • adj
acadèmic • n acadèmic m

**accelerat|e** /əkˈsel.ə.ɹeɪt/ • v
accelerar **~ion** • n acceleració
f **~or** • n accelerador m

**accent** /ˈæk.sənt, ˈæk.sent/ • n
accent m; titlla f • v accentuar

**accept** /əkˈsept/ • v acceptar
**~able** • adj acceptable

**accessib|ility** /æk.ˌses.ə.ˈbɪl.ət.i/ •
n accessibilitat f **~le** • adj
accessible

**accessory** /əkˈsesəɹi, əkˈsesɹi/ •
adj accessori • n accessori m

**accident** /ˈæk.sə.dənt/ • n
accident m **~al** • adj
accidental f • n accident m
**~ally** • adv accidentalment

**accommodation**
/ə.ˌkɒm.ə.ˈdeɪ.ʃən,
ə.ˌkɑm.ə.ˈdeɪ.ʃən/ • n
acomodació f

**accompan|y** /əˈkʌm.pə.ni/ • v
acompanyar **~iment** • n
segona f, acompanyament m

**according| to** • prep segons **~ly**
• adv apropiadament, tal com
correspon

**accordion** /əˈkɔː(ɹ).di.ən,
ə.ˈkɔɹ.di.ən/ • n acordió m

**accounta|bility**
/ə.ˌkaʊn.tə.ˈbɪl.ət.i/ • n
responsabilitat f **~nt** • n
comptable f

**accumulat|e** /əˈkjuːmjʊˌleɪt,
ə.ˈkjum.jə.ˌleɪt/ • v acumular
**~ion** • n acumulació f

**accura|te** /ˈæk.jʊ.ɹət, ˈæk.jə.ɹɪt/ •
adj exacte, precís **~cy** • n
exactitud f, precisió f **~tely** •

adv exactament, precisament,
acuradament

**accus|e** /əˈkjuːz, əˈkjuz/ • v
acusar **~ation** • n acusació f
**~ative** • adj acusatiu • n
acusatiu m, cas acusatiu m
**~ed** • n acusat m, acusada f

**achieve** /əˈtʃiːv/ • v acomplir;
obtenir, aconseguir **~ment** •
n assoliment m, consecució f

**acid** /ˈæs.ɪd/ • adj àcid • n àcid m
**~ic** • adj àcid **~ity** • n acidesa
f

**acknowledgment**
/əkˈnɒl.ɪdʒ.mənt,
əkˈnɒl.ɪdʒ.mənt/ • n
reconeixement m; agraïment
m

**acoustic** /əˈkuːstɪk/ • adj acústic
**~s** • n acústica f

**acquaintance** /əˈkweɪntəns,
ʌˈkweɪn.təns/ • n conegut m

**acqui|re** /əˈkwaɪɹ, əˈkwaɪə/ • v
adquirir **~sition** • n adquisició
f

**acre** /ˈeɪ.kə, ˈeɪ.kɚ/ • n acre m

**acrobat** /ˈæk.ɹo.bæt/ • n
acròbata f, equilibrista f **~ics**
• n acrobàcia f

**across** /əˈkɹɒs, əˈkɹɔs/ • prep a
través de

**act** /ækt, æk/ • n acte m • v
actuar; portar, comportar
**~ing** • n actuació f **~ion** • n
acció f

**activat|e** /ˈæktɪˌveɪt/ • v activar
**~ion** • n activació f

**activ|e** /ˈæk.tɪv/ • adj actiu **~ely**
• adv activament **~ist** • n
activista f **~ity** • n activitat f

**act|or** /'æk.tə, 'æk.tɚ/ ● *n* actor *m*, actriu ~**ress** ● *n* actriu *f*

**actual** /'æk(t)ʃ(əw)əl, 'ak(t)ʃ(ʊ)əl/ ● *adj* real ~**ly** ● *adv* de fet, en realitat

**acute** /ə'kjuːt, ə'kjut/ ● *adj* agut; tancat

**ad** ▷ ADVERTISEMENT

**adapt** /ə'dæpt/ ● *v* adaptar; adaptar-se ~**ation** ● *n* adaptació *f*

**add** /æd/ ● *v* afegir; sumar

**addicti|on** /ə'dɪkʃən/ ● *n* addicció *f* ~**ve** ● *adj* addictiu

**additi|on** /ə'dɪʃən/ ● *n* addició *f* ~**onal** ● *adj* addicional ~**onally** ● *adv* addicionalment ~**ve** ● *n* additiu *m*

**address** /ə'dɹɛs, 'ædɹɛs/ ● *n* adreça *f* ● *v* adreçar

**adequate** /'æ.də.kwɪt, 'æ.də.kweɪt/ ● *adj* adequat ~**ly** ● *adv* adequadament

**adhere** /æd'hɪɹ/ ● *v* adherir

**adjacent** /ə'dʒeɪ.sənt/ ● *adj* adjacent

**adjective** /'æ.dʒɪk.tɪv/ ● *adj* adjectiu ● *n* adjectiu *m*

**adjust** /ə'dʒʌst/ ● *v* ajustar ~**ment** ● *n* ajust *m*, ajustament *m*

**administer** /əd'mɪnɪstɚ/ ● *v* administrar

**administrat|ion** /əd.mɪnə'stɹeɪʃən/ ● *n* administració *f* ~**ive** ● *adj* administratiu ~**or** ● *n* administrador *m*, administradora *f*

**admir|e** /əd'maɪə, əd'maɪɪ/ ● *v* admirar ~**able** ● *adj* admirable

~**ation** ● *n* admiració *f*

**admission** /æd'mɪʃ.ən/ ● *n* admissió

**adolescen|t** /ˌædə'lɛsənt/ ● *adj* adolescent ● *n* adolescent *f* ~**ce** ● *n* adolescència *f*

**adopt** /ə'dɑpt, ə'dɒpt/ ● *v* adoptar ~**ive** ● *adj* adoptiu ~**ion** ● *n* adopció *f*

**adora|ble** /ə'dɔːɹəbəl/ ● *adj* adorable ~**tion** ● *n* adoració *f*

**adult** /'æd.ʌlt, ə'dʌlt/ ● *adj* adult ~**ery** ● *n* adulteri *m*

**advantage** /əd'vɑːn.tɪdʒ, əd'væn.tɪdʒ/ ● *n* avantatge *m*; benefici *m* ~**ous** ● *adj* avantatjós

**adventur|e** /əd'vɛntʃɚ, əd'vɛntʃə/ ● *n* aventura ~**ous** ● *adj* aventurer

**adverb** /'æd.vɜːb, 'æd.vɝb/ ● *n* adverbi *m*

**advers|e** /'æd.və(ɹ)s/ ● *adj* advers ~**ary** ● *n* adversari *m*

**advertisement** /əd'vɜːtɪsmənt, 'ædvɚˌtaɪzmənt/ ● *n* anunci *m*

**advice** /əd'vaɪs, æd'vaɪs/ ● *n* consell *m*

**advis|e** /əd'vaɪz/ ● *v* aconsellar ~**able** ● *adj* aconsellable ~**or** ● *n* assessor, conseller *m*

**advocate** /'æd.və.kət, 'æd.və.keɪt/ ● *n* advocat *m* ● *v* advocar

**aerial** /'ɛːɹ.i.əl/ ● *adj* aeri ● *n* antena *f*

**aerobic** /ɛˈɹoʊbɪk/ ● *adj* aeròbic

**aesthetic** /es.'θɛ.tɪk, ɛs.'θɛ.tɪk/ ● *adj* estètic ~**ally** ● *adv* estèticament ~**s** ● *n* estètica *f*

**affair** /ə'fɛɹ, ə'fɛə(ɹ)/ ● *n* afer *m*

**affect** /əˈfɛkt/ ● *n* afecte *m* ● *v* afectar **~ion** ● *n* afecte *m*; afecció *f* **~ionate** ● *adj* afectuós

**afford** /əˈfɔːd, əˈfɔːrd/ ● *v* permetre's

**Afghanistan** ● *n* l'Afganistan

**afraid** /əˈfreɪd/ ● *adj* amb por

**Africa** ● *n* Àfrica *f* **~n** ● *adj* africà ● *n* africà *m*, africana *f*

**after** /ˈæf.tə(r), ˈæf.tər/ ● *adv* més tard, després, acabat, en acabat ● *conj* després que, acabat que, en acabat que ● *prep* després de, acabat de, en acabat de **~noon** ● *n* tarda *f*, vesprada *f*, horabaixa *f* **~wards** ● *adv* després

**again** /əˈɡɛn, əˈɡɪn/ ● *adv* una altra vegada, de nou, un altre cop

**against** /əˈɡɛnst, əˈɡeɪnst/ ● *prep* contra; davant; en contra

**age** /eɪdʒ/ ● *n* edat *m* ● *v* envellir **of ~** ● *phr* major d'edat *f*

**agenda** /əˈdʒɛn.də/ ● *n* agenda *f*; ordre del dia *m*

**agen|t** /ˈeɪ.dʒənt/ ● *n* agent *m* **~cy** ● *n* agència *f*

**aggressi|on** /əˈɡrɛʃən/ ● *n* agressió *f* **~ve** ● *adj* agressiu **~veness** ● *n* agressivitat *f*

**agil|e** /ˈædʒ.aɪl/ ● *adj* àgil **~ity** ● *n* agulla *f*, agilitat *f*

**ago** /əˈɡoʊ, əˈɡəʊ/ ● *adv* fa

**agreement** /əˈɡriːmənt/ ● *n* acord *m*, pacte *m*; contracte *m*, conveni *m*; concordança *f*

**agreeable** /əˈɡriːəbl/ ● *adj* agradable; tractable

**agricultur|e** /ˈæɡ.rɪˌkʌltʃə, ˈæɡ.rɪˌkʌltʃər/ ● *n* agricultura *f* **~al** ● *adj* agrícola *f*

**ahead** /əˈhɛd/ ● *adv* en front de, al davant de

**aide** ▷ ASSISTANT

**AIDS** ● *n* (*abbr* Acquired ImmunoDeficiency Syndrome) sida *f*, SIDA *f*

**aim** /eɪm/ ● *v* apuntar

**air** /ˈɛə, ˈɛər/ ● *n* aire *m* ● *v* airejar **~ conditioning** ● *n* condicionament de l'aire *m* **~bag** ● *n* coixí de seguretat *m*, airbag *m* **~craft** ● *n* aeronau *f* **~line** ● *n* aerolínia *f* **~plane** ● *n* avió *m* **~port** ● *n* aeroport *m* **on ~** ● *phr* en directe

**aisle** /aɪl/ ● *n* nau *f*; passadís *m*, corredor *m*

**AKA** ● *adv* (*abbr* Also Known As) dit *m*, conegut *m*

**alarm** /əˈlɑːm, əˈlɑːrm/ ● *n* alarma *f*; despertador *m* ● *v* alarmar **~ing** ● *adj* alarmant

**Albania** ● *n* Albània *f* **~n** ● *adj* albanès ● *n* albanès *m*, albanesa *f*

**albatross** /ˈæl.bəˌtrɒs, ˈæl.bəˌtrɔːs/ ● *n* albatros *m*

**albeit** /ɔːlˈbiː.ɪt, ɔlˈbiː.ət/ ● *conj* encara que, tanmateix, però

**alcohol** /ˈæl.kə.hɒl, ˈæl.kə.hɔːl/ ● *n* alcohol *m* **~ic** ● *adj* alcohòlic ● *n* alcohòlic *m* **~ism** ● *n* alcoholisme *m*

**alert** /əˈlɜːt, əˈlɜrt/ ● *adj* vigilant ● *n* alerta *f* ● *v* alertar

**Algeria** ● *n* Algèria *f*

**alibi** /ˈæl.əˌbaɪ/ ● *n* coartada

**alien** /ˈeɪ.li.ən/ ● *adj* aliè, alié; alienígena, extraterrestre ● *n* estrany *m*, estranya *f*, foraster *m*, forastera *f*; extraterrestre *f* ~**ate** ● *v* alienar ~**ation** ● *n* alienació *f*

**alive** /əˈlaɪv/ ● *adj* viu, vivent

**all** /ɔːl, ɔl/ ● *det* tot *m*, tota *f*, tots, totes ● *n* tot **above ~** ● *phr* sobretot

**allege** /əˈlɛdʒ/ ● *v* al·legar ~**d** ● *adj* presumpte ~**dly** ● *adv* presumptament

**alleviate** /əˈli.vi.eɪt/ ● *v* mitigar, pal·liar

**alley** /ˈæ.li/ ● *n* carreró *m*

**allow** /əˈlaʊ/ ● *v* deixar

**alliance** /əˈlaɪ.əns/ ● *n* aliança *f*

**almond** /ˈɑː(l).mənd, ˈɑ(l).mənd/ ● *n* ametlla *f*; ametller *m*

**almost** /ˈɔːl.məʊst, ˈɔl.moʊst/ ● *adv* gairebé, quasi

**alone** /əˈləʊn, əˈloʊn/ ● *adj* sol, únic; tot sol; només

**already** /ɔːlˈɹɛdi, ɔlˈɹɛdi/ ● *adv* ja

**also** /ˈɔːl.səʊ, ˈɔl.soʊ/ ● *adv* també

**alter** /ˈɔːl.tə, ˈɔl.tɚ/ ● *v* alterar

**alternat|e** /ˈɒl.tɜː(ɹ).nət, ˈɔl.tɚ.nət/ ● *v* alternar ~**ive** ● *adj* alternatiu ~**ively** ● *adv* alternativament

**although** /ɔːlˈðəʊ, ɔlˈðoʊ/ ● *conj* tot i que, malgrat que, encara que

**altogether** /ˌɔːl.tʊˈɡɛð.ə(ɹ), ˌɔl.tuˈɡɛð.ɚ/ ● *adv* totalment, completament; en total

**aluminium** /ˌæl.(j)ʊˈmɪn.i.əm, ˌæl.(j)uˈmɪn.i.əm/ ● *n* alumini

**always** /ˈɔː(l).weɪz, ˈɔl.weɪz/ ● *adv* sempre

**ambassador** /æmˈbæs.ə.də(ɹ), æmˈbæs.ə.dɚ/ ● *n* ambaixador *m*

**ambigu|ous** /æmˈbɪɡjuəs/ ● *adj* ambigu ~**ity** ● *n* ambigüitat *f*

**ambitio|n** /æmˈbɪ.ʃən/ ● *n* ambició *f* ~**us** ● *adj* ambiciós

**ambulance** /ˈæm.bjə.ləns, ˈæm.bjəˌlæns/ ● *n* ambulància *f*

**amend** /əˈmɛnd/ ● *v* esmenar ~**ment** ● *n* esmena

**American** ● *adj* americà; estatunidenc, nord-americà ● *n* estatunidenc *m*, nord-americà *m*; americà *m*, americana *f* ● *n* anglès americà *m*

**amicable** /ˈæ.mi.kə.bəl/ ● *adj* amigable

**among** /əˈmʌŋ/ ● *prep* entre

**amount** /əˈmaʊnt/ ● *n* quantitat *f*

**Amsterdam** ● *n* Amsterdam

**amus|e** /əˈmjuːz/ ● *v* divertir, entretenir, distreure ~**ing** ● *adj* divertit, entretingut

**an** /æn, ən/ ● *num* un *m*, una *f*

**analogy** ● *n* analogia *f*

**analy|ze** /ˈæn.ə.laɪz/ ● *v* analitzar ~**sis** ● *n* anàlisi *f*; anàlisi matemàtica *f*

**ancest|or** /ˈæn.sɛs.tə/ ● *n* avantpassat *m* ~**ral** ● *adj* ancestral ~**ry** ● *n* llinatge *m*, ascendència *f*

**anchor** /ˈæŋ.kə, ˈæŋ.kɚ/ ● *n* àncora *f*; enllaç *m* ● *v* ancorar

**ancient** /ˈeɪn.(t)ʃənt/ ● *adj* antic, vetust

**and** /ænd, ənd/ ● *conj* i

**Andorra** ● *n* Andorra *f*

**angel** /ˈeɪn.dʒəl/ • n àngel m **~ic**
• adj angèlic, angelical

**anger** /ˈæŋɡə(ɹ), ˈæŋɡɚ/ • n ira f,
còlera f, ràbia f, enfat m,
enuig m • v enfadar, enutjar,
cabrejar

**angle** /ˈæŋ.ɡəl/ • n angle m; racó
m, cantonada f; biaix m; punt
de vista m

**Angola** • n Angola f

**angry** /ˈæŋ.ɡɹi/ • adj enfadat,
enutjat

**animal** /ˈænɪməl/ • adj animal •
n animal m; bèstia f

**animat|e** /ˈæ.nɪ.mət, ˈæ.nɪ.meɪt/ •
adj animat m • v animar **~ed**
• adj animat **~ion** • n
animació f

**ankle** /ˈæŋ.kəl/ • n turmell m

**anniversary** /ˌæni'vɜːs(ə)ɹi,
ˌænɪˈvɜs(ə)ɹi/ • n aniversari m;
aniversari de noces m

**announce** /ʌˈnaʊns, əˈnaʊns/ • v
anunciar

**annoy** /əˈnɔɪ/ • v molestar **~ing**
• v enutjós, enfadós, fastijós,
molest **~ance** • n molèstia f

**annual** /ˈæn.juːəl, ˈæn.ju.əl/ • adj
anual, anyal • n anuari m **~ly**
• adv anualment

**anonymous** /əˈnɒnəməs/ • adj
anònim

**anorak** • n anorac m

**another** /əˈnʌ.ðə(ɹ), əˈnʌ.ðɚ/ • det
un altre

**answer** /ˈɑːn.sə, ˈæn.sɚ/ • n
resposta f • v respondre

**ant** /ænt, ɛnt/ • n formiga f

**antagonis|t** /ænˈtæɡənɪst/ • n
antagonista f **~m** • n
antagonisme m

**Antarctica** • n Antàrtida f

**anteater** /ˈænt.iːtə, ˈænt.iːtɚ/ • n
ós formiguer

**antelope** /ˈæn.tɪ.ləʊp, ˈæn.tə.loʊp/
• n antílop m

**antenna** /ænˈtɛn.ə/ • n antena f

**anthology** /ænˈθɒlədʒi,
ænˈθæ.lədʒi/ • n antologia f

**anticipate** /ænˈtɪs.ɪ.peɪt,
ænˈtɪs.ə.peɪt/ • v anticipar,
preveure

**antithesis** /ænˈtɪ.θə.sɪs/ • n
antítesi f

**anxi|ous** /ˈaŋ(k)ʃəs, ˈæŋ(k).ʃəs/ •
adj ansiós **~ety** • n ansietat f
**~ously** • adv ansiosament

**any** /ˈɛni, ˈæni/ • det algun;
qualsevol f, qualssevol • pron
algun, qualque ~ **more** • adv
més, per més temps **~how** •
adv en qualsevol cas, de
qualsevol manera, tot i així
**~one** • pron qualsevol,
tothom, algú, ningú **~thing** •
pron qualsevol cosa, alguna
cosa, quelcom, tot, res **~way**
• adv de qualsevol manera,
en fi **~where** • adv onsevulga

**apart** /əˈpɑː(ɹ)t, əˈpɑɹt/ • adv a
part

**apartment** /əˈpɑːt.mənt,
əˈpɑɹt.mənt/ • n pis m

**apolog|y** /əˈpɒl.ə.dʒi/ • n
disculpa f; apologia f **~etic** •
adj apologètic **~ize** • v
apologitzar

**apparent** /əˈpæ.ɹənt/ • adj
aparent **~ly** • adv
aparentment

**appeal** /əˈpɪəl/ • n apel·lació f;
atractiu m • v apel·lar; abellir,

agradar

**appear** /əˈpɪə, əˈpɪː/ • v
aparèixer, sortir; semblar
**~ance** • n aparició; aparença

**appetite** /ˈæp.ə.taɪt/ • n gana,
apetit m

**applau|d** /əˈplɔːd, əˈpləd/ • v
aplaudir **~se** • n aplaudiment
m

**apple** /ˈæp.əl/ • n poma f

**applicable** /ˈæplɪkəbəl/ • adj
aplicable

**applied** /əˈplaɪd/ • adj aplicat

**appointment** /əˈpɔɪnt.mənt,
əˈpɔɪnt.mɪnt/ • n nomenament
m; compromís m; cita f,
consulta f

**appreciate** /əˈpɹiː.ʃi.eɪt/ • v agrair

**apprehen|d** /æ.pɹiˈhɛnd/ • v
aprehendre **~sive** • adj
aprensiu

**approach** /əˈpɹoʊtʃ, əˈpɹəʊtʃ/ • n
aproximació f, aproparment m
• v aproximar-se

**appropriate** /əˈpɹəʊ.pɹiː.ɪt,
əˈpɹoʊ.pɹi.ɪt/ • adj apropiat,
adequat **~ly** • adv
apropiadament

**approve** /əˈpɹuːv/ • v aprovar

**approximate** /əˈpɹɒk.sɪ.mət,
əˈpɹɑk.sə.mət/ • adj aproximat
**~ly** • adv aproximadament

**apricot** /ˈeɪ.pɹɪ.kɒt, ˈæ.pɹɪ.kɒt/ • n
albercoc m; albercoquer m

**April** • n abril m

**apron** /ˈeɪ.pɹən/ • n davantal m

**aqueduct** /ˈæk.wɪ.dʌkt,
ˈæk.wə.dʌkt/ • n aqüeducte m

**Arab** • adj àrab • n àrab f

**arbitrar|y** /ˈɑː.bɪ.tɹə.ɹi,
ˈɑː.bɪ.tɹɛ(ə).ɹi/ • adj arbitrari
**~ily** • adv arbitràriament

**arch** /ɑ·tʃ, ɑ·k/ • n arc m • v
arquejar

**archer** /ˈɑː(ɹ).tʃə(ɹ), ˈɑɹtʃə̩/ • n
arquer m

**architect** /ˈɑː.kɪtɛkt, ˈɑɪkɪtɛkt/ • n
arquitecte f **~ural** • adj
arquitectònic **~ure** • n
arquitectura f

**archive** /ˈɑː.kaɪv/ • n arxiu m

**area** /ˈɛə.ɹɪə, ˈæɹ.i.ə/ • n àrea f

**arena** /əˈɹiː.nə/ • n arena f

**Argentina** • n Argentina f

**argu|e** /ˈɑː.gjuː, ˈɑɹ.gju/ • v
discutir; argumentar, argüir
**~able** • adj argüible;
discutible **~ment** • n
argument m; disputa f;
argumentació f

**arithmetic** /əˈɹɪθmətɪk,
æɹɪθˈmɛtɪk/ • n aritmètica

**arm** /ɑːm, ɑɹm/ • n braç m; arma
f • v armar **~chair** • n butaca
f **~ed** • adj armat **~pit** • n
aixella f, axil·la f

**armadillo** /ˌɑːməˈdɪloʊ, ɑːməˈdɪləʊ/
• n armadillo m

**Armenia** • n Armènia f **~n** • adj
armeni • n armeni m, armènia

**armour** /ˈɑː.mə, ˈɑː.ɹ.mə/ • n arnès
m, armadura f

**army** /ˈɑː.miː, ˈɑɹ.mi/ • n exèrcit
m, host f

**around** /əˈɹaʊnd, əˈɹæwnd/ • prep
al voltant de; passant

**arrange** /əˈɹeɪndʒ/ • v
organitzar, planificar,
arreglar; arrenjar **~ment** • n

arreglada; acord *m*;
arrangement *m*
**array** /ə'ɹeɪ/ • *v* arreglar
**arrest** /ə'ɹɛst/ • *n* arrest *m*
**arriv|e** /ə'ɹaɪv/ • *v* arribar ~**al** •
*n* arribada *f*
**arrogan|t** /'æɹəgənt/ • *adj*
arrogant ~**ce** • *n* arrogància *f*
~**tly** • *adv* arrogantment
**arrow** /'æɹ.əʊ, 'æɹ.oʊ/ • *n* fletxa
*f*, sageta *f*
**artist** /'ɑːtɪst, 'ɑɹ.ɹɪst/ • *n* artista *f*
~**ic** • *adv* artístic
**artichoke** /'ɑɹ.tɪ.tʃəʊk, 'ɑː.tɪ.tʃəʊk/
• *n* carxofera, carxofa
**article** /'ɑːtɪkəl, 'ɑɹtɪkəl/ • *n* article
**articulat|e** /ɑː(ɹ)'tɪk.jʊ.lət,
ɑːɹ'tɪk.jə.lət/ • *adj* articulat *m*
~**ion** • *n* articulació *f*
**artifact** /'ɑːtɪfækt, 'ɑɹtɪfækt/ • *n*
artefacte *m*
**artificial** /ɑː(ɹ)tə'fɪʃəl/ • *adj*
artificial; fals ~**ly** • *adv*
artificialment ~ **intelligence** •
*n* intel·ligència artificial *f*
**as** /æz, əz/ • *adv* tan ... com •
*conj* com; a mesura que; com
que, ja que • *prep* com
**ascertain** /ˌæsə'teɪn, ˌæsə'teɪn/ • *v*
establir, determinar
**ash** /'æʃ/ • *n* cendra *f*, cendre
**ashamed** /ə'ʃeɪmd/ • *adj*
avergonyit
**Asia** • *n* Àsia *f* ~**n** • *adj* asiàtic •
*n* asiàtic *m*, asiàtica *f*
**ask** /'ɑːsk, 'ask/ • *v* preguntar,
demanar
**asleep** • *adj* adormit
**asparagus** /ə'spɛɹ.ə.gəs,
ə'spæɹ.ə.gəs/ • *n* esparreguera
*f*

**asphalt** /'æʃfɑlt, 'æʃfɔlt/ • *n* asfalt
*m*
**aspir|e** /ə'spaɪə(ɹ), ə'spaɪɹ/ • *v*
aspirar ~**ation** • *n* aspiració *f*
**ass** /æs/ • *n* cul *m*
**assassin** /ə'sæsɪn/ • *n* assassí *m*
~**ate** • *v* assassinar ~**ation** • *n*
assassinat *m*
**assembl|e** /ə'sɛmbl/ • *v* muntar
~**y** • *n* assemblea *f*
**asserti|ve** /ə'sɜːtɪv/ • *adj* assertiu
~**on** • *n* asserció *f*, afirmació *f*
**assess** /ə'sɛs/ • *v* avaluar
**assist** /ə'sɪst/ • *n* assistència *f*
~**ance** • *n* assistència *f* ~**ant** •
*adj* auxiliar • *n* assistente *f*
**associat|e** /ə'səʊʃɪeɪt, ə'soʊʃɪeɪt/ •
*n* associat *m* • *v* associar ~**ion**
• *n* associació *f*
**assumption** /ə'sʌmp.ʃən/ • *n*
assumpció *f*
**astonish|ing** • *adj* sorprenent
~**ment** • *n* estorament *m*,
sorpresa *f*
**astronom|y** /ə'stɹɒnə.mi/ • *n*
astronomia *f* ~**er** • *n*
astrònom *m*, astrònoma *f*
**asylum** /ə'saɪləm/ • *n* asil *m*
**asymmetrical** • *adj* asimètric
**at** /æt, ət/ • *prep* a
**ate** *(sp)* ▷ EAT
**Athens** • *n* Atenes *f*
**athlet|e** /'æθ.liːt, 'æθ.lɪt/ • *n*
atleta *f* ~**ic** • *adj* atlètic
**atlas** /'ætləs/ • *n* atles *m*
**atmosphere** /'æt.məs.fɪə(ɹ),
'ætməs.fɪɹ/ • *n* atmosfera *f*,
aerosfera *f*; ambient *m*
**atroci|ous** /ə'tɹəʊʃəs, ə'tɹoʊʃəs/ •
*adj* atroç ~**ty** • *n* atrocitat *f*

**attack** /ə'tæk/ • *n* atac *m* • *v*
atacar **~er** • *n* atacant *m*

**attain** /ə'teɪn/ • *v* aconseguir

**attempt** /ə'tɛmpt/ • *n*
temptativa *f*

**attend** /ə'tɛnd/ • *v* atendre;
assistir

**attenti|on** /ə'tɛn.ʃən/ • *n* atenció
*f* **~ve** • *adj* atent

**attic** /'ætɪk/ • *n* golfes, àtic *m*

**attitude** /'ætɪ.tjuːd, 'ætɪtud/ • *n*
positura *f*; actitud *f*

**attorney** /ə'tɜː(.ɹ)ni/ • *n* advocat

**attract** /ə'tɹækt/ • *v* atreure **~ive**
• *adj* atractiu **~ion** • *n*
atracció *f*

**atypical** /eɪ'tɪp.ɪ.kəl/ • *adj* atípic

**aubergine** ▷ EGGPLANT

**auction** /'ɔːkʃən, 'ɒkʃən/ • *n*
subhasta *f* • *v* subhastar

**audience** /'ɔːdi.əns/ • *n* públic *m*

**audio** /'ɔː.di.əʊ, 'ɔ.di.oʊ/ • *adj*
àudio

**audit** /'ɔː.dɪt/ • *n* auditoria *f*

**August** /'ɔː'gʌst/ • *n* agost *m*

**aunt** /ɑ(ː)nt, ænt/ • *n* tia *f*

**Australia** • *n* Austràlia *f* **~n** •
*adj* australià • *n* australià *m*

**Austria** • *n* Àustria *f* **~n** • *adj*
austríac • *n* austríac *m*

**authentic** /ɔː'θɛn.tɪk, ɑ.'θɛn.tɪk/ •
*adj* autèntic **~ity** • *n*
autenticitat *f*

**author** /'ɔː.θə, 'ɔ.'θɚ/ • *n* autor *m*,
autora *f*

**authority** /ɔː'θɒɹəti, ə'θɔɹəti/ • *n*
autoritat *f*

**authoriz|e** /'ɔθəɹaɪz, 'ɑθəɹaɪz/ • *v*
autoritzar **~ation** • *n*
autorització *f*

**automat|e** /'ɔːtoʊ.meɪt/ • *v*
automatitzar **~ic** • *adj*
automàtic **~ically** • *adv*
automàticament **~ion** • *n*
automatització *f*

**automobile** /'ɔː.tə.mə.biːl,
'ɔː.tə.moʊ.ˌbil/ • *n* automòbil *m*

**autonom|y** /ɔː'tɒnəmi, ɔ'tɑnəmi/
• *n* autonomia *f*; autonomy *f*
**~ous** • *adj* autònom

**autumn** /'ɔːtəm, 'ɔtəm/ • *n* tardor
*f*

**availab|le** /ə'veɪləb(ə)l/ • *adj*
disponible **~ility** • *n*
disponibilitat *f*

**average** /'ævəɹɪdʒ/ • *n* mitjana *f*

**avocado** /ævə'kɑːdəʊ, avə'kɑdoʊ/
• *n* alvocat *m*; alvocater *m*

**avoid** /ə'vɔɪd/ • *v* evitar

**await** /ə'weɪt/ • *v* esperar

**awake** /ə'weɪk/ • *adj* despert,
llevat • *v* (*sp* awoke, *pp*
awoken) llevar-se; despertar

**awaked** (*sp/pp*) ▷ AWAKE

**award** /ə'wɔːd, ə'ɹwɔːd/ • *n*
veredicte *m*; premi *m*, trofeu
*m*, medalla *f*, guardó *m* • *v*
fallar, decretar, sentenciar;
premiar, guardonar

**aware** /ə'wɛɚ, ə'wɛə/ • *adj*
conscient **~ness** • *n*
consciència *f*

**awesome** /'ɔːsəm, 'ɔs.əm/ • *adj*
esbalaïdor; fantàstic

**awful** /'ɔːfʊl, 'ɔfəl/ • *adj* horrorós

**awkward** /'ɔːkwəd, 'ɔkwəd/ • *adj*
maldestre *m*; retret

**awoke** (*sp*) ▷ AWAKE

**awoken** (*pp*) ▷ AWAKE

**axis** /'æksɪs, 'æksəs/ • *n* (*pl* axes)
eix *m*; axis *m*

A

B

**Azerbaijan** ● *n* Azerbaidjan *m*

# B

**baby** /'beɪbi/ ● *n* nadó *m*, bebè *m*; benjamí *m*

**back** /bæk/ ● *n* esquena *f* ● *v* recular; fer costat **~bone** ● *n* columna vertebral *f*, espina dorsal *f*, espinada *f*; coratge *m* **~drop** ● *n* escenari *m* **~ground** ● *n* bagatge *m*; fons *m*; antecedents; rerefons *m* **~pack** ● *n* motxilla *f* **~wards** ● *adv* enrere, endarrere

**bacon** /'beɪ.kən/ ● *n* cansalada *f*

**bad** /bæd, bæːd/ ● *adj* dolent

**badge** /bædʒ/ ● *n* xapa *f*, insígnia *f*, distintiu

**badly** /'bæd.li/ ● *adv* malament, mal

**badminton** /'bæd.mɪn.tən/ ● *n* bàdminton *m*

**bag** /bæg, 'bæːg/ ● *n* bossa *f*; coixí *m*

**Bahamas** ● *n* Bahames

**Bahrain** ● *n* Bahrain *m*

**bail** /beɪl/ ● *n* fiança *f*

**bake** /beɪk/ ● *v* fornejar **~r** ● *n* forner *m* **~ry** ● *n* fleca *f*, forn *m*

**balance** /'bæləns/ ● *n* equilibri *m*; balança *f*; balanç *m* ● *v* equilibrar, compensar

**balcony** /'bælkəni/ ● *n* balcó *m*

**bald** /bɔːld, bɒld/ ● *adj* calb

**ball** /bɔːl, bɒl/ ● *n* bola *f*; pilota *f*; pilotes, colló *m*

**ballet** /'bæleɪ, bæ'leɪ/ ● *n* ballet *m*

**balloon** /bə'luːn/ ● *n* globus *m*, baló *m*

**ballot** /'balət, 'bælət/ ● *n* papereta de vot *f*

**ban** /bæn/ ● *n* ban *m*

**banana** /bə'nɑːnə, bə'nænə/ ● *n* banana *f*, plàtan *m*

**bandage** /'bændɪdʒ/ ● *n* bena *f*, embenat *m* ● *v* embenar

**bang** /bæŋ(g)/ ● *n* serrell *m*

**Bangladesh** ● *n* Bangladesh

**banister** /'bænɪstə(ɹ)/ ● *n* arrambador; balustre *m*

**bank** /bæŋk/ ● *n* banc *m*; riba *f* **~er** ● *n* banquer *m*, banquera *f*

**banner** /'bænə, 'bænəɹ/ ● *n* bandera *f*, banderola *f*, estendard *m*, gomfaró *m*; pancarta *f*; banner *m*

**bar** /bɑː, bɑɹ/ ● *n* barra *f*

**Barbados** ● *n* Barbados *m*

**barbarian** /bɑː(ː).'beə.ɹi.ən, bɑɹ.'beəɹ.i.ən/ ● *adj* bàrbar ● *n* bàrbar *m*

**barber** /'bɑː.bə, 'bɑɹ.bəɹ/ ● *n* barber *m*

**bare|ly** /'beə(ɹ).li, 'bɛɹ.li/ ● *adv* a penes, amb prou feines **~foot** ● *adj* descalç

**bargain** /'bɑːgən, 'bɑːɹgən/ ● *n* ganga *f*, bicoca *f*

**baritone** /'bæɹ.ɹ.toʊn/ ● *n* baríton *m*

**barrel** /'bæɹəl, 'beəɹəl/ ● *n* bóta *f*, barral *m*, barril *m*, bocoi *m*; quart *m*; canó *m*

**barrier** /ˈbæɹɪ.ə(ɹ), ˈbæɹɪ.əɹ/ • *n* barrera *f*

**base** /beɪs/ • *adj* vulgar; baix, abjecte, vil, indigne, innoble; immoral • *n* base *f*; fonament *m*; basament *m*; principi *m*; caserna *f*; seu *f* • *v* basar

**baseball** /ˈbeɪs.bɔːl, ˈbeɪs.bɔl/ • *n* beisbol *m*

**basement** /ˈbeɪsmənt/ • *n* soterrani *m*

**basic** /ˈbeɪsɪk/ • *adj* bàsic **~ally** • *adv* bàsicament

**basil** /ˈbæz.əl, ˈbeɪz.əl/ • *n* alfàbrega *f*, alfàbega *f*

**basket** /ˈbɑːskɪt, ˈbæskɪt/ • *n* cistell *m*, cistella *f*; bàsquet, encistellada

**basketball** /ˈbɑːs.kɪt.bɔːl, ˈbæs.kɪt.bɔːl/ • *n* bàsquet *m*, basquetbol *m*

**bassoon** /bəˈsuːn, bəˈsun/ • *n* fagot *m*

**bat** /bæt/ • *n* ratpenat *m*, ratapinyada *f*, muricec *m*; bat *m*

**bath** /bɑːθ, beːθ/ • *n* bany **~room** • *n* cambra de bany *f*, bany *m*

**batter** /ˈbætə(ɹ), ˈbætəɹ/ • *n* batut *m*; batedor *m* • *v* arrebossar

**battery** /ˈbætəɹi/ • *n* bateria *f*

**battle** /ˈbætəl, ˈbætl̩/ • *n* batalla *f* • *v* combatre, batallar **~field** • *n* camp de batalla *m*

**bay** /beɪ/ • *n* badia *f*; bai • *v* udolar

**be** /biː, bi/ • *v* (*sp* was, *pp* been) fer; ser; ésser; tenir, tindre; estar

**beach** /biːʧ, biːʃ/ • *n* platja *f*

**bean** /biːn/ • *n* mongeta *f*, fesol *m*

**bear** /bɛə(ɹ), bɛəɹ/ • *n* ós *m*; bear • *v* (*sp* bore, *pp* borne) portar; suportar

**beard** /bɪəd, bɪɹd/ • *n* barba *f* • *v* barbar

**beast** /biːst/ • *n* bèstia *f*, fera *f*

**beat** /biːt/ • *n* batec *m* • *v* (*sp* beat, *pp* beaten) bategar

**beaten** (*pp*) ▷ BEAT

**beaut|y** /ˈbjuːti, ˈbjuɹi/ • *n* bellesa *f* **~iful** • *adj* bell *m*, bella *f*, formós *m*, formósa *f*, bonic *m*, bonica *f* **~ifully** • *adv* bellament

**beaver** /ˈbiːvə, ˈbivəɹ/ • *n* castor; conillet *m*

**became** (*sp*) ▷ BECOME

**because** /bɪˈkɒz, bɪˈkɔːz/ • *conj* perquè, ja que, car, puix, puix que

**become** /bɪˈkʌm, bɪˈkʊm/ • *v* (*sp* became, *pp* become) esdevenir; escaure

**bed** /bɛd, beːd/ • *n* llit *m*; jaç *m*; capa; buc • *v* allitar-se **~room** • *n* dormitori *m*, cambra *f* **~sheet** • *n* llençol *m* **make the ~** • *v* fer el llit

**bee** /bi, biː/ • *n* abella *f*; be *f* **~hive** • *n* arna *f*, buc *m*, casera *f*, rusc *m*

**beef** /bif, biːf/ • *n* vedella *f*

**been** (*pp*) ▷ BE

**beer** /bɪə(ɹ), bɪə/ • *n* cervesa *f*, birra *f*

**beetle** /ˈbiːtəl/ • *n* escarabat *m*

**beetroot** /ˈbiːtɹuːt, ˈbiːtɹut/ • *n* remolatxa d'hort *f*

**B**

**before** /bɪ'fɔː, bə'fɔɪ/ • *adv* abans; davant • *prep* abans de, abans que; davant; abans

**beg** /bɛg/ • *v* pidolar, mendicar; suplicar, pregar **~gar** • *n* mendicant *f*, captaire *f*

**began** *(sp)* ▷ BEGIN

**beget** /bɪ'gɛt/ • *v* (*sp* begot, *pp* begotten) engendrar; concebre

**begin** /bɪ'gɪn/ • *v* (*sp* began, *pp* begun) començar, iniciar **~ning** • *n* començament *m*, inici *m*, principi *m*

**begot** *(sp)* ▷ BEGET

**begotten** *(pp)* ▷ BEGET

**begun** *(pp)* ▷ BEGIN

**behavior** /bɪ'heɪvjɚ, bɪ'heɪvjə/ • *n* conducta *f*, comportament *m*

**behaviour** *(British)* ▷ BEHAVIOR

**behind** /bɪ'haɪnd, biː'haɪnd/ • *adv* darrere

**Beijing** • *n* Pequín

**being** /'biːɪŋ, 'bɪŋ/ • *n* ésser *m*

**Belarus** • *n* Bielorússia *f*, Bielarús *m*

**Belgi|um** • *n* Bèlgica *f* **~an** • *adj* belga • *n* belga *f*

**belie|ve** /bɪ'liːv/ • *v* creure **~f** • *n* creença *f* **~ver** • *n* creient *f* **~vable** • *adj* creïble

**Belize** • *n* Belize *m*

**bell** /bɛl/ • *n* campana *f*

**belly** /'bɛli/ • *n* buc *m*, abdomen *m*, panxa *f*, ventre

**belong** /bɪ'lɒŋ, bɪ'lɔŋ/ • *v* pertànyer

**beloved** /bɪ'lʌvd, bɪ'lʌvɪd/ • *adj* estimat *m*, estimada *f*

**below** /bɪ'ləʊ, bə'loʊ/ • *adv* sota; ensota • *prep* sota

**belt** /bɛlt/ • *n* cinturó *m*; corretja *f*; cop *f*; regió *f*

**bench** /bɛntʃ/ • *n* banc *m*; banqueta *f*

**bend** /bɛnd, bɪnd/ • *n* banda *f* • *v* (*sp* bent, *pp* bent) inclinar-se

**beneath** /bɪ'niːθ/ • *adv* sota

**benefactor** /'bɛnəˌfæktɚ/ • *n* benfactor *m*

**benefi|t** /'bɛn.ə.fɪt/ • *n* benefici *m* • *v* beneficiar **~cial** • *adj* beneficiós **~ciary** • *n* beneficiari *m*

**benign** /bɪ'naɪn/ • *adj* benigne

**Benin** • *n* Benín *m*

**bent** /bɛnt/ • *adj* tort • (*also*) ▷ BEND

**Berlin** • *n* Berlín

**Bern** • *n* Berna *f*

**berry** /'bɛɪi/ • *n* baia *f*

**beseech** /bɪ'siːtʃ/ • *v* (*sp* besought, *pp* besought) pregar

**beseeched** *(sp/pp)* ▷ BESEECH

**besides** /bə'saɪdz/ • *adv* a més; a més a més; d'altra banda

**besought** *(sp/pp)* ▷ BESEECH

**best** /bɛst/ • *adj* el millor **~seller** • *n* best-seller *m* **at ~** • *phr* com a molt, com a màxim

**bet** /bɛt/ • *n* aposta *f*, juguesca *f* • *v* (*sp* bet, *pp* bet) apostar

**betray** /bə'tɹeɪ/ • *v* trair

**betted** *(sp/pp)* ▷ BET

**better** /'bɛtə, 'bɛtəɪ/ • *adj* millor • *v* millorar • (*also*) ▷ GOOD

**between** /bɪ'twiːn, bə'twin/ • *prep* entre

**bias** /'baɪəs/ • *n* biaix *m* **~ed** • *adj* esbiaixat, tendenciós, parcial

**Bible** /'baɪbəl/ • *n* Bíblia *f*

**bibliography** /bɪblɪʊŋɡɹəfi/ • *n* bibliografia *f*
**bicycle** /ˈbaɪsɪkl̩/ • *n* bicicleta *f*
**big** /bɪɡ/ • *adj* gran, gros
**bike** /baɪk/ • *n* bici *f*; moto *f*
**bikini** /bɪˈkiːni/ • *n* biquini *m*
**bill** /bɪl/ • *n* bec *m*; factura *f*, compte *m*
**billion** /ˈbɪljən/ • *n* mil milió, miliard *m*, mil milions *m*; bilió *f*
**bind** /baɪnd/ • *v* (*sp* bound, *pp* bound) lligar
**biodegradable** /baɪoʊdəˈɡɹeɪdəbl̩/ • *adj* biodegradable
**biodiversity** /ˌbaɪoʊdaɪˈvɜːsəti, ˌbaɪ.oʊˌdaɪˈvɜː(ɹ).sɪ.ti/ • *n* biodiversitat *f*
**biograph|y** /baɪˈɒɡɹəfi, baɪˈɑːɡɹəfi/ • *n* biografia *f* **~ical** • *adj* biogràfic **auto~y** • *n* autobiografia *f*
**biolog|y** /baɪˈɒlədʒi, baɪˈɒlədʒi/ • *n* biologia *f* **~ical** • *n* biològic **~ist** • *n* biòleg *m*, biòloga *f*
**bird** /bɜːd, bɝd/ • *n* au, ocell; noia *f*
**birth** /bɜːθ, bɝθ/ • *n* naixença *f*; part *m* **~day** • *n* aniversari *m*, natalici *m*
**biscuit** /ˈbɪskɪt/ • *n* galeta *f*
**bishop** /ˈbɪʃəp/ • *n* bisbe *m*; alfil *m*
**bit** /bɪt/ • *n* mos *m*; mica *f*, poquet *m* • (*also*) ▷ BITE
**bite** /baɪt, bʌɪt/ • *n* mossegada *f* • *v* (*sp* bit, *pp* bitten) mossegar
**bitten** (*pp*) ▷ BITE
**bitter** /ˈbɪtə, ˈbɪtəɹ/ • *adj* amarg **~sweet** • *adj* agredolç • *n* dolçamara *f*

**bizarre** /bɪˈzɑː(ɹ), bɪˈzɑɹ/ • *adj* estrany, estrafolari
**black** /blæk/ • *adj* negre; fosc • *n* negre *m*; negra *f*
**blackberry** /ˈblækbəɹi, ˈblækbeɹi/ • *n* esbarzer *m*; móra *f*
**blackbird** /ˈblækbəːd, ˈblækˌbɚd/ • *n* merla *f*, tord negre *m*
**blackboard** /ˈblækbɔːd, ˈblækbɔːd/ • *n* pissarra *f*
**blackmail** • *n* xantatge *m*
**bladder** /ˈblædə, ˈblærə/ • *n* bufeta *f*, veixiga *f*
**blame** /bleɪm/ • *n* culpa *f* • *v* culpar
**blanket** /ˈblæŋkɪt/ • *n* manta *f*
**bled** (*sp/pp*) ▷ BLEED
**bleed** /bliːd/ • *v* (*sp* bled, *pp* bled) sagnar; dessagnar
**blend** /blɛnd/ • *n* mescla *f*
**bless** /blɛs/ • *v* (*sp* blessed, *pp* blessed) beneir
**blessed** (*sp/pp*) ▷ BLESS
**blest** (*sp/pp*) ▷ BLESS
**blew** (*sp*) ▷ BLOW
**blind** /blaɪnd/ • *adj* cec, orb • *n* persiana • *v* cegar **~fold** • *n* bena **~ness** • *n* ceguesa *f*
**block** /blɒk, blak/ • *n* cub *m*, bloc *m*; illa *f*; bloqueig *m* • *v* bloquejar, blocar
**blog** /blɒg, blɑg/ • *n* blog *m*
**blond** /blɒnd, blɑnd/ • *n* ros
**blood** /blʌd, blɵd/ • *n* sang *f* **~y** • *adj* sagnant; maleït
**blow** /bləʊ, bloʊ/ • *n* cop *m* • *v* (*sp* blew, *pp* blown) bufar; llepar
**blown** (*pp*) ▷ BLOW
**blue** /bluː, blu/ • *adj* blau; verd • *n* blau *m*

**B**

**blunt** /blʌnt/ • *adj* rom • *n* porro *m*, peta *m*

**blush** /blʌʃ/ • *n* coloret *m* • *v* posar-se vermell, tornar-se vermell, enrojolar-se

**board** /bɔːd, bɔːɪd/ • *n* post *f*, tauler *m*; mesa *f*, junta *f*; bord *m* • *v* embarcar, pujar ~ **game** • *n* joc de tauler *m*

**boat** /bəʊt, boʊt/ • *n* vaixell *m*

**bod|y** /ˈbɒdi, ˈbɑdi/ • *n* cos *m*; cadàver *m*; carrosseria, buc ~**ily** • *adj* corporal, corpori ~**yguard** • *n* guardaespatlles *f* ~**ybuilder** • *n* culturista *f*

**Bogota** • *n* Bogotà

**boil** /bɔɪl/ • *v* bullir ~**ing** • *adj* bullent

**boisterous** /ˈbɔɪstərəs/ • *adj* sorollós *m*, escandalós *m*

**bold** /bəʊld, boʊld/ • *adj* agosarat; negreta *f*

**Bolivia** • *n* Bolívia *f*

**bolt** /bɒlt, boʊlt/ • *n* balda *f*; llampec *m*

**bomb** /bɒm, bɑm/ • *n* bomba *f*; tartana *f*; monument *m* • *v* bombardejar

**bond** /bɒnd, bɒnd/ • *n* aparell *m*

**bone** /boʊn/ • *n* os *m* • *v* desossar

**book** /bʊk, buːk/ • *n* llibre *m*; àlbum *m*; llibres • *v* reservar; anotar ~**mark** • *n* punt de llibre *m*; adreça d'interès *f*

**boom** /buːm, bʊm/ • *n* boom *m*

**boost** /buːst/ • *n* impuls *m* • *v* impel·lir, empènyer; bitllar

**boot** /but, buːt/ • *n* bota *f* • *v* vomitar

**border** /ˈbɔədə, bɔːdə/ • *n* vora *f*, orla *f*; sanefa *f*; frontera *f* • *v* vorejar

**bore** *(sp)* ▷ BEAR

**bored** /bɔːd, bɔːɪd/ • *adj* avorrit

**boring** /ˈbɔːrɪŋ/ • *adj* avorrit

**born** /bɔːn, bɔɪn/ • *adj* nat • *(also)* ▷ BEAR

**borne** *(pp)* ▷ BEAR

**borrow** /ˈbɒrəʊ, ˈbɑroʊ/ • *n* caiguda *f* • *v* manllevar, amprar

**Bosnia** • *n* Bòsnia *f* ~**n** • *adj* bosnià *m*, bosniana *f*

**boss** /bɒs, bɔs/ • *n* patró *m*

**both** /bəʊθ, boʊθ/ • *conj* tant ... com ... • *det* ambdós, tots dos

**bother** /ˈbɒðəɪ/ • *v* molestar

**Botswana** • *n* Botswana *f*

**bottle** /ˈbɒ.təl, ˈbɑ.təl/ • *n* ampolla *f*, botella *f*; coratge *m*, audàcia *m* • *v* embotellar

**bottom** /ˈbɒtəm, ˈbɑtəm/ • *n* fons *m*; cul *m*

**bought** *(sp/pp)* ▷ BUY

**bounce** /baʊns/ • *v* botre

**bound** /baʊnd/ • *n* límit *m* • *(also)* ▷ BIND ~**ary** • *n* frontera *f*

**bow** /bəʊ, boʊ/ • *n* arc *m*; corba; reverència *f*, inclinació *f*; proa *f*, prora • *v* corbar, doblegar, vinclar, blincar; corbar-se, doblegar-se, vinclar-se, blincar-se ~**tie** • *n* corbatí *m*

**bowl** /bəʊl, boʊl/ • *n* bol *m* ~**ing** • *n* bitlles *m*

**box** /bɒks, bɑks/ • *n* cop de puny *m*; capsa *f*, caixa *f*; llotja *f*; garita *f*; boix *m* • *v* boxejar,

boxar; empaquetar, encapsar
~ **office** • *n* taquilla *f*
**boy** /bɔɪ, bɔːə/ • *n* noi *m*, al·lot
*m*, xiquet *m*, xic *m*, xicot *m*;
minyó *m*; home *m* **~friend** • *n*
xicot *m*, nòvio *m*; amic *m*
**bra** /brɑː/ • *n* sostenidors
**bracelet** /ˈbreɪslət/ • *n* braçalet *m*
**bracket** /ˈbrækɪt/ • *n* mènsula *f*
**brain** /breɪn/ • *n* cervell *m*
**brake** /breɪk/ • *n* fre *m* • *v* frenar
**branch** /brɑːntʃ, bræntʃ/ • *n*
branca *f*; sucursal *f*
**brand** /brand, brænd/ • *n* marca
*f*
**brandy** /ˈbrændi/ • *n* brandi *m*,
conyac *m*
**brass** /brɑːs, bræs/ • *n* llautó;
metall *m*; pasta *f*
**brave** /breɪv/ • *adj* valent,
coratjós, audaç
**Brazil** • *n* Brasil
**bread** /bred/ • *n* pa *m* • *v*
arrebossar
**break** /breɪk/ • *n* escapada *f*;
entrada *f* • *v* (*sp* broke, *pp*
broken) trencar; trencar el
servei; escapar-se, internar-se
**~able** • *adj* trencable **~ in** • *v*
irrompre **~ out** • *v* esclatar
**~down** • *n* avaria *f*, pana *f*
**~fast** • *n* esmorzar *m* • *v*
esmorzar **~through** • *n* avenç
*m*, progrés *m*
**breast** /brest/ • *n* pit *m*, mama *f*,
mamella, teta, sina **~feed** • *v*
alletar **~feeding** • *n*
alletament *m*
**breath** /brɛθ/ • *n* respiració *f*;
alè *m* **~e** • *v* respirar, alenar
**bred** *(sp/pp)* ▷ BREED

**breed** /briːd/ • *n* raça, varietat •
*v* (*sp* bred, *pp* bred) criar;
engendrar
**breez|e** /briːz/ • *n* brisa *f* **~y** •
*adj* airejós; airós
**brick** /brɪk/ • *n* maó *m* **~layer** •
*n* paleta *f*
**bride** /braɪd/ • *n* núvia *f* **~groom**
• *n* nuvi *m*
**bridge** /brɪdʒ/ • *n* pont *m*;
bridge *m*
**brief** /briːf/ • *adj* breu; concís **~ly**
• *adv* breument
**bright** /braɪt/ • *adj* brillant, clar
**brilliant** /ˈbrɪljənt/ • *adj* brillant;
clar
**bring** /brɪŋ/ • *v* (*sp* brought, *pp*
brought) portar
**British** • *adj* britànic
**broadcast** /ˈbrɔːdkɑːst, ˈbrɔːdkæst/
• *n* emissió *f*; programa *m* • *v*
emetre, transmetre
**broadcast** /ˈbrɔːdkɑːst, ˈbrɔːdkæst/
• *n* emissió *f*; programa *m* • *v*
(*sp* broadcast, *pp* broadcast)
emetre, transmetre
**broadcasted** *(sp/pp)* ▷
BROADCAST
**broccoli** /ˈbrɒkəli, ˈbrɑːkəli/ • *n*
bròcoli *m*
**broke** /broʊk, brʊk/ • *adj* pelat
• *(also)* ▷ BREAK
**broken** /ˈbroʊkən/ • *adj* trencat;
espatllat • *(also)* ▷ BREAK
**bronze** /brɒnz, brɑːnz/ • *adj*
bronze • *n* bronze *m*
**broth** /brɒθ, brɑːθ/ • *n* brou *m*
**brother** /ˈbrʌðə(r), ˈbrʌðər/ • *n*
germà *m* **~hood** • *n*
fraternitat *f*, germanor *f*
**~in-law** • *n* cunyat *m*

**brought** *(sp/pp)* ▷ BRING

**brown** /braʊn/ ● *adj* marró ● *n* marró *m* ● *v* s'enrossir; enrossir

**Brunei** ● *n* Brunei *m*

**brush** /brʌʃ/ ● *n* raspall *m*; raspallar

**Brussels** ● *n* Brussel·les ~ **sprout** ● *n* col de Brussel·les *f*

**brutal** /bruːtəl/ ● *adj* brutal

**BTW** *(abbr)* ▷ BY THE WAY

**bubble** /bʌb.əl/ ● *n* bombolla *f*

**buck** /bʌk/ ● *n* cérvol *m*, boc *m*

**bucket** /bʌkɪt/ ● *n* cubell *m*, galleda *f*; cubellada *f*; catúfol *m*

**buddy** /bʌd.i/ ● *n* company *m*

**budget** /bʌdʒ.ɪt/ ● *n* pressupost *m*

**bug** /bʌg/ ● *n* xinxa *f*; cuca *f*; error *m*, defecte *m*; febre *f*, mania *f*

**build** /bɪld/ ● *v* *(sp* built, *pp* built) construir, edificar ~**ing** ● *n* construcció *f*; edifici *m*

**built** *(sp/pp)* ▷ BUILD

**bulb** /bʌlb/ ● *n* bulb *m*

**Bulgaria** ● *n* Bulgària *f* ~**n** ● *adj* búlgar ● *n* búlgar *m*, búlgara *f*

**bulk** /bʌlk/ ● *adj* massiu ● *n* gruix *m*

**bull** /bʊl/ ● *n* toro *m*; butlla *f*; segell *m*

**bullet** /bʊl.ɪt/ ● *n* bala *f* ~**proof** ● *adj* antibales; infal·lible *f*

**bumblebee** /bʌmbḷbi/ ● *n* borinot *m*

**bump** /bʌmp/ ● *n* sotrac *m*; nyanyo *m*

**bunch** /bʌntʃ/ ● *n* raïm *m*, grapat *m*; colla *f*

**burden** /bɜːdn, bɜ́dn/ ● *n* càrrega *f*, carga

**bureaucracy** /bjʊə.rɒk.rəsi, bjʊ.rɑːkrəsi/ ● *n* burocràcia *f*

**burn** /bɜ́n, bɜːn/ ● *n* cremada *f* ● *v* *(sp* burnt, *pp* burnt) cremar

**burned** *(sp/pp)* ▷ BURN

**burning** /bɜ́nɪŋ, bɜːnɪŋ/ ● *adj* ardent

**burnt** *(sp/pp)* ▷ BURN

**burst** /bɜ́st, bɜːst/ ● *v* *(sp* burst, *pp* burst) petar, rebentar

**Burundi** ● *n* Burundi *m*

**bur|y** /bɛ.ri, bʌ.ri/ ● *v* enterrar ~**ial** ● *n* enterrament *m*

**bus** /bʌs/ ● *n* autobús *m*; bus *m*

**bush** /bʊʃ/ ● *n* arbust *m*

**business** /bɪz.nɪs, bɪz.nəs/ ● *n* negoci *m*

**bust** /bʌst/ ● *n* bust *m*

**busted** *(sp/pp)* ▷ BUST

**busy** /bɪzi/ ● *adj* ocupat

**but** /bʌt, bʊt/ ● *conj* però; encara que; menys, excepte

**butcher** /bʊtʃ.ə(r), bʊtʃ.ɚ/ ● *n* carnisser *m*, carnissera *f*

**butt** /bʌt/ ● *n* natja *f*; punta *f*, burilla *f* ● *v* tossar

**butter** /bʌtəɹ, bʌtə/ ● *n* mantega *f*

**butterfly** /bʌtə(r)flaɪ/ ● *n* papallona *f*, papalló *m*, papaió *m*, babaiana *f*, paloma *f*, palometa *f*

**button** /bʌtn/ ● *n* botó *m*; insígnia *f*; poncella *f* ● *v* botonar

**buy** /baɪ/ ● *v* *(sp* bought, *pp* bought) comprar ~**er** ● *n* comprador *m*

**by** /baɪ/ ● *prep* per a; per

**bye** /baɪ/ • *interj* adéu

**cabbage** /ˈkæbɪdʒ/ • *n* col *f*
**cabinet** /ˈkæ.bɪ.nɪt, ˈkæ.bə.nət/ • *n* armari *m*; gabinet *m*
**cable** /ˈkeɪ.bl̩/ • *n* cable *m* • *v* cablejar; lligar
**cactus** /ˈkæktəs/ • *n* (*pl* cacti) cactus *m*
**café** /ˈkæˈfeɪ, ˈkæfeɪ/ • *n* cafè *m*, cafeteria *f*
**cage** /keɪdʒ/ • *n* gàbia *f* • *v* engabiar
**Cairo** • *n* Caire *m*
**cake** /keɪk/ • *n* pastís *m*
**calculat|e** /ˈkælkjʊleɪt/ • *v* calcular **~ion** • *n* càlcul *m* **~or** • *n* calculadora *f*
**calendar** /ˈkæl.ən.də, ˈkæl.ən.dɚ/ • *n* calendari *m*, calendàriu; agenda *f*
**calf** /kɑːf, kæf/ • *n* (*pl* calves) vedell *m*; panxell *m*
**call** /kɔːl, kɔl/ • *n* visita *f*; crit *m*, crida *f*, xiscle *m*; telefonada *f*, trucada *f* • *v* cridar; xisclar, xillar; telefonar, trucar, tocar; visitar
**calm** /kɑːm, kɑ(l)m/ • *adj* calm • *n* calma *f* • *v* calmar
**calves** (*pl*) ▷ CALF
**Cambodia** • *n* Cambodja *f*
**came** (*sp*) ▷ COME
**camel** /ˈkæməl/ • *n* camell *m*

**camera** /ˈkæmərə/ • *n* càmera *f* **~man** • *n* cameràman *m*
**Cameroon** • *n* Camerun *m*
**camp** /kæmp, æ/ • *n* campament *m*, càmping *m* • *v* acampar
**campaign** /kæmˈpeɪn/ • *n* campanya *f*
**campus** /ˈkæmpəs/ • *n* campus *m*
**can** /kæn, kən/ • *n* llauna *f* • *v* (*sp* could, *pp* -) poder, poguer; enllaunar
**Canad|a** • *n* Canadà *m* **~ian** • *adj* canadenc • *n* canadenc *m*, canadenca *f*
**canal** /kəˈnæl, kəˈnɛl/ • *n* canal *m*
**canary** /kəˈnɛəɪɪ/ • *n* canari
**Canberra** • *n* Canberra
**cancel** /ˈkænsl̩/ • *v* cancel·lar **~lation** • *n* cancel·lació *f*
**cancer** /ˈkænsə, ˈkæːnsə/ • *n* càncer *m*
**candidate** /ˈkæn.dɪdət, ˈkæn.dɪ.deɪt/ • *n* candidat *m*
**candle** /ˈkændəl/ • *n* espelma *f*, candela *f*
**candy** /ˈkændɪ/ • *n* caramel *m*, llaminadura *f*
**cannabis** /ˈkænəbɪs/ • *n* cànem *m*, cànnabis *m*
**canoe** /kəˈnuː/ • *n* canoa *f*
**canvas** /ˈkæn.vəs/ • *n* lona *f*; llenç *m*, tela *f*
**cap** /kæp/ • *n* gorra *f*
**capable** /ˈkeɪpəbl̩/ • *adj* capaç
**capacity** /kəˈpæsɪtɪ/ • *n* capacitat *f*
**Cape Verde** • *n* Cap Verd *m*
**caper** /ˈkeɪpə, ˈkeɪpə/ • *n* tàpera *f*; taperera *f*

**capital** /ˈkæp.ɪ.təl/ • adj capital; excel·lent; majúscula • n capital m; capitell m

**capitalis|m** /ˈkapɪt(ə)lɪz(ə)m, ˈkæpɪtl̩ˌɪzm/ • n capitalisme ~t • adj capitalista

**captain** /ˈkæp.tɪn, ˈkæp.tən/ • n capità m • v capitanejar; pilotar

**capture** /ˈkæp.tʃɚ, ˈkæp.tʃə/ • n captura f • v capturar

**car** /kɑː, kɑɪ/ • n cotxe m, automòbil m; vagó m; cabina f

**carbohydrate** /kɑːbəʊˈhaɪdɹeɪt, kɑːboʊˈhaɪdɹeɪt/ • n carbohidrat m, hidrat de carboni m

**carbon** /ˈkɑːbən/ • n carboni m; carbó m

**card** /kɑːd, kɑɪd/ • n targeta f ~ **game** • n joc de cartes m

**cardigan** /ˈkɑːdɪgən/ • n càrdigan m, rebeca f

**care** /kɛə, kɛ(ə)ɪ/ • n cura f, compte m ~**less** • adj imprudent, negligent ~**ful** • adj cautelós; curós ~**fully** • adv acuradament ~**taker** • n conserge m

**career** /kəˈɪɪɪ, kəˈɪɪə/ • n carrera f

**cargo** • n càrrega f

**carp** /kɑːp, kɑɪp/ • n carpa f

**carpenter** /ˈkɑːˌpən.tə, ˈkɑɪpəntɚ/ • n fuster m, fustera f

**carpet** /ˈkɑːpɪt, ˈkɑɪpɪt/ • n moqueta f, catifa f

**carriage** /ˈkæɹɪdʒ/ • n carruatge m, cotxe m; vagó m

**carrier** /ˈkæ.ɹɪ.ə, ˈkæ.ɹɪ.ɚ/ • n portador m; portadora f

**carrot** /ˈkæɹ.ət/ • n pastanaga f, safanòria f

**carry** /ˈkæ.ɹi/ • v portar

**cart** /kɑːt, kɑɪt/ • n carretó m, carret m, carreta f

**cartoon** /kɑːˈtuːn, kɑːˈtuːn/ • n vinyeta f, tira còmica f; caricatura f; cartó m; dibuixos animats

**carv|e** /kɑːv, kɑːv/ • v tallar ~**ing** • n entallament m

**case** /keɪs/ • n cas m; causa f; caixa f, capsa f; maleta f; vitrina f • v empaquetar

**cash** /kæʃ/ • n efectiu m

**cashier** /kəˈʃɪə/ • n caixer m • v destituir

**casino** /kæˈsinoʊ/ • n casino m

**cast** /kɑːst, kæst/ • n motlle m; llançament m; repartiment m; enguixat • v (sp cast, pp cast) dirigir; llençar; fondre; votar

**castle** /ˈkɑːsəl, ˈkæsəl/ • n castell m • v enrocar

**casual** /ˈkæʒuəl, ˈkaʒuəl/ • adj casual; ocasional; informal

**casualty** /ˈkaʒ(ʊ)əlti/ • n baixa f

**catalogue** /ˈkæt.ə.lɒg, ˈkætəlɔg/ • n catàleg m

**category** /ˈkætəˌgɔɹi, ˈkætɪg(ə)ɹi/ • n categoria f

**caterpillar** /ˈkætəpɪlə(ɹ), ˈkædəɹˌpɪlɚ/ • n eruga f

**cathedral** /kəˈθiːdɹəl/ • n catedral f

**Catholic** • adj catòlic • n catòlic m

**cattle** /ˈkæt(ə)l/ • n bestiar m

**cauliflower** /ˈkɒl.iˌflaʊ.ə, ˈkɔl.ɪˌflaʊ.ɚ/ • n coliflor f, bròquil blanc m

**caus|e** /kɔːz, kɔz/ • *n* causa *f* **~al**
  • *adj* causal
**caustic** /'kɔːstɪk/ • *adj* càustic
**cautious** /'kɔːʃəs/ • *adj* cautelós,
  caut
**cave** /keɪv/ • *n* cova *f*
**cease** /siːs/ • *v* cessar
**ceiling** /'siːlɪŋ/ • *n* sostre *m*
**celebrat|e** /'sɛl.ɪ.bɹeɪt/ • *v*
  celebrar **~ion** • *n* celebració *f*
**celebrity** /sɪ'lɛbɹɪti/ • *n* celebritat
  *f*
**celery** /'sɛl.ə.ɹi/ • *n* api *m*
**cell** /sɛl/ • *n* pila *f*; calabós *m*,
  cel·la *f*; cèl·lula *f*
**cello** /'tʃɛləʊ, 'tʃɛloʊ/ • *n* violoncel
  *m*
**cemetery** *(British)* ▷ GRAVEYARD
**censor** /'sɛn.sə, 'sɛn.sɚ/ • *n*
  censor *m* • *v* censurar
**cent** /sɛnt/ • *n* centau, cèntim
**cent|er** /'sɛn.tɚ, 'sɛn.tə(ɹ)/ • *n*
  centre *m*; pivot *f*; central *m*
  **~ral** • *adj* central
**centre** *(British)* ▷ CENTER
**century** /'sɛn.tʃə.ɹi/ • *n* segle *m*,
  centúria *f*
**ceramic** /sə'ɹæmɪk/ • *adj* ceràmic
  • *n* ceràmica *f* **~s** • *n*
  ceràmica *f*
**cereal** • *n* cereal *m*; cereals
**ceremon|y** /'sɛɹɪməni,
  'sɛɹəmoʊni/ • *n* cerimònia *f*
  **~ial** • *adj* cerimonial
**certain** /'sɜːtn̩, 'sɜtn̩/ • *adj* cert
  **~ly** • *adv* certament **~ty** • *n*
  certesa *f*
**certifiable** • *adj* certificable;
  boig

**certificat|e** /sər'tɪfɪkɪt,
  sər'tɪfɪ.keɪt/ • *n* certificat *m*
  **~ion** • *n* certificació *f*
**Chad** • *n* Txad *m*
**chain** /'tʃeɪn/ • *n* cadena *f*
**chair** /tʃɛə(ɹ), tʃeəɹ/ • *n* cadira *f*;
  càtedra *f* • *v* presidir
**chalk** /tʃɔːk, tʃɔk/ • *n* creta *f*;
  guix *m*; magnèsia *f*
**challeng|e** /'tʃæl.ɪndʒ/ • *n*
  desafiament *m*, repte *m* • *v*
  desafiar **~ing** • *adj* desafiador
**chamber** /'tʃeɪmbə(ɹ)/ • *n*
  cambra *f*; recambra *f*
**chameleon** /kə'miːliːən/ • *n*
  camaleó *m*
**champion** /'tʃæmpiən/ • *n*
  campió *m* **~ship** • *n*
  campionat *m*
**chance** /tʃæns, tʃɑːns/ • *n*
  oportunitat *f*; atzar *m*;
  probabilitat *f* • *v* arriscar-se
**chancellor** /'tʃɑːnsələ, 'tʃænsələ/ •
  *n* canceller *f*
**change** /'tʃeɪndʒ/ • *n* canvi *m* • *v*
  canviar; modificar
**channel** /'tʃænəl/ • *n* canal *m* • *v*
  canalitzar
**chao|s** /'keɪ.ɒs, 'keɪ.ɑs/ • *n* caos
  *m* **~tic** • *adj* caòtic
**chapter** /'tʃæptə, 'tʃæptɚ/ • *n*
  capítol *m*; divisió *f*
**character** /'kɛɹəktɚ, 'kæɹəktə/ • *n*
  personatge *m*; caràcter *m*;
  tarannà
**characteri|ze** /'kɛɹəktəɹaɪz,
  'kæɹəktəɹaɪz/ • *v* caracteritzar
  **~stic** • *adj* característic • *n*
  característica *f*
**charge** /'tʃɑːdʒ, tʃɑɹdʒ/ • *n*
  càrrega *f*; cost *m*, preu *f*;

encàrrec *f* • *v* acusar, inculpar
**~r** • *n* carregador *m*
**charity** /'tʃɛɹəti/ • *n* caritat *f*
**charm** /tʃɑːm, tʃɑːm/ • *n* amulet
*m*; encant **~ing** • *adj*
encantador, encisador
**charter** /'tʃɑːtə, 'tʃɑɹɹə/ • *v*
noliejar
**chase** /tʃeɪs/ • *n* persecució *f* • *v*
perseguir, empaitar, encalçar
**chat** /tʃæt/ • *n* xat *m* • *v* xerrar
**cheap** /tʃiːp, tʃiːp/ • *adj* barat
**cheat** /tʃiːt/ • *n* trampós; truc •
*v* trampejar, mentir; enganyar
**check** /tʃɛk/ • *n* compte *m*;
inspecció *f* • *v* comprovar,
verificar; comparar **~mate** •
*interj* escac i mat
**cheek** /tʃiːk/ • *n* galta *f* **~y** • *adj*
descarat
**cheese** /tʃiːz, tʃiːz/ • *n* formatge
*m*
**chef** /ʃɛf/ • *n* xef *m*
**chemi|stry** /'kɛm.ɪ.stɹi/ • *n*
química *f* **~cal** • *adj* químic
**~st** • *n* químic *m*, química *f*
**cherry** /'tʃɛɹi/ • *n* cirera *f*; cirerer
*m*
**chess** /tʃɛs/ • *n* escacs **~board** •
*n* àbac *m*
**chest** /tʃɛst/ • *n* arca *f*, cofre *f*;
pit *m*, tòrax *m*
**chestnut** /'tʃɛs.nʌt/ • *adj* castany,
marró • *n* castanya *f*; castany
*m*, marró *m*
**chew** /tʃuː, tʃu/ • *v* mastegar,
masticar **~ing gum** • *n* xiclet
*m*
**chicken** /'tʃɪkɪn/ • *n* pollastre *m*,
gallina *f*, gall *m*, butza

**chief** /tʃiːf/ • *adj* principal • *n*
cap *m*
**child** /tʃaɪld/ • *n* (*pl* children)
nen **~hood** • *n* infància *f*,
infantesa
**children** *(pl)* ▷ CHILD
**Chile** • *n* Xile *m* **~an** • *adj* xilè •
*n* xilè *m*, xilena *f*
**chilling** /'tʃɪlɪŋ/ • *adj* refrescant;
esgarrifós, glaçador
**chimney** /'tʃɪmni/ • *n* xemeneia *f*
**chimpanzee** /tʃɪm'pæn.zi/ • *n*
ximpanzé *m*
**chin** /tʃɪn/ • *n* mentó *m*
**Chin|a** /tʃaɪnə/ • *n* Xina *f* **~ese** •
*adj* xinès • *n* xinès *m*; xinesos;
xinesa *f*
**chisel** /'tʃɪzəl/ • *n* cisell *m*
**chivalrous** /'ʃɪv.əl.ɹʌs/ • *adj*
cavalleresc, cavallerós
**chocolate** /'tʃɒk(ə)lɪt, 'tʃɒːk(ə)lət/
• *adj* xocolata • *n* xocolata *f*;
bombó *m*, xocolatina *f*
**choice** /tʃɔɪs/ • *n* tria *f*
**choir** /kwaɪə(ɹ), kwaɪə/ • *n* cor *m*
**cholesterol** • *n* colesterol *m*
**choose** /tʃuːz/ • *v* (*sp* chose, *pp*
chosen) triar, escollir, elegir
**choreograph|y** /ˌkɔ.ɹiˈɒɡ.ɹə.fi/ •
*n* coreografia *f* **~er** • *n*
coreògraf *m*
**chose** *(sp)* ▷ CHOOSE
**chosen** *(pp)* ▷ CHOOSE
**Christian** • *adj* cristià • *n* cristià
*m*, cristiana *f* **~ity** • *n*
cristianisme *m*
**Christmas** • *n* Nadal *m*
**chronic** /'kɹɒnɪk/ • *adj* crònic
**chronology** /kɹəˈnɒl.ə.dʒi/ • *n*
cronologia *f*
**church** /tʃɜːtʃ, tʃɜtʃ/ • *n* església *f*

**cider** /ˈsaɪ.dər, ˈsaɪ.də/ • n sidra f

**cigarette** /ˌsɪ.gə.ˈrɛt/ • n cigarret m

**cinema** /ˈsɪn.ə.mə, ˈsɪn.ɪ.mə/ • n cinema m

**cinnamon** /ˈsɪn.ə.mən, ˈsɪn.mɪn/ • adj canyella f, canella f • n canyeller m, caneller m; canyella f, canella f

**circ|le** /ˈsɜːkəl/ • n cercle m; disc; ulleres ~ular • adj circular

**circuit** /ˈsɜː.kɪt, ˈsɜ.kət/ • n circuit m

**circumspect** /ˈsɜː.kəm.spɛkt, ˈsɜ.kəm.spɛkt/ • adj circumspecte

**circumstance** /ˈsɜːkəmst(ə)ns, ˈsɜ.kəm.ˌstæns/ • n circumstància f

**circus** /ˈsɜː.kəs, ˈsɜkəs/ • n circ m

**citizen** /ˈsɪtɪzən/ • n ciutadà m ~ship • n ciutadania f

**city** /ˈsɪti, sɪti/ • n ciutat f ~ hall • n ajuntament m

**civic** /ˈsɪvɪk/ • adj cívic

**civil** /ˈsɪv.əl/ • adj civil

**civilization** /ˌsɪv.ɪ.laɪˈzeɪ.ʃən, ˌsɪv.ə.ləˈzeɪ.ʃən/ • n civilització f; civilitat f • n civilització f

**claim** /kleɪm/ • n pretensió

**clam** /klæm/ • n cloïssa f

**clarif|y** /ˈklæɹɪfaɪ/ • v aclarir ~ication • n aclariment m

**clarinet** /ˌklæɹɪˈnɛt/ • n clarinet m

**clarity** /ˈklæɹɪti/ • n claredat f

**class** /klɑːs, klæs/ • n classe f; promoció f; curs m

**classic** /ˈklæ.sɪk/ • adj clàssic

**classification** /ˌklæsɪfɪˈkeɪʃən/ • n classificació f

**clause** /klɔːz/ • n clàusula f

**claw** /klɔː, klɔ/ • n urpa f; arpa f; pinça f; garfi m • v esgarrapar; garfir

**clay** /kleɪ/ • n argila f, fang m

**clean** /kliːn, klin/ • adj net; pur; sa • v netejar; arreglar, ordenar ~ **sth up** • v netejar ~er • n netejador m

**clear** /klɪə(ɹ), klɪɪ/ • adj clar • v aclarir-se; rebutjar ~ly • adv clarament

**cleavage** /ˈkliːvɪdʒ, ˈklivɪdʒ/ • n escot m

**clerk** /klɑːk, klɜk/ • n clergue m; oficinista f

**clever** /ˈklɛvər/ • adj llest

**click** /klɪk/ • n clic m • v clicar, fer clic

**client** /ˈklʌɪənt, ˈklaɪ.ənt/ • n client f ~ele • n clientela f

**cliff** /klɪf/ • n penya-segat m

**climate** /ˈklaɪmɪt/ • n clima m ~ change • n canvi climàtic

**climb** /klaɪm/ • n pujada f, ascensió f • v escalar ~er • n enfiladissa f

**clinic** /ˈklɪnɪk/ • n clínica f ~al • adj clínic

**clipboard** • n porta-retalls m

**cloak** /ˈkloʊk/ • n capa f; mantell m • v emboçar

**clock** /klɒk, klɑk/ • n rellotge m; comptaquilòmetres m • v cronometrar; mesurar la velocitat de

**close** /kləʊz, kloʊz/ • adj pròxim • v cloure, tancar ~d • adj tancat

**closure** /ˈkləʊ.ʒə(ɹ), ˈkloʊ.ʒɜ/ • n clausura f

**cloth** /klɔθ, klɑθ/ • *n* tela *f*; drap *m* **~es** • *n* roba **~ing** • *n* roba *f*

**cloud** /klaʊd/ • *n* núvol; polseguera *f* **~y** • *adj* ennuvolat, nuvolós; nebulós

**club** /klʌb/ • *n* bastó *m*; club *m*; trèvol *m* • *v* bastonejar

**clumsy** /ˈklʌmzi/ • *adj* maldestre, barroer, sapastre

**coach** /kəʊtʃ, koʊtʃ/ • *n* entrenador *m*, entrenadora *f*; autocar *m*

**coal** /kəʊl, koʊl/ • *n* carbó *m*; brasa *f*

**coast** /kəʊst, koʊst/ • *n* costa *f* **~al** • *adj* coster, costaner, costal

**coat** /koʊt, kəʊt/ • *n* abric *m*, casaca *f*; cobertura *f* • *v* cobrir

**cocaine** /koʊˈkeɪn/ • *n* cocaïna *f*

**cock** /kɒk, kak/ • *n* mascle *m*; colom *m*; clau *f*

**cockroach** • *n* escarabat *m*, panerola *f*

**cocktail** • *n* còctel *m*

**coconut** /ˈkoʊ.kə.nʌt, ˈkəʊ.kə.nʌt/ • *n* coco *m*

**cod** /kɒd, kad/ • *n* bacallà *m*

**code** /kəʊd, koʊd/ • *n* codi *m*; clau *f*

**coffee** /ˈkɒ.fi, ˈkɔː.fi/ • *adj* cafè, marró • *n* cafè *m*; marró *m*

**cognitive** /ˈkɒɡnɪtɪv/ • *adj* cognitiu

**coheren|t** /kəʊˈhɪərənt, koːˈhiːrənt/ • *adj* coherent **~ce** • *n* coherència *f*

**cohort** /ˈkəʊ.hɔː(ɹ)t, ˈkoʊ.hɔɹt/ • *n* cohort *f*

**coin** /kɔɪn/ • *n* moneda *f* • *v* encunyar

**coincide** /ˌkoʊɪnˈsaɪd/ • *v* coincidir

**cold** /kəʊld, koʊld/ • *adj* fred • *n* fred *m*; constipat *m*, refredat *m*

**collaborat|e** /kəˈlæbəɹeɪt, kəˈlæbəɹeɪt/ • *v* col·laborar **~or** • *n* col·laborador *m* **~ion** • *n* col·laboració *f*

**collage** /kɒˈlɑːʒ, kəˈlɑʒ/ • *n* collage *m*

**collapse** /kəˈlæps/ • *n* col·lapse *m* • *v* enfonsar-se, derruir-se; col·lapsar; plegar; col·lapsar-se

**collar** /ˈkɒl.ə, ˈkɑ.lər/ • *n* coll *m*; collar *m*; collera *m*, jou *m* • *v* collar

**colleague** /ˈkɑliːɡ/ • *n* col·lega, company

**collect** /kəˈlɛkt/ • *v* reunir, ajuntar, recollir, agrupar, aplegar, arreplegar, replegar; col·leccionar **~ive** • *adj* col·lectiu **~or** • *n* col·leccionador *m*, col·leccionista *f*; col·lector *m* **~ion** • *n* col·lecció *f*

**collision** /kəˈlɪʒən/ • *n* col·lisió *f*

**colloquial** /kəˈləʊ.kwi.əl, kəˈloʊ.kwi.əl/ • *adj* col·loquial

**Colombia** • *n* Colòmbia *f* **~n** • *adj* colombià • *n* colombià *m*, colombiana *f*

**colon** /ˈkəʊlən, ˈkoʊlən/ • *n* dos punts; còlon *m*

**colon|y** /ˈkɒl.əni, ˈkɑləni/ • *n* colònia **~ial** • *adj* colonial

**color** /ˈkʌl.ər, ˈkʌl.ə(ɹ)/ • *n* color *f* • *v* acolorir

**colossal** /kə'lɒsəl/ • *adj* colossal

**colour** *(British)* ▷ COLOR

**column** /'kɒləm, 'kɑləm/ • *n* columna *f* **~ist** • *n* columnista *f*

**coma** /'kəʊmə, 'koʊmə/ • *n* coma *m*; cabellera *f*

**comb** /kəʊm, koʊm/ • *n* pinta *f* • *v* pentinar

**combat** /'kɒm.bæt, 'kɑm.bæt/ • *n* batalla *f*, combat *m* • *v* combatre **~ive** • *adj* combatiu **~ant** • *n* combatent *f*

**combination** /kɒmbɪ'neɪʃən/ • *n* combinació *f*

**come** /kʌm/ • *v* (*sp* came, *pp* come) venir; escórrer-se **~ across sth** • *v* ensopegar amb

**comedy** /'kɑm.ə.di/ • *n* comèdia *f*

**comfort** /'kʌm.fət, 'kʌm.fərt/ • *n* comoditat *f*, confort *m*; consol *m*; benestar *m* • *v* consolar; confortar **~able** • *adj* còmode

**comic** /'kɒmɪk, 'kɑmɪk/ • *adj* còmic • *n* còmic *m*

**comma** /'kɒm.ə, 'kɑm.ə/ • *n* coma *f*

**command** /kə'mɑːnd, kə'mænd/ • *n* ordre *f*, manat *m* • *v* ordenar, manar **~er** • *n* comandant *m*

**commence** /kə'mɛns/ • *v* començar

**comment** /'kɒmɛnt, 'kɑmɛnt/ • *n* comentari *m* • *v* comentar **~ary** • *n* comentari *m*

**commerc|e** /'kɑm.ɚs, 'kɒm.əs/ • *n* comerç *m* **~ial** • *adj* comercial • *n* anunci *m*

**commission** /kə'mɪʃən/ • *n* comissió *f*, encàrrec *m* • *v* encarregar, comissionar **~er** • *n* comissionat *m*

**commit** /kə'mɪt/ • *v* validació, transferència • *v* confiar, consignar; tancar, empresonar; cometre; comprometre **~ment** • *n* compromís *m*

**committee** /kə'mɪt.i, kɒmɪ'tiː/ • *n* comitè *m*

**common** /'kɒmən, 'kɑmən/ • *adj* comú *m*, comuna *f* • *n* comuna *f* **~ly** • *adv* comunament **in ~** • *phr* en comú

**communicat|e** /kə'mjuːnɪkeɪt/ • *v* combregar **~ion** • *n* comunicació *f*

**communis|m** /'kɒm.ju.nɪzm̩/ • *n* comunisme *m* **~t** • *adj* comunista *f*

**community** /kə'mjuːnɪti, k(ə)'mjunəti/ • *n* comunitat *f*

**Comoros** • *n* Comores

**companion** /kəm'pænjən/ • *n* acompanyant *m*

**company** /'kʌmp(ə)ni, 'kʌmpəni/ • *n* companyia *f*

**compar|e** /kəm'pɛɚ, kəm'pɛə/ • *v* comparar **~able** • *adj* comparable **~ative** • *adj* comparatiu *m* comparatiu *m* **~ison** • *n* comparació *f*

**compass** /'kʌm.pəs/ • *n* brúixola *f*; àrea *f*, àmbit *m*

**compassion** /kəm'pæʃ.ən/ • *n* compassió *f* **~ate** • *adj* compassiu

**compelling** /kəm'pɛlɪŋ/ • *adj*
convincent

**compensation** /ˌkɒmpɛnˈseɪʃən/
• *n* compensació *f*

**compet|e** /kəmˈpiːt/ • *v*
competir **~ition** • *n*
competència *f*; competició *f*
**~itive** • *adj* competitiu

**competen|t** /ˈkɒmpətənt/ • *adj*
competent **~ce** • *n*
competència *f*

**compilation** /ˌkɒmpɪˈleɪʃən/ • *n*
compilació *f*, recopilació *f*

**complain** /kəmˈpleɪn/ • *v*
queixar-se **~t** • *n* queixa *f*

**complement** /ˈkɒmpləmənt,
ˈkɑmpləmənt/ • *v*
complementar **~ary** • *adj*
complementari

**complete** /kəmˈpliːt/ • *adj*
complet *m*, completa *f* • *v*
complir **~ly** • *adv*
completament; totalment

**complex** /kəmˈplɛks, ˈkɒm.plɛks/
• *adj* complex • *n* complex *m*
**~ity** • *n* complexitat *f*

**complicat|e** • *v* complicar **~ed** •
*adj* complicat **~ion** • *n*
complicació *f*

**compose** /kəmˈpoʊz, kəmˈpəʊz/ •
*v* compondre **~r** • *n*
compositor *m*, compositora *f*

**compound** /ˈkɒmpaʊnd,
ˈkɑmpaʊnd/ • *adj* compost • *n*
compost *m*

**comprehension** /ˌkɒmpɹɪˈhɛnʃn,
ˌkɑmpɹɪˈhɛnʃn/ • *n* comprensió
*f*

**compromise** /ˈkɒmpɹəˌmaɪz,
ˈkɑmpɹəˌmaɪz/ • *n* compromís
*m*

**compulsory** • *adj* obligatori

**compute** /kəmˈpjuːt/ • *v*
computar **~r** • *n* ordinador *m*;
computador *m*, calculador *m*

**comrade** /ˈkɒmɹeɪd, ˈkɑmɹæd/ • *n*
camarada *f*

**conceal** /kənˈsiːl/ • *v* amagar,
ocultar

**conceited** • *adj* presumptuós

**conce|ive** /kənˈsiːv/ • *v* concebre
**~ption** • *n* concepció *f*

**concentrat|e** /ˈkɒn.sən.tɹeɪt,
ˈkɑn.sən.tɹeɪt/ • *v* concentrar
**~ion** • *n* concentració *f*

**concept** /ˈkɒn.sɛpt/ • *n* concepte
*m* **~ual** • *adj* conceptual

**concern** /kənˈsɜn, kənˈsɜːn/ • *n*
preocupació *f*, consternació *f*
• *v* preocupar

**concert** /ˈkənsɜt, kənˈsɜːt/ • *n*
concert *m*

**conclu|de** /kənˈkluːd/ • *v*
concloure **~sion** • *n* conclusió
*f*

**concrete** /ˈkɒnkɹiːt, ˌkɑnˈkɹiːt/ •
*adj* concret • *n* formigó

**condemn** /kənˈdɛm/ • *v*
condemnar

**condescending** /ˌkɒn.dɪ.sɛnd.ɪŋ,
ˌkɑndəˈsɛndɪŋ/ • *adj*
condescendent

**condition** /kənˈdɪʃən/ • *n*
condició *f* • *v* condicionar **~al**
• *adj* condicional • *n*
condicional *m*

**condom** /ˈkɒn.dɒm, ˈkɑn.dəm/ • *n*
preservatiu *m*, condó *m*,
condom *m*

**conduct** /ˈkɒndʌkt, ˈkɑndʌkt/ • *n*
conducta *f*

**cone** /kəʊn, koʊn/ • *n* con *m*; pinya *f*

**confess** /kənˈfɛs/ • *v* confessar **~ion** • *n* confessió *f*

**confiden|t** /ˈkɒnfɪdənt, ˈkɑːnfɪdənt/ • *adj* confiat **~ce** • *n* confiança *f*

**configuration** • *n* configuració *f*

**confinement** • *n* confinament *m*

**confirm** /kənˈfɜːm, kənˈfɜːm/ • *v* confirmar **~ation** • *n* confirmació *f*

**conflict** /ˈkɒn.flɪkt, ˈkɑn.flɪkt/ • *n* conflicte

**confrontation** /ˌkɒnfɹənˈteɪʃən/ • *n* confrontació *f*, confrontament *m*, enfrontament *m*, afrontament *m*

**confus|e** /kənˈfjuːz/ • *v* confondre **~ed** • *adj* confús *m*, desconcertat **~ing** • *adj* confús **~ion** • *n* confusió *f*

**congratulations** /kənˌɡɹætʃəˈleɪʃ(ə)nz, kənˌɡɹatʃəˈleɪʃ(ə)nz/ • *interj* felicitats, enhorabona *f*

**congregat|e** /ˈkɒŋ.ɡɹə.ɡeɪt/ • *v* congregar **~ion** • *n* congregació *f*

**conjunction** /kənˈdʒʌŋkʃən/ • *n* conjunció *f*

**connotation** /ˌkɒnəˈteɪʃən, ˌkɒnəˈteɪʃən/ • *n* connotació *f*

**conquer** /ˈkɒŋkə, ˈkɑŋkɚ/ • *v* conquerir, conquistar

**conscientious objector** • *n* objector de consciència *m*

**consci|ous** /ˈkɒnˈʃəs, ˈkɒn.ʃəs/ • *adj* conscient **~ence** • *n* consciència

**consecutive** /kɒnsɛkjʊtɪv/ • *adj* consecutiu

**consent** /kənˈsɛnt/ • *n* consentiment *m* • *v* consentir

**consequen|tly** /ˈkɒnsɪˌkwɛntli, ˈkɑːnsɪˌkwɛntli/ • *adv* conseqüentment **~ce** • *n* conseqüència *f*

**conservati|on** /ˌkɒnsə(ɹ)ˈveɪʃən/ • *n* conservació *f* **~ve** • *adj* conservador; republicà

**conserve** /ˈkɒnsɜː(ɹ)v, kənˈsɜː(ɹ)v/ • *v* conservar

**consider** /kənˈsɪdə, kənˈsɪdɚ/ • *v* considerar **~able** • *adj* apreciable, considerable **~ably** • *adv* considerablement

**considerate** /kənˈsɪdəɹət/ • *adj* considerat

**consist** /kənˈsɪst/ • *v* consistir **~ent** • *adj* consistent **~ently** • *adv* consistentment **~ency** • *n* consistència *f*

**consolidate** /kənˈsɒlɪdeɪt/ • *v* consolidar

**conspiracy** /kənˈspɪɹəsi/ • *n* conspiració *f*

**constant** /ˈkɒnstənt, ˈkɑnstənt/ • *adj* constant • *n* constant *f* **~ly** • *adv* constantment

**constituen|t** • *adj* constituent **~cy** • *n* circumscripció *f*

**constitution** /ˌkɒnstɪˈtjuːʃən, ˌkɑnstɪˈtuʃən/ • *n* constitució *f* **~al** • *adj* constitucional

**constraint** /kənˈstɹeɪnt/ • *n* restricció *f*

**construct** /ˈkɒn.stɹʌkt, ˈkɑn.stɹʌkt/ • *v* construir **~ion** • *n* construcció *f*

**consult** /kɒnsʌlt, 'kɑnsʌlt/ • v
consultar **~ation** • n consulta
f

**consum|er** /kən'sju:mə,
kən'sumɚ/ • n consumidor m
**~ption** • n consum m

**contain** /kən'teɪn/ • v contenir
**~er** • n contenidor m

**contemporary** • adj
contemporani • n
contemporani

**content** /kɒn'tɛnt, 'kɑn.tɛnt/ •
adj content • n contingut m

**contest** /kɒn.tɛst, 'kɑn.tɛst/ • n
concurs m, competició f **~ant**
• n concursant f

**context** /kɒntɛkst, 'kɑ:ntɛkst/ • n
context m

**continent** /'kɒntɪnənt, 'kɑntɪnənt/
• n continent m

**continu|e** /kən'tɪnju:/ • v
continuar **~ous** • adj continu
**~ally** • adv continuadament

**contract** /'kɒntɹækt, 'kɑntɹækt/ •
n contracte m • v contreure
**~ion** • n contracció f

**contradict** /kɒntɹə'dɪkt/ • v
contradir **~ory** • adj
contradictori **~ion** • n
contradicció f

**on the contrary** • phr
contràriament, al contrari,
per contra

**contrast** /'kɒntɹɑːst, 'kɑnt(ʃ)ɹæst/
• n contrast m

**contribut|e** /kən't(ʃ)ɹɪbju:t,
kən't(ʃ)ɹɪb(j)ət/ • v contribuir
**~ion** • n contribució f

**control** /kən'tɹəʊl, kən't(ʃ)ɹoʊl/ •
n control m • v controlar

**controversial** /kɒn.tɹə.'vɜː.ʃəl,
kɑn.tɹə.'vɝ.ʃəl/ • adj
controvertit, polèmic

**convenien|t** /kən'vi:nɪənt,
kən'vinjənt/ • adj convenient
**~ce** • n conveniència f

**convention** /kən'vɛn.ʃən/ • n
convenció **~al** • adj
convencional

**conversation** /ˌkɒn.və'seɪ.ʃən,
ˌkɑːn.vɚ'seɪ.ʃən/ • n conversa f,
conversació f

**conver|t** /'kɒn.vɜːt, 'kɑn.vɝt/ • v
convertir **~sion** • n
transformació f

**convict** /kən'vɪkt, 'kɒnvɪkt/ • v
condemnar **~ion** • n convicció
f

**convinc|e** /kən'vɪns/ • v
convèncer **~ed** • adj
convençut **~ing** • adj
convincent

**cook** /kʊk, kuk/ • n cuiner m, xef
m • v cuinar; coure; coure's

**cookie** /'kʊki/ • n galeta f; coca
f

**cool** /ku:l/ • adj fresc; fred m,
freda f; guai; tranqui

**cooperat|e** /koʊ'ɒpəɹeɪt/ • v
cooperar **~ion** • n cooperació
f **~ive** • adj cooperatiu • n
cooperativa f

**coordinator** • n coordinador

**copper** /'kɒp.ə, 'kɒp.ə/ • adj
courenc • n coure m, aram m

**copy** /'kɒpi, 'kɑpi/ • n còpia f;
exemplar m • v copiar

**cord** /kɔːd, kɔːd/ • n corda f,
cordill m; cable m

**coriander** /ˌkɒɹiˈændə/ • n
coriandre m, celiandre m

**cork** /kɔːk/ • *n* suro *m*; tap *m*

**corn** /kɔːn, kɔːn/ • *n* call *m*

**corner** /ˈkɔːnə, ˈkɔːnə(ɹ)/ • *n* racó *m*; cantonada *f*; amagatall *m* • *v* arraconar **~stone** • *n* pedra cantonera *f*; pedra angular *f*

**corpora** *(pl)* ▷ CORPUS

**corpus** /ˈkɔːpəs, ˈkɔːpəs/ • *n* (*pl* corpora) corpus *m*

**correct** /kəˈɹɛkt/ • *adj* correcte, condret • *v* corregir **~ion** • *n* correcció *f* **~ly** • *adv* correctament

**correlation** /kɒɹəˈleɪʃən, kɒɹəˈleɪʃən/ • *n* correlació *f*

**correspond** /ˌkɒɹəˈspɒnd, ˌkɒɹəˈspɒnd/ • *v* correspondre **~ence** • *n* correspondència *f* **~ent** • *n* corresponsal *f* **~ing** • *adj* corresponent

**corridor** /ˈkɒɹɪˌdɔː(ɹ), ˈkɒɹəˌɹɪdɔː/ • *n* passadís *m*, corredor *m*

**corrupt** /kəˈɹʌpt/ • *adj* corrupte • *v* corrompre

**cost** /kɒst, kɔst/ • *n* cost *m* • *v* (*sp* cost, *pp* cost) costar **~ly** • *adj* costós

**Costa Rica** • *n* Costa Rica *f*

**cotton** /ˈkɒt.n̩, ˈkɒt.n̩/ • *adj* de cotó • *n* cotó *m*

**couch** /kaʊtʃ/ • *n* sofà *m*

**cough** /kɒf, kɔːf/ • *n* tos *f* • *v* tossir

**could** *(sp)* ▷ CAN

**council** /ˈkaʊn.səl/ • *n* consell *m*

**count** /kaʊnt/ • *n* comptatge *m*, compte *m*; comte *m* • *v* comptar; valdre

**counter** /ˈkaʊntə, ˈkaʊntə/ • *n* fitxa *f*, getó *m*; taulell *m*;

comptador *m*; comptavoltes *m*

**country** /ˈkʌntɹi, ˈkʌntɹi/ • *adj* campestre • *n* país *m*; camp *m*

**county** /ˈkaʊnti/ • *n* comtat *m*; comarca *f*

**couple** /ˈkʌpəl/ • *n* parella • *v* acoblar

**courage** /ˈkʌɹɪdʒ/ • *n* coratge *m*, valor *m* **~ous** • *adj* coratjós, valent

**courgette** /kʊɹˈʒɛt, kʊəˈʒɛt/ • *n* carabassó

**course** /kɔːs, kɔːɹs/ • *n* curs *m*; plat *m*; itinerari *m*, ruta *f*, recorregut *m*; trajectòria *f*; rumb *m* • *v* cursar, recórrer

**court** /kɔːt, kɔɹt/ • *n* pati *m*; cort *f*; tribunal *m*; pista de joc *f* • *v* cortejar

**courte|ous** /ˈkɜːti.əs, ˈkɜːti.əs/ • *adj* cortès **~sy** • *n* cortesia *f*

**cousin** /ˈkʌz.n̩, ˈkʌz.ɪn/ • *n* cosí *m*, cosina *f*

**cover** /ˈkʌvə, ˈkʌvə/ • *n* tapa *f* **~ed** • *adj* cobert

**cow** /kaʊ/ • *n* vaca *f*; bruixa *f*, foca *f*; marró *m*, pedra *f*

**coward** /ˈkaʊəd, ˈkaʊəd/ • *n* covard **~ly** • *adj* covard • *adv* covardament

**crab** /kɹæb/ • *n* cranc *m*, carranc *m*; cabra

**crack** /kɹæk/ • *n* esquerda *f*, escletxa *f*; badall *m* • *v* esquerdar

**craft** /kɹɑːft, kɹæft/ • *v* fet a mà **~sman** • *n* artesà *m*

**cranberry** /ˈkɹænb(ə)ɹi/ • *n* nabiu de grua *m*; nabiu

**crash** /kɹæʃ/ • n xoc m, patacada f

**crawl** /kɹɔːl, kɹɔl/ • v arrossegar-se, gatejar

**crayon** /'kɹeɪ.ən, 'kɹeɪ.ɒn/ • n llapis de color m

**crazy** /'kɹeɪzi/ • adj boig • n boig m

**cream** /kɹiːm/ • n nata f, crema f ~y • adj cremós

**creat|e** /kɹiː'eɪt/ • v crear ~ion • n creació f ~or • n creador m

**creativ|e** /kɹiː'eɪtɪv/ • adj creatiu • n creatiu ~ity • n creativitat f

**credib|le** /'kɹɛdəbl/ • adj creïble ~ility • n credibilitat f

**credit** /'kɹɛdɪt/ • v reconeixement m ~ card • n targeta de crèdit f

**credulous** /'kɹɛdjələs/ • adj crèdul

**creepy** /'kɹiːpi, 'kɹipi/ • adj esborronador

**crew** /kɹuː/ • n tripulació f; marineria f; equip m; banda f, colla f; tripulant m • (also) ▷ CROW

**cricket** /'kɹɪk.ɪt/ • n grill m; criquet m

**crim|e** /kɹaɪm/ • n crim m, delicte m ~inal • adj criminal • n criminal f

**crisis** /'kɹaɪsɪs/ • n (pl crises) crisi f

**criterion** /kɹaɪ'tɪəɹi.ən/ • n criteri m

**criti|c** /'kɹɪt.ɪk/ • n crític m ~que • n crítica f ~cize • v criticar

**critical** /'kɹɪtɪkəl/ • adj crític ~ly • adv críticament

**Croatia** • n Croàcia ~n • adj croat • n croat m, croata f

**crocodile** /'kɹɑkədaɪl, 'kɹɒkədaɪl/ • n cocodril m

**crooked** /kɹʊkt/ • adj tort, tortuós

**crop** /kɹɒp, kɹɑp/ • n pap m

**cross** /kɹɒs, kɹɔs/ • n creu f ~roads • n encreuament m, cruïlla f ~walk • n pas de vianants m ~word • n mots encreuats

**crow** /kɹəʊ, kɹoʊ/ • n còrvid m; corb m

**crowd** /kɹaʊd/ • n multitud f, gentada f, gernació f ~ed • adj abarrotat

**crowed** (sp/pp) ▷ CROW

**crown** /kɹaʊn/ • n corona f; capçada f

**crucial** /'kɹuːʃəl/ • adj crucial

**crude** /kɹuːd/ • adj cru; groller

**cruel** /kɹuːəl/ • adj cruel ~ty • n crueltat f

**cruise** /kɹuːz/ • n creuer m

**crush** /kɹʌʃ/ • v aixafar

**cry** /kɹaɪ/ • n plor m; crit m • v plorar; cridar

**crystal** /'kɹɪstəl/ • n cristall m

**Cuba** • n Cuba f ~n • adj cubà • n cubà m

**cube** /kjuːb, kjub/ • n cub m • v cubicar, elevar al cub

**cuckoo** /'kʊkuː, 'kuːkuː/ • n cucut m

**cucumber** /'kjuːˌkʌmbəɹ, 'kjuːˌkʌmbə/ • n cogombre m, cogombrera f

**cuddle** /'kʌd.l̩/ • v acaronar

**cue** /kjuː/ • n estímul m; cu f; tac m

**cuff** /kʌf/ • n puny m

**cultivate** /ˈkʌltɪveɪt/ • v conrear, cultivar

**cultur|e** /ˈkʌltʃə, ˈkʌltʃə/ • n cultura f; cultiu m ~al • adj cultural

**cumin** /ˈkʌmɪn, ˈkumɪn/ • n comí m

**cup** /kʌp/ • n tassa f; copa f

**cupboard** /ˈkʌbəd, ˈkʌbəd/ • n canterano m, calaixera f, armari m

**cupcake** /ˈkʌpkeɪk/ • n cupcake m

**curio|us** /ˈkjʊəri.əs, ˈkjɜːi.əs/ • adj curiós m, curiosa ~sity • n curiositat f

**curly** /ˈkɜːli, ˈkɜːli/ • adj arrissat

**currency** /ˈkʌɹ.ən.si/ • n moneda f

**current** /ˈkʌɹənt/ • adj actual • n riu m, corrent m ~ly • adv actualment

**curtain** /ˈkɜːtn̩, ˈkɜːtn̩/ • n cortina f; teló m

**curve** /kɜːv, kɜːv/ • n revolt m; corba f; corbes

**cushion** /ˈkʊʃən/ • n coixí m

**custody** /ˈkʌstədiː/ • n custòdia f

**custom** /ˈkʌstəm/ • adj personalitzat • n costum m

**customer** /ˈkʌstəmə, ˈkʌstəmə/ • n client f

**cut** /kʌt/ • n costura f • v (sp cut, pp cut) tallar; retallar ~ting • adj mordaç

**cute** /kjuːt/ • adj bufó; maco

**CV** • n (abbr Curriculum Vitae) cv m

**cycle** /ˈsaɪkəl/ • n cicle m

**cycling** /ˈsaɪk(ə)lɪŋ/ • n ciclisme m

**cylinder** /ˈsɪlɪndə(ɹ), ˈsɪləndə/ • n cilindre m

**cymbal** /ˈsɪmbəl/ • n platerets

**Cypr|us** • n Xipre ~iot • adj xipriota • n xipriota f

**Czech** • adj txec • n txec m, txeca f ~ **Republic** • n República Txeca f, Txèquia f

# D

**dad** /dæd/ • n papa m

**dairy** /ˈdɛəɹi/ • n lleteria, vaqueria (specifically, cows), cabreria; lactis

**dam** /dæm/ • n presa f

**damag|e** /ˈdæmɪdʒ/ • n dany m • v danyar ~ing • adj perjudicial

**damn** /dæm/ • adj maleït • adv malaïdament • interj cagondena • v maleir

**damp** /dæmp/ • adj humit • n humitat f

**dance** /dæns, dɑːns/ • n ball m, dansa f • v ballar, dansar ~r • n ballador m, ballarí m

**danger** /ˈdeɪn.dʒə(ɹ), ˈdeɪndʒə/ • n perill m ~ous • adj perillós

**Danish** • adj danès • n danès m

**dare** /dɛə(ɹ), dɛə/ • v gosar, atrevir-se ~devil • adj temerari

**dark** /dɑːɹk, dɑːk/ • adj fosc; obscur • n foscor f, obscuritat f ~ness • n foscor f; tenebres; negror f

**data** /'deɪtə, 'dætə/ • *n*
informació *f*, dades **~base** • *n*
base de dades *f*

**date** /deɪt/ • *n* dàtil *m*; data *f*;
cita *f* • *v* sortir, quedar

**daughter** /'dɔːtə(ɹ), 'dɔːtəɹ/ • *n*
filla *f* **~-in-law** • *n* nora *f*

**dawn** /dɔːn, dɔːn/ • *n* aurora *f*;
alba *m*; albada *f*; albors *v*
clarejar; néixer

**da|y** /deɪ/ • *n* dia *m*, jorn *m*;
jornada *f* **~ily** • *adj* diari • *adv*
diàriament • *n* diari *m*

**dazzling** /'dæz.l̩.ɪŋ/ • *adj*
enlluernador

**deactivate** /ˌdiːˈæktɪveɪt/ • *v*
desactivar ~ • *v* desactivar

**dead** /dɛd/ • *adj* mort • *n* morts
*m* **~ly** • *adj* mortal, letal,
mortifer

**deaf** /dɛf, diːf/ • *adj* sord • *n* els
sords **~ening** • *adj* ensordidor

**deal** /diːl/ • *n* tracte *m* • *v* (*sp*
dealt, *pp* dealt) repartir;
comerciar, vendre, comprar;
tractar

**dealt** *(sp/pp)* ▷ DEAL

**dean** /diːn/ • *n* degà *m*

**dear** /dɪɹ, dɪə/ • *adj* estimat,
benvolgut

**death** /dɛθ/ • *n* mort *f*; la mort
**~ penalty** • *n* pena de mort *f*

**debat|e** /dɪˈbeɪt/ • *n* debat *m* • *v*
debatre **~able** • *adj* discutible

**debris** /'dɛbɹiː, dəˈbɹiː/ • *n* restes

**debt** /dɛt/ • *n* deute *m*

**debut** /'dɛbjuː, deɪˈbjuː/ • *n* debut
*m* • *v* debutar

**decade** /'dɛkeɪd/ • *n* dècada *f*,
decenni *m*

**deceive** /dɪˈsiːv/ • *v* enganyar,
decebre

**December** • *n* desembre *m*

**decency** /'diːsənsi/ • *n* decència *f*

**decepti|on** /dɪˈsɛpʃən/ • *n*
engany *m* **~ve** • *adj* enganyós,
decebedor, deceptiu

**decide** /dɪˈsaɪd/ • *v* decidir

**decisi|on** /dɪˈsɪʒən/ • *n* decisió *f*
**~ve** • *adj* decisiu

**deck** /dɛk/ • *n* terra *m*; baralla *f*;
coberta *f*

**declar|e** /dɪˈkleə, dɪˈklɛɹ/ • *v*
declarar **~ation** • *n* declaració
*f*

**decl|ine** /dɪˈklaɪn/ • *n* declivi *m*,
caiguda *f* • *v* declinar-se;
debilitar-se; declinar, refusar
**~ension** • *n* declinació *f*

**decorat|e** /'dɛkəɹeɪt/ • *v* decorar
**~ion** • *n* decoració *f* **~ive** •
*adj* decoratiu

**decrease** /dɪˈkɹiːs, 'diːkɹiːs/ • *n*
disminució *f*, decreixença *f* •
*v* decréixer, disminuir

**dedicat|e** /'dɛdɪkeɪt/ • *v* dedicar;
destinar; dedicar-se;
inaugurar **~ion** • *n*
dedicatòria *f*

**deed** /diːd/ • *n* fet *m*, acte *m*;
escriptura *f*, acta *f*

**deep** /diːp/ • *adj* profund;
pregon; greu; intens; fondo
**~ly** • *adv* profundament

**deer** /dɪə, dɪɹ/ • *n* cérvol *m*

**defeat** /dɪˈfiːt/ • *n* venciment *m*;
derrota *f* • *v* vèncer

**defect** /'diːfɛkt, dɪˈfɛkt/ • *n*
defecte *m* **~ive** • *adj* defectiu,
defectuós

**defence** *(British)* ▷ DEFENSE

**defen|d** /dɪˈfɛnd, dɛˈfɛnd/ • v
defensar, defendre **~der** • n
defensor m **~se** • n defensa f
**~seless** • adj indefens

**deficien|t** /dɪˈfɪʃənt/ • adj
deficient **~cy** • n deficiència f;
dèficit m

**deficit** /ˈdɛfɪsɪt, ˈdɛfəsɪt/ • n
dèficit m

**defin|e** /dɪˈfaɪn/ • v definir
**~ition** • n definició f

**definit|e** /ˈdɛfɪnɪt/ • adj definit m
**~ely** • adv definitivament;
decididament **~ive** • adj
definitiu

**deforestation** /dɪˌfɒɹɪsˈteɪʃən/ • n
desforestació f

**defrost** /diːˈfɹɒst/ • v
descongelar; desglaçar,
desgelar

**degree** /dɪˈgɹiː/ • n grau m; títol
m, diploma m

**delay** /dɪˈleɪ/ • n retard m,
demora f, endarreriment m •
v endarrerir, demorar

**delegate** /ˈdɛlɪgət, ˈdɛlɪˌgeɪt/ • n
delegat m, delegada f

**delete** /dɪˈliːt/ • v esborrar

**deliberat|e** /dɪˈlɪbəɹət, dəˈlɪbəɹət/
• adj deliberat **~ely** • adv
deliberadament;
prudentment **~ion** • n
deliberació f

**delicate** /ˈdɛlɪkət/ • adj delicat

**delicious** /dɪˈlɪʃəs, dəˈlɪʃəs/ • adj
deliciós, gustós, saborós **~ly** •
adv deliciosament

**delight** /dəˈlaɪt/ • n delit m, plaer
m **~ed** • adj encantat m

**delightful** /dəˈlaɪtˌfəl/ • adj
encantador

**deliver** /dɪˈlɪvə(ɹ), dɪˈlɪvɚ/ • v
entregar, lliurar **~y** • n
lliurament m, entrega f

**demand** /dɪˈmɑːnd, dɪˈmænd/ • v
exigir **~ing** • adj exigent

**democra|cy** /dɪˈmɒkɹəsi,
dɪˈmɑkɹəsi/ • n democràcia f
**~tic** • adj democràtic

**demographic** /dɛməˈgɹæfɪk/ •
adj demogràfic

**demon** /ˈdiːmən/ • n dimoni,
diable **~ic** • adj demoníac

**demonstrat|e** /ˈdɛmənstɹeɪt/ • v
demostrar **~ive** • adj
demostratiu

**demoralize** /dɪˈmɒɹəlaɪz/ • v
desmoralitzar

**Denmark** • n Dinamarca f

**denounce** /dɪˈnaʊns/ • v
denunciar

**dens|e** /dɛns/ • adj dens **~ity** •
n densitat f

**dentist** /ˈdɛntɪst/ • n dentista

**den|y** /dɪˈnaɪ/ • v negar **~ial** • n
desmentiment m

**depart** /dɪˈpɑːt, dɪˈpɑɹt/ • v
departir, deixar

**depend** /dɪˈpɛnd/ • v dependre
**~ent** • adj dependent **~ence** •
n dependència f

**depiction** • n representació f

**deposit** /dɪˈpɒzɪt, dɪˈpɑzɪt/ • n
jaciment m; dipòsit m • v
dipositar

**depress** /dɪˈpɹɛs/ • v deprimir
**~ed** • adj deprimit **~ing** • adj
depriment **~ion** • n depressió
f **~ive** • adj depressiu m

**depth** /dɛpθ/ • n profunditat

**deriv|e** /dəˈɹaɪv/ • v derivar
**~ation** • n derivació f

**descen|d** /dɪ'sɛnd/ • v descendir
~**t** • n baixada f ~**dant** • n
descendent m

**descri|be** /də'skɹaɪb/ • v
descriure ~**ptive** • adj
descriptiu ~**ption** • n
descripció f

**desert** /dɪ'zɜ:(ɪ)t, dɪ'zɜɹt/ • adj
desert • n desert m • v
desertar ~**er** • n desertor m

**deserve** /dɪ'zɜ:v, dɪ'zɜ'v/ • v
merèixer, meritar

**design** /dɪ'zaɪn/ • n disseny m • v
dissenyar ~**er** • n dissenyador
m

**desir|e** /dɪ'zaɪə, dɪ'zaɪɪ/ • n desig
m • v desitjar ~**able** • adj
desitjable

**desktop** /'dɛsktɒp/ • n escriptori
m; sobretaula m

**despair** /dɪ'spɛə(ɹ), dɪ'spɛəɹ/ • n
desesperació

**desperat|e** /'dɛsp(ə)ɹət/ • adj
desesperat ~**ely** • adv
desesperadament ~**ion** • n
desesperació f

**despite** /dɪ'spaɪt/ • n malgrat,
tot i que, encara que, tot i

**dessert** /dɪ'zɜ:t, dɪ'zɜ't/ • n
postres, darreries

**destination** /dɛstɪ'neɪʃən/ • n
destinació f

**destiny** /'dɛstɪni/ • n destí m,
planeta f

**destr|oy** /dɪ'stɹɔɪ/ • v destruir
~**uction** • n destrucció f
~**uctive** • adj destructiu

**detail** /'di:teɪl, 'dɪˌteɪl/ • n detall
m • v detallar ~**ed** • adj
detallat

**detain** /dɪ'teɪn/ • v detenir,
detindre

**detect** /dɪ'tɛkt/ • v detectar ~**ion**
• n detecció f ~**ive** • n
detectiu m

**determine** /dɪ'tɜ:mɪn, dɪ'tɜ'mɪn/ •
v determinar ~**d** • adj
determinat

**devastat|e** /'dɛvəsteɪt/ • v
devastar ~**ing** • adj
devastador

**develop** /dɪ'vɛ.ləp, 'dɛv.ləp/ • v
desenvolupar ~**er** • n
desenvolupador m ~**ment** • n
desenvolupament m

**device** /də'vaɪs/ • n dispositiu m,
mecanisme m

**devil** /'dɛvəl, 'dɛvɪl/ • n dimoni m,
diable m

**devise** • v divisar, copçar,
preveure

**devot|e** /dɪ'vəʊt/ • v consagrar
~**ion** • n devoció f

**diabetes** /ˌdaɪə'bi:ti:z/ • n
diabetis f

**diagnos|e** /'daɪəg'nəʊz,
daɪəg'noʊs/ • v diagnosticar
~**is** • n diagnòstic m, diagnosi
f

**diagram** /'daɪ.ə.gɹæm/ • n
diagrama m

**dialogue** /'daɪəlɒg, 'daɪələg/ • n
diàleg m • v dialogar

**diamond** /'daɪ(ə)mənd/ • n
diamant m; camp interior m

**diary** /'daɪəɹi/ • n diari m

**dictatorship** /dɪk'teɪtə(ɹ)ʃɪp,
'dɪkteɪtəɹʃɪp/ • n dictadura f

**dictionary** /'dɪkʃ(ə)n(ə)ɹi,
'dɪkʃənɛɹi/ • n diccionari m

**did** *(sp)* ▷ DO

**didactic** /daɪˈdæk.tɪk/ • *adj* didàctic

**die** /daɪ/ • *n* encuny *m*; dau *m* • *v* morir

**diet** /ˈdaɪət/ • *n* dieta *f*

**differ** /ˈdɪfə/ • *v* diferir

**differen|t** /ˈdɪf.rənt/ • *adj* diferent **~ce** • *n* diferència *f* **~tly** • *adv* diferentment

**difficult** /ˈdɪfɪkəlt/ • *adj* difícil **~y** • *n* dificultat *f*

**diffus|e** /dɪˈfjuːz, dɪˈfjuz/ • *adj* difús **~ion** • *n* difusió *f*

**dig** /dɪg/ • *n* excavació *f* • *v* (*sp* dug, *pp* dug) cavar, excavar

**digest** /daɪˈdʒɛst/ • *v* digerir **~ive** • *adj* digestiu • *n* digestiu *m*

**digit** /ˈdɪdʒɪt/ • *n* dit *m*; xifra *f* **~al** • *adj* digital **~ally** • *adv* digitalment

**digni|ty** /ˈdɪgnɪti/ • *n* dignitat *f* **~fied** • *adj* digne

**dilemma** /daɪˈlɛmə/ • *n* dilema *m*

**diligent** /ˈdɪlɪdʒənt/ • *adj* diligent **~ly** • *adv* diligentment

**dill** /dɪł/ • *n* anet *m*

**dimension** /daɪˈmɛnʃən, daɪˈmɛnʃn̩/ • *n* dimensió *f*

**diminish** /dɪˈmɪnɪʃ/ • *v* disminuir

**din|e** /daɪn/ • *v* sopar **~ner** • *n* sopar *m*; menjar *m*; dinar *m*; banquet *m* **~ing room** • *n* menjador *m*

**dinosaur** /ˈdaɪnəsɔː(ɹ)/ • *n* dinosaure *m*

**dip** /dɪp/ • *n* gual *m* • *v* sucar

**diploma** /dɪˈpləʊmə/ • *n* diploma *m*, títol *m*

**diploma|t** /ˈdɪ.plə.mæt/ • *n* diplomàtic *m*, diplomàtica *f*

**~cy** • *n* diplomàcia *f* **~tic** • *adj* diplomàtic

**direct** /d(a)ɪˈɹɛkt/ • *adj* directe • *v* dirigir; adreçar **~ion** • *n* direcció *f* **~ly** • *adv* directament **~or** • *n* director *m*, directora *f*

**dirt** /dɜːt, dɜt/ • *n* terra *f* **~y** • *adj* brut • *v* embrutar

**disabled** /dɪsˈeɪbəld/ • *adj* invàlid; minusvàlid, discapacitat

**disadvantage** /ˌdɪsədˈvɑːntɪdʒ, ˌdɪsədˈvæntɪdʒ/ • *n* desavantatge *m*

**disagreement** /ˌdɪsəˈgɹiːmənt/ • *n* desacord *m*

**disappear** /dɪsəˈpɪə, dɪsəˈpɪɹ/ • *v* desaparèixer **~ance** • *n* desaparició

**disappoint** /dɪsəˈpɔɪnt/ • *v* decebre **~ed** • *adj* decebut **~ment** • *n* decepció *f*

**disast|er** /dɪˈzæs.tə, dɪˈzɑːs.tə(ɹ)/ • *n* desastre *m* **~rous** • *adj* desastrós

**disc** *(British)* ▷ DISK

**discipline** /ˈdɪ.sə.plɪn/ • *n* disciplina *f* • *v* disciplinar

**disclose** /dɪsˈkləʊz/ • *v* revelar; divulgar

**disconnect** /dɪskəˈnɛkt/ • *v* desconnectar

**discount** /dɪsˈkaʊnt, ˈdɪskaʊnt/ • *n* descompte *m*, rebaixa *f*

**discover** /dɪsˈkʌvə, dɪsˈkʌvə/ • *v* descobrir **~y** • *n* descobriment *m*

**discrete** /dɪsˈkɹiːt/ • *adj* discret

**discriminat|e** /dɪsˈkɹɪmɪneɪt/ • *v* discriminar **~ion** • *n* discriminació f

**discuss** /dɪsˈkʌs/ • v discutir, debatre **~ion** • n discussió f

**disease** /dɪˈziːz, dɪˈziz/ • n malaltia f

**disguise** /dɪsˈgaɪz, dɪˈskaɪz/ • n disfressa f • v disfressar

**dish** /dɪʃ/ • n vaixella f; plat m; antena parabòlica f **~washer** • n rentaplats m

**dishonest** /dɪˈsɒnɪst, dɪˈsɑnɪst/ • adj deshonest

**disk** /dɪsk/ • n disc m; disc dur m

**dislike** /dɪsˈlaɪk/ • v desagradar, no agradar

**dismiss** /dɪsˈmɪs, dɪzˈmɪs/ • v destituir, acomiadar, despedir; rebutjar

**disorder** /dɪsˈɔːdə(ɹ), dɪsˈɔːɹdɚ/ • n desordre m; trastorn m

**displace** /dɪsˈpleɪs/ • v desnonar; suplantar; desplaçar, desallotjar **~ment** • n desplaçament m

**display** /dɪsˈpleɪ/ • n espectacle m; monitor m • v exhibir

**disposable** /dɪsˈpəʊzəbl̩, dɪsˈpoʊzəbl̩/ • adj disponible

**dispute** /dɪsˈpjuːt/ • v disputar

**disruption** /dɪsˈɹʌpʃən/ • n interrupció f; desordre m

**distan|t** /ˈdɪstənt/ • adj distant **~ce** • n distància; llunyania f • v distanciar-se, allunyar-se

**distinct** /dɪsˈtɪŋkt/ • adj distint **~ion** • n distinció f **~ive** • adj distintiu

**distinguish** /dɪsˈtɪŋgwɪʃ/ • v distingir **~ed** • adj distingit

**distort** /dɪsˈtɔːt, dɪsˈtɔːɹt/ • v deformar; tergiversar,

distorsionar **~ion** • n distorsió f

**distract** /dɪsˈtɹækt/ • v distreure **~ion** • n distracció f

**distribution** /ˌdɪstɹəˈbjuːʃən/ • n distribució f

**district** /ˈdɪstɹɪkt/ • n comarca f, districte

**disturb** /dɪsˈtɜːb/ • v molestar

**div|e** /ˈdaɪv/ • n estirada f • v capbussar-se **~er** • n bus f **~ing** • n salts

**divers|e** /daɪˈvɜːs, diˈvɜs/ • adj divers **~ify** • v diversificar **~ity** • n diversitat f

**divert** /daɪˈvɜːt, daɪˈvɜt/ • v desviar

**divi|de** /dɪˈvaɪd/ • v dividir **~dend** • n dividend m **~sion** • n divisió f

**divine** /dɪˈvaɪn/ • adj diví

**divorce** /dɪˈvɔːs, dɪˈvɔɹs/ • n divorci m • v divorciar **~d** • adj separat; divorciat

**dizzy** /ˈdɪzi/ • adj marejat; vertiginós

**DNA** • n (abbr DeoxyriboNucleic Acid) ADN

**do** /duː, du/ • n do m; fer; anar; fer-ho ~ **away with sth** • v desfer-se

**doctorate** /ˈdɒk.tə.ɹɪt, ˈdɑk.tə.ɹət/ • n doctorat m

**doctrine** /ˈdɒktɹɪn, ˈdɒktɹɪn/ • n doctrina f

**document** /ˈdɒkjʊmənt, ˈdɑkjʊmənt/ • n document m • v documentar **~ation** • n documentació f

**documentary** /ˌdɒk.jəˈmɛn.tɹi, ˌdɑː.kjəˈmɛn.tɚ.i/ • adj

documental

**dog** /dɒg, dɔg/ • *n* gos, ca *m*, gossa *f*, cutxu

**doll** /dɒl, dal/ • *n* nina *f*

**dollar** /ˈdɒlə, ˈdalɚ/ • *n* dòlar *m*

**dolphin** /ˈdɒlfɪn, ˈdalfɪn/ • *n* dofí *m*

**domestic** /dəˈmɛstɪk/ • *adj* domèstic; interior ~**ate** • *v* domesticar

**dominate** /ˈdɒməˌneɪt, ˈdɑːməˌneɪt/ • *v* dominar

**don|ation** /dəʊˈneɪʃən, doʊˈneɪʃən/ • *n* donació *f*, donatiu *m* ~**or** • *n* donador *m*, donadora *f*, donant *f*

**done** *(pp)* ▷ DO

**donkey** /ˈdɒŋki, ˈdaŋki/ • *n* ase *m*, somera *f*, burro *m*, burra *f*, ruc *m*, ruca *f*

**door** /dɔː, dɔɹ/ • *n* porta *f* ~**bell** • *n* timbre

**dormitory** /ˈdɔːmɪˌtɔːri/ • *n* dormitori *m*

**dose** /dəʊs, doʊs/ • *n* dosi *f*

**dot** /dɒt, dat/ • *n* punt *m*

**double** /ˈdʌb.əl/ • *adj* doble • *v* doblar

**doubt** /daʊt, dʌʊt/ • *n* dubte *m* • *v* dubtar ~**ful** • *adj* dubtós

**dough** /dəʊ, doʊ/ • *n* pasta *f*, massa *f*

**dove** /dʌv/ • *n* colom *m*

**down** /daʊn/ • *adj* deprimit, moix; baix • *adv* avall • *n* intent *m*; plomissol *m* ~**load** • *n* baixada • *v* baixar, descarregar ~**stairs** • *adv* a baix, escala avall

**dozen** /ˈdʌzn̩/ • *n* dotzena *f*

**draft** /dɹɑːft, dɹæft/ • *n* esborrany *m*; esbós *m*; calat *m*; tiro *m*, corrent *f*, correntia *f*

**drag** /dɹæg/ • *n* pipada *f* • *v* arrossegar

**dragon** /ˈdɹægən/ • *n* drac *m*, víbria *f* ~**fly** • *n* libèl·lula *f*, cavall de serp *m*, espiadimonis *m*, tallanassos *m*, teixidor *m*, barratgina

**drainage** /ˈdɹeɪnədʒ/ • *n* drenatge *m*

**drama** /ˈdɹɑːmə, ˈdɹɑmə/ • *n* drama *m* ~**tic** • *adj* dramàtic ~**tically** • *adv* dramàticament

**drank** *(sp)* ▷ DRINK

**draw** /dɹɔː, dɹɑ/ • *v* (*sp* drew, *pp* drawn) dibuixar; empatar ~**ing** • *n* dibuix *m*

**drawer** /ˈdɹɔː(ɹ), dɹɔɹ/ • *n* calaix *m*

**drawn** *(pp)* ▷ DRAW

**dread** /dɹɛd/ • *v* témer

**dream** /dɹiːm, dɹim/ • *n* somni *m* • *v* (*sp* dreamt, *pp* dreamt) somiar

**dreamed** *(sp/pp)* ▷ DREAM

**dreamt** *(sp/pp)* ▷ DREAM

**dress** /dɹɛs/ • *n* vestit *m* • *v* vestir; vestir-se ~**ing gown** • *n* batí *m*, bata *f*

**drew** *(sp)* ▷ DRAW

**drift** /dɹɪft/ • *n* vagar, vagarejar

**drill** /dɹɪl/ • *n* trepant *m* • *v* perforar, foradar

**drink** /dɹɪŋk/ • *n* beguda *f*, glop *m* • *v* (*sp* drank, *pp* drunk) beure

**drive** /dɹaɪv/ • *v* (*sp* drove, *pp* driven) conduir ~**r** • *n* conductor *m*; controlador de dispositiu *m*

**driven** *(pp)* ▷ DRIVE
**drool** /dɹuːl/ • *v* salivar
**drop** /dɹɒp, dɹɑp/ • *n* gota *f*
**drought** /dɹaʊt/ • *n* sequera *f*, secada *f*, seca *f*
**drove** *(sp)* ▷ DRIVE
**drown** /dɹaʊn/ • *v* ofegar; submergir
**drug** /dɹʌg/ • *n* droga *f*
**drum** /dɹʌm/ • *n* tambor *m*; barril *m* • *v* tamborinejar
**drunk** /dɹʌŋk/ • *adj* borratxo, embriac, begut • *n* borratxo *m*, embriac *m* • *(also)* ▷ DRINK
**dry** /dɹaɪ/ • *adj* eixut, sec • *v* assecar, eixugar **~er** • *n* assecadora *f* **tumble ~er** • *n* assecadora *f*
**dual** /ˈdjuːəl, ˈd(j)uːəl/ • *adj* dual; doble
**dub** /dʌb/ • *v* doblar **~bing** • *n* doblatge *m*
**Dublin** • *n* Dublín
**duck** /dʌk/ • *n* ànec *m* • *v* ajupir-se
**dude** /d(j)uːd, duːʊd/ • *n* paio *m*, tio *m*
**dug** *(sp/pp)* ▷ DIG
**dull** /dʌl/ • *adj* insuls *m*, fat
**dumb** /dʌm/ • *adj* estúpid
**duration** /djʊˈɹeɪʃn, dəˈɹeɪʃn/ • *n* durada *f*, duració *f*
**during** /ˈdjʊəɹɪŋ, ˈdʊəɹɪŋ/ • *prep* durant
**dust** /dʌst/ • *n* pols *f* • *v* desempolsar; espolsar; empolsar
**Dutch** • *adj* neerlandès, holandès • *n* neerlandès *m*, holandès *m*; neerlandesa *f*, holandesa *f*

**duty** /ˈdjuːti, duːˈti/ • *n* obligació, deure *m*; servei; taxa
**dynamic** /daɪˈnæ.mɪk/ • *adj* dinàmic *m* • *n* dinàmica *f* **~s** • *n* dinàmica *f*

**each** /iːtʃ, itʃ/ • *det* cada, cada un de, cadascun de
**eagerness** /ˈiɡənəs, ˈiːɡənəs/ • *n* ànsia *f*, afany *m*
**eagle** /ˈiːɡəl/ • *n* àliga *f*, àguila *f*
**ear** /ɪə, ɪɹ/ • *n* orella *f*; espiga *f* • *v* espigar, espiguejar
**early** /ˈɜli, ˈɜːli/ • *adj* d'hora • *adv* aviat
**earn** /ɜːn, ɜn/ • *v* guanyar; cobrar **~est** • *adj* seriós
**earth** /ɜːθ, ɜθ/ • *n* terra *f*, sòl *m*; massa *f* **~quake** • *n* terratrèmol *m*, sisme *m* **on ~** • *phr* dimonis, diables
**easily** /ˈiːzɪli, ˈiːzə.liː/ • *adv* fàcilment
**east** /iːst/ • *n* est *m*, llevant *m*, orient *m* **~ern** • *adj* oriental; llevant
**easy** /ˈiːzi, ˈizi/ • *adj* fàcil **~going** • *adj* calmat, tranquil, relaxat
**eat** /iːt, it/ • *v* *(sp* ate, *pp* eaten) menjar **~er** • *n* menjador
**eaten** *(pp)* ▷ EAT
**echo** /ˈɛkəʊ, ˈɛkoʊ/ • *n* *(pl* echoes) eco *m*

**ecolog|y** /ɛˈkɒlədʒi, iˈkɑ.lə.dʒi/ •
*n* ecologia *f* **~ical** • *adj*
ecològic

**econom|y** /iˈkɒn.ə.mi, iˈkɑn.ə.mi/
• *n* economia *f* **~ic** • *adj*
econòmic **~ically** • *adv*
econòmicament **~ics** • *n*
economia *f* **~ist** • *n*
economista *f*

**ecosystem** /ˈiːkəʊ sɪstəm,
ˈikoʊ sɪstəm/ • *n* ecosistema *m*

**Ecuador** • *n* Equador *m*

**edge** /ɛdʒ/ • *n* vora *f*

**Edinburgh** • *n* Edimburg

**edit** /ˈɛdɪt/ • *n* edició *f*,
modificació *f* • *v* editar **~ion**
• *n* edició *f* **~or** • *n* editor *m*,
editora *f* **~orial** • *adj* editorial

**educat|e** /ˈɛdʒəkeɪt, ˈɛdjʊkeɪt/ • *v*
educar, instruir **~ed** • *adj*
educat **~ion** • *n* educació *f*
**~ional** • *adj* educatiu; didàctic

**eel** /iːl/ • *n* anguila *f*

**eerie** /ˈɹi, ˈɹəi/ • *adj* misteriós;
espantós

**effect** /ɪˈfɛkt, əˈfɛkt/ • *n* efecte *m*
• *v* efectuar **~ive** • *adj* eficaç;
efectiu **~iveness** • *n* eficàcia *f*

**efficien|t** /ɪˈfɪʃənt, əˈfɪʃənt/ • *adj*
eficient **~cy** • *n* eficiència *f*;
rendiment *m* **~tly** • *adv*
eficientment

**effort** /ˈɛfət, ˈɛfət/ • *n* esforç *m*
**~less** • *adj* fàcil

**egg** /ɛg, eɪg/ • *n* ou *m*; òvul *m*

**eggplant** • *n* alberginiera *f*;
alberginia *f*

**ego** /ˈiːgəʊ, ˈigoʊ/ • *n* jo *m*, ego *m*

**Egypt** • *n* Egipte *m* **~ian** • *adj*
egipci • *n* egipci *m*

**eight** /eɪt/ • *n* vuit *m* • *num* vuit;
vuitena *f* **~een** • *num* divuit
**~h** • *adj* vuitè **~y** • *num*
vuitanta

**either** /ˈaɪð.ə(ɹ), aɪ/ • *adv* tampoc

**El Salvador** • *n* El Salvador *m*

**elaborate** /ɪˈlæbəɹət, ɪˈlæbəɹeɪt/ •
*v* aprofundir

**elastic** /ɪˈlæstɪk/ • *adj* elàstic **~ity**
• *n* elasticitat *f*

**elbow** /ˈɛl.bəʊ, ˈɛl.boʊ/ • *n* colze
*m*; cop de colze *m*

**elder** /ˈɛldə, ˈɛldə/ • *n* grans;
ancian *m*; saüc *m* **~ly** • *adj*
ancià *m*

**elect|ion** /ɪˈlekʃ(ə)n/ • *n* elecció *f*
**~oral** • *adj* electoral

**electric** /ɪˈlɛktɹɪk/ • *adj* elèctric
**~al** • *adj* elèctric **~ity** • *n*
electricitat *f* **~ian** • *n*
electricista *f*

**electronic** /ˌɛl.ɛkˈtɹɒn.ɪk,
ɪˌlɛkˈtɹɑn.ɪk/ • *adj* electrònic **~s**
• *n* electrònica *f*

**elegant** /ˈɛl.ə.gənt/ • *adj* elegant
**~ly** • *adv* elegantment

**elephant** /ˈɛləfənt/ • *n* elefant *m*

**elevation** /ˌɛlɪˈveɪʃən/ • *n*
elevació *f*; alçat *m*

**eleven** /ɪˈlɛv.ən/ • *num* onze

**eligible** /ˈɛlɪdʒəb(ə)l/ • *adj*
elegible

**eliminate** /ɪˈlɪmɪneɪt/ • *v* eliminar

**elite** /ɪˈliːt/ • *n* elit *f*

**else** /ɛls, ɛlts/ • *adj* més, altre

**email** /ˈiːmeɪl/ • *n* correu
electrònic *m*

**embark** /ɪmˈbɑː(ɹ)k/ • *v* embarcar

**embarrass|ed** /ɪmˈbæɹ.əst/ • *adj*
avergonyit *m*, avergonyida *f*
**~ment** • *n* avergonyiment *m*

**embassy** /'ɛmbəsi/ • *n* ambaixada *f*

**embed** /ɛm'bɛd/ • *v* encastar

**embrace** /ɪm'bɹeɪs/ • *n* abraçada *f* • *v* abraçar

**emerge** /iˈmɜːdʒ/ • *v* emergir; sorgir **~nce** • *n* emergència *f*; propietats emergents *f* **~ncy** • *n* emergència *f*, urgència *f*

**eminence** /'ɛmɪnəns/ • *n* eminència *f*

**emit** /i'mɪt/ • *v* emetre **~ssion** • *n* emissió

**emotion** /ɪ'moʊʃən, ɪ'məʊʃən/ • *n* emoció *f* **~al** • *adj* emocional **~ally** • *adv* emocionalment

**emperor** /'ɛmpəɹə, 'ɛmpəɹɚ/ • *n* emperador *m*

**emphasi|s** /'ɛmfəsɪs/ • *n* (*pl* emphases) èmfasi *f* **~ze** • *v* emfatitzar

**empire** /'ɛmpaɪə, 'ɛm,paɪɹ/ • *n* imperi *m*

**employee** /ɛmplɔɪ'iː/ • *n* empleat *m*

**empress** /'ɛmpɹəs/ • *n* emperadriu *f*

**empt|y** /'ɛmpti/ • *adj* buit • *v* buidar **~iness** • *n* buidor *f*, buidesa *f*

**enable** /ɪ'neɪbəl/ • *v* habilitar

**encounter** /ɪn'kaʊntə, ɪn'kaʊntɚ/ • *n* trobada *f*; encontre *m*

**encourag|e** /ɪn'kʌɹɪdʒ, ɪn'kɜːɹɪdʒ/ • *v* encoratjar **~ing** • *adj* encoratjador

**encyclopedia** /ən,saɪ.klə'pi.di.ə, ɪn,saɪ.klə'pi(ː).di.ə/ • *n* enciclopèdia *f*

**end** /ɛnd/ • *n* final *m*, fi *f* • *v* acabar **~ up** • *v* acabar-se;

acabar **~ing** • *n* fi *f*, final *m* **~less** • *adj* interminable; inacabable

**endeavor** /ɪn'dɛv.ə, ɛn'dɛv.ɚ/ • *n* esforç *m*

**endure** /ɪn'djʊə(ɹ), ɪn'd(j)ʊɹ/ • *v* aguantar

**enemy** /'ɛnəmi/ • *adj* enemic • *n* enemic *m*

**energ|y** /'ɛnədʒi, 'ɛnɚdʒi/ • *n* energia *f* **~etic** • *adj* enèrgic, ple d'energia; energètic

**engaged** /ɪn'ɡeɪdʒd/ • *adj* promès; comunicar

**engine** /'ɛndʒɪn/ • *n* motor *m* **~er** • *n* enginyer *m* **~ering** • *n* enginyeria

**English** • *adj* anglès • *n* anglès *m*, anglesa *f*

**engrav|e** • *v* gravar **~ing** • *n* gravat

**engrossed** /ɛn.'ɡɹoʊst/ • *adj* absort

**enjoy** /ɪn'dʒɔɪ, ɛn'dʒɔɪ/ • *v* gaudir

**enormous** /iˈnɔː(ɹ)məs/ • *adj* enorme

**enough** /ɪ'nʌf/ • *adv* suficientment, prou • *det* suficient • *interj* prou! • *pron* prou

**enrich** /ɪn'ɹɪtʃ/ • *v* enriquir **~ment** • *n* enriquiment *m*

**enroll** /ɛn'ɹoʊl, ɪn'ɹəʊl/ • *v* inscriure; matricular, enrolar

**enslave** • *v* esclavitzar

**entail** /ɛn'teɪl/ • *v* implicar

**enter** /'ɛntə(ɹ), 'ɛntɚ/ • *v* entrar

**enterprise** /'ɛntɚ,pɹaɪz/ • *n* empresa *f*

**entertain** /,ɛntə'teɪm, ,ɛntɚ'teɪm/ • *v* entretenir, divertir,

distreure **~ing** • *adj* divertit
**~ment** • *n* entreteniment *m*
**enthusias|m** /ɪnˈθjuːzɪæz(ə)m,
-θuː-/ • *n* entusiasme *m* **~t** • *n*
entusiasta *f* **~tic** • *adj*
entusiàstic
**entire** /ɪnˈtaɪə, ɪnˈtaɪə/ • *adj* enter
**~ly** • *adv* totalment,
enterament
**entrance** /ˈɛn.tɹəns/ • *n* entrada
*f* • *v* encantar, embadalir
**entrepreneur** /ˌɒn.tɹə.pɹəˈnɜː,
ˌɑn.t(ʃ)ɹə.pɹəˈnʊər/ • *n*
emprenedor *m* **~ship** • *n*
emprenedoria *f*
**entry** /ˈɛntɹɪ, ˈɛntɹi/ • *n* entrada
*f*; accés *m*
**envelope** /ˈɛn.və.ləʊp, ˈɛn.vəˌloʊp/
• *n* sobre *m*, sobre de carta *m*
**environment** /ɪnˈvaɪɹə(n)mənt/ •
*n* medi *m*, ambient *m*, entorn
*m*; medi ambient *m* **~al** • *adj*
ambiental, mediambiental
**env|y** /ˈɛnvi/ • *n* enveja *f* • *v*
envejar **~ious** • *adj* envejós
**epic** /ˈɛp.ɪk/ • *adj* èpic • *n*
epopeia *f*
**epidemic** /ˌɛpɪˈdɛmɪk/ • *adj*
epidèmic • *n* epidèmia *f*
**episode** /ˈɛpɪsəʊd, ˈɛ.pəˌsoʊd/ • *n*
episodi *m*; capítol *m*
**equal** /ˈiːkwəl/ • *adj* igual • *v*
equivaldra **~ity** • *n* igualtat *f*
**~ly** • *adv* igualment
**equation** /ɪˈkweɪʒən/ • *n* equació
*f*
**equestrian** • *adj* eqüestre
**equipment** /ɪˈkwɪpmənt/ • *n*
equipament *m*; equipatge *m*,
equip *m*

**equity** /ˈɛk.wɪ.ti/ • *n* patrimoni
net *m*
**era** /ˈɪə.ɹə, ˈɛ.ɹə/ • *n* era *f*, època *f*,
període *m*
**erase** /ɪˈɹeɪz, ɹˈeɪs/ • *v* esborrar
**~r** • *n* goma *f*, goma
d'esborrar *f*
**erect** /ɪˈɹɛkt/ • *adj* erecte **~ion** •
*n* erecció *f* **~ile** • *adj* erèctil
**~ile dysfunction** • *n* disfunció
erèctil *f*
**Eritrea** • *n* Eritrea
**erosion** /əˈɹoʊʒən, əˈɹəʊʒən/ • *n*
erosió *f*
**error** /ˈɛɹə(ɹ), ˈɛɹə/ • *n* error *m*,
errada
**eruption** /ɪˈɹʌpʃən/ • *n* erupció *f*
**escalator** /ˈɛs.kə.leɪ.tə, ˈɛs.kə.leɪ.tɚ/
• *n* escala mecànica *f*
**escape** /ɪˈskeɪp/ • *n* fuita *f* • *v*
escapar; eludir
**especially** /ɪˈspɛʃ(ə)li, ɛkˈspɛʃ(ə)li/
• *adv* sobretot, especialment
**essay** /ˈɛˌseɪ/ • *n* redacció *f*
**essen|ce** /ˈɛsəns/ • *n* bessó *m*
**~tial** • *adj* essencial **~tially** •
*adv* en essència
**establish** /ɪˈstæb.lɪʃ/ • *v* establir
**~ment** • *n* establiment *m*
**estate** /ɪsˈteɪt/ • *n* propietat *f*,
béns
**estimation** /ɛstɪˈmeɪʃən/ • *n*
estimació *f*
**Estonia** • *n* Estònia **~n** • *adj*
estonià *m*, estoniana *f*
**etern|al** /ɪˈtɜːnəl, ɪˈtɜːnəl/ • *adj*
etern, eternal **~ity** • *n*
eternitat *f*
**ethic|al** /ˈɛθɪkəl/ • *adj* ètic **~s** • *n*
ètica *f*
**Ethiopia** • *n* Etiòpia *f*

ethnic /'εθ.nɪk/ ● adj ètnic; pagà

EU (abbr) ▷ EUROPEAN UNION

euro /'jʊərəʊ, 'jʊːrəʊ/ ● n euro m

Europe ● n Europa f ~an ● adj
europeu m, europea f ● n
europeu m, europea f

European Union ● n Unió
Europea f

evacuat|e ● v evacuar ~ion ● n
evacuació f

evasi|ve /ɪ'veɪsɪv/ ● adj evasiu
~on ● n evasió f

evaluate /ɪ'valjʊeɪt, ɪ'valjə͵weɪt/ ●
v avaluar

even /'iːvən, 'iːvən/ ● adj pla;
igual; parell ● adv fins i tot,
àdhuc; encara

evening /'iːvnɪŋ, 'iːvnɪŋ/ ● n tarda
f, vespre m

event /ɪ'vɛnt/ ● n esdeveniment
m ~ually ● adv finalment

every /'ɛv.(ə.)ɹi/ ● det cada
~body ● pron tothom ~one ●
pron tothom, cada u, cadascú
~thing ● pron tot ~where ●
adv a tot arreu, pertot

eviden|t /'ɛ.vɪ.dənt/ ● adj
evident ~tly ● adv
evidentment ~ce ● n prova f

evil /'iːvɪl, 'iːvəl/ ● adj malvat,
dolent, maliciós, malèfic, roí ●
n mal m

evoke /ɪ'vəʊk, ɪ'vɒʊk/ ● v evocar

evolution /͵iːvə'luːʃ(ə)n,
͵ɛvə'luʃ(ə)n/ ● n evolució f
~ary ● adj evolutiu

evolve ● v progressar;
desenvolupar

exact /ɪg'zækt/ ● adj exacte;
precís ~ly ● adv exactament

exaggerat|e /ɛg'zæ.dʒə.ɹeɪt/ ● v
exagerar ~ion ● n exageració
f

exam ▷ EXAMINATION

examination /ɪg͵zæmɪ'neɪʃən/ ● n
examen m

example /ɪg'zɑːmpl̩, əg'zæːmpuːl/ ●
n exemple m for ~ ● phr per
exemple, com ara

exceed /ɪk'siːd/ ● v excedir

excellen|t /'ɛksələnt/ ● adj excel·
lent ~ce ● n excel·lència f

except /ɪk'sɛpt, ɛ'ksɛpt/ ● prep
excepte, llevat ~ion ● n
excepció f ~ional ● adj
excepcional

excess /ək'sɛs/ ● n excés m ~ive
● adj excessiu

exchange /ɛks'tʃeɪndʒ/ ● n
intercanvi m ● v intercanviar

excit|ed /ɪk'saɪtɪd/ ● adj
entusiasmat, emocionat;
excitat ~ing ● adj excitant

excla|im /ɛk'skleɪm/ ● v
exclamar ~mation mark ● n
signe d'exclamació m, signe
d'admiració m

exclu|de /ɪks'kluːd/ ● v excloure
~sion ● n exclusió f ~sive ●
adj exclusiu ~sively ● adv
exclusivament

excuse /ɪk'skjuːz, ɪks'kjuz/ ● n
excusa f ● v excusar

execut|e /'ɛksɪ͵kjuːt/ ● v
executar; arrancar, arrencar
~ion ● n execució f

exercise /'ɛk.sə.saɪz, 'ɛk.sər.saɪz/ ●
n exercici m ● v exercitar;
exercir

exhausted /ɪg'zɔstɪd, ɪg'zɔːstɪd/ ●
adj exhaust

exhibit 41 facade

**exhibit** /ɪgˈzɪbɪt, ɪgˈzibət/ ● *v*
exhibir; exposar

**exile** /ˈɛgˌzaɪl/ ● *n* exili *m*,
bandejament *m*,
desterrament *m*; exiliat *m*,
exiliada *f*, bandejat *m* ● *v*
exiliar, bandejar, desterrar

**exist** /ɪgˈzɪst/ ● *v* existir **~ing** ●
*adj* existent **~ence** ● *n*
existència *f*

**exit** /ˈɛgzɪt/ ● *n* sortida *f*, eixida *f*
● *v* sortir, eixir

**exotic** /ɪgˈzɒtɪk, ɪgˈzɑtɪk/ ● *adj*
exòtic

**expectation** /ˌɛkspɛkˈteɪʃən/ ● *n*
expectativa *f*

**expenditure** ● *n* despesa *f*

**expensive** /ɪkˈspɛnsɪv/ ● *adj* car

**experience** /ɪkˈspɪɹiəns,
ɪkˈspɪəˌɹiəns/ ● *n* experiència *f*
● *v* experimentar

**experimental** /ˌɪkspɛɹəˈmɛntəl/ ●
*adj* experimental

**expert** /ˈɛkspət/ ● *adj* expert ● *n*
expert *m*

**expla|in** /ɪkˈspleɪn/ ● *v* explicar
**~nation** ● *n* explicació *f*

**explicit** /ɪkˈsplɪsɪt/ ● *adj* explícit
**~ly** ● *adv* explícitament

**explo|de** /ɪkˈspləʊd, ɪkˈsploʊd/ ●
*v* esclatar, explotar **~sion** ● *n*
explosió *f* **~sive** ● *adj* explosiu
● *n* explosiu *m*

**exploit** /ˈɛkspləɪt, ɪksˈpləɪt/ ● *n*
fita *f*, proesa *f*, gesta *f* ● *v*
explotar **~ation** ● *n*
explotació *f*

**explor|e** /ɪkˈspləː, ɪkˈspləɹ/ ● *v*
explorar **~ation** ● *n* exploració
*f* **~er** ● *n* explorador *m*

**export** /ˈɛks.pɔːt, ˈɛks.pɔɹt/ ● *v*
exportar **~er** ● *n* exportador
*m*

**express** /ɪkˈspɹɛs/ ● *v* expressar
**~ive** ● *adj* expressiu **~ion** ● *n* expressió *f*

**exten|d** /ɛkˈstɛnd/ ● *v* extendre
**~sion** ● *n* extensió *f* **~sive**
● *adj* extens **~sively** ● *adv*
extensament

**external** /ɛksˈtɜːnəl, ɛksˈtɜːnəl/ ●
*adj* extern *m*, externa *f*

**extinct** /ɪkˈstɪŋkt/ ● *adj* extint
**~ion** ● *n* extinció

**extract** /ˈɛkstɹækt, ɪksˈtɹækt/ ● *v*
extreure

**extraordinar|y** /ɪksˈtɹɔː(ɹ)dɪˌnɛɹi/
● *adj* extraordinari **~ily** ● *adv*
extraordinàriament

**extrem|e** /ɪkˈstɹiːm/ ● *adj*
extrem ● *n* extrem *m* **~ely** ●
*adv* extremadament **~ist** ● *adj*
extremista ● *n* extremista

**eye** /aɪ/ ● *n* ull *m* **~brow** ● *n* cella
*f* **~lash** ● *n* pestanya *f* **~lid** ●
*n* parpella *f* **~sight** ● *n* vista *f*

**fable** /ˈfeɪbəl/ ● *n* faula *f*
**fabric** /ˈfæb.ɹɪk/ ● *n* tela *f*
**fabulously** /ˈfæbjʊləsli/ ● *adv*
fabulosament
**facade** /fəˈsaːd, fəˈsɑːd/ ● *n*
façana *f*, fatxada *f*, frontera *f*

**fac|e** /feɪs/ • *n* cara *f*, faç *f*; rictus *m*, gest *m*; faceta *f* • *v* encarar; enfrontar-se **~ial** • *adj* facial

**fact** /fækt/ • *n* fet **in ~** • *phr* de fet, en realitat

**faction** /'fæk.ʃən/ • *n* facció *f*

**fail** /feɪl/ • *v* fracassar **~ure** • *n* fracàs *m*

**faint** /feɪnt/ • *adj* feble *f*, dèbil *f*; tènue *f* • *n* desmai • *v* acubar-se

**fair** /fɛə, fɛər/ • *adj* bell; just; equitatiu • *n* fira *f* **~ly** • *adv* francament, verdaderament; justament; força

**faith** /feɪθ/ • *n* fe *f* **~ful** • *adj* fidel, lleial **~fully** • *adv* fidelment

**fake** /feɪk/ • *v* falsejar

**falcon** /'fɔː(l)kən, 'fælkən/ • *n* falcó *m*

**fall** /fɔːl, fɔl/ • *n* caiguda *f* • *v* (*sp* fell, *pp* fallen) caure

**fallen** (*pp*) ▷ FALL

**false** /fɔːls, fɔls/ • *adj* fals, incorrecte; postís, artificial

**fam|e** /feɪm/ • *n* fama *f* **~ous** • *adj* famós; cèlebre

**famil|ly** /'fæm(ɪ)li, 'fæm(ə)li/ • *adj* marieta *m* • *n* família *f*; familiar **~iar** • *adj* familiar

**fan** /fæn/ • *n* ventall *m*, vano *m*, palmito *m*; ventilador *m*; fan *f*, aficionat • *v* ventar **~atic** • *adj* fanàtic • *n* fanàtic *m*

**fancy** /'fæn.si/ • *n* fantasia *f*

**fantastic** /fæn'tæstɪk/ • *adj* fantàstic

**fantasy** /'fæntəsi/ • *n* fantasia *f*

**FAQ** • *n* (*abbr* Frequently Asked Questions) PMF

**far** /fɑː, fɑɪ/ • *adj* llunyà; extrem • *adv* lluny; enllà, ença

**fare** /fɛə(ɪ), fɛər/ • *n* tarifa *f*

**farm** /fɑːm, fɑːm/ • *n* granja *f* **~er** • *n* granger *m*

**fascinat|e** • *v* fascinar **~ing** • *adj* fascinador, fascinant **~ion** • *n* fascinació *f*

**fast** /fɑːst, fæst/ • *adj* ferm; ràpid, veloç • *adv* fermament; ràpid, ràpidament, veloçment • *v* dejunar **~er** • *n* dejunador *m*, dejunadora *f*

**fat** /fæt/ • *adj* gras

**fat|e** /feɪt/ • *n* destí *m*; planeta *f* **~al** • *adj* fatal

**father** /'fɑː.ðə(ɪ), 'fɑː.ðə/ • *n* pare *m* **~-in-law** • *n* sogre *m*

**fatigue** /fə'tiːg/ • *n* fatiga *f* • *v* fatigar

**fault** /fɔːlt, fɔlt/ • *n* errada *f*, culpa *f*, defecte *m*, error *m*; falta; falla *f*

**favor** /'feɪvə, 'feɪvə/ • *n* favor *m* • *v* afavorir

**favour** (*British*) ▷ FAVOR

**favourable** /'feɪv(ə)ɹəbəl/ • *adj* favorable

**favourite** /'feɪv.ɹɪt/ • *adj* favorit, preferit

**fear** /fɪə, fɪəɹ/ • *n* por *f*, paüra *f*, basarda *f*, temor *f*; respecte *m* • *v* témer, tenir por de; respectar

**feat** /fiːt/ • *n* gesta *f*, acompliment *m*, proesa *f*, consecució *f*, feta *f*, fita *f*

**feather** /'fɛð.ə(ɪ), 'fɛð.ə/ • *n* ploma *f*

**feature** /'fiːtʃə, 'fitʃɚ/ ● *n* tret *m*

**February** ● *n* febrer *m*

**fed** *(sp/pp)* ▷ FEED

**federal** /'fɛdərəl/ ● *adj* federal

**feeble** /'fiːbəl/ ● *adj* feble *f*, dèbil *f*

**feed** /'fiːd/ ● *n* pinso ● *v* (*sp* fed, *pp* fed) alimentar **~back** ● *n* resposta *f*

**feeling** /'fiːlɪŋ, 'filɪŋ/ ● *n* sensació *f*; sentiment *m*

**feet** *(pl)* ▷ FOOT

**fell** *(sp)* ▷ FALL

**female** /'fiːˌmeɪl/ ● *adj* femení *m*, femenina *f*; femella ● *n* femella *f*

**feminine** /'fɛmɪnɪn/ ● *n* femení *m*

**feminis|t** /'fɛmənɪst/ ● *adj* feminista *f* **~m** ● *n* feminisme *m*

**fence** /fɛns/ ● *n* tanca *f*; perista *f* ● *v* esgrimir

**fennel** /'fɛnəl/ ● *n* fonoll *m*

**ferocious** /fəˈroʊʃəs/ ● *adj* ferotge

**ferry** /'fɛɹi, 'fɛɹi/ ● *n* bac *m*, rai *m*

**fertil|e** /'fɜːtaɪl, 'fɜːtəl/ ● *adj* fèrtil **~ity** ● *n* fertilitat *f* **~izer** ● *n* adob *m*

**fervent** /'fɜːvənt, 'fɜːˌvənt/ ● *adj* fervent

**festivity** ● *n* festivitat *f*

**fever** /'fiːvə, 'fivɚ/ ● *n* febre *f* **~ish** ● *adj* febril

**few** /fjuː, fju/ ● *det* poc **~er** ● *det* menys

**fibre** /'faɪbə(ɹ)/ ● *n* fibra *f*

**fiction** /'fɪkʃən/ ● *n* ficció *f* **~al** ● *adj* ficcional

**field** /fiːld, fild/ ● *n* camp *m*; terreny *m*; cos *m*

**fierce** /fiəs, fɪɹs/ ● *adj* ferotge; feroç

**fift|een** /fɪfˈtiːn, fɪfˈtiːn/ ● *num* quinze **~h** ● *adj* cinquè, quint ● *n* cinquè *m*, quint *m*; quinta *f* **~y** ● *num* cinquanta

**fig** /fɪɡ/ ● *n* figuera *f*; figa *f*

**fight** /faɪt/ ● *n* lluita *f*, combat *m* ● *v* (*sp* fought, *pp* fought) lluitar, barallar-se; combatre **~er** ● *n* caça *m*

**figure** /'fɪɡjə, 'fɪɡə/ ● *n* figura *f*; xifra *f* ● *v* figurar-se

**Fiji** ● *n* Fiji

**file** /faɪl/ ● *n* arxiu *m*, fitxer *m*; columna *f*; llima *f*

**fill** /fɪl/ ● *v* empastar **~ sth in** ● *v* reemplaçar

**film** /fɪlm, 'fɪləm/ ● *n* pel·lícula *f* ● *v* filmar **~maker** ● *n* cineasta *f*

**filter** /'fɪltə, 'fɪltɚ/ ● *n* filtre *m* ● *v* filtrar

**filth** /fɪlθ/ ● *n* immundícia, porqueria *f* **~y** ● *adj* impur; obscè, groller

**final** /'faɪnəl/ ● *adj* final *f* ● *n* final *m* **~ly** ● *adv* finalment

**financ|e** /'f(a)ɪˌnæns/ ● *n* finances **~ial** ● *adj* financer **~ially** ● *adv* financerament

**finch** /fɪntʃ/ ● *n* pinsà *m*

**find** /faɪnd/ ● *v* (*sp* found, *pp* found) trobar

**fine** /faɪn, fæn/ ● *n* multa *f* ● *v* multar

**finger** /'fɪŋɡə, 'fɪŋɡə/ ● *n* dit *m* **~nail** ● *n* ungla *f* **~tip** ● *n* punta dels dits

**finish** /'fɪnɪʃ/ ● *n* meta *f*, fita *f*, fi *f* ● *v* acabar, finir, terminar;

finalitzar

**Fin|land** • *n* Finlàndia *f* **~nish** • *adj* finlandès *m*; finès • *n* finès *m*, finlandès *m*

**fire** /ˈfaɪ.ə(ɪ), ˈfaɪə.ə(ɪ)/ • *n* foc *m*; incendi *m* • *v* coure; acomiadar; disparar **~arm** • *n* arma de foc *f* **~fighter** • *n* bomber *m*, bombera *f* **~place** • *n* llar de foc *f* **~work** • *n* for d'artifici *m*, foc d'artifici *m*

**firm** /fɜɪm, fɜːm/ • *adj* ferm **~ly** • *adv* fermament

**first** /fɜːst, fɜst/ • *adj* primer *m* • *n* primer *m* **~ly** • *adv* primerament

**fiscal** /ˈfɪskəl/ • *adj* fiscal

**fish** /fɪʃ, fəʃ/ • *n* (*pl* fish) peix *m* • *v* pescar **~erman** • *n* pescador *m*, pescadora *f* **~ing** • *n* pesca *f*

**fist** /fɪst/ • *n* puny *m* • *v* apunyalar

**fit** /fɪt/ • *adj* adequat; apte

**five** /faɪv, fɑːv/ • *n* cinc *m* • *num* cinc

**fix** /fɪks/ • *v* arreglar; fixar; preparar **~ed** • *adj* fix

**flag** /flæg, fleɪg/ • *n* bandera *f*

**flamboyant** /flamˈbɔɪənt, flæmˈbɔɪ(j)ənt/ • *adj* flamant

**flame** /fleɪm/ • *n* flama *f*

**flamingo** /fləˈmɪŋgoʊ/ • *n* flamenc *m*

**flash** /flæʃ/ • *n* flaix *m*

**flat** /flæt/ • *adj* pla; xato *m* • *n* bemoll; punxada, avaria

**flavor** /ˈfleɪvə, ˈfleɪvɚ/ • *n* gust *m*, sabor *m*

**flavour** (*British*) ▷ FLAVOR

**flawless** /ˈflɔːləs, ˈflɑːləs/ • *adj* perfecte **~ly** • *adv* perfectament

**flea** /fliː/ • *n* puça *f*

**fled** (*sp/pp*) ▷ FLEE

**flee** /fliː/ • *v* (*sp* fled, *pp* fled) fugir; esvair-se

**fleet** /fliːt/ • *n* flota *f*, estol *m*

**flesh** /flɛʃ/ • *n* carn *f* **in the ~** • *phr* en carn i òs, en persona

**flew** (*sp*) ▷ FLY

**flexib|le** /ˈflɛk.sɪ.bəl/ • *adj* flexible **~ility** • *n* flexibilitat *f*

**flight** /flaɪt/ • *n* vol *m*; fuga *f*, fugida *f* **~ attendant** • *n* hostessa *f*, cambrer d'avions *m*

**fling** /flɪŋ/ • *n* aventura *f*

**flirt** /flɜːt, flɜt/ • *v* flirtar, flirtejar

**float** /fləʊt, floʊt/ • *n* taloja *f*; carrossa *f* • *v* flotar

**flood** /flʌd/ • *n* inundació *f*, aiguat

**floor** /flɔː, flɔɪ/ • *n* sòl *m*, terra *m*

**florist** /ˈflɒ.ɪɪst/ • *n* florista *f*

**flour** /ˈflaʊə, ˈflaʊɚ/ • *n* farina *f* • *v* enfarinar

**flow** /fləʊ, floʊ/ • *n* flux *m*; cabal *m* • *v* fluir

**flower** • *n* flor *f* • *v* florir

**flown** (*pp*) ▷ FLY

**fluid** /ˈfluːɪd/ • *n* fluid *m*

**flung** (*sp/pp*) ▷ FLING

**flute** /fluːt/ • *n* flauta *f*; canaladura *f*, estria *f*

**fly** /flaɪ/ • *n* mosca *f*; bragueta *f* • *v* (*sp* flew, *pp* flown) volar; fugir; pilotar; onejar **~ing** • *adj* volador *m*, voladora *f*

**focus** /ˈfəʊ.kəs, ˈfoʊ.kəs/ • *n* (*pl* foci) focus *m* • *v* enfocar

**fog** /fɒɡ, fɑɡ/ • *n* boira *f* **~gy** •
*adj* enboirat *m*

**fold** /fəʊld, foʊld/ • *n* plegament
*m*; plec *m*, séc *m* • *v* doblegar,
plegar **~ing** • *adj* plegador,
plegable • *n* plegatge *m*

**follow** /ˈfɒləʊ, ˈfɑloʊ/ • *v* seguir
**~er** • *n* seguidor *m* **~ing** • *adj*
següent

**food** /fuːd, fud/ • *n* menjar *m*,
aliment *m*

**fool** /fuːl/ • *n* beneit *m*, idiota;
boig • *v* enganar

**foolish** /ˈfuːlɪʃ/ • *adj* ximple

**foot** /fʊt/ • *n* (*pl* feet) pota *m*;
peu *m* **~ball** • *n* futbol *m*;
pilota de futbol *m*, pilota
**on ~** • *phr* a peu

**for** /fɔː(ɹ), fɔɹ/ • *conj* per • *prep*
per a

**forbad** (*sp*) ▷ FORBID

**forbade** (*sp*) ▷ FORBID

**forbid** /fə(ɹ)ˈbɪd/ • *v* (*sp* forbad,
*pp* forbid) denegar

**forbidden** (*pp*) ▷ FORBID

**force** /fɔɹs, fɔːs/ • *n* força *f* **in ~** •
*phr* vigent

**forecast** /ˈfɔɹkæst, ˈfɔːkɑːst/ • *n*
calendari *m*

**forecasted** (*sp/pp*) ▷ FORECAST

**forehead** /ˈfʊɹɪd, ˈbɑɹɛd/ • *n* front
*m*

**foreign** /ˈfʊɹɪn, ˈfɔɹən/ • *adj*
estrany *m*, estranya *f*; foraster
*m*, forastera *f*, estranger *m*,
estrangera *f* **~er** • *n* foraster
*m*, forastera, estrangera *f*

**forest** /ˈfɒɹɪst, ˈfɔɹɪst/ • *n* bosc *m*,
forest *f*, selva

**forever** /fəˈɹɛvə(ɹ), fəˈɹɛvəɹ/ • *adv*
per sempre, per a sempre

**forge** /fɔːʤ, fɔɹʤ/ • *n* farga *f*,
forja *f* • *v* forjar

**forget** /fəˈɡɛt, fəˈɡɛt/ • *v* (*sp*
forgot, *pp* forgotten) oblidar;
descuidar-se, oblidar-se **~ful** •
*adj* oblidadís, oblidós

**forgive** /fə(ɹ)ˈɡɪv, fəˈɡɪv/ • *v*
perdonar

**forgot** (*sp*) ▷ FORGET

**forgotten** (*pp*) ▷ FORGET

**fork** /fɔːɹk/ • *n* forca *f*; forquilla
*f*; bifurcació *f* • *v* bifurcar-se;
bifurcar

**form** /fɔːm, fɔɹm/ • *n* forma *f*;
formulari *m* • *v* formar

**formal** /ˈfɔɹməl, ˈfɔːməl/ • *adj*
formal; solemne,
convencional **~ly** • *adv*
formalment **~ity** • *n*
formalitat *f*, formalisme *m*

**format** /ˈfɔː(ɹ).mæt, ˈfɔːɹ.mæt/ • *n*
format • *v* formatar

**former** /ˈfɔɹmə, ˈfɔːmə/ • *adj*
previ **~ly** • *adv* anteriorment

**formula** /ˈfɔː.mjʊ.lə, ˈfɔɹ.mjə.lə/ •
*n* fórmula *f*

**formulat|e** • *v* formular **~ion** •
*n* formulació *f*

**forsake** /fɔɹˈseɪk/ • *v* (*sp* forsook,
*pp* forsaken) abandonar

**forsaken** (*pp*) ▷ FORSAKE

**forsook** (*sp*) ▷ FORSAKE

**fort** /fɔɹt, fɔːt/ • *n* fort *m*

**forth** /fɔːθ, fɔɹθ/ • *adv* envant

**fortnight** /ˈfɔːt.naɪt, ˈfɔɹt.naɪt/ •
*adv* quinzena *f*

**fortunately** • *adv*
afortunadament; feliçment

**fortune** /ˈfɔːtʃuːn, ˈfɔɹtʃən/ • *n*
fortuna *f*, destí *m*

**forty** /ˈfɔɹti/ • *num* quaranta

**forum** /ˈfɔːɹəm/ • *n* fòrum *m*

**forward** /ˈfɔːwəd, ˈfɔɹwəɹd/ • *n* atacant *m*, davanter *m*; ala *f*; aler *m*

**fossil** /ˈfɒsəl, ˈfɑːsəl/ • *n* fòssil *m*

**foster** /ˈfɒstə, ˈfɑstəɹ/ • *v* criar; cultivar ~ **care** • *n* acolliment familiar *m*

**fought** *(sp/pp)* ▷ FIGHT

**found** /faʊnd/ • *v* fundar • *(also)* ▷ FIND **~ation** • *n* fundació *f*; fonaments **~er** • *n* fundador *m*; fonedor *m*

**four** /fɔː, fo(ː)ɹ/ • *n* quatre *m* • *num* quatre; qüern *f* **~teen** • *num* catorze **~th** • *adj* quart

**fox** /fɒks, fɑks/ • *n* guineu *f*, guilla *f*, rabosa *f*

**fraction** /ˈfɹækʃən/ • *n* fracció

**fragil|e** /ˈfɹædʒaɪl, ˈfɹædʒəl/ • *adj* fràgil **~ity** • *n* fragilitat *f*

**fragment** /ˈfɹægmənt, fɹægˈmɛnt/ • *n* fragment *m* • *v* fragmentar

**frame** /fɹeɪm/ • *n* estructura *f*; constitució; marc *m* • *v* emmarcar; enquadrar, contextualitzar

**framework** /ˈfɹeɪmwɜːk, ˈfɹeɪmwɜk/ • *n* infraestructura *f*

**France** • *n* França *f*

**frank** /fɹæŋk/ • *adj* franc

**fraud** /fɹɔːd, fɹɑd/ • *n* frau *m*

**freckle** /ˈfɹɛkəl/ • *n* piga *f*

**free** /fɹiː/ • *adj* lliure; desocupat • *adv* gratis, gratuïtament • *v* alliberar **~dom** • *n* llibertat *f* **~ly** • *adv* lliurement **for ~** • *phr* de franc

**freeze** /ˈfɹiːz/ • *n* glaçada *f*, gelada *f* • *v* (*sp* froze, *pp* frozen) gelar, glaçar, congelar **~r** • *n* congelador *m*

**French** /fɹɛntʃ/ • *adj* francès • *n* francès *m*; els francesos

**frequen|t** /ˈfɹiːkwənt/ • *v* freqüentar **~tly** • *adv* freqüentment **~cy** • *n* freqüència *f*

**fresh** /fɹɛʃ/ • *adj* fresc; fresca *f*

**Friday** • *n* divendres *m*

**fridge** ▷ REFRIGERATOR

**friend** /fɹɛnd, frɪnd/ • *n* amic *m*, amiga *f*; conegut *m*, coneguda *f* **~ly** • *adj* amistós • *adv* amistosament **~ship** • *n* amistat *f*

**frighten** /ˈfɹaɪtn̩/ • *v* espantar, espaventar, esporuguir, esgarrifar **~ed** • *adj* atemorit

**frog** /fɹɒg, fɹɑg/ • *n* granota *f*

**from** /fɹɒm, fɹʌm/ • *prep* de, des de

**front** /fɹʌnt/ • *n* front *m*, cara *f*; façana principal *f*

**frontier** /fɹʌnˈtɪɹ, fɹʌnˈtɪə/ • *adj* fronterer • *n* frontera *f*

**frown** /fɹaʊn/ • *v* arrufar les celles; arrufar el nas

**froze** *(sp)* ▷ FREEZE

**frozen** /ˈfɹəʊzən/ • *adj* gelat • *(also)* ▷ FREEZE

**fruit** /fɹuːt, fɹut/ • *n* fruit *m*; fruita *f*; marieta, maricó

**frustrat|e** /fɹəˈstɹeɪt, ˈfɹʌstɹeɪt/ • *v* frustrar **~ed** • *adj* frustrat **~ion** • *n* frustració *f*

**fry** /fɹaɪ/ • *n* aleví *m* • *v* fregir **~ing pan** • *n* paella *f*

**fuck** /fʌk, fʊk/ ● *interj* merda!, collons! ● *n* clau *m* ● *v* follar, cardar, fotre, fer un clau, fotre un clau, tirar-se

**fuel** /'fju:əl/ ● *n* carburant *m*, combustible *m*

**fulfill** /fʊl'fil/ ● *v* complir

**full** /fʊl/ ● *adj* ple; complet; total, sencer; tip **~y** ● *adv* plenament; completament

**fun** /fʌn, fʌn/ ● *adj* divertit ● *n* diversió *f* **~ny** ● *adj* divertit

**function** /'fʌŋ(k)ʃən, 'fʌŋkʃən/ ● *n* funció *f* ● *v* funcionar

**funding** /'fʌndɪŋ/ ● *n* finançament *m*

**fundamental** ● *adj* fonamental ● *n* fonamental *f*

**funeral** /'fju:nərəl, 'fjunərəl/ ● *n* funeral *m*, funerals

**furious** /'fjʊə.ɹɪəs, 'fjʊɹ.i.əs/ ● *adj* furiós

**furthermore** /'fɜː(ɹ).ðə(ɹ).mɔː(ɹ)/ ● *adv* a més, a més a més, endemés

**fussy** /'fʌ.si/ ● *adj* perepunyetes

**future** /'fju:tʃə, 'fju:tʃɚ/ ● *adj* futur ● *n* avenir *m*, futur *m*

**fuzzy** /'fʌzi/ ● *adj* arrissat, borrós

**gain** /ɡeɪn/ ● *n* guany *m*

**galaxy** /'ɡaləksi, 'ɡæləksi/ ● *n* galàxia *f*

**gallery** /'ɡæləɹi/ ● *n* galeria *f*

**gallon** /'ɡælən/ ● *n* galó *m*

**Gambia** ● *n* Gàmbia

**gambler** ● *n* jugador *m*

**game** /ɡeɪm/ ● *n* joc *m*; partida *f*; caça *f*

**garage** /'ɡæɹɑː(d)ʒ, 'ɡæɹɪdʒ/ ● *n* garatge *m*

**garden** /'ɡɑɹdn̩, 'ɡɑːdn̩/ ● *n* jardí *m*; parc *m*, jardí públic **~er** ● *n* jardiner *m*, jardinera *f* **~ing** ● *n* jardineria *f*

**garlic** /'ɡɑːlɪk, 'ɡɑɹlɪk/ ● *n* all *m* ● *v* allejar

**garnish** /'ɡɑːmɪʃ, 'ɡɑːnɪʃ/ ● *n* guarnició *f*, guarniment *m* ● *v* guarnir

**gas** /ɡæs/ ● *n* gas *m* **~ station** ● *n* gasolinera *f*

**gasoline** /'ɡæs.ə.lin/ ● *n* gasolina *f*, benzina *f*

**gate** /ɡeɪt/ ● *n* taquilla *f*, porta *f*, reixat *m*

**gather** /'ɡæðə, 'ɡæðə/ ● *v* recollir

**gave** *(sp)* ▷ GIVE

**gay** /ɡeɪ/ ● *adj* gai, gaia ● *n* gai *m*

**gazelle** /ɡə'zɛl/ ● *n* gasela *f*

**geese** *(pl)* ▷ GOOSE

**gender** /'dʒɛndə, 'dʒɛndɚ/ ● *n* gènere *m*; sexe *m*

**gene** /dʒiːn/ ● *n* gen *m*

**general** /'dʒɛnɹəl, 'dʒɛnərəl/ ● *adj* general ● *n* general *m* **~ly** ● *adv* generalment **~ize** ● *v* generalitzar **~ization** ● *n* generalització *f*

**generation** /ˌdʒɛnə'ɹeɪʃən/ ● *n* generació *f* **~al** ● *adj* generacional

**generic** /dʒɪ'nɛɹɪk/ ● *adj* genèric

**generous** /ˈdʒen(ə)ɹəs/ ● *adj* generós **~ly** ● *adv* generosament

**genetic** /dʒəˈnetɪk/ ● *adj* genètic

**genius** /ˈdʒin.jəs, ˈdʒiː.nɪəs/ ● *n* geni *m*

**genocide** /ˈdʒenəsaɪd/ ● *n* genocidi *m*

**genre** /ˈ(d)ʒɑnɹə, ˈ(d)ʒɒnɹə/ ● *n* gènere *m*

**gentl|y** /ˈdʒentli/ ● *adv* suaument **~eman** ● *n* cavaller *m*

**genuine** /ˈdʒenjuː.ɪn/ ● *adj* genuí

**geograph|y** /dʒiˈɒgɹəfi, dʒiˈɑgɹəfi/ ● *n* geografia *f* **~ic** ● *adj* geogràfic

**geometr|y** /dʒiˈɑmətɹi, dʒiːˈɒmɪtɹi/ ● *n* geometria *f* **~ic** ● *adj* geomètric

**Georgia** ● *n* Geòrgia *f*

**German** ● *adj* alemany ● *n* alemany *m*, alemanya *f*; germànic; alt alemany *m* **~y** ● *n* Alemanya *f*, Alemània *f*

**gesture** /ˈdʒestʃə, ˈdʒes.tʃɚ/ ● *n* gest *m*

**get** /ɡet/ ● *v* (*sp* got, *pp* got) aconseguir, obtenir; rebre; convertir-se en, esdevenir; arribar; copsar, clissar; ser **~ sth across** ● *v* evidenciar, patentitzar **~ along** ● *v* dur-se bé; desfer-se'n **~ on sth** ● *v* embarcar, muntar; pujar; progressar; envellir; dur-se bé; som-hi **~ up** ● *v* llevar-se

**gherkin** /ˈɡɡkɪn, ˈɡɜːkɪn/ ● *n* cogombret *m*

**ghetto** /ˈɡetəʊ, ˈɡetoʊ/ ● *n* gueto *m*, call *m*, jueria *f*

**giant** /ˈdʒaɪ.ənt/ ● *adj* gegant, gegantí ● *n* gegant *m*

**gift** /ɡɪft/ ● *n* regal; do *m*, dot *m* ● *v* regalar

**gig** /ɡɪɡ/ ● *n* carrossí

**gigantic** /dʒaɪˈɡæntɪk/ ● *adj* gegantí, gegantesc

**gild** /ɡɪld/ ● *v* (*sp* gilded, *pp* gilded) daurar

**gilded** (*sp/pp*) ▷ GILD

**gilt** (*sp/pp*) ▷ GILD

**gin** /dʒɪn/ ● *n* ginebra *f*, gin *m*

**ginger** /ˈdʒɪndʒə, ˈdʒɪndʒɚ/ ● *adj* pèl-roig ● *n* gingebre *m*

**giraffe** /dʒɪˈɹɑːf, dʒəˈɹæf/ ● *n* girafa *f*

**girl** /ɡɜːl, ɡɜ̩l/ ● *n* noia *f*, nena *f*, xiqueta, al·lota *f* **~friend** ● *n* nòvia *f*, xicota *f*; amiga *f*

**give** /ɡɪv/ ● *v* (*sp* gave, *pp* given) donar **~ in** ● *v* cedir, rendir-se **~ up** ● *v* rendir

**given** (*pp*) ▷ GIVE

**glad** /ɡlæd/ ● *adj* alegre **~ly** ● *adv* gustosament

**glance** /ɡlɑːns, ɡlæns/ ● *n* cop d'ull *m*, ullada, llambregada *f* ● *v* donar un cop d'ull, llambregar

**glass** /ɡlɑːs, ɡlæs/ ● *n* vidre *m*; got, vas *m*

**glasses** ▷ SPECTACLES

**gleaming** /ˈɡliːmɪŋ/ ● *adj* llampant

**global** /ˈɡləʊbəl, ˈɡloʊbəl/ ● *adj* globular; mundial, global **~ warming** ● *n* escalfament global *m*

**glob|e** /ɡləʊb, ɡloʊb/ ● *n* globus *m* **~al** ● *adj* globular; mundial, global

**glor|y** /ˈɡlɔːɹi, ˈɡlo(ː)ɹi/ • *n* glòria *f* **~ious** • *adj* gloriós

**glossary** /ˈɡlɒsəɹi/ • *n* glossari *m*

**glove** /ɡlʌv/ • *n* guant *m*

**glue** /ɡluː/ • *v* encolar

**gnaw** /nɔː/ • *v* (*sp* gnawed, *pp* gnawed) rosegar

**gnawed** (*sp/pp*) ▷ GNAW

**gnawn** (*pp*) ▷ GNAW

**go** /ɡəʊ, ɡoʊ/ • *n* volta *f*, torn *m*; temptativa *f*, intent *m*; aprovació *f*; go *m* • *v* (*sp* went, *pp* gone) dir; anar; sortir amb; fer; funcionar; desaparèixer, anar-se'n; destruir **~ out** • *v* sortir

**goal** /ɡəʊl, ɡoʊl/ • *n* objectiu *m*, meta *f*; porteria *f*; gol *m*

**goat** /ɡəʊt, ɡoʊt/ • *n* cabra *f*

**God** /ɡɒd, ɡɔd/ • *n* Déu *m*

**god** /ɡɒd, ɡɔd/ • *n* déu *m*

**gold** /ɡəʊld, ɡoʊld/ • *adj* daurat **~en** • *adj* d'or, daurat; daurada *f* • *v* daurar-se **~fish** • *n* carpí *m*

**golf** /ɡɒlf, ɡɒf/ • *n* golf *m* **~er** • *n* golfista *f*

**gone** (*pp*) ▷ GO

**good** /ɡʊd, ɡʊ(d)/ • *adj* bo, bon • *interj* bo • *n* bo *m*, bona *f* **~ afternoon** • *phr* bona tarda **~ evening** • *n* bon vespre **~ morning** • *interj* bon dia **~bye** • *interj* adéu, adéu-siau **~ness** • *n* bondat *f*, bonesa *f* **~s** • *n* béns **for ~** • *phr* d'una vegada per totes

**goose** /ɡuːs/ • *n* (*pl* geese) oca *f*

**gore** /ɡɔː, ɡɔɹ/ • *v* banyegar

**gorgeous** /ˈɡɔːdʒəs, ˈɡɔɹdʒəs/ • *adj* esplèndit, magnífic, maquíssim .

**gorilla** /ɡəˈɹɪl.ə/ • *n* goril·la *m*

**gossip** /ˈɡɒs.ɪp, ˈɡɑs.ɪp/ • *n* tafaner, xafarder; xafarderia *f* • *v* xafardejar

**got** (*sp*) ▷ GET

**gotten** (*pp*) ▷ GET

**govern** /ˈɡʌvɚn, ˈɡʌvən/ • *v* governar **~ment** • *n* govern *m* **~or** • *n* governador *m*; regulador *m*

**grab** /ɡɹæb/ • *n* agafament *m*; agafador *m*

**grace** /ɡɹeɪs/ • *n* gràcia *f* **~fully** • *adv* graciosament

**gradual** /ˈɡɹædʒuəl, ˈɡɹædʒuəl/ • *adj* gradual **~ly** • *adv* gradualment

**grain** /ɡɹeɪn/ • *n* gra *m*; cereal *m*; veta *f*

**gram** /ɡɹæm/ • *n* gram *m*

**grand|child** • *n* nét *m*, néta *f* **~son** • *n* nét *m* **~daughter** • *n* néta *f* **~father** • *n* avi *m* **~mother** • *n* àvia *f*, iaia *f* **grandiloquent** /ɡɹænˈdɪl.ə.kwənt/ • *adj* grandiloqüent *n*

**grandiose** • *adj* grandiós

**grant** /ɡɹɑːnt, ɡɹænt/ • *v* admetre

**grape** /ɡɹeɪp/ • *n* raïm *m* **~fruit** • *n* aranger *m*; aranja *f*

**graphic** /ˈɡɹæfɪk/ • *adj* gràfic • *n* gràfic *m*; gràfics

**grasp** /ɡɹɑːsp, ɡɹæsp/ • *v* comprendre

**grass** /ɡɹɑːs, ɡɹæs/ • *n* herba *f* **~hopper** • *n* llagosta *f*, saltamartí *m*

**grateful** /'ɡɹeɪtfəl/ • *adj* agraït

**grave** /ɡɹeɪv/ • *adj* seriós; greu • *n* sepulcre *m* **~yard** • *n* cementiri *m*, camp sant, tenca d'hora

**gravity** /'ɡɹævɪti/ • *n* gravetat *f*

**gray** /ɡɹeɪ/ • *adj* gris • *n* gris *m*

**greas|e** /ɡɹis, ɡɹiːs/ • *v* greixar **~y** • *adj* greixós

**great** /ɡɹeɪt/ • *adj* gran, enorme; genial, fabulós

**Gree|ce** • *n* Grècia *f* **~k** • *adj* grec, hel·lè *m* • *n* grec *m*, grega *f*

**greed** /ɡɹid/ • *n* avaricia *f*, cobdícia *f* **~y** • *adj* avariciós, cobdiciós, cobejós, àvid

**green** /ɡɹiːn, ɡɹin/ • *adj* verd • *n* verd *m* **~house** • *n* hivernacle *m* **~house effect** • *n* efecte hivernacle *m*

**greet** /ɡɹiːt/ • *v* saludar **~ing** • *n* salut *m*

**gregarious** /ɡɹɪˈɡɛə.ɹɪ.əs, ɡɹɪˈɡɛɹ.i.əs/ • *adj* gregari

**grew** (*sp*) ▷ GROW

**grid** /ɡɹɪd/ • *n* quadrícula *f*

**grill** /ɡɹɪl/ • *n* graella *f*

**grind** /'ɡɹaɪnd/ • *v* (*sp* ground, *pp* ground) moldre, triturar

**grip** /ɡɹɪp/ • *v* agafar, empunyar

**grocer|y** /'ɡɹəʊsəɹi, 'ɡɹoʊs(ə)ɹi/ • *n* adrogueria *f*, ultramarins **~ies** • *n* queviures

**gross** /ɡɹəʊs, ɡɹoʊs/ • *n* grossa

**ground** /ɡɹaʊnd/ • *adj* mòlt • *n* terra *m*, sòl *m*; fons *m*; camp *m*; punt de terra *m* • (*also*) ▷ GRIND

**group** /ɡɹuːp/ • *n* grup *m*

**grow** /ɡɹəʊ, ɡɹoʊ/ • *v* (*sp* grew, *pp* grown) créixer; cultivar; tornar-se **~ up** • *v* créixer, fer-se gran **~ing** • *adj* creixent **~th** • *n* creixement *m*

**grown** (*pp*) ▷ GROW

**grumpy** /'ɡɹʌmpi/ • *adj* rondinaire

**guarantee** /ˌɡæɹənˈtiː/ • *n* garantia • *v* garantir

**guard** /ɡɑːd, ɡɑɹd/ • *n* guarda, guàrdia; escorta *f* **~ian** • *n* guardià *m*, guàrdia *m*; tutor *m*

**Guatemala** • *n* Guatemala *f*

**guerrilla** /ɡəˈɹɪlə/ • *n* guerrilla *f*

**guess** /ɡɛs/ • *n* conjetura *f* • *v* endevinar; obtenir; suposar

**guest** /ɡɛst/ • *n* convidat *m*, hoste *m*; invitat *m*

**guide** /ɡaɪd/ • *n* guia *f* • *v* guiar

**guilt** /ɡɪlt/ • *n* culpabilitat *f*, culpa *f* **~y** • *adj* culpable; reprovable

**guinea pig** /ˈɡɪni pɪɡ/ • *n* cobaia, conillet d'índia

**guitar** /ɡɪˈtɑː(ɹ), ɡɪˈtɑɹ/ • *n* guitarra *f* **~ist** • *n* guitarrista *f*

**gum** /ɡʌm/ • *n* geniva *f*

**gun** /ɡʌn/ • *n* pistola *f*; escopeta *f*; canó *m*; obús *m* • *v* disparar **~powder** • *n* pólvora

**gut** /ɡʌt/ • *v* estripar, esbudellar

**gutter** /ˈɡʌt.ə, ˈɡʌt.ɚ/ • *n* cuneta *f*; canal

**guy** /ɡaɪ/ • *n* paio *m*

**Guyana** • *n* Guyana *f*

**gymnast** /'dʒɪm.næst/ • *n* gimnasta *f* **~ics** • *n* gimnàstica *f*

**gymnasium** /dʒɪmˈneɪ.zi.əm/ • *n* gimnàs *m*

**gynecolog|y** /ˌgaɪnɪˈkɒlədʒi, ˌgaməˈkɑlədʒi/ • n ginecologia f **~ical** • adj ginecològic

**ha** /hɑː/ • interj ha
**habit** /ˈhæbɪt, ˈhæbət/ • n costum; hàbit m **~ual** • adj habitual
**habitat** /ˈhæbɪtæt/ • n hàbitat m
**had** (sp/pp) ▷ HAVE
**hail** /heɪl/ • n calamarsa • v calamarsejar
**hair** /hɛə/ • n cabell m, pèl m **~dresser** • n perruquer m
**Haiti** • n Haiti m
**hake** /heɪk/ • n lluç m
**half** /hɑːf, hæf/ • adj mig • n (pl halves) meitat f **~ time** • n mitja part f
**hallucin|ate** • v al·lucinar **~ogenic** • adj al·lucinogen • n al·lucinogen m **~ation** • n al·lucinació f
**halves** (pl) ▷ HALF
**ham** /hæm, ˈhæːm/ • n pernil m
**hammer** /ˈhæm.ə(ɹ), ˈhæmər/ • n martell m • v martellejar; clavar
**hamster** /ˈhæm(p)stər/ • n hàmster m
**hand** /hænd/ • n mà f; busca f, maneta f, agulla f **~bag** • n bossa de mà f **~ball** • n handbol m **~cuffs** • n manilles **~ful** • n grapat m **~y** • adj

pràctic; a mà at ~ • phr a mà on ~ • phr a mà **on the one** ~ • phr d'una banda
**handl|e** /ˈhæn.dl/ • n nansa f, mànec m, maneta m, tirador f **~ing** • n manipulació
**hang** /hæŋ, æ/ • v (sp hung, pp hung) penjar; encallar-se, bloquejar-se, penjar-se; encallar, bloquejar ~ **out** • v passar l'estona ~ **up** • v penjar **~over** • n ressaca f
**hangar** /ˈhæŋə, ˈhæŋər/ • n hangar m
**happen** /ˈhæpən/ • v passar, ocórrer, succeir
**happ|y** /ˈhæpiː, ˈhæpi/ • adj feliç, content, alegre; afortunat; satisfet **~ily** • adv feliçment, afortunadament; alegrement **~iness** • n felicitat f
**harass** /həˈɹæs, ˈhæɹəs/ • v molestar, fastiguejar, vexar
**harbor** /ˈhɑːbər, ˈhɑːbə/ • n port m, refugi m • v refugiar
**hard** /hɑːd, hɑɪd/ • adj dur; complicat, difícil; dura **~ly** • adv a penes
**hardware** /ˈhɑːdˌwɛə, ˈhɑːdˌwɛɹ/ • n ferreteria f, ferramenta f; maquinari m
**hare** /hɛə/ • n llebre f
**harm** /hɑːm, hɑːm/ • n dany m **~ful** • adj nociu **~less** • adj inofensiu
**harmon|y** /ˈhɑːməni, ˈhɑːməni/ • n harmonia f **~ious** • adj harmònic **~ica** • n harmònica f
**harp** /hɑːp, hɑɪp/ • n arpa f

**harpsichord** /ˈhɑː(ɹ)p.sɪ.kɔː(ɹ)d, ˈhɑɹp.sɪ.kɔɹd/ • n clavicèmbal m, clavecí m

**harsh** /hɑɹʃ, hɑːʃ/ • adj aspre f; sever m, severa f • v criticar

**harvest** /ˈhɑɹ.vəst, ˈhɑːvɪst/ • n collita f • v collir, segar **~er** • n colliter m

**hat** /hæt/ • n barret m, capell m

**hat|e** /heɪt/ • v odiar **~eful** • adj odiós **~red** • n odi m

**have** /hæv, həv/ • v (sp had, pp had) tenir **~ to** • v haver de

**Hawaii** • n Hawai m, Hawaii m; illes Hawaii, illes Hawai

**hawk** /hɔːk, hɔk/ • n falcó

**hay** /heɪ/ • n fenc m

**hazard** /ˈhæzəɹd, ˈhazəd/ • n risc m; perill m **~ous** • adj atzarós

**he** /hiː, hi/ • det ell • n he f

**head** /hɛd/ • adj cap • n seny m, cap m; punta f; cabota f; capçal m; líder f; director m, directora f; capçalera f; capça f; capçada f; fava f; testa f, closca f • v comandar, dirigir, encapçalar, liderar; cabotejar **~ache** • n mal de cap m; maldecap m **~phones** • n auriculars **~quarters** • n quarter general m; central m, seu f

**heal** /hiːl/ • v curar, guarir

**health** /hɛlθ/ • n salut, sanitat f **~y** • adj salubre

**hear** /hɪə(ɹ), hɪɹ/ • v (sp heard, pp heard) sentir, oir **~ing** • n oïda f

**heard** (sp/pp) ▷ HEAR

**heart** /hɑːt, hɑɹt/ • n cor; si m

**heat** /hiːt/ • n calor; bòfia • v escalfar **~ing** • n calefacció f; escalfament m

**heaven** /ˈhɛvən/ • n cel

**heavy** /ˈhɛ.vi, ˈhɛ.vi/ • adj pesat, greu

**hectare** /ˈhɛktɛː, ˈhɛktɛɪ/ • n hectàrea f

**hedgehog** /ˈhɛdʒhɒg/ • n eriçó m

**heel** /hiːl/ • n taló m; crostó m • v estalonar

**height** /haɪt/ • n altura f; alçada f, estatura f **~en** • v aixecar

**heir** /ɛəɹ/ • n hereu m

**held** (sp/pp) ▷ HOLD

**helicopter** /ˈhɛli̩kɒptə(ɹ), ˈhɛl.i̩kɒp.tə(ɹ)/ • n helicòpter m

**hell** /hɛl/ • n infern m

**hello** /həˈləʊ, hɛˈloʊ/ • interj hola; digui, si, mani'm; hola?, na maria?; conill!

**helmet** /ˈhɛlmɪt/ • n casc m, elm m

**help** /hɛlp/ • interj socors, auxili • n ajuda f • v ajudar, aidar **~ful** • adj útil **~less** • adj indefens **~er** • n ajudant m, ajudador m

**hen** /hɛn/ • n gallina f; au femella f

**her** /ˈhɜː(ɹ), ˈhɜʃ/ • det seu, seva **~self** • pron es; mateix

**herb** /hɜːb, (h)ʒb/ • n herba f

**here** /hɪə(ɹ), hɪɹ/ • adv aquí, ací

**hero** /ˈhɪɹoʊ, ˈhɪɹɹəʊ/ • n (pl heroes) heroi m, heroïna f **~ic** • adj heroic **~in** • n heroïna f **~ine** • n heroïna f

**herring** /ˈhɛɹɪŋ/ • n areng m

**hesitat|e** /ˈhɛzɪteɪt/ • v hesitar, dubtar; titubejar **~ion** • n hesitació f, vacil·lació f

**hey** /heɪ/ • interj ep, ei; eh

**hi** /haɪ/ • interj hola

**hid** (sp) ▷ HIDE

**hidden** /ˈhɪd(ə)n/ • adj amagat • (also) ▷ HIDE

**hide** /haɪd/ • v (sp hid, pp hidden) amagar

**hierarch|y** /ˈhaɪ.ə.ɹɑː(ɹ).ki/ • n jerarquia f **~ical** • adj jeràrquic

**high** /haɪ/ • adj alt, elevat; drogat **~light** • n llum f • v emfasitzar, remarcar, ressaltar; marcar, subratllar **~ly** • adv altament

**hik|e** /haɪk/ • n caminada f **~er** • n excursionista f **~ing** • n senderisme m

**hilarious** /hɪˈlɛəɹiəs, hɪˈlɛɹiəs/ • adj hilarant

**hill** /hɪl/ • n puig m, turó m

**himself** /hɪmˈsɛlf/ • pron es; mateix

**hip** /hɪp/ • n maluc m

**hire** /haɪə, haɪɹ/ • v llogar; contractar

**his** /hɪz, həz/ • det seu • pron el seu m, la seva f, els seus, les seves

**histor|y** /ˈhɪst(ə)ɹi/ • n història f; historial m **~ic** • adj històric **~ical** • adj històric **~ically** • adv històricament **~ian** • n historiador m

**hit** /hɪt/ • adj cop m; èxit m • v (sp hit, pp hit) colpejar, batre, pegar; xocar; encertar

**hockey** /ˈhɒki/ • n hoquei m

**hog** /hɒɡ, hɑɡ/ • n suid m, marrà m; tacany m

**hold** /həʊld, hoʊld/ • v (sp held, pp held) aguantar, sostenir

**hole** /həʊl, hoʊl/ • n forat m • v foradar

**holiday** /ˈhɒlɪdeɪ, ˈhɒləˌdeɪ/ • n festa f; dia de festa, dia feriat; vacances

**holy** /ˈhəʊli, ˈhoʊli/ • adj sagrat, sagrada f, sant m, santa f

**home** /(h)əʊm, hoʊm/ • adv a casa • n llar m, casa f; asil m; meta f **~land** • n pàtria f **~less** • adj sensellar, sensesostre **~made** • adj casolà m, casolana f **~sick** • adj enyorat **~work** • n deures at **~** • phr a casa

**Honduras** • n Hondures f

**honest** /ˈɒnɪst, ˈɔːnɪst/ • adj honest, sincer **~ly** • adv honestament **~y** • n honradesa f, honestedat f

**honey** /ˈhʌni/ • n mel f **~ bee** • n abella de la mel f, abella mel·lífera f **~moon** • n lluna de mel f

**honor** /ˈɑːnə, ˈɒnə/ • n honor m

**honorable** /ˈɒnəɹəbl̩, ˈɑnəɹəbl̩/ • adj honorable

**honour** (British) ▷ HONOR

**hoof** /hʊf/ • n (pl hooves) peülla f

**hook** /hʊk, huːk/ • n garfi m, ganxo m • v enganxar **~er** • n prostituta; talonador m

**hooves** (pl) ▷ HOOF

**hope** /həʊp, hoʊp/ • n esperança f • v esperar **~less** • adj desesperat

**horizon** /həˈɹaɪzən/ • *n* horitzó *m*
**~tal** • *adj* horitzontal

**hormon|e** /ˈhɔːməʊn, ˈhɔːɹmoʊn/
• *n* hormona *f* **~al** • *adj*
hormonal

**horn** /hɔːn, hɔɹn/ • *n* banya *f*;
corn *m*; clàxon *m*

**horrible** /ˈhɒɹɪbəl, ˈhɔɹɪbəl/ • *adj*
horrible, hòrrid, esgarrifós

**horror** /ˈhɒɹɚ, ˈhɔɹɚ/ • *n* horror
*m*; terror

**horse** /hɔːs, hɔɹs/ • *n* cavall *m*,
euga *f*

**hospitality** /ˌhɒs.pɪˈtæl.ɪ.ti,
ˌhɒs.pɪˈtæl.ɪ.ti/ • *n* hospitalitat *f*

**hospital** /ˈhɒs.pɪ.tl̩, ˈɒs.pɪ.tl̩/ • *n*
hospital *m* **~ize** • *v*
hospitalitzar **~ization** • *n*
hospitalització *f*

**host** /həʊst, hoʊst/ • *n* amfitrió
*m*, amfitriona *f* • *v* allotjar
**~ess** • *n* amfitriona *f*

**hostage** /ˈhɒstɪdʒ/ • *n* ostatge *f*

**hostil|e** /ˈhɒstaɪl, ˈhɒstəl/ • *adj*
hostil **~ity** • *n* hostilitat *f*

**hot** /hɒt, hɑt/ • *adj* calent

**hotel** /həʊˈtɛl, hoʊˈtɛl/ • *n* hotel *m*

**hour** /ˈaʊə(ɹ), ˈaʊɚ/ • *n* hora *f*

**hous|e** /haʊs, haʊs/ • *n* casa *f* •
*v* allotjar **~ehold** • *n* seguici
*m*, familiars **~ing** • *n*
habitatge *m*, allotjament *m*;
vivenda *f* **on the ~e** • *phr* per
compte de la casa

**how** /haʊ, hæʊ/ • *adv* com; que

**however** /haʊˈɛvə, haʊˈɛvɚ/ • *adv*
tanmateix, nogensmenys

**howl** /haʊl/ • *n* udol *m* • *v*
udolar

**hug** /hʌg/ • *n* abraçada *f* • *v*
abraçar

**huge** /hjuːdʒ, juːdʒ/ • *adj* enorme

**human** /ˈ(h)juːmən, ˈ(h)juːmən/ •
*adj* humà **~e** • *adj* humà
**~itarian** • *adj* humanitari *m*,
humanitària *f* **~ity** • *n*
humanitat *f* **~ being** • *n* ésser
humà *m*, humà *m*

**humbl|e** /ˈhʌmbəl, ˈʌmbəl/ • *adj*
humil *f* • *v* humiliar **~y** • *adv*
humilment

**humour** /ˈhjuː.mə(ɹ), ˈhjuːmɚ/ • *n*
humor *m*

**hundred** /ˈhʌndɹəd, ˈhʌndɚd/ •
*num* cent *f*

**hung** *(sp/pp)* ▷ HANG

**Hungar|y** • *n* Hongria *f* **~ian** •
*adj* hongarès • *n* hongarès *m*,
hongaresa *f*

**hunger** /ˈhʌŋgɚ, ˈhʌŋgə/ • *n*
gana *f*, fam *m*

**hungry** /ˈhʌn.gɹi/ • *adj* afamat

**hunt** /hʌnt/ • *n* caça *f*, cacera *f*
• *v* caçar; caça; caça **~er** • *n*
caçador *m* **~ing** • *n* caça *f*

**hurricane** /ˈhʌɹɪkən, ˈhʌɹɪˌkeɪn/ •
*n* huracà *m*

**hurry** /ˈhʌ.ɹi, r/ • *n* presa *f* • *v*
cuitar, fer via; accelerar,
apressar **~ up** • *v* afanyar,
donar-se pressa, fer via

**hurt** /hɜːt, hɜt/ • *adj* ferit *m*; ofès
*m* • *v* (*sp* hurt, *pp* hurt)
doldre, doler; ferir

**husband** /ˈhʌzbənd/ • *n* marit *m*

**husky** /ˈhʌs.ki/ • *adj* ronc *m*

**hut** /hʌt/ • *n* cabana *f*, cabanya
*f*

**hydrogen** /ˈhaɪdɹədʒ(ə)n,
ˈhaɪdɹədʒən/ • *n* hidrogen *m*

**hyena** /haɪˈiːnə/ • *n* hiena *f*

**hyperbole** /haɪˈpɜːbəli/ • *n*
hipèrbole *f*

**hypothe|sis** /haɪˈpɒθɪsɪs/ • *n* (*pl*
hypotheses) hipòtesi *f* **~tical**
• *adj* hipotètic

**hysterical** /hɪˈstɛrɪkəl/ • *adj*
histèric

# I

**I** • *pron* jo

**ice** /aɪs, ʌɪs/ • *n* gel *m* **~ cream** •
*n* gelat *m*; carapulla *f*

**Iceland** • *n* Islàndia *f*

**icon** /ˈaɪ.kən, ˈaɪ.kɑːn/ • *n* icona *f*
**~ic** • *adj* icònic

**idea** /aɪˈdɪə, aɪˈdi.ə/ • *n* idea *f* **~l** •
*adj* ideal • *n* ideal *m* **~list** • *n*
idealista *f* **~listic** • *adj*
idealista **~lism** • *n* idealisme *m*

**identif|y** /aɪˈdɛn.tɪ.faɪ/ • *v*
identificar; identificar-se
**~ication** • *n* identificació *f*

**identi|ty** /aɪˈdɛntəti/ • *n*
identitat *f* **~cal** • *adj* idèntic

**ideolog|y** /aɪ.di.ˈɑl.ə.dʒi/ • *n*
ideologia **~ical** • *adj*
ideològic, ideològica *f*

**idiot** /ˈɪd.i.(j)ɪt/ • *n* idiota *f* **~ic** •
*adj* idiota

**if** /ɪf/ • *conj* si

**ignor|e** /ɪgˈnɔːr, ɪgˈnɔːr/ • *v* ignorar
**~ance** • *n* ignorància *f* **~ant** •
*adj* ignorant

**iguana** /ɪˈgjuɑːnə, ɪˈgwɑnə/ • *n*
iguana *f*

**ill** /ɪl/ • *adj* malalt **~ness** • *n*
malaltia *f*

**illegal** /ɪˈliːgəl, ɪˈli.gəl/ • *adj* il·
legal **~ly** • *adv* il·legalment
**~ity** • *n* il·legalitat *f*

**illegitimate** /ɪlɪˈdʒɪtɪmət,
ələˈdʒɪtɪtɪmət/ • *adj* il·legítim

**illiterate** /ɪˈlɪtərət/ • *adj* illetrat,
analfabet • *n* analfabet *m*

**illogical** • *adj* il·lògic **~ly** • *adv*
il·lògicament

**illusion** /ɪˈl(j)uːʒ(ə)n, ɪˈl(j)uːzj(ə)n/
• *n* il·lusió *f*, illusió

**image** /ˈɪmɪdʒ/ • *n* imatge *f* **~ry**
• *n* imatgeria *f*

**imagin|e** /ɪˈmædʒ.ɪn/ • *v*
imaginar **~ary** • *adj* imaginari
**~ative** • *adj* imaginatiu **~ation**
• *n* imaginació *f*

**immatur|e** • *adj* immadur **~ity**
• *n* immaduresa *f*

**immediate** /ɪˈmiː.di.ɪt, ɪˈmiːdɪət/ •
*adj* immediat; pròxim **~ly** •
*adv* immediatament

**immens|e** /ɪˈmɛns/ • *adj* immens
**~ely** • *adv* immensament **~ity**
• *n* immensitat *f*

**immigra|nt** /ˈɪmɪgrənt/ • *n*
immigrant *f* **~tion** • *n*
immigració *f*

**imminent** /ˈɪmɪnənt/ • *adj*
imminent

**immune** /ɪˈmjuːn/ • *adj* immune
**~ system** • *n* sistema
immunitari *m*

**impact** /ˈɪmpækt, ɪmˈpækt/ • *v*
impactar

**impartial** /ɪmˈpɑːʃəl/ • *adj*
imparcial **~ity** • *n*
imparcialitat *f*

**impatien|t** /ɪmˈpeɪʃənt/ ● *adj* impacient **~tly** ● *adv* impacientment **~ce** ● *n* impaciència *f*

**impersonal** /ɪmˈpɜːsənəl/ ● *adj* impersonal

**implementation** ● *n* implementació *f*

**imply** /ɪmˈplaɪ/ ● *v* implicar; insinuar

**import** /ˈɪm.pɔːt, ˈɪm.pɔːt/ ● *v* importar

**importan|t** /ɪmˈpɔːtənt, ɪmˈpɔːtənt/ ● *adj* important **~tly** ● *adv* notablement; importantment **~ce** ● *n* importància *f*

**impossib|le** /ɪmˈpɒsɪbəl/ ● *adj* impossible; insuportable ● *n* impossible **~ility** ● *n* impossibilitat *f*

**impress|ed** /ɪmˈprɛst/ ● *adj* impressionat; imprès; requisat **~ive** ● *adj* impressionant **~ion** ● *n* impressió *f*

**imprison** /ɪmˈprɪzən/ ● *v* empresonar **~ment** ● *n* empresonament *m*

**improve** /ɪmˈpruːv/ ● *v* millorar **~ment** ● *n* millora *f*

**impuls|e** /ˈɪmpʌls/ ● *n* impuls *m*; antull *m*, capritx *m*, capricei *m*; impulsió *f* **~ive** ● *adj* impulsiu

**in** /ɪn, ən/ ● *adv* dins; cap endintre ● *prep* en; dins; d'aquí a **~ love** ● *phr* enamorat

**inactiv|e** /ɪnˈæktɪv/ ● *adj* inactiu **~ity** ● *n* inactivitat *f*

**inadequate** ● *adj* inadequat

**inappropriate** /ˌɪnəˈprəʊprɪ.ət, ˌɪnəˈprəʊprɪ.ət/ ● *adj* inapropiat

**incentive** /ɪnˈsɛntɪv/ ● *n* incentiu *m*

**inch** /ɪntʃ/ ● *n* polzada *f*; centímetre *m*

**incisive** /ɪnˈsaɪsɪv/ ● *adj* incisiu

**inclination** /ˌɪn.klɪˈneɪ.ʃən/ ● *n* inclinació *f*; desnivell *m*

**inclu|de** /ɪnˈkluːd/ ● *v* incloure **~sion** ● *n* inclusió *f*

**income** /ˈɪnˌkʌm/ ● *n* renda *f*

**incompetent** ● *adj* incompetent

**inconsiderate** /ˌɪnkənˈsɪdərɪt/ ● *adj* inconsiderat

**inconsisten|t** /ˌɪnkənˈsɪstənt/ ● *adj* inconsistent **~cy** ● *n* inconsistència *f*

**incorporate** /ɪŋˈkɔːpəre(ɪ)t, ɪŋˈkɔː(ɹ).pəd.eɪt/ ● *v* incorporar

**incorrect** /ˌɪnkəˈrɛkt/ ● *adj* incorrecte

**increas|e** /ɪnˈkriːs, ˈɪnkriːs/ ● *n* augment *m* ● *v* augmentar **~ing** ● *adj* creixent **~ingly** ● *adv* cada vegada més

**incredibl|e** /ɪnˈkrɛdəbəl/ ● *adj* increïble **~y** ● *adv* increïblement

**incur** /ɪnˈkɜː, ɪnˈkɜː/ ● *v* incórrer

**indeed** /ɪnˈdiːd/ ● *adv* certament, efectivament, en efecte ● *interj* és clar, i tant

**independen|t** /ˌɪndɪˈpɛndənt/ ● *adj* independent **~tly** ● *adv* independentment **~ce** ● *n* independència *f*

**index** /ˈɪndɛks/ ● *n* (*pl* indices) índex *m* ● *v* indexar

**India ●** *n* Índia *f* **~n ●** *adj* indi **●** *n* indi; índia *f*

**indicat|e** /ˈɪndɪkeɪt/ **●** *v* indicar **~ive ●** *adj* indicatiu **~or ●** *n* indicador de gir *m*

**indices** *(pl)* ▷ INDEX

**indigenous** /ɪnˈdɪdʒnəs, ɪnˈdɪdʒənəs/ **●** *adj* indígena

**indirect** /ˌɪndəˈrɛkt, ˌɪndəˈrɛkt/ **●** *adj* indirecte **~ly ●** *adv* indirectament

**indiscreet ●** *adj* indiscret

**individual** /ˌɪndɪˈvɪdʒuəl, ˌɪndɪˈvɪdʒʊəl/ **●** *adj* individual **●** *n* individu **~ly ●** *adv* individualment **~ist ●** *n* individualista *f* **~ism ●** *n* individualisme *m*

**indolent** /ˈɪn.dəl.ənt/ **●** *adj* indolent

**Indonesia ●** *n* Indonèsia *f* **~n ●** *adj* indonesi **●** *n* indonesi *m*, indonèsia *f*

**induce** /ɪnˈduːs, ɪnˈdjuːs/ **●** *v* induir

**indulgent** /ɪnˈdʌldʒənt/ **●** *adj* indulgent

**industr|y** /ˈɪndəstɹi/ **●** *n* indústria *f* **~ial ●** *adj* industrial

**inequality** /ˌɪnɪˈkwɒlɪti/ **●** *n* desigualtat *f*

**inevitabl|e** /ɪnˈɛvɪtəbəl/ **●** *adj* inevitable **~y ●** *adv* inevitablement

**inexpensive ●** *adj* barat

**infamous** /ˈɪnfəməs/ **●** *adj* infame

**infantry** /ˈɪnfəntɹi/ **●** *n* infanteria *f*

**infect** /ɪnˈfɛkt/ **●** *v* infectar, contagiar **~ious ●** *adj* infecciós **~ion ●** *n* infecció *f*

**inferiority ●** *n* inferioritat *f*

**inflation** /ɪnˈfleɪʃən/ **●** *n* inflament *f*; inflació *f*

**inflict** /ɪnˈflɪkt/ **●** *v* infligir

**influence** /ˈɪn.fl(j)u.əns/ **●** *n* influència *f* **●** *v* influenciar; influir

**informati|ve** /ɪnˈfɔːmətɪv/ **●** *adj* informatiu **~on ●** *n* informació *f*

**informal** /ɪnˈfɔːm(ə)l, ɪnˈfɔːm(ə)l/ **●** *adj* informal **~ly ●** *adv* informalment **~ity ●** *n* informalitat *f*

**infrastructure** /ˈɪnfɹəˌstɹʌk(t)ʃɚ/ **●** *n* infraestructura *f*

**ingredient** /ɪnˈgɹiːdi.ənt/ **●** *n* ingredient *m*

**inhabitant** /ɪnˈhæ.bɪ.tənt/ **●** *n* habitant *m*

**inherent** /ɪnˈhɪəɹənt/ **●** *adj* inherent

**inherit** /ɪnˈhɛɹɪt/ **●** *v* heretar

**inhibit ●** *v* inhibir **~ion ●** *n* inhibició *f*

**initial** /ɪˈnɪʃəl/ **●** *adj* inicial **●** *n* inicial; inicials; caplletra; obertura

**initiative** /ɪˈnɪʃətɪv/ **●** *n* iniciativa *f*

**inject** /ɪnˈdʒɛkt/ **●** *v* injectar **~ion ●** *n* injecció *f*

**injur|e** /ˈɪndʒɚ, ˈɪndʒə/ **●** *v* ferir **~y ●** *n* ferida *f*, injúria *f*

**injured** *(sp/pp)* ▷ INJURE

**injustice** /ɪnˈdʒʌs.tɪs/ **●** *n* injustícia *f*

**ink** /ɪŋk/ **●** *n* tinta *f* **●** *v* tintar; signar; tatuar

**inmate ●** *n* internat *m*, intern *m*; resident *f*

**inner** /ˈɪnɚ, ˈɪnə/ **●** *adj* interior

**innocen|t** /'ɪnəsn̩t/ ● *adj* innocent ~**ce** ● *n* innocència *f*

**innovat|e** /'ɪnəveɪt/ ● *v* innovar ~**ive** ● *adj* innovador ~**ion** ● *n* innovació *f*

**inquiry** /ɪn'kwaɪəɹi, ɪn'kwaɪ(ə)ɹi/ ● *n* indagació *f*, perquisició *f*

**insanity** /ɪn'sænɪti/ ● *n* insanitat *f*, bogeria *f*

**insect** /'ɪnsɛkt/ ● *n* insecte ~**icide** ● *n* insecticida *m*

**insensitive** /ɪn'sɛnsɪtɪv/ ● *adj* insensible

**insertion** /ɪn'sɝʃən/ ● *n* inserció *f*

**inside** /'ɪnsaɪd/ ● *adj* dins ● *n* interior *m* ● *prep* dins

**insist** /ɪn'sɪst/ ● *v* insistir ~**ence** ● *n* insistència *f*

**inspect** /ɪn'spɛkt/ ● *v* inspeccionar ~**ion** ● *n* inspecció *f*

**inspiring** ● *adj* inspirador

**instability** ● *n* inestabilitat *f*

**install** /ɪn'stɔːl/ ● *v* instal·lar ~**ation** ● *n* instal·lació *f*

**instantly** /'ɪnstəntli/ ● *adv* instantàniament

**instinct** /'ɪn.stɪŋkt/ ● *n* instint *m* ~**ive** ● *adj* instintiu

**institut|e** /'ɪnstɪt(j)uːt/ ● *n* institut *m* ● *v* instituir ~**ion** ● *n* institució *f* ~**ionalize** ● *v* institucionalitzar ~**ionalization** ● *n* institucionalització *f*

**instruct** /ɪn'stɹʌkt/ ● *v* instruir ~**ion** ● *n* instrucció *f* ~**or** ● *n* instructor *m*

**instrument** /'ɪnstɹəmənt/ ● *n* instrument *m* ~**al** ● *adj* instrumental

**insufficient** ● *adj* insuficient

**insult** /ɪn'sʌlt, 'ɪn.sʌlt/ ● *n* insult *m* ● *v* insultar ~**ing** ● *adj* insultant

**insurance** /ɪn.'ʃɔɹ.ɪns/ ● *n* assegurança *f*

**intact** /ɪn'tækt/ ● *adj* intacte

**integrity** /ɪn'tɛgɹəti/ ● *n* integritat *f*; enteresa *f*

**integrate** ● *v* integrar

**intellectual** /ˌɪntə'lɛk(t)ʃʊəl/ ● *adj* intel·lectual ● *n* intel·lectual *f*

**intelligen|t** /ɪn'tɛlɪdʒənt/ ● *adj* intel·ligent ~**tly** ● *adv* intel·ligentment ~**ce** ● *n* intel·ligència *f*, seny *m*, llestesa *f*

**intention** /ɪn'tɛnʃən/ ● *n* intenció *f* ~**al** ● *adj* intencionat ~**ally** ● *adv* intencionadament, intencionalment

**intens|e** /ɪn'tɛns/ ● *adj* intens ~**ely** ● *adv* intensament ~**ify** ● *v* intensificar ~**ity** ● *n* intensitat *f* ~**ive** ● *adj* intensiu

**interact** /ɪntɚ'ækt/ ● *v* interactuar, relacionar-se ~**ion** ● *n* interacció *f* ~**ive** ● *adj* interactiu

**interest** /'ɪntɚɪst, 'ɪntəɹəst/ ● *n* interès *m* ~**ed** ● *adj* interessat ~**ing** ● *adj* interessant

**interface** /'ɪntɚfeɪs, 'ɪntɚˌfeɪs/ ● *n* interfície *f*

**interfere** /ˌɪntɚ'fɪɹ, ˌɪntɚ'fɪə/ ● *v* interferir ~**nce** ● *n* interferència *f*

**interim** /'ɪntəɹɪm/ ● *adj* interí

**interior** /ɪn'tɪɹiɚ, ɪn'tɪɹiɹə/ ● *adj* interior ● *n* interior *m*

**interjection** /ɪn.tɚ'dʒɛk.ʃən, ˌɪn.tɚ'dʒɛk.ʃən/ ● *n* interjecció *f*

**intermediate** /ˌɪntə(ɹ)ˈmidiːət, ˌɪntə(ɹ)ˈmidˌiert/ • *adj* intermedi

**internal** /ɪnˈtɜːnəl/ • *adj* intern **~ly** • *adv* internament; interiorment

**international** /ˌɪntəˈnæʃ(ə)n(ə)l, ˌɪntəˈnæʃ(ə)n(ə)l/ • *adj* internacional **~ly** • *adv* internacionalment

**Internet** • *n* Internet *f*, xarxa *f*

**interpret** /ɪnˈtɜːpɹɪt, ɪnˈtɜːpɹɪt/ • *v* interpretar **~ation** • *n* interpretació *f* **~er** • *n* intèrpret *f*

**interrogat|e** • *v* interrogar **~ion** • *n* interrogatori *m*

**interrupt** /ˌɪntəˈɹʌpt, ˈɪntəˌɹʌpt/ • *v* interrompre

**interven|e** • *v* intervenir **~tion** • *n* intervenció *f*

**interview** /ˈɪntəvjuː, ˈɪntəvjuː/ • *n* entrevista *f*, interviu *m* • *v* entrevistar **~er** • *n* entrevistador *m*

**intestine** /ɪnˈtɛstɪn, ɪnˈtɛstəm/ • *n* intestí *m*, budell *m*

**intima|te** /ˈɪn.tɪ.mət, ˈɪn.tɪ.meɪt/ • *adj* íntim **~cy** • *n* intimitat *f*

**intolerant** • *adj* intolerant

**intonation** /ɪntəˈneɪʃən/ • *n* entonació *f*

**intrigu|e** /ɪnˈtɹiːg, ɪnˈtɹiːg/ • *n* intriga • *v* intrigar **~ing** • *adj* intrigant

**introduc|e** /ˌɪntɹəˈdus, ˌɪntɹəˈdjuːs/ • *v* introduir **~tory** • *adj* introductori **~tion** • *n* introducció *f*; presentació *f*

**intuiti|on** /ˌɪntjʊˈɪʃən, ɪntuwˈɪʃɪn/ • *n* intuïció *f* **~ve** • *adj* intuïtiu

**inva|de** /ɪnˈveɪd/ • *v* envair **~der** • *n* invasor **~sion** • *n* invasió *f*

**invent** /ɪnˈvɛnt/ • *v* inventar **~ive** • *adj* inventiu; enginyós **~ion** • *n* invenció *f*, invent *m*; inventiva *f*

**inventory** /ˈɪn.vən.tɹi, ˈɪn.vən.tɔːɹi/ • *n* inventari *m* • *v* inventariar

**invest** /ɪnˈvɛst/ • *v* invertir; investir **~ment** • *n* inversió *f*

**investigat|e** /ɪnˈvɛs.tɪ.geɪt/ • *v* investigar **~ion** • *n* investigació *f* **~or** • *n* investigador *m*

**invisible** /ɪnˈvɪzəb(ə)l/ • *adj* invisible

**invite** /ɪnˈvaɪt/ • *n* invitació • *v* invitar, convidar

**invoice** /ˈɪn.vɔɪs/ • *n* factura *f*

**invoke** /ɪnˈvoʊk/ • *v* invocar

**iodine** /ˈaɪ.əˌdaɪn, -dɪn/ • *n* iode *m*

**Iran** • *n* Iran *m* **~ian** • *adj* iranià • *n* iranià *m*

**Iraq** • *n* Iraq *m* **~i** • *adj* iraquià • *n* iraquià *m*

**Ir|eland** • *n* Irlanda *f* **~ish** • *adj* irlandès • *n* irlandès *m*, gaèlic irlandès *m*; irlandesos

**iron** /ˈaɪən, ˈaɪən/ • *adj* de ferro • *n* ferro *m*; planxa *f* • *v* planxar

**iron|y** /ˈaɪə.ɹən.i, ˈaɪ.ɹə.ni/ • *n* ironia *f* **~ic** • *adj* irònic **~ically** • *adv* irònicament

**irrelevant** • *adj* irrellevant

**irresistible** /ˌɪɹɪˈzɪstəbl/ • *adj* irresistible

**irritati|ng** • *adj* irritant **~on** • *n* irritació *f*

**Islam** • *n* islam *m*, islamisme *m* **~ic** • *adj* islàmic *m*, islàmica *f*

**island** /'aɪlənd/ • *n* illa *f*
**isolat|e** /'aɪsəleɪt, 'aɪsələt/ • *v* aïllar, isolar **~ed** • *adj* aïllat **~ion** • *n* aïllament *m*, isolament *m*; isolació *f*
**Israel** • *n* Israel *m* **~i** • *adj* israelià • *n* israelià *m*
**issue** /'ɪsjuː, 'ɪʃ(j)u/ • *v* lliurar
**Istanbul** • *n* Istanbul
**~s** • *det* seu *m* • *pron* seu **~self** • *pron* es; mateix
**Ital|y** • *n* Itàlia *f* **~ian** • *adj* italià • *n* italià *m*, italiana *f*
**itchy** /'ɪtʃi/ • *adj* picar

# J

**jackdaw** /'dʒæk,dɔː, 'dʒæk,dɔ/ • *n* gralla *f*
**jacket** /'dʒæk.ɪt, 'dʒækɪt/ • *n* jaqueta *f*
**jam** /dʒæm, 'dʒæːm/ • *n* melmelada *f*; esmaixada *f*
**Jamaica** • *n* Jamaica *f* **~n** • *adj* jamaicà • *n* jamaicana *f*
**January** • *n* gener *m*
**Japan** • *n* Japó *m* **~ese** • *adj* japonès • *n* japonès *m*, japonesa *f*
**jaw** /dʒɔː, dʒɔ/ • *n* mandíbula *f*, maixella *f*
**jay** /dʒeɪ/ • *n* gaig; jota *f*
**jazz** /dʒæz/ • *n* jazz *m*
**jealous** /'dʒɛləs/ • *adj* gelós **~y** • *n* gelosia *f*
**jeans** /dʒiːnz/ • *n* texans *m*

**jelly** /'dʒɛl.i/ • *n* gelatina *f*; melmelada *f*
**jellyfish** /'dʒɛli,fɪʃ/ • *n* medusa *f*
**jet** /dʒɛt/ • *n* raig *m*; atzabeja *f*, gaieta *f*; atzabegenc
**Jew** • *n* jueu *m*, jueva *f* **~ish** • *adj* jueu
**jewel** /'dʒuː.əl, dʒul/ • *n* gemma *f*; joia *f* **~er** • *n* joier *m*
**job** /dʒɒb, dʒɑb/ • *n* treball *m*, feina *f*
**join** /dʒɔɪn/ • *n* unió • *v* unir-se, afegir-se
**joint** /dʒɔɪnt/ • *adj* conjunt • *n* juntura *f*; articulació *f*; cau *m*; porret *m* **~ly** • *adv* conjuntament
**joke** /dʒəʊk, dʒoʊk/ • *n* acudit *m*; broma *f*
**Jordan** • *n* Jordània *f*; Jordà *m*
**journal** /'dʒɜːnəl/ • *n* diari *m*; gaseta *f*
**journalis|t** /'dʒɜːnəlɪst, 'dʒɜːnəlɪst/ • *n* periodista *f* **~m** • *n* periodisme *m*
**joy** /dʒɔɪ/ • *n* alegria *f*, joia *f* **~ful** • *adj* joiós
**judg|e** /dʒʌdʒ/ • *n* jutge *m*; àrbitre *m* • *v* jutjar **~ment** • *n* judici, jutjament *m*; seny *m*, esma, coneixement *m*; veredicte
**judicial** /dʒu'dɪʃəl/ • *adj* judicial, judiciari
**judo** /'dʒuːdəʊ, 'dʒudoʊ/ • *n* judo *m*
**jug** /dʒʌg/ • *n* gerra *f*; popa *f*, pitrera *f*
**juic|e** /dʒuːs, dʒus/ • *n* suc *m* **~y** • *adj* sucós
**July** • *n* juliol *m*

**jump** /dʒʌmp/ • *n* salt *m*;
sobresalt *m* • *v* saltar;
sobresaltar

**June** • *n* juny *m*

**jungle** /'dʒʌŋgəl/ • *n* jungla *f*

**Jupiter** • *n* Júpiter *m*

**jur|y** /'dʒʊəri/ • *n* jurat *m* **~or** •
*n* jurat *m*

**just** /dʒʌst/ • *adj* just • *adv*
simplement, només, sols;
acabar de; just

**justice** /'dʒʌs.tɪs/ • *n* justesa *f*,
justícia *f*

**justif|y** /'dʒʌstɪfaɪ/ • *v* justificar
**~ication** • *n* justificació *f*

**kangaroo** /kaŋ.gə'ruː, ˌkæŋ.gə'ru/
• *n* cangur *m*

**Kazakhstan** • *n* Kazakhstan

**keen** /kiːn, kin/ • *adj* entusiasta

**keep** /kiːp/ • *n* torre mestra *f*,
torre de l'homenatge *f*,
homenatge *m* • *v* (*sp* kept, *pp*
kept) desar, guardar; seguir,
continuar

**kept** (*sp/pp*) ▷ KEEP

**kestrel** /'kɛstɹəl/ • *n* falcó *m*;
xoriguer *m*, xoriguer gros *m*,
xoriguer comú *m*

**key** /kiː, ki/ • *adj* clau • *n* clau *f*;
tecla *f* **~board** • *n* teclat *m* •
*v* teclejar **~ring** • *n* clauer *m*

**kick** /kɪk/ • *n* puntada *f*, guitza,
coça, xut • *v* donar un cop de
peu, donar una puntada,
xutar

**kid** /kɪd/ • *n* cabrit *m*

**kidnap** • *n* segrest, rapte • *v*
segrestar, raptar

**kidney** /'kɪdni/ • *n* ronyó *m*

**kill** /kɪl/ • *n* assassinat *m*; mort •
*v* matar, assassinar

**kilo** /'kiːləʊ, 'kiloʊ/ • *n* quilo *m*
**~metre** • *n* quilòmetre *m*,
kilòmetre *m*

**kind** /kaɪnd/ • *adj* maco; amable
• *n* tipus *m*, gènere *m*, classe *f*
**~ly** • *adv* amablement **~ness**
• *n* bondat *f*, cortesia *f*,
gentilesa *f*

**king** /kɪŋ, ŋ/ • *n* rei *m* • *v*
coronar **~dom** • *n* regne *m*

**kiss** /kɪs/ • *n* petó *m*, bes *m*,
besada *f* • *v* besar, petonejar

**kitchen** /'kɪtʃən/ • *n* cuina *f*

**kite** /kaɪt/ • *n* milà *m*; estel,
milotxa *f*

**kiwi** /'kiːwi/ • *n* kiwi *m*

**knee** /niː, ni/ • *n* genoll *m*

**kneel** /niːl/ • *v* (*sp* knelt, *pp*
knelt) agenollar-se

**kneeled** (*sp/pp*) ▷ KNEEL

**knelt** (*sp/pp*) ▷ KNEEL

**knew** (*sp*) ▷ KNOW

**knickers** ▷ PANTIES

**knife** /naɪf/ • *n* (*pl* knives)
ganivet *m*, coltell *m*; daga *f*,
punyal *m* • *v* acoltellar,
apunyalar

**knives** (*pl*) ▷ KNIFE

**knock** /nɒk, nɑk/ • *n* cop *m* • *v*
colpejar, batre, tustar

**knot** /nɒt/ • *n* nus *m*; grop *m*;
territ gros *m*

**know** /nəʊ, noʊ/ • *v* (*sp* knew, *pp* known) saber

**knowledge** /ˈnɒlɪdʒ, ˈnɑlɪdʒ/ • *n* coneixement *m*; coneixements **~able** • *adj* erudit; entès

**known** *(pp)* ▷ KNOW

**knuckle** /ˈnʌkəl/ • *n* artell *m*, nus *m*

**kookaburra** /ˈkʊkəˌbʌɹə, ˈkʊkəˌbaɹə/ • *n* cucaburra *m*

**Korea** • *n* Corea *f* **~n** • *adj* coreà • *n* coreà *m*; coreana *f*

**Kosovo** • *n* Kosovo *m*

**Kuwaiti** • *adj* kuwaitià

**Kyrgyzstan** • *n* Kirguizistan *m*

**label** /ˈleɪbəl/ • *n* etiqueta *f* • *v* etiquetar **~ing** • *n* etiquetatge *m*

**laboratory** /ˈlæbɹəˌtɹɪ, ləˈbɒɹət(ə)ɹiː/ • *n* laboratori

**lack** /lak, læk/ • *n* falta *f*, manca *f* • *v* faltar, mancar

**ladder** /ˈladə, ˈlædəɹ/ • *n* escala *f*; escalafó *m*; carrera *f*

**lady** /ˈleɪdi/ • *n* senyora **~bird** • *n* marieta *f*

**laid** *(sp/pp)* ▷ LAY

**lain** *(pp)* ▷ LIE

**lake** /leɪk/ • *n* llac *m*; laca *f*

**lamb** /læm/ • *n* xai *m*, anyell, corder *m*

**lame** /leɪm/ • *adj* coix; sonso

**lamp** /læmp/ • *n* làmpada *f* **~post** • *n* farola *f*

**land** /lænd/ • *n* terra *f*; terreny • *v* aterrar; atracar **~ing** • *n* aterratge *m*; replà **m~lord** • *n* amo *m*, mestressa *f*

**landscape** /ˈlandskeɪp/ • *n* paisatge *m*; apaïsat *m*

**lane** /leɪn/ • *n* carril *m*

**language** /ˈlæŋgwɪdʒ, æ/ • *n* idioma *m*, llengua *f*; llenguatge *m*; codi *m*

**Laos** • *n* Laos *m*

**lap** /læp/ • *n* doblec *m*; falda *f*; volta *f* **~top** • *n* ordinador portàtil *m*, portàtil *m*

**lard** /lɑːd, lɑːɹd/ • *n* llard

**large** /lɑːdʒ, ˈlɑːɹdʒ/ • *adj* llarg **at ~** • *phr* escàpol

**larva** /ˈlɑːˌvə, ˈlɑːˌvə/ • *n* larva *f*

**laser** /ˈleɪz.ə(ɹ), ˈleɪzəɹ/ • *n* làser *m*

**last** /lɑːst, læst/ • *adj* darrer *m*

**late** /leɪt/ • *adj* tard **~r** • *adj* futur • *adv* després; posteriorment • *interj* fins aviat

**Latin** • *adj* llatí; romà; llatina • *n* llatí

**latter** /ˈlæt.ə(ɹ), ˈlæt.əɹ/ • *adj* segon, ponent

**Latvia** • *n* Letònia *f* **~n** • *adj* letó • *n* letó *m*; letona *f*

**laugh** /lɑːf, lɑːf/ • *n* riure *m* • *v* riure; riure's de **~ter** • *n* riure, rialla

**launch** /lɔːnʧ, lɑːnʧ/ • *n* llançament; llanxa *f* • *v* llançar

**laund|ry** /ˈlɔːn.dɹi, ˈlɑn.dɹi/ • *n* bugada *f* **~erette** • *n* bugaderia *f*

**law** /lɔː, lɔ/ • *n* llei, dret **~yer** • *n* advocat *m*, advocada *f* **~suit** • *n* plet *m*, litigi *m*

**lawn** /lɔːn, lɔn/ • *n* gespa *f*

**lay** /leɪ/ • *adj* profà; laic • (*also*) ▷ LIE

**layer** /leɪə, 'leɪ.ər/ • *n* capa *f*

**lazy** /'leɪzi/ • *adj* mandrós, peresós

**lead** /led/ • *n* plom *m* • *v* (*sp* led, *pp* led) dirigir, conduir, portar; encapçalar, anar al capdavant **~er** • *n* líder *f*, dirigent *m* **~ership** • *n* lideratge *m*

**leaf** /liːf/ • *n* (*pl* leaves) fulla *f*; full *m*

**league** /liːg/ • *n* lliga *f*; llegua *f* • *v* alligar

**lean** /liːn/ • *adj* magre • *v* (*sp* leant, *pp* leant) inclinar; abocar; repenjar-se, recolsar-se, arrambar-se

**leaned** (*sp/pp*) ▷ LEAN

**leant** (*sp/pp*) ▷ LEAN

**leap** /liːp/ • *n* salt • *v* (*sp* leapt, *pp* leapt) saltar

**leaped** (*sp/pp*) ▷ LEAP

**leapt** (*sp/pp*) ▷ LEAP

**learn** /lɜːn, lɜn/ • *v* (*sp* learnt, *pp* learnt) aprendre; estudiar **~er** • *n* aprenent *f* **~ing** • *n* aprenentatge

**learned** (*sp/pp*) ▷ LEARN

**learnt** (*sp/pp*) ▷ LEARN

**at least** • *phr* almenys, pel cap baix

**leather** /'leðə, 'leðər/ • *n* cuir *m*

**leave** /liːv/ • *n* permís *m*; comiat *m* • *v* (*sp* left, *pp* left) dipositar; deixar; sortir, partir

**leaves** (*pl*) ▷ LEAF

**Leban|on** • *n* Líban *m* **~ese** • *adj* libanès • *n* libanès *m*

**led** (*sp/pp*) ▷ LEAD

**leek** /liːk/ • *n* porro *m*

**left** /left/ • *adj* esquerre; esquerrà • *n* esquerra *f* **~handed** • *n* esquerrà • (*also*) ▷ LEAVE

**leg** /leg, leɪg/ • *n* cama *f*; petge *m*

**legacy** /'legəsi, 'leɪgəsi/ • *n* llegat *m*

**legal** /'liː.gəl, 'liɡəl/ • *adj* legal, jurídic *m* **~ly** • *adv* legalment **~ity** • *n* legalitat *f* **~ization** • *n* legalització *f*

**legend** /'ledʒ.ənd/ • *n* llegenda *f* **~ary** • *adj* llegendari

**legislat|e** /'ledʒɪs.leɪt/ • *v* legislar **~ive** • *adj* legislatiu **~or** • *n* legislador **~ion** • *n* legislació *f*

**legitimate** /lɪ'dʒɪtɪmət, lə'dʒɪtɪmeɪt/ • *adj* legítim

**legume** /lɪ'gjuːm/ • *n* llegum *m*

**leisure** /'leʒə(r), 'liːʒər/ • *n* lleure *m*, oci *m*

**lemon** /'lemən/ • *n* llimona *f*; llimoner *m*, llimonera *f*

**length** /leŋ(k)θ/ • *n* longitud *f* **~en** • *v* allargar

**lens** /lenz/ • *n* lent *f*

**lentil** /'lentəl/ • *n* llentilla *f*

**leopard** /'lepəd, 'lepərd/ • *n* lleopard *m*

**lesbian** /'lezbi.ən/ • *adj* lesbiana *f*; lesbià *m* • *n* lesbiana *f*

**Lesotho** • *n* Lesotho

**less** /les/ • *adj* menys • *prep* menys

**lesson** /'lesn/ • *n* lliçó *f*

**let** /lɛt/ • *v* (*sp* let, *pp* let)
permetre, deixar
**lethal** /'liː.θəl/ • *adj* letal, mortal
**letharg|y** /'lɛθədʒi, 'lɛθɚdʒi/ • *n*
letargia *f* **~ic** • *adj* letàrgic
**letter** /'lɛtə(ɹ), 'lɛtɚ/ • *n* lletra *f*,
caràcter *m*; carta *f*
**lettuce** /'lɛtɪs/ • *n* enciam *m*,
lletuga *f*
**level** /'lɛv.əl/ • *adj* anivellat;
uniforme • *n* nivell *m*, llivell *m*
• *v* anivellar
**liab|le** /'laɪəbəl/ • *adj*
responsable; subjecte **~ility** •
*n* responsabilitat *f*
**liar** /'laɪ.ə, 'laɪ.ɚ/ • *n* mentider *m*
**liberal** /'lɪbɹəl, 'lɪbəɹəl/ • *adj*
liberal **~ism** • *n* liberalisme *m*
**liberat|e** /'lɪbəɹeɪt/ • *v* alliberar
**~ion** • *n* alliberament *m*,
alliberació *f*
**Liberia** • *n* Libèria *f*
**liberty** /'lɪbɚti/ • *n* llibertat *f*
**librar|y** /'laɪbɹəɹi, 'laɪbɹəɹi/ • *n*
biblioteca *f* **~ian** • *n*
bibliotecari *m*
**Libya** • *n* Líbia *f*
**lice** (*pl*) ▷ LOUSE
**licence** (*British*) ▷ LICENSE
**license** /'laɪsəns/ • *n* llicència *f*,
permís *m*
**lid** /lɪd/ • *n* tapa *f*
**lie** /laɪ/ • *n* situació *f*; mentida *f*
• *v* (*sp* lay, *pp* lain) jeure;
trobar-se; mentir **~ down** • *v*
ajeure's
**Liechtenstein** • *n* Liechtenstein
**life** /laɪf/ • *n* (*pl* lives) vida *f*
**~guard** • *n* socorrista *f* **~style**
• *n* estil de vida *m* **~time**;
eternitat *f*

**lift** /lɪft/ • *n* ascensor *m* • *v* alçar
**light** /laɪt, lʌɪt/ • *adj* lleuger,
light; clar; tallat • *n* llum;
flama, metxa • *v* (*sp* lit, *pp* lit)
encendre, il·luminar **~ly** • *adv*
lleugerament **~ing** • *n*
enllumenat *m* **~house** • *n* far
*m* **~ning** • *n* llampec *m*,
rellamp *m*; llamp *m* **~ bulb** • *n*
bombeta *f*
**lighted** (*sp/pp*) ▷ LIGHT
**like** /laɪk/ • *adj* semblant *f* • *adv*
com • *n* preferències • *part*
com • *v* agradar
**likelihood** /'laɪklihʊd/ • *n*
probabilitat *f*
**limb** /lɪm/ • *n* membre *m*
**lime** /laɪm/ • *n* calç *f*; envescada
*f*
**limit** /'lɪmɪt/ • *n* límit *m* • *v*
limitar
**line** /laɪn/ • *n* línia *f*; recta *v*
folrar
**linen** /'lɪnən/ • *n* lli *m*
**linger** • *v* romandre; perviure;
rumiar
**lingerie** /'læn.ʒə.ɹi, ˌlɑn.(d)ʒəˈɹeɪ/ •
*n* llenceria *f*
**link** /lɪŋk/ • *n* enllaç *m*, vincle *m*;
baula *f*; link *m*; torxa *f* • *v*
lligar, enllaçar, vinclar
**lion** /'laɪən/ • *n* lleó *m* **~ess** • *n*
lleona *f*
**lip** /lɪp/ • *n* llavi *m* **~stick** • *n*
pintallavis *m*
**liquid** /'lɪkwɪd/ • *adj* líquid • *n*
líquid *m*
**Lisbon** • *n* Lisboa *f*
**list** /lɪst/ • *n* llista *f* • *v* llistar,
allistar
**listen** /'lɪs.ən/ • *v* escoltar

**lit** *(sp/pp)* ▷ LIGHT

**literal** /ˈlɪt(ə)ɹəl/ • *adj* literal **~ly** • *adv* literalment

**literary** /ˈlɪtəɹəɹi, ˈlɪtə(ə)ɹi/ • *adj* literari

**litera|te** /ˈlɪtəɹət/ • *adj* alfabet; lletrat **~cy** • *n* alfabetisme *m*

**literature** /ˈlɪ.tə.ɹɪ.tʃə(ɹ), ˈlɪ.tə.ɹ.tʃɚ/ • *n* literatura *f*

**Lithuania** • *n* Lituània *f* **~n** • *adj* lituà • *n* lituà *m*

**litre** /ˈliː.tə, ˈli.tɚ/ • *n* litre *m*

**little** /ˈlɪtəl, ˈlɪtl̩/ • *adj* petit • *adv* poc • *det* una mica de

**liv|e** /lɪv/ • *adj* viu; en viu • *adv* en directe • *v* viure **~ely** • *adj* vivaç *f* **~ing** • *adj* viu

**liver** /ˈlɪvə(ɹ)/ • *n* fetge *m*

**lives** *(pl)* ▷ LIFE

**lizard** /ˈlɪz.əd, ˈlɪz.ɚd/ • *n* llangardaix *m*, sargantana *f*

**llama** /ˈlɑː.mə, ˈlɑmə/ • *n* llama *f*

**load** /loʊd, ləʊd/ • *v* carregar

**loaf** /ləʊf, loʊf/ • *v* gandulejar

**loan** /ləʊn, loʊn/ • *n* préstec *m* • *v* prestar

**loaves** *(pl)* ▷ LOAF

**lobby** /ˈlɒbi, ˈlɑbi/ • *n* lobby *m*

**lobster** /ˈlɒb.stə, ˈlɑb.stɚ/ • *n* llagosta *f*, llamàntol *m*, escamarlà *m*

**local** /ˈləʊkəl, ˈloʊkl̩/ • *adj* local **~ly** • *adv* localment **~ize** • *v* localitzar

**location** /loʊˈkeɪʃən, ləʊˈkeɪʃən/ • *n* ubicació

**lock** /lɒk, lɑk/ • *n* cadenat *m*; resclosa *f*; floc *m*, ble *m* **~er** • *n* armari **~smith** • *n* manyà *m*

**log out** • *v* sortir

**logic** /ˈlɒdʒɪk, ˈlɑdʒɪk/ • *n* lògica *f* **~al** • *adj* lògic **~ally** • *adv* lògicament

**logistical** • *adj* logístic

**London** • *n* Londres

**lonely** /ˈləʊnli, ˈloʊnli/ • *adj* solitari *m*

**long** /lɒŋ, lɔːŋ/ • *adj* llunyà, llong • *v* enyorar **~-term** • *adj* a llarg termini **~ing** • *n* enyorança

**look** /lʊk, luːk/ • *n* ullada *f*, cop d'ull *m*, mirada *f* • *v* mirar; semblar; cercar, buscar; encarar **~ sth up** • *v* cercar **~ for sb/sth** • *v* cercar, buscar **~ forward to sth** • *v* esperar amb il·lusió

**loom** /luːm, lum/ • *n* teler *m*

**loop** /luːp/ • *n* bucle *m*, cicle *m* **~hole** • *n* espitllera *f*

**loose** /luːs/ • *v* deslligar; descordar; afluixar; alliberar; tirar

**lord** /lɔːd, lɔɹd/ • *n* castellà; senyor • *v* senyorejar

**los|e** /luːz/ • *v* (*sp* lost, *pp* lost) perdre **~s** • *n* pèrdua *f*

**lost** /lɒst, lɔːst/ • *adj* perdut • *(also)* ▷ LOSE

**lottery** /ˈlɒtəɹi, ˈlɑtɚi/ • *n* loteria *f*

**loud** /laʊd/ • *adj* fort, alt; estrident, sorollós *m*; cridaner *m*, llampant *m* **~ly** • *adv* sorollosament

**lous|e** /laʊs/ • *n* (*pl* lice) poll *m* **~y** • *adj* pèssim, horrible; pollós

**lov|e** /lʌv, lɔːv/ • *n* amor *f*; res, zero *m* • *v* estimar, voler;

agradar; fer l'amor **~ing** ● *adj* amorós **~ingly** ● *adv* amorosament **~ely** ● *adj* encantador; preciós **~able** ● *adj* amable **~er** ● *n* amant *f*; amistançat *m* **in ~e** ● *phr* enamorat

**low** /ləʊ, loʊ/ ● *adj* baix ● *adv* baix **~er** ● *v* baixar, abaixar; disminuir; reduir

**loyal** /ˈlɔɪəl/ ● *adj* lleial **~ly** ● *adv* lleialment **~ty** ● *n* lleialtat *f*

**luck** /lʌk, lʊk/ ● *n* sort *f* **~y** ● *adj* afortunat **~ily** ● *adv* afortunadament, per sort

**luggage** /ˈlʌɡɪdʒ/ ● *n* equipatge *m*, bagatge *m*

**lunch** /lʌntʃ/ ● *n* dinar *m* ● *v* dinar **~box** ● *n* carmanyola *f*

**lung** /ˈlʌŋ/ ● *n* pulmó *m*

**lust** /lʌst/ ● *n* luxúria *f*

**Luxembourg** ● *n* Luxemburg *m*

**luxurious** /lʌɡˈʒʊr.i.əs/ ● *adj* luxós; luxuriós

**lynx** /lɪŋks/ ● *n* linx *m*

**lyrics** /ˈlɪɹ.ɪks/ ● *n* lletra *f*

**Macedonia** ● *n* Macedònia *f*; República de Macedònia *f* **~n** ● *adj* macedònic, macedoni ● *n* macedoni *m*, macedònic *m*, macedònia *f*, macedònica *f*

**machine** /məˈʃiːn/ ● *n* màquina *f*; auto *m*, automòbil *m* **~ry** ● *n* maquinària *f*

**mad** /ˈmæd, ˈmæːd/ ● *adj* boig *m*, boja *f*

**Madagascar** ● *n* Madagascar *m*

**made** *(sp/pp)* ▷ MAKE

**Madrid** ● *n* Madrid

**magazine** /mæɡəˈzin, mæɡəˈziːn/ ● *n* revista *f*; arsenal; carregador

**maggot** /ˈmæɡət/ ● *n* asticot *m*

**magic** /ˈmadʒɪk, ˈmædʒɪk/ ● *adj* màgic *m* ● *n* màgia *f* **~al** ● *adj* màgic

**magnet** /ˈmæɡnət/ ● *n* imant *m* **~ic** ● *adj* magnètic

**magnificent** /mæɡˈnɪfəsənt/ ● *adj* magnífic *m*

**magnifying glass** ● *n* lupa *f*

**mail|box** ● *n* bústia *f* **~man** ● *n* carter *m*

**main** /meɪn/ ● *adj* principal *f* **~land** ● *n* continent *m*, terra ferma *f* **~ly** ● *adv* principalment

**maint|ain** /meɪnˈteɪn/ ● *v* mantenir **~enance** ● *n* manteniment *m*

**major** /ˈmeɪ.dʒə(ɹ), ˈmeɪ.dʒæ/ ● *adj* major ● *n* major *m* **~ity** ● *n* majoria *f*; majoria d'edat *f*

**make** /meɪk/ ● *v* *(sp* made, *pp* made) fer **~r** ● *n* fabricant *m*, faedor *m* **~up** ● *n* maquillatge *m*

**Malawi** ● *n* Malawi

**Malaysia** ● *n* Malàisia *f* **~n** ● *adj* malaisi

**Maldives** ● *n* Maldives

**male** /meɪl/ ● *adj* masculí *m*, masculina *f*, mascle *m*, mascla *f* ● *n* mascle *m*

**mallard** /'mæl.ɑ:(ɹ)d, 'mælərd/ • *n* ánade azulón / ánade real

**Malt|a** • *n* Malta *f* **~ese** • *adj* maltès *m*, maltesa *f*

**mammoth** /'mæməθ/ • *adj* mastodòntic • *n* mamut *m*

**man** /mæn/ • *n* (*pl* man) home *m*, humà *m*, ésser humà *m* **-ly** • *adj* viril

**manage** /'mænɪdʒ/ • *v* sortir-se'n **~ment** • *n* administració *f*, gestió *f*; direcció *f*, gerència *f*; maneig *m*

**mandat|e** /'mæn.deɪt/ • *n* mandat *m* **~ory** • *adj* obligatori

**mandolin** /'mændəlɪn/ • *n* mandolina *f*

**manifest** /'mæn.ɪ.fɛst/ • *adj* manifest • *n* manifest • *v* manifestar

**manipulat|e** /mə'nɪpjʊleɪt/ • *v* manipular **~ive** • *adj* manipulador

**manner** /'mænə, 'mænər/ • *n* manera *f*; maneres

**manually** • *adv* manualment

**manuscript** /'mænjə,skrɪpt/ • *adj* manuscrit *m*; original *m*

**many** /'mɛni, 'mɪni/ • *det* molt, moltes

**map** /mæp/ • *n* mapa *m*, plànol *m*

**marathon** /'mærəθən, 'mærə,θɑn/ • *n* marató *f*

**marble** /'mɑ:bəl, 'mɑɹbəl/ • *n* marbre *m*; bala *f*

**March** /mɑ:tʃ, mɑɹtʃ/ • *n* març *m*

**march** /mɑ:tʃ, mɑɹtʃ/ • *n* marxa *f*; manifestació *f*; pas *m*; marca *f* • *v* marxar

**mare** /mɛə, mɛəɹ/ • *n* euga *f*, egua *f*

**margin** /'mɑ:dʒɪn, 'mɑ:ɹdʒ(ə)n/ • *n* marge *m* **~al** • *adj* marginal

**marine** /mə'ɹiːn/ • *adj* marí

**mark** /mɑ:k/ • *n* marca *f*; nota; marc *m* • *v* tacar; puntuar; marcar; advertir, observar

**market** /'mɑ:kɪt, 'mɑɹkɪt/ • *n* mercat *m* **~ing** • *n* màrqueting *m*

**marmot** /'mɑɹ.mət/ • *n* marmota *f*

**marr|y** /'mæɹɪ, 'mæɹi/ • *v* casar-se; casar; pegar **~iage** • *n* matrimoni *m*; casament *m*, boda *f* **~ied** • *adj* casat

**Mars** • *n* Mart *m*

**martial** /'mɑ:ʃəl, 'mɑɹʃəl/ • *adj* marcial

**mashed potatoes** • *n* puré de patates *m*

**mask** /mɑ:sk, mæsk/ • *n* màscara *f*, careta *f*; mascarada *f* • *v* emmascarar

**mass** /mæs/ • *n* massa *f*; missa *f* **~ive** • *adj* massiu

**massacre** /'mæs.ə.kə, 'mæs.ə.kə(ɹ)/ • *n* massacre *m* • *v* massacrar

**master** /'mɑ:stə, 'mæstər/ • *n* mestre *m* **~piece** • *n* obra mestra *f*

**match** /mætʃ/ • *n* partit *m*, matx *m*; misto *m* • *v* coincidir, concordar, correspondre

**material** /mə'tɪɹɪəl, mə'tɪəɹɪəl/ • *adj* material **~ize** • *v* materialitzar **~ism** • *n* materialisme *m* **~istic** • *adj* materialista

**maternal** /mə'tɜ:nəl, mə'tɜ:nəl/ ● *adj* maternal

**mathematic|s** /mæθ(ə)'mætɪks/ ● *n* matemàtiques, matemàtica **~al** ● *adj* matemàtic *m*

**maths** ▷ MATHEMATICS

**matrix** /'meɪtɪks, 'mætɪks/ ● *n* (*pl* matrices) matriu *f*

**matter** /'mætə, 'mætə/ ● *v* importar

**mattress** /'mætɪs/ ● *n* matalàs *m*

**matur|e** /mə'tjʊə, mə'tʃʊ(ə)ɹ/ ● *adj* madur; raonat ● *v* madurar; vèncer **~ity** ● *n* maduresa *f*

**Mauritania** ● *n* Mauritània *f*

**maxim|um** /'mæksɪməm/ ● *adj* màxim **~ize** ● *v* maximitzar

**May** /meɪ/ ● *n* maig *m*

**may** /meɪ/ ● *v* (*sp* might, *pp* -) poder

**maybe** /'meɪbi/ ● *adv* potser

**mayonnaise** /'meɪ.ə.neɪz, 'mæn.eɪz/ ● *n* maionesa *f*

**mayor** /'meɪ.ə, 'mɛə/ ● *n* alcalde *m*, alcaldessa *f*, batlle *m*, batllessa *f*

**me** /mi:, mi/ ● *pron* em, me; mi

**meal** /mi:l/ ● *n* àpat *m*

**mean** /mi:n/ ● *adj* mig *m* ● *n* mitjana ● *v* (*sp* meant, *pp* meant) pretendre; significar; voler dir **~ing** ● *n* significat *m*; sentit *m* **~ingful** ● *adj* significatiu **~ingless** ● *adj* sense sentit

**meant** *(sp/pp)* ▷ MEAN

**meanwhile** /'mi:nwaɪl, 'mi:nhwaɪl/ ● *adv* mentrestant; entretant

**measure** /'mɛʒə, 'mɛʒə/ ● *n* mesura *f* ● *v* mesurar, amidar

**meat** /mi:t, mit/ ● *n* carn *f*; bessó *m* **~ball** ● *n* mandonguilla *f*

**mechani|cal** /mɪ'kænɪk(ə)l, mə'kæ.nə.kəl/ ● *adj* mecànic **~sm** ● *n* mecanisme *m*

**medal** /'mɛdəl/ ● *n* medalla *f*

**medic|ine** /'mɛd.sɪn, 'mɛ.dɪ.sɪn/ ● *n* medicament; medicina *f* **~al** ● *adj* mèdic **~ation** ● *n* medicament *m*

**medieval** /,mɛd.i.'i:.vəl, mɪd.'i.vəl/ ● *adj* medieval

**meditat|e** ● *v* meditar **~ion** ● *n* meditació *f*

**medium** /'mi:dɪəm/ ● *adj* mitjà ● *n* medi *m*; mitjà *m*; mèdium

**meet** /mi:t, mit/ ● *v* (*sp* met, *pp* met) quedar; conèixer; reunir

**meeting** /'mi:tɪŋ, 'mitɪŋ/ ● *n* reunió *f*; trobada *f*

**melod|y** /'mɛl.ə.di, 'mɛl.ə.di/ ● *n* melodia *f* **~ic** ● *adj* melòdic

**melon** /'mɛlən/ ● *n* meló *m*

**melt** /mɛlt/ ● *v* (*sp* melted, *pp* molten) fondre

**melted** *(sp/pp)* ▷ MELT

**member** /'mɛmbə, 'mɛmbə/ ● *n* membre *m*; membre viril *m*

**memor|y** /'mɛm(ə)ɹi, 'mɪm(ə)ɹi/ ● *n* memòria *f*; record *m* **~able** ● *adj* memorable **~ize** ● *v* memoritzar

**men** *(pl)* ▷ MAN

**mental** /'mɛntəl/ ● *adj* mental **~ly** ● *adv* mentalment

**mention** /'mɛnʃən/ ● *v* mencionar, esmentar

**menu** /'mɛnju:, 'mɛnju/ ● *n* menú *m*; carta *m*

**merchant** /'mɜːtʃənt, 'mɜːtʃənt/ • *n* mercader *m*

**mercurial** /məˈkjʊə.ɪɪəl, mɜˈkjʊ.ɹi.əl/ • *adj* mercurial

**Mercury** /'mɜː.kjʊ.ɹi, 'mɜkjəɹi/ • *n* Mercuri *m*

**merc|y** /'mɜːsi, 'mɜsi/ • *n* misericòrdia ~**iless** • *adj* despietat

**mere** /mɪə, mɪə/ • *adj* mer ~**ly** • *adv* merament, simplement

**merit** /'mɛɹɪt/ • *n* mèrit *m* • *v* merèixer

**mess** /mɛs/ • *n* garbuix *m*, embolic

**message** /'mɛsɪdʒ/ • *n* missatge *m*, notícia *f*

**met** *(sp/pp)* ▷ MEET

**metal** /'mɛtəl/ • *n* metall; metal ~**lic** • *adj* metàl·lic

**metaphor** /'mɛt.ə.fɔː(ɹ), 'mɛt.ə.fɔ(ə)ɹ/ • *n* metàfora *f* ~**ical** • *adj* metafòric

**meteorite** /'miː.tɪ.ə.ɹaɪt, 'mi.ti.ə.ɹaɪt/ • *n* meteorit *m*

**meteorolog|y** /ˌmiː.tɪəˈɹɒlədʒi, ˌmiti.əˈɹɔːlədʒi/ • *n* meteorologia *f* ~**ist** • *n* meteoròleg *m*

**meter** /'miːtəɹ, 'miːtə/ • *n* comptador *m*

**method** /'mɛθəd/ • *n* mètode *m* ~**ical** • *adj* metòdic ~**ology** • *n* metodologia *f*

**meticulous** /mɪˈtɪkjilɪs/ • *adj* meticulós, minuciós

**metre** *(British)* ▷ METER

**metropolitan** /mɛtɹəˈpɒlɪtən, mɛtɹəˈpɒlɪtən/ • *adj* metropolità

**Mexic|o** • *n* Mèxic *m* ~**an** • *adj* mexicà *m*, mexicana *f*

**mice** *(pl)* ▷ MOUSE

**Micronesia** • *n* Micronèsia *f*

**microwave** /'maɪkɹəˌweɪv, 'maɪkɹəʊˌweɪv/ • *n* microona *f* ~ **oven** • *n* forn de microones *m*

**middle** /'mɪdəl, 'mədəl/ • *adj* mitjà • *n* mig *m*; cintura *f* ~ **finger** • *n* dit del mig *m* ~ **name** • *n* segon prenom *m*, nom del mig *m* ~**man** • *n* mitjancer *m*

**Middle Ages** • *n* edat mitjana *f*

**midnight** /'mɪdnʌɪt, 'mɪdˌnaɪt/ • *n* mitjanit *f*

**midwife** /'mɪd.waɪf/ • *n* llevadora *f*

**mighty** /'maɪti/ • *adj* poderós

**migrat|ory** /'maɪ.ɡɹə.tə.ɹi, 'maɪˈɡɹeɪ.tə.ɹi/ • *adj* migratori ~**ion** • *n* migració *f*

**mild** /'maɪld/ • *adj* suau

**mile** /maɪl/ • *n* milla *f*

**military** /'mɪl.ɪ.tɹi, 'mɪl.ɪ.tɛɹ.i/ • *adj* militar • *n* exèrcit *m*

**milk** /mɪlk/ • *n* llet *f* • *v* munyir ~**shake** • *n* batut de llet *m* ~**y** • *adj* lletós

**Milky Way** • *n* Via Làctia *f*

**mill** /mɪl/ • *n* molí *m* • *v* moldre

**millilitre** • *n* mil·lilitre *m*

**millimeter** • *n* mil·límetre *m*

**million** /'mɪljən/ • *num* milió *m*

**millipede** /'mɪləpɪd/ • *n* milpeu *m*

**mind** /maɪnd/ • *n* ment *f*

**mine** /maɪn/ • *n* mina *f* • *pron* el meu *m*, la meva *f* • *v* minar

**miner** /'maɪnə/ • *n* minaire *f*, miner *m*

**mineral** /ˈmɪ.nəɪ.əl/ • *adj* mineral *f* • *n* mineral *m*; aigua mineral *f*

**minimal** /ˈmɪnəməl/ • *adj* mínim; minimalista **~ist** • *adj* minimalista **~ism** • *n* minimalisme *m*

**minim|um** /ˈmɪnɪməm/ • *n* mínim *m* **~ize** • *v* minimitzar

**mining** /ˈmaɪnɪŋ/ • *n* mineria *f*

**miniskirt** /ˈmɪnɪskəːt/ • *n* minifaldilla *f*

**minist|er** /ˈmɪnɪstə, ˈmɪnɪstɚ/ • *n* ministre de l'església *m*; ministre *m* **~ry** • *n* ministeri *m*

**mink** /mɪŋk/ • *n* visó *m*

**minor** /ˈmaɪnə, ˈmaɪnɚ/ • *n* menor, menor d'etat **~ity** • *n* minoria; minoritat

**mint** /mɪnt/ • *adj* menta • *n* seca *f*; menta *f* • *v* encunyar

**minute** /ˈmɪnɪt/ • *adj* menut, diminut, minúscul • *n* minut *m*; segon *m*, moment *m*; acta *f*

**mirac|le** /ˈmɪɹəkəl, ˈmiɹəkəl/ • *n* miracle *m* **~ulous** • *adj* miraculós

**mirror** /ˈmɪɹ.ə, ˈmiɹ.ɚ/ • *n* mirall *m*, espill *m*; còpia *f* • *v* duplicar, copiar

**miser|y** /ˈmɪz(ə)ɹɪ, ˈmɪz(ə)ɹi/ • *n* misèria *f* **~able** • *adj* trist *m*, desgraciat

**mislead** /ˈmɪsˈliːd/ • *v* desencaminar; enganyar

**miss** /mɪs/ • *v* fallar; trobar a faltar, enyorar

**missile** /ˈmɪsaɪl/ • *n* projectil *m*; míssil

**mission** /ˈmɪʃ(ə)n/ • *n* missió *f* **~ary** • *n* missioner *m*

**mist** /mɪst/ • *n* boira *f*

**mistress** /ˈmɪstɹɪs/ • *n* mestressa *f*; amistançada *f*

**mix** /mɪks/ • *v* barrejar, mesclar **~er** • *n* batedora *f* **~ture** • *n* barreja *f*, mescla *f*; mixtura *f*

**moan** /məʊn, moʊn/ • *n* gemec *m* • *v* gemegar; llamentar-se, plànyer-se

**mob** /mɒb, mɑb/ • *n* xusma *f*, xurma *f*

**mobil|e** /ˈməʊbaɪl, ˈmoʊbəl/ • *adj* mòbil • *n* mòbil *m* **~ity** • *n* mobilitat *f*

**mode** /məʊd, moʊd/ • *n* moda

**model** /ˈmɒdḷ, ˈmɑdḷ/ • *n* model *f*; maqueta *f*

**moderat|e** /ˈmɒdəɹət, ˈmɑdəɹət/ • *adj* moderat • *v* moderar **~or** • *n* moderador *m* **~ion** • *n* moderació *f*

**modern** /ˈmɒd(ə)n, ˈmɑdɚn/ • *adj* modern **~ity** • *n* modernitat *f* **~ize** • *v* modernitzar **~ism** • *n* modernisme *m*

**modest** /ˈmɑdəst/ • *adj* modest **~y** • *n* modèstia *f*

**modify** /ˈmɒdɪfaɪ, ˈmɑdɪfaɪ/ • *v* modificar

**Moldova** • *n* Moldàvia *f*

**mole** /məʊl, moʊl/ • *n* piga *f*; talp *m*; mol *m*

**molecul|e** /ˈmɒləkjuːl, ˈmɑləkjul/ • *n* molècula *f* **~ar** • *adj* molecular

**molten** *(pp)* ▷ MELT

**moment** /ˈməʊmənt, ˈmoʊmənt/ • *n* moment *m*, instant *m*;

moment de força m **~um** • n impuls m

**Monaco** • n Mònaco m

**Monday** • n dilluns m

**money** /ˈmʌni/ • n diner m **~ laundering** • n blanqueig de diners m

**Mongolia** • n Mongòlia f **~n** • adj mongol

**mongoose** /ˈmɒŋguːs, ˈmɑŋgus/ • n mangosta f

**monitor** /ˈmɒnɪtə/ • n monitor m

**monk** /mʌŋk/ • n monjo m

**monkey** /ˈmʌŋki/ • n mico m

**monologue** • n monòleg m

**monopoly** /məˈnɒpəˌli, məˈnɑpəˌli/ • n monopoli m

**monster** /ˈmɒnstə(ɹ), ˈmɑnstɚ/ • adj monstruós • n monstre m; dimoni m

**Montenegro** • n Montenegro m

**month** /mʌnθ/ • n mes m **~ly** • adj mensual • adv mensualment

**monument** /ˈmɒnjəmənt/ • n monument m **~al** • adj monumental

**mood** /muːd/ • n humor f; ànim m **in the ~** • phr tenir ganes de, estar d'humor per

**moon** /muːn/ • n lluna f **~light** • n llum de lluna f

**moose** /muːs/ • n ant m

**mop** /mɒp, mɑp/ • n pal de fregar m; ganyota f

**moral** /ˈmɒɹəl, ˈmɔɹəl/ • adj moral • n moralitat f **~ly** • adv moralment **~ity** • n moralitat f

**morbid** /ˈmɔːbɪd, ˈmɔɹbɪd/ • adj mòrbid m, mòrbida f

**more** /mɔː, mɔɹ/ • adv més • det més

**morning** /ˈmɔːnɪŋ, ˈmɔɹnɪŋ/ • n matí m; matinada f

**Morocc|o** • n Marroc m **~an** • adj marroquí

**moron** /ˈmɔːɹɒn/ • n imbècil f, retardat; subnormal f, idiota f

**mortal** /ˈmɔːtəl/ • adj mortal • n mortal f **~ity** • n mortalitat f

**mortgage** /ˈmɔːɡɪdʒ, ˈmɔɹɡɪdʒ/ • n hipoteca f • v hipotecar

**mosaic** /məʊˈzeɪɪk, moʊˈzeɪɪk/ • n mosaic m

**Moscow** • n Moscou f

**mosque** /mɑsk, mɒsk/ • n mesquita f

**most** /məʊst, moʊst/ • adv el/la/els/les més **~ly** • adv sobretot, per damunt de tot **at ~** • phr com a màxim, pel cap alt, a tot estirar

**motel** /moʊˈtɛl/ • n motel m

**moth** /mɒθ, mɔθ/ • n arna f

**mother** /ˈmʌðə(ɹ), ˈmʌðɚ/ • n mare f **~ tongue** • n llengua materna f **~-in-law** • n sogra f

**motion** /ˈməʊʃən, ˈmoʊʃən/ • n moviment m; moció f

**motivat|e** /ˈməʊtɪveɪt, ˈmoʊtɪveɪt/ • v motivar **~ion** • n motivació f

**motive** /ˈməʊtɪv, ˈmoʊtɪv/ • n motiu m

**motor** /ˈməʊtə, ˈmoʊtɚ/ • adj motor • n motor m **~ist** • n motorista f **~cycle** • n motocicleta f, moto f

**mountain** /ˈmaʊntɪn, ˈmaʊntən/ • n muntanya f; munt m, tou m

~ous • *adj* muntanyós ~eer •
*n* alpinista *f* ~eering • *n*
alpinisme *m* ~ bike • *n*
bicicleta de muntanya *f*
mouse /maʊs, mʌʊs/ • *n* (*pl*
mice) ratolí *m*
mouth /maʊθ, mʌʊθ/ • *n* boca *f*;
embocadura *f*,
desembocadura *f* ~ful • *n*
mossegada *f*, bocí *m*, mos *m*
mov|e /muːv/ • *n* mudament *m*,
mudança *f* • *v* moure,
mudar, traslladar; emocionar
~ement • *n* moviment *m* ~ing
• *adj* commovedor
movie /ˈmuːvi/ • *n* pel·lícula *f*,
film *m*
mow /məʊ, moʊ/ • *v* (*sp*
mowed, *pp* mown) segar
mowed (*sp/pp*) ▷ MOW
mown (*pp*) ▷ MOW
Mozambique • *n* Moçambic
much /mʌtʃ/ • *adv* molt
mud /mʌd/ • *n* fang *m*, llot *m* •
*v* enllotar, enfangar
muddy /ˈmʌdi/ • *adj* fangós
mule /mjuːl/ • *n* mul *m*, mula *f*,
matxo *m*
multipl|y /ˈmʌltɪplaɪ/ • *v*
multiplicar ~e • *adj* múltiple
~ication • *n* multiplicació *f*
mum /mʌm/ • *n* mama
municipal /mjuˈnɪsɪpəl/ • *adj*
municipal ~ity • *n* municipi
murder /ˈmɜːdə(ɹ), ˈmɝ.dɚ/ • *n*
assassinat *m* • *v* assassinar ~ •
*n* assassinat *m* • *v* assassinar
~er • *n* assassí *m*
musc|le /ˈmʌs.əl/ • *n* múscul *m*
~ular • *adj* muscular;
musculós

museum /mjuːˈziːəm, mjuˈzi.əm/ •
*n* museu *m*
mushroom /ˈmʌʃˌɹuːm/ • *n* bolet
*m*, fong *m*
music /ˈmjuːzɪk, ˈmjuzɪk/ • *n*
música *f* ~al • *adj* musical *f*
~ian • *n* músic *m*
Muslim • *adj* musulmà • *n*
musulmà *m*
mussel /ˈmʌsəl/ • *n* musclo
must /mʌst, məs(t)/ • *n* most • *v*
*v* deure
mustard /ˈmʌstəɹd/ • *n* mostassa
*f*
mute /mjuːt/ • *adj* mut • *n* mut
*m*, muda *f*
mutual /ˈmjuːtʃuəl/ • *adj* mutu
my /maɪ, mɪ/ • *det* meu *m*
Myanmar • *n* Myanmar *m*
myself /maɪˈsɛlf/ • *pron* em;
mateix
myster|y /ˈmɪstəɹi/ • *n* misteri *m*
~ious • *adj* misteriós
myth /mɪθ/ • *n* mite *m*, mites
~ical • *adj* mític ~ology • *n*
mitologia *f* ~ological • *adj*
mitològic

nail /neɪl/ • *n* ungla *f*; clau *m* • *v*
clavar
naive /naɪˈiːv/ • *adj* ingenu *m*,
càndid *m*; naïf
naked /ˈneɪkɪd, ˈnɛkɪd/ • *adj*
despullat, nu ~ness • *n* nuesa
*f*

**name** /neɪm/ • *n* nom *m*;
reputació *f* • *v* anomenar;
escollir; especificar, precisar;
denominar

**Namibia** • *n* Namíbia

**nap** /nap, næp/ • *n* becaina *f*,
migdiada

**napkin** /'næp.kɪn/ • *n* tovalló *m*,
torcaboques *m*

**narrat|e** /nə'ɹeɪt, 'næɹeɪt/ • *v*
narrar, explicar **~ive** • *adj*
narratiu *n* narració *f*,
narrativa *f* **~or** • *n* narrador *m*

**narrow** /'næɹoʊ, 'næɹəʊ/ • *adj*
estret *m*, estreta *f*, angost

**nasty** /na:.sti, 'nɑː.sti/ • *adj* brut;
menyspreable

**nation** /'neɪʃən/ • *n* nació *f*;
estat *m* **~al** • *adj* nacional

**NATO** • *n* (*abbr* North Atlantic
Treaty Organization) OTAN *f*

**natur|e** /'neɪtʃə, 'neɪtʃɚ/ • *n*
natura *f*; natural *m* **~al** • *adj*
natural **~ally** • *adv*
naturalment

**naughty** /'nɔːti, 'nɔti/ • *adj*
trapella, entremaliat

**Nauru** • *n* Nauru

**naval** /'neɪvəl/ • *adj* naval

**navel** /'neɪvəl/ • *n* melic *m*,
llombrígol *m*

**navigat|e** /'næv.ɪ.geɪt/ • *v*
navegar **~ion** • *n* navegació *f*,
nàutica *f*

**near** /nɪə(ɹ), nɪɹ/ • *v* apropar,
aproximar **~ly** • *adv* gairebé,
quasi

**neat** /niːt/ • *adj* pulcre; sol; pur;
net; enginyós

**necess|ary** /'nɛsəˌsɛɹi, 'nɛsəsɹi/ •
*adj* necessari **~arily** • *adv*
necessàriament **~ity** • *n*
necessitat *f*

**neck** /nɛk/ • *n* coll *m*; broc *m*
**~tie** • *n* corbata *f*

**nectarine** /'nɛk.tə.ɹin/ • *n*
nectarina *f*

**need** /niːd/ • *n* necessitat *f* • *v*
necessitar, requerir; haver de,
caldre **~less** • *adj* innecessari

**needle** /'niː.dl/ • *n* agulla *f*

**negativ|e** /'nɛgətɪv, 'nɛ(e)gəˌɹɪv/ •
*adj* negatiu *m*; estrictament
negatiu *m* **~ity** • *n* negativitat
*f*

**neglect** /nɪ'glɛkt/ • *n* negligència
*f* • *v* negligir

**negotiat|e** /nə'gəʊ.ʃi.eɪt,
nə'goʊ.ʃi.eɪt/ • *v* negociar **~ion**
• *n* negociació *f*

**neighbo|ur** /'neɪbə, 'neɪbɚ/ • *n*
veí *m*; proïsme *m* **~rhood** • *n*
barri *m*

**neighbourhood** (*British*) ▷
NEIGHBORHOOD

**Nepal** • *n* Nepal *m* **~i** • *adj*
nepalès *m*, nepalesa *f* • *n*
nepalès *m*, nepalesa *f*

**Neptune** • *n* Neptú *m*

**nerv|e** /nɜv, nɜːv/ • *n* nervi *m*
**~ous** • *adj* nerviós

**nest** /nɛst/ • *n* niu *m*

**net** /nɛt/ • *adj* net • *n* xarxa *f*;
malla *f* **~work** • *n* xarxa *f*

**Netherlands** • *adj* holandès • *n*
els Països Baixos, Holanda *f*

**neutral** /'njuːtɹəl, 'nuːtɹəl/ • *adj*
neutral; neutre **~ity** • *n*
neutralitat *f*

**never** /'nɛv.ə(ɹ), 'nɛ.vɚ/ • *adv* mai

**nevertheless** /'nɛvəðəles,
'nɛvɚðəlɛs/ • *adv*

nogensmenys, no obstant,
tanmateix, ara bé

**new** /njuː, n(j)u/ • *adj* novell,
nou; nounat **~born** • *adj*
nounat • *n* nounat *m*,
nounada *f* **~ly** • *adv*
novament **~lywed** • *adj*
noucasat • *n* noucasat *m*,
noucasada *f*

**New York** • *adj* novaiorquès •
*n* Nova York *f*

**New Zealand** • *n* Nova Zelanda
**~er** • *n* neozelandès *m*

**news** /njuːz/ • *n* (*pl* news)
notícies; telenotícies *m*,
informatiu *m*, diari *m* **~paper**
• *n* diari *m*, periòdic *m*

**next** /nɛkst/ • *adj* proper,
següent; que ve • *prep* al
costat

**NGO** • *n* (*abbr*
Non-Governmental
Organization) ONG *f*

**Nicaragua** • *n* Nicaragua *f* **~n** •
*adj* nicaragüenc • *n*
nicaragüenc *m*, nicaragüenca
*f*

**niche** /niːʃ, nɪtʃ/ • *n* nínxol *m*

**Nigeria** • *n* Nigèria **~n** • *adj*
nigerià

**night** /naɪt/ • *n* nit *f*; vetllada *f*,
vespre *m*; vesprada *f*, foscant
*m*; fosca *f*, obscuritat *f* **~mare**
• *n* malson *m*

**nightingale** /ˈnaɪtɪŋgeɪl/ • *n*
rossinyol *m*

**nin|e** /naɪn/ • *n* nou *m* • *num*
nou; novena *f* **~eteen** • *num*
dinou **~th** • *adj* novè • *n* novè
*m*, novena *f* **~ety** • *num*
noranta

**nipple** /ˈnɪp(ə)l/ • *n* mugró *m*

**no** • *det* cap, gens; no, prohibit
• *n* negativa *f*, no *m* • *part*
cap, gens; no, prohibit **~ one**
• *pron* ningú **~ way** • *interj*
de cap manera; impossible
**~body** • *n* ningú *f*

**nob|le** /ˈnəʊbəl, ˈnoʊbəl/ • *adj*
noble **~ility** • *n* noblesa *f*

**nod** /nɒd, nɑd/ • *n* capejada *f* •
*v* fer que sí amb el cap,
assentir amb el cap, capejar;
capcinejar, pesar figues

**nois|e** /nɔɪz/ • *n* soroll *m* **~y** •
*adj* sorollós

**nominate** /ˈnɒm.ɪ.neɪt,
ˈnɑm.ɪ.neɪt/ • *v* nominar

**none** /nʌn/ • *pron* cap **~theless**
• *adv* nogensmenys, no
obstant

**nonsense** /ˈnɒnsɛns, ˈnɒnsəns/ •
*n* bajanada *f*, bestiesa *f*,
estirabot *m*

**noodle** /ˈnuːdl̩/ • *n* fideu *m*;
cervell *m*

**normal** /ˈnɔːməl, ˈnɔːməl/ • *adj*
normal • *n* normal **~ly** • *adv*
normalment **~ity** • *n*
normalitat *f*

**north** /nɔːθ, nɔɹθ/ • *n* nord *m*,
septentrió *m* • *adj*
septentrional **~erner** • *n*
septentrional *f*, nordista *f*
**~west** • *n* nord-oest **~east** • *n*
nord-est *m*

**Norw|ay** • *n* Noruega *f* **~egian**
• *adj* noruec *m*, noruega *f* • *n*
noruec *m*, noruega *f*

**nose** /nəʊz, noʊz/ • *n* nas *m*

**nostril** /ˈnɒstɹɪl/ • *n* nariu *m*

**nosy** /ˈnəʊziː, ˈnoʊzi/ • *adj* dotor

**not** /nɒt, nat/ • *adv* no

**notabl|e** /ˈnəʊtəbəl, ˈnoʊtəbəl/ • *adj* notable **~y** • *adv* notablement

**note** /nəʊt, noʊt/ • *n* nota *f* • *v* notar **~book** • *n* llibreta *f*, quadern *m*

**nothing** /ˈnʌθɪŋ/ • *pron* res **~ness** • *n* no-res *m*

**notice** /ˈnəʊtɪs, ˈnoʊtɪs/ • *n* atenció *f*; anunci *m*, nota *f*; avís *m*; acomiadament *m*, dimissió *f*; ressenya *f* • *v* fixar-se en, notar; adonar-se

**notification** /ˌnəʊtɪfɪˈkeɪʃən, ˌnoʊtɪfɪˈkeɪʃən/ • *n* notificació *f*

**notion** /ˈnəʊʃən, ˈnoʊʃən/ • *n* noció *f*

**notori|ous** • *adj* notori **~ously** • *adv* notòriament **~ety** • *n* notorietat *f*

**noun** /naʊn, næːn/ • *n* substantiu *m*

**novel** /ˈnɒvl̩, ˈnɑvəl/ • *n* novel·la *f* **~ist** • *n* novel·lista *f*

**November** • *n* novembre *m*

**now** /naʊ/ • *adv* ara • *interj* ara, ja • *n* ara *m* **~adays** • *adv* actualment, avui dia; avui en dia **for ~** • *phr* per ara

**nowhere** • *adv* enlloc

**nucle|us** /ˈnjuːˌkli.əs, ˈnuːˌkli.əs/ • *n* (*pl* nuclei) nucli *m* **~ar** • *adj* nuclear

**number** /ˈnʌmbə, ˈnʌmbɚ/ • *n* nombre; xifra *f*; número *m* • *v* numerar; comptar, sumar

**numer|al** /ˈnjuːmərəl, ˈnuːmərəl/ • *n* número *m*, xifra; numeral *m* **~ical** • *adj* numèric **~ous** • *adj* nombrós

**nurs|e** /nɜːs, nɜs/ • *n* infermer *m* • *v* alletar **~ing** • *n* infermeria *f*

**nut** /nʌt/ • *n* nou *f*; ou **~meg** • *n* nou moscada *f*; túnel *m*

**nutritio|nal** • *adj* nutritiu, nutricional **~us** • *adj* nutritiu, nutrient, nutrici, alimentós, alimentador

**nymph** /nɪmf/ • *n* nimfa *f*

**o'clock** /əˈklɒk, əˈklɑk/ • *adv* la una

**oak** /oʊk, əʊk/ • *n* roure *m*

**oat** /əʊt/ • *n* civada *f*

**obes|e** /oʊˈbiːs, əʊˈbiːs/ • *adj* obès **~ity** • *n* obesitat

**obe|y** /oʊˈbeɪ, əʊˈbeɪ/ • *v* obeir **~dient** • *adj* obedient **~dience** • *n* obediència

**object** /ˈɒb.dʒɛkt, ˈɑb.dʒɛkt/ • *n* objecte *m* **~ion** • *n* objecció *f* **~ive** • *adj* objectiu • *n* objectiu *m* **~ivity** • *n* objectivitat *f*

**oblig|e** /əˈblaɪdʒ/ • *v* obligar **~ation** • *n* obligació *f*; compromís *m*

**oboe** /ˈoʊboʊ/ • *n* oboè *m*

**observ|e** /əbˈzɜːv, əbˈzɜv/ • *v* observar; seguir **~er** • *n* observador *m* **~atory** • *n* observatori *m* **~ation** • *n* observació *f*; registre *m*, anotació *f*; comentari *m*

**obsess|ion** /əbˈsɛʃən/ • *n* obsessió *f* **~ed** • *adj* obsessionat **~ive** • *adj* obsessiu

**obstacle** /ˈɒbstəkl/ • *n* obstacle *m*

**obtain** /əbˈteɪn/ • *v* obtenir

**obvious** /ˈɒ(b).vi.əs, ˈɒ(b).vɪəs/ • *adj* obvi **~ly** • *adv* òbviament

**occasional** /əˈkeɪʒənəl/ • *adj* ocasional **~ly** • *adv* ocasionalment

**occup|y** /ˈɒkjʊpaɪ, ˈɒkjəpaɪ/ • *v* ocupar **~ation** • *n* ocupació *f*

**occur** /əˈkɜː, əˈkɝ/ • *v* ocórrer

**ocean** /ˈəʊ.ʃən, ˈoʊ.ʃən/ • *n* oceà *m* **~ic** • *adj* oceànic

**Oceania** • *n* Oceania *f*

**octave** /ˈɒktɪv, ˈɑktɪv/ • *n* octava *f*; vuitada *f*

**October** • *n* octubre *m*

**octopus** /ˈɒkt.ə.pʊs, ˈɑːkt.ə.pʊs/ • *n* pop *m*

**odd** /ɒd, ɑd/ • *adj* estrany *m*; imparell, senar; i escaig

**of** /ɒv, əv/ • *prep* de

**off** /ɒf, ɔːf/ • *adj* tallat, apagat, tancat; passat, dolent

**offence** *(British)* ▷ OFFENSE

**offen|d** /əˈfɛnd/ • *v* ofendre **~se** • *n* ofensa *f*, insult *m* **~sive** • *adj* ofensiu *m*, ofensiva *f*

**offer** /ˈɒfə(ɹ), ˈɔfɚ/ • *n* oferta *f* • *v* ofrenar; oferir **~ing** • *n* oferiment *m*

**office** /ˈɒfɪs, ˈɔfɪs/ • *n* ofici *m*; càrrec *m*; oficina *f*

**official** /əˈfɪʃəl/ • *adj* oficial • *n* funcionari *m* **~ly** • *adv* oficialment

**offset** /ˈɒf.sɛt, ˈɑf.sɛt/ • *n* decalatge *m*, decalatges

**often** /ˈɒf(t)ən, ˈɔf(t)ən/ • *adv* sovint

**oil** /ɔɪl/ • *n* oli *m*; benzina *f*, petroli *m* • *v* greixar

**OK** • *adj* d'acord

**old** /ˈəʊld, ˈoʊld/ • *adj* vell, antic; gran; tenir + period of time

**olive** /ˈɒlɪv, ˈɑlɪv/ • *n* oliva *f* **~ oil** • *n* oli d'oliva *m* **~ tree** • *n* olivera *f*

**Olympic** • *adj* olímpic **~s** • *n* olimpíada *f*, olimpíades

**omelette** /ˈɒm.lɪt, ˈɒm.lət/ • *n* truita *f*, truita a la francesa *f*

**on** /ɒn, ɑn/ • *prep* sobre

**once** /wʌn(t)s, wʌns/ • *adv* una vegada • *conj* un cop **~ again** • *adv* una vegada més, de nou, novament **~ and for all** • *adv* d'una vegada

**one** /wʌn, wan/ • *adj* un; u; mateix; únic **~** • *n* u *m* • *num* un • *pron* 'expressed by nominalization when following an adjective; un, hom

**onion** /ˈʌnjən, ˈʌnjɪn/ • *n* ceba *f*

**only** /ˈəʊn.li, ˈəʊn.lɪ/ • *adj* únic • *adv* només, sols, solament, únicament

**open** /ˈəʊ.pən, ˈoʊ.pən/ • *adj* obert; lliure • *n* open *m* • *v* obrir, descloure **~ly** • *adv* obertament **~ing** • *n* obertura *f* **in the ~** • *phr* a la serena

**opera** /ˈɒp.ə.ɹ.ə, ˈɑ.red.ə/ • *n* òpera *f*

**operati|ng system** /ˈɒpə(ˌ)ɪeɪtɪŋ (ˌ)sɪstəm, ˈɒpəˌɪeɪtɪŋ ˌsɪstəm/ • *n* sistema operatiu *m* **~on** • *n* operació *f* **~onal** • *adj* operatiu

**opinion** /əˈpɪnjən/ • *n* opinió *f*

**opportunity** /ˌɒp.əˈtjuː.nɪ.ti, ˌɑpəˈtunəti/ • *n* oportunitat *f*

**oppose** /əˈpəʊz, əˈpoʊz/ • *v* oposar

**opposit|e** /ˈɒpəzɪt, ˈɑp(ə)sɪt/ • *adj* oposat • *n* contrari *m* • *prep* davant de **~ion** • *n* oposició *f*

**optic|al** /ˈɒptɪkəl, ˈɑptɪkəl/ • *adj* òptic **~ian** • *n* òptic *m*

**optimis|tic** /ˌɒptɪˈmɪstɪk, ˌɑptɪˈmɪstɪk/ • *adj* optimista **~m** • *n* optimisme *m*

**option** /ˈɒpʃən, ˈɑpʃən/ • *n* opció *f* **~al** • *adj* opcional

**or** /ɔː(ɹ), ɔɪ/ • *conj* o, o bé

**oral** /ˈɔːɹəl, ˈɔɹəl/ • *adj* oral, bucal; verbal

**orange** /ˈɒɹɪn(d)ʒ, ˈɑɹɪndʒ/ • *adj* ataronjat, carabassa • *n* taronger *m*; taronja *f*

**orbit** • *n* òrbita *f* • *v* orbitar

**orchestra** • *n* orquestra *f* **~l** • *adj* orquestral

**order** /ˈɔːdə, ˈɔɹdɚ/ • *n* ordre *m*; comanda *f*; orde *m* • *v* ordenar; demanar

**ordinar|y** /ˈɔːdɪnəɹi, ˈɔɹdɪnɛɹi/ • *adj* ordinari **~ily** • *adv* ordinàriament

**oregano** /ɒɹɪˈɡɑːnəʊ, ɔɪˈɛɡənoʊ/ • *n* orenga *f*

**organ** /ˈɔɹ.ɡən, ˈɔː.ɡən/ • *n* òrgan *m*; orgue *m*

**organic** /ɔːˈɡænɪk, ɔɹˈɡænɪk/ • *adj* orgànic

**organism** /ˈɔː.ɡən.ɪ.zəm, ˈmez.ɹ.ɡən/ • *n* organisme *m*

**organization** /ˌɔː(ɹ)ɡə.naɪˈzeɪʃən, ˌɔɹɡənɪˈzeɪʃən/ • *n* organització *f*

**organize** /ˈɔɹɡənaɪz, ˈɔːɡənaɪz/ • *v* organitzar **~d** • *adj* organitzat **~r** • *n* organitzador *m*

**orientation** /ˌɔɹiɛnˈteɪʃən/ • *n* orientació *f*

**origin** /ˈɒɹ.ɪ.dʒɪn, ˈɔɹ.ɪ.dʒɪn/ • *n* origen *m* **~ally** • *adv* originàriament

**Oslo** • *n* Oslo

**ostentatious** /ˌɒs.tɛnˈteɪ.ʃəs/ • *adj* ostentós

**ostrich** /ˈɒs.tɹɪtʃ, ˈɔs.tɹɪtʃ/ • *n* estruç *m*

**other** /ˈʌðə(ɹ), ʊðə/ • *det* un altre *m*, una altra *f* **~s** • *n* altres **~wise** • *adv* altrament

**otter** /ˈɒt.ə, ˈɑtɚ/ • *n* llúdria *f*, llúdriga *f*

**ounce** /aʊns/ • *n* unça *f*

**our** /ˈaʊə(ɹ), ˈaʊɚ/ • *det* nostre **~selves** • *pron* ens; mateix

**out** /aʊt, æt/ • *adj* disponible • *n* eliminació *f* **~come** • *n* resultat *m* **~going** • *adj* sortint **~let** • *n* sortida *f*; desguàs *m*; punt de venda *m* **~rage** • *n* atrocitat *f*; ultratge *m*; ràbia *f*, indignació *f* • *v* indignar **~rageous** • *adj* xocant, cruel, immoral, escandalós **~side** • *adv* fora **~skirts** • *n* afores, extraradi *m* **~standing** • *adj* destacat; excepcional; sobresortint; pendent

**oven** /ˈʌ.vn̩/ • *n* forn *m*

**over|seas** /ˌəʊvəˈsiːz, ˌoʊvəˈsiːz/ ● *adj* ultramar **~sight** ● *n* oblit *m*; supervisió *f* **~whelm** ● *v* superar; agobiar **~whelming** ● *adj* aclaparador

**owe** /əʊ, oʊ/ ● *v* deure

**owl** /aʊl/ ● *n* òliba *f*, mussol, tawny owl gamarús, eagle owl gran duc

**own** /ˈəʊn, ˈoʊn/ ● *adj* mateix, propi **~er** ● *n* propietari *m* **~ership** ● *n* propietat *f*, possessió *f*

**ox** /ˈɑks, ˈɒks/ ● *n* bou *m*

**oxygen** /ˈɒksɪdʒən/ ● *n* oxigen *m*

**oxymoron** /ˌɒksɪˈmɔːrɒn, ˌaksɪˈmɔːrɑn/ ● *n* oxímoron *m*

**oyster** /ˈɔɪ.stə(r), ˈɔɪ.stɚ/ ● *n* ostra *f*

**ozone** ● *n* ozó *m*

# P

**pace** /peɪs/ ● *n* pas *m*; passa *f*; ritme *m* ● *prep* amb tot el respecte per **~maker** ● *n* marcapassos *m*

**pack** /pæk/ ● *v* fer **~age** ● *n* paquet *m*; empaquetatge *m* ● *v* empaquetar

**page** /peɪdʒ, paːʒ/ ● *n* pàgina *f*; patge *m*

**paid** *(sp/pp)* ▷ PAY

**pain** /peɪn/ ● *n* dolor *m*; pena *f* **~ful** ● *adj* dolorós **~less** ● *adj* indolor **~staking** ● *adj* acurat **~killer** ● *n* analgèsic *m*

**paint** /peɪnt/ ● *n* pintura *f* ● *v* pintar **~er** ● *n* pintor *m* **~ing** ● *n* quadre *m*, pintura *f* **~brush** ● *n* pinzell *m*

**pair** /peə(r)/ ● *n* parella *f*; parell *m*

**Pakistan** ● *n* Pakistan **~i** ● *adj* pakistanès ● *n* pakistanès *m*

**palace** /ˈpæləs, ˈpælɪs/ ● *n* palau *m*

**Palau** ● *n* Palau

**pale** /peɪl/ ● *adj* pàl·lid ● *n* pal

**Palestin|e** ● *n* Palestina *f* **~ian** ● *adj* palestí, palestinenc ● *n* palestí *m*, palestinenc *m*

**palm** /paːm, pɑm/ ● *n* palmell *m*

**Panama** ● *n* Panamà *m* **~nian** ● *adj* panameny ● *n* panameny *m*, panamenya *f*

**pancake** /ˈpæn.keɪk/ ● *n* crep americana *f*

**panda** /ˈpandə, ˈpændə/ ● *n* panda *m*

**panel** /ˈpænəl/ ● *n* panell *m*; panel *m*

**panic** /ˈpænɪk/ ● *n* pànic **~ attack** ● *n* atac de pànic *m*

**pant** /pænt/ ● *v* panteixar

**pant|s** /pænts/ ● *n* pantaló *m*, pantalons, calçons; bragues, calçotets, calçons blancs **~ies** ● *n* calces, calçons

**paper** /ˈpeɪpə, ˈpeɪpɚ/ ● *n* paper *m*; article *m* ● *v* empaperar **~work** ● *n* paperassa *f*, paperada *f* **on ~** ● *phr* sobre paper

**parable** /ˈpaɪəbəl, ˈpæɪ.ə.bəl/ ● *n* paràbola *f*

**parachute** /ˈpæɪəʃuːt/ ● *n* paracaigudes *m*

**parade** /pə'ɹeɪd/ • *n* desfilada *f*

**parakeet** /'paɹəkiːt/ • *n* periquito *m*

**parallel** /'pæɹəˌlɛl, 'pɛɹəˌlɛl/ • *adj* paral·lel **~ism** • *n* paral·lelisme *m*

**parameter** /pə'ɹæm.ɪ.tə/ • *n* paràmetre *m*

**parent** /'pɛəɹʊnt/ • *n* progenitor *f*, genitor *f*, pares; pare *m*, mare *f*

**parenthesis** /pə'ɹɛnθəsɪs/ • *n* (*pl* parentheses) parèntesi *m*

**Paris** • *n* París *m*; Paris *m*

**parish** /'pæɹɪʃ/ • *n* parròquia **~ioner** • *n* parroquià *m*

**park** /pɑɹk/ • *n* parc *m*, parc natural *m*; vedat *m*

**parliament** /'pɑːləmənt, 'pɑɪləmənt/ • *n* parlament *m* **~ary** • *adj* parlamentari

**parody** /'pæɹədi/ • *n* paròdia *f* • *v* parodiar

**parrot** /'pæɹət/ • *n* lloro *m*, papagai *m*

**parsley** /'pɑː(ɹ)sli/ • *n* julivert *m*

**part** /pɑɹt, pɑɪt/ • *n* part *f* **~ial** • *adj* parcial **~ially** • *adv* parcialment **~ridge** • *n* perdiu *f*

**participate** /pɑː'tɪsɪpeɪt/ • *v* participar

**particle** /'pɑːtɪk(ə)l, 'pɑɪtɪkəl/ • *n* partícula *f*

**partner** /'pɑːtnə(ɹ), 'pɑɪtnə/ • *n* parella *f*

**party** /'pɑː.ti, 'pɑɪ.ti/ • *n* part *f*; festa *f*, sarau *m*

**pass** /pɑːs, pæs/ • *v* passar; ser aprovat; aprovar

**passage** /'pæsɪdʒ/ • *n* passatge *m*

**passenger** /'pæsəndʒɚ, 'pæsəndʒə/ • *n* passatger *m*

**passing** /'pɑːsɪŋ/ • *adj* passatger • *n* passada *f*

**passion** /'pæʃən/ • *n* passió *f* **~ate** • *adj* apassionat **~ately** • *adv* apassionadament

**passive** /'pæs.ɪv/ • *adj* passiu *m* **~ly** • *adv* passivament

**passport** /'pɑːspɔːt, 'pæspɔɹt/ • *n* passaport *m*

**password** /'pæswɜːɹd, 'pɑːswɜː(ɹ)d/ • *n* contrasenya *f*

**past** /pɑːst, pæst/ • *adj* passat • *n* passat *m*

**pasta** /'pæstə, 'pɑstə/ • *n* pasta *f*

**paste** /peɪst/ • *v* enganxar

**pastime** /'pæs.taɪm/ • *n* passatemps *m*

**pastor** /'pɑːstə, 'pæstə/ • *n* pastor *m*

**patch** /pætʃ/ • *n* pedaç *m* • *v* apedaçar

**patent** /'peɪtənt, 'pætənt/ • *adj* patent • *v* patentar

**paternal** /pə'tɜː(ɹ)nəl/ • *adj* patern *m*

**path** /pɑːθ, pæθ/ • *n* sendera *f*, sender *m*; camí *m*, trajectòria *f*; ruta *f*

**patien|t** /'peɪʃ(ə)nt, 'peɪʃənt/ • *adj* pacient **~tly** • *adv* pacientment **~ce** • *n* paciència *f*; solitari *m*

**patrol** /pə'tɹəʊl, pə'tɹoʊl/ • *n* patrulla *f* • *v* patrullar

**pattern** /'pat(ə)n, 'pætɹɹn/ • *n* mostra *f*, model *m*, patró

**pause** /pɔːz, pɔz/ • *n* pausa *f*

**pay** /peɪ/ • *v* (*sp* paid, *pp* paid) pagar **~ment** • *n* pagament *m*

**PC** *(abbr)* ▷ COMPUTER

**pea** /piː/ • *n* pesolera *f*; pèsol *m* **chick~** • *n* cigronera *f*, ciuró; cigró *m*

**peace** /piːs/ • *n* pau *f* **~ful** • *adj* pacífic; assossegat **~fully** • *adv* pacíficament

**peach** /piːtʃ/ • *n* presseguer *m*; préssec *m*

**peacock** /ˈpiːkɑk, ˈpiːkɒk/ • *n* paó *m*

**peak** /piːk/ • *n* punta *f*, visera *f*; pic *m*; cim *m*

**peanut** /ˈpiːˌnʌt, ˈpiːnət/ • *n* cacauet *m*

**pear** /peə, peə˞/ • *n* pera *f*; perera *f*

**peasant** /ˈpɛzənt/ • *n* camperol, pagès *m*

**peculiar** /prˈkjuljə˞, prˈkjuːljə/ • *adj* peculiar

**pedestrian** /pəˈdɛstɹiːən/ • *n* vianant *m*

**peephole** /ˈpiːphəʊl, piphoʊl/ • *n* espiera *f*, espiell *m*

**pelican** /ˈpɛlɪkən/ • *n* pelicà *m*

**pen** /pɛn, pɪn/ • *n* bolígraf *m*

**penalty** • *n* càstig *m*

**pencil** /ˈpɛnsəl, ˈpɛnsɪl/ • *n* llapis *m* **~ sharpener** • *n* maquineta de fer punta

**pending** /ˈpɛndɪŋ/ • *adj* pendent

**pendulum** /ˈpɛndʒələm, ˈpɪndʒələm/ • *n* pèndol *m*

**penetrat|e** /ˈpɛnɪtɹeɪt, ˈpɛnɪˌtɹeɪt/ • *v* penetrar **~ion** • *n* penetració *f*

**penguin** /ˈpɛŋgwɪn, ˈpɪŋgwɪn/ • *n* pingüí *m*

**penis** /ˈpiːnɪs, ˈpɪnɪs/ • *n* penis *m*

**penned** *(sp/pp)* ▷ PEN

**pension** /ˈpɛnʃ(ə)n/ • *n* pensió *f*

**pensive** /ˈpɛn.sɪv/ • *adj* pensatiu

**pent** *(sp/pp)* ▷ PEN

**people** /ˈpiːpəl, ˈpipəl/ • *n* gent *f*; poble *m*; família *f*, els meus • *v* poblar; poblar-se

**pepper** /ˈpɛpə, ˈpɛpə˞/ • *n* pebrotera *f*; pebre *m*; pebrot *m*

**per** /pɜ(ɹ), pɝ/ • *prep* per; via; segons

**perce|ive** /pəˈsiːv, pə˞ˈsiv/ • *v* percebre **~ption** • *n* percepció *f*

**percent** /pəˈsɛnt, pɹˈsɛnt/ • *n* per cent **~age** • *n* percentatge *m*

**perch** /pɜːtʃ, pɝtʃ/ • *n* perca *f*

**perfect** /ˈpɜː.fɪkt, ˈpɝfɪkt/ • *adj* perfecte; perfet • *v* perfeccionar **~ion** • *n* perfecció *f* **~ly** • *adv* perfectament

**perform** /pəˈfɔːm, pə˞ˈfɔɹm/ • *v* realitzar; actuar **~ance** • *n* actuació *f*, execució *f*; representació *f*

**perhaps** /pəˈhæps, pə˞ˈhæps/ • *adv* potser, tal vegada, possiblement

**period** /ˈpɪəɹɪəd/ • *interj* i punt • *n* període *m* **~ic** • *adj* periòdic **~ic table** • *n* taula periòdica *f* **~ically** • *adv* periòdicament

**permanen|t** /ˈpɜːmənənt, ˈpɝːmənənt/ • *adj* permanent **~tly** • *adv* permanentment **~ce** • *n* permanència *f*

**permission** /pəˈmɪʃən, pə˞ˈmɪʃən/ • *n* permís *m*, autorització *f*

P

**persever|e** ● *v* perseverar
**~ance** ● *n* perseverança *f*
**Persian** ● *adj* persa *f*, persà *m*,
persana *f* ● *n* persa *m*, farsi *m*;
persà *m*, persana *f*; gat persa
*m*
**persist** /pəˈsɪst/ ● *v* persistir **~ent**
● *adj* persistent **~ence** ● *n*
persistència *f*
**person** /ˈpɜːsən, ˈpɜːsən/ ● *n* (*pl*
people) persona *f* **~al** ● *adj*
personal; corporal **~ally** ● *adv*
personalment **~alize** ● *v*
personalitzar **~alization** ● *n*
personalització *f* **~ality** ● *n*
personalitat *f*
**perspective** /pəˈspɛktɪv/ ● *n*
perspectiva *f*
**persua|de** /pəˈsweɪd, pəˈsweɪd/ ●
*v* persuadir **~sive** ● *adj*
persuasiu **~sion** ● *n* persuasió
*f*
**Peru** ● *n* Perú **~vian** ● *adj* peruà
● *n* peruà *m*, peruana *f*
**pesticide** /ˈpɛstɪsaɪd, ˈpɛstɪˈsaɪd/ ●
*n* plaguicida *m*, pesticida *m*
**pet** /pɛt/ ● *n* mascota *f*
**petition** /pəˈtɪʃən/ ● *n* petició *f*
**pharmac|y** /ˈfɑːməsi, ˈfɑːməsi/ ●
*n* farmàcia *f* **~eutical** ● *adj*
farmacèutic **~ist** ● *n*
farmacèutic *m*
**phase** /feɪz/ ● *n* fase *f*
**pheasant** /ˈfɛzənt/ ● *n* faisà *m*
**phenomenon** /fɪˈnɒmənɒn,
fɪˈnɑmənən/ ● *n* (*pl*
phenomena) fenomen *m*
**Philippines** ● *n* Filipines
**philosoph|y** /fɪˈlɒsəfi, fɪˈlɑsəfi/ ●
*n* filosofia **~er** ● *n* filòsof *m*,
filòsofa *f* **~ical** ● *adj* filosòfic

**phone** /fəʊn, foʊn/ ● *n* fon *m* ● *v*
telefonar, trucar
**phonetic** /fəˈnɛtɪk/ ● *adj* fonètic
**~s** ● *n* fonètica *f*
**photo** ▷ PHOTOGRAPH
**photograph** /ˈfəʊtəɡɹɑːf,
ˈfoʊtəɡɹæf/ ● *n* fotografia *f*,
foto *f* ● *v* fotografiar **~er** ● *n*
fotògraf *m* **~y** ● *n* fotografia *f*
**phrase** /freɪz/ ● *n* sintagma *m*;
frase *f*
**physical** /ˈfɪzɪkəl/ ● *adj* físic **~ly** ●
*adv* físicament
**physician** /fɪˈzɪʃən/ ● *n* metge *m*,
metgessa *f*
**physic|s** /ˈfɪzɪks/ ● *n* física *f* **~ist**
● *n* físic *m*
**pian|o** /piˈænoʊ, piˈænəʊ/ ● *n*
piano *m* **~ist** ● *n* pianista *f*
**pick** /pɪk/ ● *n* pic *m*
**picky** /ˈpɪki/ ● *adj* exigent
**picture** /ˈpɪktʃə, ˈpɪk(t)ʃɚ/ ● *n* foto
*f*, fotografia *f*; cinema *m*
**pie** /paɪ/ ● *n* pastís *m*
**piece** /piːs/ ● *n* peça *f*, tros *m*
**pig** /pɪɡ/ ● *n* porc *m*; golafre *m*
**pigeon** /ˈpɪdʒɪn, ˈpɪdʒən/ ● *n*
colom *m*
**pike** /paɪk/ ● *n* pica *f*; lluç de riu
*m*
**pile** /paɪl/ ● *n* pila *f*
**pill** /pɪl/ ● *n* píndola *f*
**pillow** /ˈpɪləʊ/ ● *n* coixí *m*
**pilot** /ˈpaɪlət/ ● *adj* pilot *f* ● *v*
pilotar; provar
**pinch** /pɪntʃ/ ● *n* pessic ● *v*
pessigar; pispar
**pine** /paɪn/ ● *n* pi *m*
**pineapple** /ˈpaɪnæpəl/ ● *n*
ananàs *m*; pinya *f*
**pink** /pɪŋk/ ● *adj* rosa ● *n* rosa *m*

**pioneer** /ˌpaɪəˈnɪər/ • n pioner m, pionera f

**pipe** /paɪp/ • n gaita f; tub m, canonada f

**piranha** /pɪˈrɑːnjə, pɪˈrɑnjə/ • n piranya f

**pira|te** /ˈpaɪ(ə)rɪt/ • n pirata m • v piratejar **~cy** • n pirateria f

**pistol** /ˈpɪstəl/ • n pistola f

**pit** /pɪt/ • n sot; pinyol m

**pitch** /pɪtʃ/ • n reïna f; llançament m • v llançar **~er** • n llançador m; gerra f

**pit|y** /ˈpɪti/ • n llàstima f **~iful** • adv lamentable; miserable

**pizza** /ˈpiːt.sə, ˈpɪtsə/ • n pizza f

**place** /pleɪs/ • n lloc m, indret m • v col·locar

**placid** /ˈplæs.ɪd/ • adj plàcid

**plagiarism** /ˈpleɪdʒəˌrɪzm/ • n plagi m

**plague** /pleɪg/ • n pesta f

**plaice** /pleɪs/ • n capellà m

**plain** /pleɪn/ • adj senzill; natural, simple; net • n plana f, planura f, planície f

**plan** /plæn/ • n pla m • v planejar **~ner** • n agenda f **~ning** • n planificació f

**plane** /pleɪn/ • n pla m; ribot m

**planet** /ˈplænɪt, ˈplænət/ • n planeta m **~arium** • n planetari m

**plant** /plɑːnt, plænt/ • n planta f • v plantar

**plaster** /ˈplɑːstə, ˈplæstər/ • n argamassa f • v arrebossar

**plastic** /ˈplɑːstɪk, ˈplæstɪk/ • adj plàstic • n plàstic

**plate** /pleɪt/ • n plat m; làmina f; matrícula f; planxa f; placa f • v xapar

**platform** /ˈplætfɔːm, ˈplætfɔːrm/ • n tarima f; plataforma f; programa m; andana f

**platypus** /ˈplætɪpəs, ˈplætɪˌpʊs/ • n ornitorinc m

**play** /pleɪ/ • n joc m; obra f; jugada f • v jugar; participar; tocar; actuar **~er** • n jugador m **~ful** • adj enjogassat, juganer

**plea** /pliː/ • n súplica f

**pleas|e** /pliːz, pliz/ • adv si us plau, per favor • v plaure, complaure, agradar **~ant** • adj agradable, plaent **~ed** • adj content **~ure** • n plaer m • v agradar

**pledge** /pledʒ/ • n promesa f, jurament m; penyora f, garantia f • v prometre; penyorar, empenyorar

**plot** /plɒt, plɑt/ • n solar, marjal, terreny m; gràfica f, traçada f; complot m, conspiració f; argument m, trama f • v conspirar; planejar; traçar; marcar

**pluck** /plʌk/ • n perseverància f

**plug** /plʌg/ • n clavilla f, endoll m **~ in** • v endollar

**plum** /plʌm/ • adj pruna • n pruna f; pruner m, prunera f; color pruna; pilotes, ous

**plunge** /plʌndʒ/ • n immersió f • v submergir

**plus** /plʌs/ • adj més, positiu • prep més

**poach** /poʊtʃ/ • v escaldar

**pocket** /ˈpɑkɪt, ˈpɒkɪt/ • *n* butxaca *f*; tronera *f* • *v* embutxacar

**poem** /ˈpəʊɪm, ˈpoʊəm/ • *n* poema *m*, poesia *f*, oda *f*

**poet** /ˈpəʊɪt, ˈpoʊət/ • *n* poeta *f* **~ic** • *adj* poètic **~ry** • *n* poesia *f*; poeticitat *f*

**point** /pɔɪnt/ • *n* punt *m* **~ sb/sth out** • *v* assenyalar, apuntar; indicar **~ed** • *adj* punxegut **~ of view** • *n* punt de vista *m*

**poison** /ˈpɔɪz(ə)n/ • *n* verí *m*, metzina *f* • *v* emmetzinar, enverinar **~ing** • *n* enverinament *m* **~ous** • *adj* verinós, tòxic

**poke|y** /ˈpoʊki/ • *n* garjola *f* **~r** • *n* pòquer *m*

**Pol|and** • *n* Polònia *f* **~ish** • *adj* polonès • *n* polonès *m*

**pole** /pəʊl, poʊl/ ; pol *m*

**police** /pˈ(ə)liːs, ˈpliːs/ • *n* policia *f* **~ station** • *n* comissaria *f*, comissaria de policia *f*

**policy** /ˈpɒləsi, ˈpaləsi/ • *n* política *f*; pòlissa *f*

**polish** /ˈpɒlɪʃ, ˈpalɪʃ/ • *v* polir

**polite** /pəˈlaɪt/ • *adj* cortès **~ness** • *n* educació cortesia *f*

**politic|s** /ˈpɑl.ɪˌtɪks, ˈpɒl.ɪˌtɪks/ • *v* política *f* **~al** • *adj* polític **~ally** • *adv* políticament **~ian** • *n* polític *m*, política *f*

**poll** /pɑl, pɒl/ • *n* enquesta *f*

**pollution** /pəˈl(j)uːʃn̩/ • *n* contaminació *f*, pol·lució *f*; pol·luent *m*

**polo** /ˈpoʊloʊ, ˈpəʊləʊ/ • *n* polo *m*

**pond** /pɒnd, pand/ • *n* bassa *f*

**pony** /ˈpəʊni, ˈpoʊni/ • *n* poni *m*

**pool** /pul, puːl/ • *n* gorg *m*, toll *m*; bassal *m* • *(also)* ▷ SWIMMING POOL

**poor** /poː, pʊə(ɹ)/ • *adj* pobre • *n* pobres

**pop** /pɒp, pap/ • *n* papi, papa *m*

**poppy** /ˈpɒpi, ˈpapi/ • *n* rosella *f*

**popular** /ˈpɒpjʊlə, ˈpapjələɹ/ • *adj* popular **~ity** • *n* popularitat *f*

**population** /ˌpɒpjʊˈleɪʃən, ˌpɑpjuːˈleɪʃən/ • *n* població *f*

**porcelain** /ˈpɔːɹ.sə.lɪn, ˈpɔː.sə.lɪn/ • *n* porcellana *f*

**porcupine** /ˈpɔː(ɹ)kjʊˌpaɪn/ • *n* porc espí *m*

**port** /pɔːt, pɔːt/ • *n* port *m*; babor

**portion** /ˈpɔːʃən, ˈpɔːʃən/ • *n* porció *f*

**portrait** /ˈpɔːtɹɪt, ˈpɔːtɹeɪt/ • *n* retrat *m*

**Portug|al** • *n* Portugal *m* **~uese** • *adj* portuguès, portugalès • *n* portuguès *m*, portuguesa *f*, portugalès *m*, portugalesa *f*

**position** /pəˈzɪʃ(ə)n/ • *n* posició *f*

**positive** /ˈpɒzɪtɪv, ˈpazɪtɪv/ • *adj* positiu • *n* positiu *m*

**possess** /pəˈzɛs/ • *v* posseïr **~ive** • *adj* possessiu **~ion** • *n* possessió *f*, propietat *f*

**possib|le** /ˈpɒsɪbl̩, ˈpasəbl̩/ • *adj* possible **~ility** • *n* possibilitat *f* **~ly** • *adv* possiblement

**post** /pəʊst, poʊst/ • *n* pivot *f* **~ office** • *n* oficina de correus *f*, oficina postal *f*

**poster** /ˈpoʊstə/ • *n* pòster *m*; cartell *m*

**postman** *(British)* ▷ MAILMAN

**postpone** /poʊstˈpoʊn/ • v
posposar, ajornar

**pot** /pɒt, pɑt/ • n olla f **~tery** • n
terrissa f

**potato** /pəˈteɪtəʊ, pəˈteɪtoʊ/ • n
(pl potatoes) patata f **~ crisp**
• n patata xip f

**potential** /pəˈtenʃəl/ • adj
potencial **~ly** • adv
potencialment

**pound** /paʊnd/ • n lliura f

**pour** /pɔː, pɔɹ/ • v abocar

**poverty** /ˈpɒvəti, ˈpɑːvəti/ • n
pobresa f

**powder** /ˈpaʊ.də(ɹ)/ • n pols f

**power** /ˈpaʊə(ɹ), paə/ • n poder
m; potència f **~ful** • adj
potent, poderós

**practical** /ˈpɹæktɪkəl/ • adj
pràctic **~ly** • adv
pràcticament; gairebé

**practice** /ˈpɹæktɪs/ • n pràctica f

**practise** /ˈpɹæktɪs/ • v practicar

**praise** /pɹeɪz/ • n alabança f,
lloança f • v lloar

**pray** /pɹeɪ/ • v resar, pregar **~er**
• n oració, pregària; rés m

**precede** /pɹəˈsiːd/ • v precedir
**~nt** • n precedent m

**precious** /ˈpɹeʃəs/ • adj preciós

**precis|e** /pɹɪˈsaɪs/ • adj precís
**~ely** • adv precisament **~ion** •
n precisió f

**predecessor** /ˈpɹiːdɪsesə(ɹ),
ˈpɹiːdɪsesɚ/ • n antecessor m

**predict** /pɹɪˈdɪkt/ • v predir **~ion**
• n predicció f

**predominant** • adj
predominant **~ly** • adv
predominantment

**preface** /ˈpɹefəs/ • n prefaci m

**prefer** /pɹɪˈfɜ, pɹɪˈfɜː/ • v preferir
**~ably** • adv preferiblement
**~ence** • n preferència f

**prefix** /ˈpɹiːfɪks/ • n prefix m

**pregnan|t** /ˈpɹegnənt/ • adj
embarassat, encinta f,
prenyat, gràvid **~cy** • n
embaràs m, prenyat m

**prejudice** /ˈpɹedʒədɪs/ • n
prejudici m

**preliminary** /pɹɪˈlɪmɪneɹi,
pɹɪˈlɪmɪnəɹi/ • adj preliminar

**premiere** /pɹəˈmɪɹ, ˈpɹɛmjeə/ • n
estrena f • v estrenar

**premium** /ˈpɹiːmiəm/ • n prima f

**prepare** /pɹɪˈpeə, pɹɪˈpeəɹ/ • v
preparar; fer; preparar-se **~d**
• adj preparat, disposat

**preposition** /ˌpɹepəˈzɪʃən/ • n
preposició f

**prescription** /pɹəˈskɹɪpʃən/ • n
recepta f

**presen|t** /ˈpɹezənt, pɹɪˈzent/ • adj
actual, present • n present m
• v presentar **~ce** • n
presència f **~ter** • n
presentador m

**preserv|e** /pɹəˈzɜːv, pɹəˈzɜːv/ • n
reserva natural f • v
preservar; conservar **~ation** •
n preservació f

**presiden|t** /ˈpɹezɪdənt/ • n
president m, presidenta f **~cy**
• n presidència f **~tial** • adj
presidencial

**press** /pɹes/ • n premsa f;
impressora f • v prémer **~ure**
• n pressió f • v pressionar

**prestig|e** /pɹeˈstiː(d)ʒ/ • n prestigi
m **~ious** • adj prestigiós

**presumably** /pɹɪˈzjuːməbli, pɹɪˈzuːməbli/ • *adv* presumiblement

**preten|d** /pɹɪˈtɛnd/ • *v* fingir, fer veure **~tious** • *adj* pretensiós; ostentós

**pretty** /ˈpɹɪti, ˈpɜti/ • *adj* bonic • *adv* força

**prevent** /pɹɪˈvɛnt, pɹəˈvɛnt/ • *v* impedir **~ive** • *adj* preventiu; profilàctic **~ion** • *n* prevenció *f*

**previous** /ˈpɹiːvi.əs, ˈpɹiːvɪəs/ • *adj* previ, anterior; prematur **~ly** • *adv* anteriorment, prèviament

**prey** /pɹeɪ/ • *n* presa

**price** /pɹaɪs, pɹʌɪs/ • *n* preu *m* **~less** • *adj* no tenir preu

**prickly** • *adj* espinós; malhumorós

**pride** /pɹaɪd/ • *n* orgull

**priest** /pɹiːst/ • *n* sacerdot *m*, capellà *m*

**primar|y** /ˈpɹaɪmɛɹi, ˈpɹaɪˌmɛɹi/ • *adj* primari *m*, primària *f* • *n* primària *f*; primari *m*, bàsic *m*, fonamental *m* **~ily** • *adv* primàriament

**prime** /pɹaɪm/ • *adj* primer

**prince** /pɹɪns, pɹɪnts/ • *n* príncep *m* **~ss** • *n* princesa

**principal** /ˈpɹɪnsɪpəl, ˈpɹɪnsɪpəl/ • *n* director *m*, directora *f*

**principle** /ˈpɹɪnsɪpəl/ • *n* principi *m* **in ~** • *phr* en principi

**print** /pɹɪnt/ • *v* imprimir **~er** • *n* impressora *f*

**prior** /ˈpɹaɪɚ/ • *n* prior *m*

**priorit|y** /pɹaɪˈɒɹɪti, pɹaɪˈɔɹiti/ • *n* prioritat *f* **~ize** • *v* prioritzar

**prison** /ˈpɹɪzən/ • *n* presó *f* **~er** • *n* pres *m*, presoner *m*

**priva|te** /ˈpɹaɪvɪt/ • *adj* privat, personal **~cy** • *n* privacitat *f*, privadesa *f* **~tely** • *adv* privadament **~tization** • *n* privatització *f*

**privilege** /ˈpɹɪv(ɪ)lɪdʒ/ • *n* privilegi *m*

**prize** /pɹaɪz/ • *n* botí *m*; premi *m*

**pro** /pɹəʊ, pɹoʊ/ • *n* pro *m* • *prep* pro

**probab|le** /ˈpɹɑbəbl̩, ˈpɹɒbəbl̩/ • *adj* probable **~ility** • *n* probabilitat *f* **~ly** • *adv* probablement

**problem** /ˈpɹɒbləm, ˈpɹɒblɪm/ • *n* problema *m* **~atic** • *adj* problemàtic; dubtós, incert

**procedur|e** /pɹəˈsiːdʒɚ, pɹəˈsɪdʒɚ/ • *n* procediment *m* **~al** • *adj* procedimental

**process** /ˈpɹəʊsɛs, ˈpɹɑˌsɛs/ • *n* procés *m* **~ing** • *n* processament *m* **~or** • *n* processador *m*

**proclamation** • *n* proclamació *f*

**produc|e** /pɹəˈdjuːs, pɹəˈdus/ • *v* produir **~er** • *n* productor *m*, productora *f* **~t** • *n* producte *m* **~tion** • *n* producció *f* **~tive** • *adj* productiu **~tivity** • *n* productivitat *f*

**profession** /pɹəˈfɛʃən/ • *n* professió *f*, ofici *m* **~al** • *adj* professional; perit • *n* professional

**professor** /pɹəˈfɛsə, pɹəˈfɛsɚ/ • *n* professor *m*, professora *f*

**proficien|t** /pɹəˈfɪʃ.ənt, pɹoʊˈfɪʃ.ənt/ • *adj* perit, capaç,

versat **~cy** • *n* habilitat,
competència *f*

**profit** /ˈpɹɒfɪt, ˈpɹɑfɪt/ • *n* benefici
*m* **~able** • *adj* profitós,
rendible

**program** /ˈpɹəʊɡɹæm,
ˈpɹoʊˌɡɹæm/ • *n* programa *m*
**~mer** • *n* programador *m*

**programme** *(British)* ▷ PROGRAM

**progress** /ˈpɹəʊɡɹɛs, ˈpɹɑɡɹɛs/ • *n*
progrés **~ive** • *adj*
progressista; progressiu
**~ively** • *adv* progressivament
**~ion** • *n* progressió *f*

**prohibit** /pɹəˈhɪbɪt, pɹoʊˈhɪbɪt/ • *v*
prohibir **~ion** • *n* prohibició *f*,
interdicció *f*

**project** /ˈpɹɒdʒɛkt, ˈpɹɑdʒˌɛkt/ • *n*
projecte *m* **~or** • *n* projector
*m*

**prologue** /ˈpɹəʊlɒɡ, ˈpɹoʊˌlɔɡ/ • *n*
pròleg *m*

**prominen|t** /ˈpɹɑmɪnənt,
ˈpɹɒmɪnənt/ • *adj* prominent
**~ce** • *n* prominència *f*

**promis|e** /ˈpɹɒmɪs, ˈpɹɑmɪs/ • *n*
promesa *f* • *v* prometre **~ing**
• *adj* prometedor

**prompt** /pɹɒmpt, pɹɑmpt/ • *adj*
ràpid; puntual • *v* incitar;
apuntar; causar

**pronoun** /ˈpɹəʊnaʊn, ˈpɹoʊˌnaʊn/
• *n* pronom *m*

**pron|ounce** /pɹəˈnaʊns/ • *v*
pronunciar **~unciation** • *n*
pronunciació *f*, pronúncia *f*

**proof** /pɹuːf, pɹuf/ • *n* prova *f*

**propaganda** /ˌpɹɒpəˈɡændə/ • *n*
propaganda *f*

**proper** /ˈpɹɒp.ə, ˈpɹɑ.pə/ • *adj*
adequat

**property** /ˈpɹɒp.ət.i, ˈpɹɑp.ɚt.i/ •
*n* propietat *f*, possessió *f*;
immoble *m*; pertinença *f*

**proportion** /pɹəˈpɔːʃən,
pɹəˈpɔːʃən/ • *n* proporció *f* **~al**
• *adj* proporcional

**propos|e** /pɹəˈpəʊz, pɹəˈpoʊz/ • *v*
proposar **~al** • *n* proposta *f*

**prose** /ˈpɹəʊz/ • *n* prosa *f*

**prosecut|e** • *v* perseguir **~or** •
*n* fiscal *f*

**prospect** /ˈpɹɒspɛkt, ˈpɹɑspɛkt/ •
*n* prospeccions • *v* fer
prospeccions; prospectar

**prosperity** /pɹɑˈspɛɹ.ti,
pɹɒˈspɛɹ.ti/ • *n* prosperitat *f*

**protagonist** /pɹəˈtæ.ɡə.nɪst,
pɹoʊˈtæ.ɡə.nɪst/ • *n*
protagonista *f*

**protect** /pɹəˈtɛkt/ • *v* protegir
**~ion** • *n* protecció *f*

**protein** /ˈpɹəʊtiːn, ˈpɹoʊtiːn/ • *n*
proteïna *f*

**protest** /ˈpɹəʊˌtɛst, ˈpɹoʊˌtɛst/ • *n*
protesta *f* • *v* protestar **~er** •
*n* protestant *f*, manifestant *f*

**Protestant** • *adj* protestant • *n*
protestant *f*

**proud** /pɹaʊd/ • *adj* orgullós;
arrogant

**prove** /pɹuːv/ • *v* (*sp* proved, *pp*
proven) provar, demostrar

**proved** *(sp/pp)* ▷ PROVE

**proven** *(pp)* ▷ PROVE

**provide** /pɹəˈvaɪd/ • *v* proveir

**provinc|e** /ˈpɹɑvɪns, ˈpɹɒvɪns/ • *n*
província *f* **~ial** • *adj*
provincial

**provisional** /pɹəˈvɪʒənəl/ • *adj*
provisional, provisori

**provo|ke** /pɹəˈvəʊk, pɹəˈvoʊk/ • *v* provocar **~cative** • *adj* provocador, provocatiu

**prudence** /ˈpɹuːdəns/ • *n* prudència *f*

**prune** /pɹuːn/ • *n* pruna seca *f* • *v* podar, esporgar

**pseudonym** /ˈs(j)uːdəʊ.nɪm, ˈsudoʊnɪm/ • *n* pseudònim *m*

**psychiatr|y** /saɪˈkaɪ.ə.tɹi/ • *n* psiquiatria *f* **~ic** • *adj* psiquiàtric **~ist** • *n* psiquiatre *m*

**psycholog|y** /saɪˈkɑlədʒi, saɪˈkɒlədʒi/ • *n* psicologia *f* **~ical** • *adj* psicològic **~ist** • *n* psicòleg *m*

**pub** /pʌb, pʊb/ • *n* bar *m*, taverna *f*

**public** /ˈpʌblɪk/ • *adj* públic **~ly** • *adv* públicament **~ity** • *n* publicitat *f* **~ation** • *n* publicació *f*

**publish** /ˈpʌblɪʃ/ • *v* publicar **~er** • *n* editorial *f*, editor *m*

**puff pastry** • *n* pasta de full *f*, pasta fullada *f*

**pull** /pʊl/ • *v* tirar

**pulse** /pʌls, pʊls/ • *n* pols *m*; pulsació

**pump** /pʌmp/ • *n* bomba *f* • *v* bombar

**pumpkin** /ˈpʌmpkɪn/ • *n* carbassera *f*, carabassera *f*; carbassa *f*, carabassa *f*

**punch** /pʌntʃ/ • *n* cop de puny *m*; ponx *m* • *v* apunyegar; perforar

**punctual** /ˈpʌŋktjʊəl, ˈpʌŋktʃuəl/ • *adj* puntual **~ity** • *n* puntualitat *f*

**punctuation** /pʌŋk.tʃuˈeɪ.ʃən/ • *n* puntuació *f* **~ mark** • *n* signe de puntuació *m*

**punish** /ˈpʌnɪʃ/ • *v* castigar, punir **~ment** • *n* punició *f*, puniment *m*; càstig *m*

**puny** /pjuːni/ • *adj* feble, escarransit, desnerit

**pupil** /pjuːpəl/ • *n* alumne *m*, alumna *f*, pupil *m*, pupil·la *f*

**pure** /pjʊə, ˈpjɔːɹ/ • *adj* pur

**purple** /ˈpɜː(ɹ).pəl, ˈpɜ́pəl/ • *adj* porpra, purpuri • *n* porpra *f*, púrpura *f*

**on purpose** • *phr* a propòsit

**purr** /pɜː(ɹ)/ • *v* roncar, ronronejar

**purse** /pɜːs, pɝs/ • *n* moneder *m*

**pursuit** /pəˈsjuːt, pɝˈsuːt/ • *n* perseguiment *m*

**push** /pʊʃ/ • *n* empenta *f* • *v* empènyer, empentar

**put** /pʊt/ • *v* posar, ficar, metre **~ sth out** • *n* eliminació *f* • *v* apagar

**puzzle** /ˈpʌzəl/ • *n* trencaclosques *m*

**pyramid** /ˈpɪɹəmɪd/ • *n* piràmide *f*

**python** /ˈpaɪθən, ˈpaɪθɑːn/ • *n* pitó *m*

**Qatar** • *n* Qatar *m*
**quail** /kweɪl/ • *n* guatlla *f*

**qualifi|cation** /ˌkwɒlɪfɪˈkeɪʃn/ ● *n*
qualificació *f* **~ed** ● *adj*
qualificat

**quality** /ˈkwɒlɪti, ˈkwæliti/ ● *adj*
de qualitat ● *n* qualitat *f*;
quality *f*

**quantity** /ˈkwɒn.tɪ.ti, ˈkwɑn(t)iti/
● *n* quantitat *f*

**quarrel** /ˈkwɒɹəl, ˈkwɔɹəl/ ● *n*
baralla *f*; queixa *f* ● *v*
barallar-se, discutir

**quarter** /ˈkwɔːtə, ˈk(w)ɔɹ.tɚ/ ● *n*
quart *m*, quarter *m*

**quarterback** ● *n* rerequart *m*

**queen** /kwiːn/ ● *n* gata *f*; reina
*f*; marieta *f*

**question** /ˈkwɛstʃən/ ● *n*
pregunta *f*, qüestió *f* ● *v*
interrogar; qüestionar **~naire**
● *n* qüestionari *m* **~ mark** ● *n*
interrogant, signe
d'interrogació *m*

**queue** /kjuː, kju/ ● *n* cua *f*, fila *f*

**quick** /kwɪk/ ● *adv* corrents ● *n*
carn viva *f* **~ly** ● *adv*
ràpidament

**quiet** /ˈkwaɪ.ɪt, ˈkwaɪ.ət/ ● *adj*
silenciós, tranquil; quiet; poc,
mica ● *v* calmar **~ly** ● *adv*
silenciosament

**quince** /kwɪns/ ● *n* codony *m*;
codonyer *m*

**quit** /kwɪt/ ● *adj* sortir, eixir;
deixar, aturar

**quite** /kwaɪt/ ● *adv*
completament, del tot;
totalment, exactament;
verdaderament; bastant

**quitted** *(sp/pp)* ▷ QUIT

**quote** /kwəʊt/ ● *n* citació

# R

**rabbi** /ˈɹæ.baɪ/ ● *n* rabí *m*

**rabbit** /ˈɹæbɪt, ˈɹæbət/ ● *n* conill *m*

**rabble** /ˈɹæbəl/ ● *n* gentalla *f*,
gentola *f*

**race** /ɹeɪs/ ● *n* arrel *f*; raça *f*;
cursa *f*

**racial** /ˈɹeɪʃəl/ ● *adj* racial

**racis|t** /ˈɹeɪsɪst/ ● *adj* racista ● *n*
racista *f* **~m** ● *n* racisme *m*

**rack** /ɹæk/ ● *n* poltre *m*; pitrera

**radar** /ˈɹeɪdɑː(ɹ)/ ● *n* radar *m*

**radiant** /ˈɹeɪdi.ənt/ ● *adj* radiant
● *n* radiant *m*

**radiation** /ˌɹeɪ.di.ˈeɪ.ʃən,
ˌɹaɪ.di.ˈaɪ.ʃən/ ● *n* radiació *f*

**radical** /ˈɹædɪkəl/ ● *adj* radical ●
*n* radical *f*

**radio** /ˈɹeɪdi.əʊ, ˈɹeɪdi.oʊ/ ● *n*
ràdio *f* **~active** ● *adj*
radioactiu **~activity** ● *n*
radioactivitat *f*

**radish** /ˈɹædɪʃ, ˈɹædɪʃ/ ● *n*
ravenera *f*; rave *m*

**radius** /ˈɹeɪ.di.əs/ ● *n* (*pl* radii)
radi *m*

**rage** /ɹeɪdʒ/ ● *n* ràbia *f*

**rail** /ɹeɪl/ ● *n* carril *m*

**rain** /ɹeɪn/ ● *n* pluja *f* ● *v* ploure
**~bow** ● *n* arc de Sant Martí
*m*, arc iris *m* **~coat** ● *n*
impermeable *m* **~y** ● *adj*
plujós

**raise** /ɹeɪz/ ● *v* alçar; criar

**raisin** /ˈɹeɪzn̩, ˈɹiːzən/ ● *n* pansa *f*

**rally** /ˈɪæ.li/ • *n* manifestació *f*; intercanvi de cops *m*, piloteig *m*

**ran** *(sp)* ▷ RUN

**ranch** /ɪæntʃ/ • *n* ranxo *m*

**random** /ˈɪændəm/ • *adj* aleatori • *n* fulano *m* **~ly** • *adv* aleatòriament, a l'atzar

**rang** *(sp)* ▷ RING

**range** /ɪeɪmdʒ/ • *n* rang *m*; fogó *m*; ventall *m*, gamma *f*; camp de tir *m*; camp de Mart *m*; distància *f*; abast *m*; devesa *f*; àmbit *m*; interval *m*; amplitud *f*; hàbitat *m*; llista *f*; serralada *f*

**rank** /ɪæŋk/ • *adj* ranci • *n* rang *m*; fila *f* **~ing** • *n* rànquing *m*

**rap|e** /ɪeɪp/ • *n* violació *f* **~ist** • *n* violador *m*

**rapid** /ˈɪæpɪd/ • *adj* ràpid • *n* ràpid *m* **~ly** • *adv* ràpidament

**rare** /ɪeə, ɪeəɪ/ • *adj* rar; cru **~ly** • *adv* rarament

**rat** /ɪæt/ • *n* rata *f*, rat *m* • *v* delatar, acuar

**rather** /ˈɪɑː.ðə, ˌɪɑːˈðɜː(ɪ)/ • *adv* preferiblement; força, bastant

**rational** /ˈɪæʃ(ə)nəl/ • *adj* racional **~ly** • *adv* racionalment **~ity** • *n* racionalitat *f* **~ize** • *v* racionalitzar

**raven** /ˈɪeɪvən/ • *n* corb *m*

**raw** /ɪɔː, ɪɔ/ • *adj* cru

**ray** /ɪeɪ/ • *n* raig *m*; semirecta; rajada *f*

**reach** /ɪiːtʃ/ • *n* abast *m* • *v* abastar

**reaction** /ɪiˈækʃən/ • *n* reacció *f*

**read** /ɪid, ɪiːd/ • *v* (*sp* read, *pp* read) llegir; llegir-se; sentir; estudiar **~er** • *n* lector *m*

**ready** /ˈɪedi/ • *adj* llest; disposat

**real|ly** /ˈɪəlɪ, ˈɪɪli/ • *adv* realment, de debò **~ity** • *n* realitat *f*

**realis|m** /ɪi.əlɪzm/ • *n* realisme **~tic** • *adj* realista

**realize** /ˈɪi.ə.laɪz, ˈɪɪə.laɪz/ • *v* adonar-se

**realm** /ɪɛlm/ • *n* domini *m*

**reason** /ˈɪiːzən/ • *n* raó *f* • *v* raonar **~able** • *adj* raonable **~ably** • *adv* raonablement **~ing** • *n* raonament *m*

**reassure** /ɪiəˈʃʊə(ɪ), ɪiəˈʃʊɪ/ • *v* tranquil·litzar

**rebel** /ˈɪebəl/ • *n* rebel *f* **~lion** • *n* rebel·lió *f*

**rebuild** /ɪiːbɪld/ • *v* reconstruir

**recall** /ɪiˈkɔːl, ɪiˈkɔl/ • *v* evocar; recordar

**receipt** /ɪiˈsiːt/ • *n* recepció *f*; rebut *m*, rebuda *f*; recepta *f*

**receive** /ɪiˈsiːv/ • *v* rebre

**recent** /ˈɪiːsənt/ • *adj* fresc, recent **~ly** • *adv* recentment, últimament, darrerament

**recepti|onist** /ɪiˈsɛpʃənəst/ • *n* recepcionista *f* **~ve** • *adj* receptiu

**recipe** /ˈɪɛs.ɪ.pi/ • *n* recepta *f*

**recognize** /ˈɪɛkəɡnaɪz, ˈɪɛkənaɪz/ • *v* reconèixer

**recommend** /ˌɪɛkəˈmɛnd/ • *v* recomanar **~ation** • *n* recomanació *f*

**reconciliation** /ˌɪɛkənˌsɪlɪˈeɪʃən/ • *n* reconciliació *f*

**recorder** • *n* flauta dolça *f*

**recovery** /ɹɪˈkʌvəɹi/ ● *n* recuperació *f*

**recruit** /ɹɪˈkɹuːt/ ● *v* reclutar ~**ment** ● *n* reclutament

**recycl|e** /ɹəˈsaɪkəl/ ● *v* reciclar ~**ing** ● *n* reciclatge *m*

**red** /ɹɛd/ ● *adj* roig, vermell; pèl-roig ● *n* vermell *m*, roig *m*; roja *f*; vi negre *m*

**reduc|e** /ɹɪˈdjuːs, ɹɪˈduːs/ ● *v* reduir ~**tion** ● *n* reducció *f*

**redundan|t** /ɹɪˈdʌn.dənt/ ● *adj* redundant ~**cy** ● *n* redundància *f*

**refer** /ɹɪˈfɜː, ɹɪˈfɜ/ ● *v* referir ~**ence** ● *n* referència *f* ● *v* referenciar

**referee** /ˌɹɛf.əˈɹiː, ˌɹɛfəˈɹiː/ ● *n* àrbitre *m*

**referendum** /ˌɹɛfəˈɹɛndəm/ ● *n* (*pl* referenda) referèndum *m*

**reflecti|ve** ● *adj* reflector, reflectant ~**on** ● *n* reflexió *f*; reflex *m*

**reform** /ɹɪˈfɔːm/ ● *n* reforma *f* ● *v* reformar

**refrigerator** /ɹɪˈfɹɪdʒəˌɹeɪtə, ɹɪˈfɹɪdʒəˌɹeɪɹə/ ● *n* frigorífic *m*

**refuge** /ˈɹɛfjuːdʒ/ ● *n* refugi *m* ● *v* refugiar-se ~**e** ● *n* refugiat *m*, refugiada *f*

**refuse** /ˈɹɛfjuːs/ ● *n* rebuig *m* ● *v* refusar, rebutjar

**regain** ● *v* reconquerir

**regardless** /ɹɪˈɡɑɪd.lɪs/ ● *adv* malgrat tot

**regime** /ɹəˈʒim/ ● *n* règim *m*

**region** /ˈɹiːdʒn̩/ ● *n* regió *f* ~**al** ● *adj* regional

**regularly** /ˈɹɛɡjələɹi, ˈɹɛɡjʊləli/ ● *adv* regularment

**regulator** /ˈɹɛɡ.juːˌleɪt.ə/ ● *n* regulador *m*

**rehabilitation** ● *n* rehabilitació *f*

**rehears|e** /ɹɪˈhɜ́s/ ● *v* reproduir; assajar ~**al** ● *n* assaig *m*

**reign** /ɹeɪn/ ● *n* regnat *m* ● *v* regnar

**reindeer** /ˈɹeɪndɪə, ˈɹeɪndɹɪ/ ● *n* ren *m*

**reinforcement** ● *n* reforç *m*, reforçament *m*

**reject** /ɹɪˈdʒɛkt, ˈɹiːdʒɛkt/ ● *v* rebutjar, refusar ~**ion** ● *n* rebuig *m*, refús *m*

**relat|e** /ɹɪˈleɪt/ ● *v* indentificar-se ~**ionship** ● *n* relació *f* ~**ive** ● *adj* relatiu ● *n* parent *m*, parenta *f* ~**ively** ● *adv* relativament

**relax** /ɹɪˈlæks/ ● *v* relaxar, afluixar; relaxar-se, afluixar-se ~**ed** ● *adj* relaxat ~**ing** ● *adj* relaxant ~**ation** ● *n* relaxació *f*

**release** /ɹɪˈliːs/ ● *n* versió *f*; estrena *f*; alliberat *m*; alliberament *m* ● *v* amollar; alliberar; estrenar, publicar, llançar

**relevan|t** /ˈɹɛləvənt/ ● *adj* rellevant, pertinent ~**ce** ● *n* rellevància *f*

**reliability** ● *n* fiabilitat *f*

**relic** /ˈɹɛlɪk/ ● *n* relíquia *f*

**relie|f** /ɹɪˈliːf/ ● *n* consol *m*, alleujament *m*; relleu *m* ~**ved** ● *adj* alleujat

**religio|n** /ɹɪˈlɪdʒən/ ● *n* religió *f* ~**us** ● *adj* religiós

**reluctance** ● *n* reluctància

**remain** /ɹɪˈmeɪn/ • v quedar-se, restar **~der** • n resta f, residu m **~ing** • adj romanent, restant, sobrer **~s** • n restes

**remarkable** /ɹɪˈmɑɹkəbl̩, ɹɪˈmɑːkəbl̩/ • adj remarcable

**remedy** /ˈɹɛmədi/ • n remei m; correcció f, correctiu m • v remeiar

**rememb|er** /ɹɪˈmɛmbɚ, ˈmɛmbɚ/ • v recordar, rememorar **~rance** • n recordatori m, memòria f

**remind** /ɹəˈmaɪnd/ • v recordar **~er** • n recordatori m, record m

**remote** /ɹɪˈməʊt, ɹɪˈmoʊt/ • adj remot **~ly** • adv remotament **~ control** • n comandament a distància m

**remove** /ɹɪˈmuːv/ • v treure

**render** /ˈɹɛn.də, ˈɹɛn.dɚ/ • v traduir

**renew** /ɹɪˈnjuː/ • v renovar **~al** • n renovació f **~able** • adj renovable

**rent** /ɹɛnt/ • n lloguer m • v llogar

**repair** /ɹɪˈpɛə, ɹɪˈpɛɚ/ • v reparar

**repe|at** /ɹɪˈpiːt/ • v repetir **~atedly** • adv repetidament **~tition** • n repetició f

**replace** /ɹɪˈpleɪs/ • v reemplaçar **~ment** • n substitut m; reemplaçament m

**reply** /ɹɪˈplaɪ/ • n resposta

**report** /ɹɪˈpɔɹt, ɹɪˈpɔːt/ • n informe m • v informar; notificar, fer saber; ser responsable; presentar-se **~er** • n reporter m

**represent** /ˌɹɛp.ɹɪˈzɛnt/ • v representar **~ation** • n representació f

**reproduc|e** /ˌɹiˌpɹoʊˈdjus, ˌɹiˌpɹoʊˈdus/ • v reproduir; reproduir-se **~tion** • n reproducció f

**republic** /ɹɪˈpʌblɪk/ • n república f **~an** • adj republicà • n republicà m, republicana f

**Republican** /ɹɪˈpʌblɪkən/ • adj republicà • n republicà m

**repulsive** • adj repulsiu

**reputation** /ˌɹɛpjʊˈteɪʃən/ • n reputació f

**request** /ɹɪˈkwɛst/ • n petició f, sol·licitud f • v demanar

**requirement** /ɹɪˈkwʌɪəm(ə)nt, ɹɪˈkwaɪmənt/ • n requisit m, menester m, exigència f

**rescue** /ˈɹɛs.kjuː/ • n rescat m • v rescatar

**research** /ɹɪˈsɜːtʃ, ˈɹiːsɚtʃ/ • n recerca m **~er** • n investigador m

**resembl|e** /ɹɪˈzɛmb(ə)l/ • v semblar **~ance** • n semblança f

**reserved** /ɹɪˈzɜvd, ɹɪˈzɜːvd/ • adj reservat m

**reside** /ɹɪˈzaɪd/ • v residir **~nce** • n residència f, domicili; seu social f **~ntial** • adj residencial

**residue** /ˈɹɛzɪduː, ˈɹɛzɪdjuː/ • n residu m

**resign** /ɹɪˈzaɪn/ • v dimitir

**resist** /ɹɪˈzɪst/ • v resistir **~ant** • adj resistent • n resistent m **~ance** • n resistència f

**resol|ve** /ɹɪˈzɒlv, ɹɪˈzɑlv/ • n resolució f • v resoldre, solucionar **~ute** • *adj* resolut

**respect** /ɹɪˈspɛkt/ • *n* respecte *m*
• *v* respectar **~ful** • *adj*
respectuós **~ive** • *adj*
respectiu **~ively** • *adv*
respectivament

**respon|d** /ɹɪˈspɒnd, ɹəˈspɑnd/ • *v*
respondre **~se** • *n* resposta *f*

**responsib|le** /ɹɪˈspɒnsəbl̩,
ɹɪˈspɑnsəbəl/ • *adj* responsable
**~ility** • *n* responsabilitat *f*

**rest** /ɹɛst/ • *n* descans *m*, repòs
*m*; resta *f* • *v* descansar,
reposar **~less** • *adj* intranquil;
inquiet; desvetllat

**restaurant** /ˈɹɛs.t(ə).ɹɒ̃,
ˈɹɛs.t(ə).ɹɑnt/ • *n* restaurant *m*

**restrict** /ɹɪˈstɹɪkt/ • *v* restringir
**~ive** • *adj* restrictiu **~ion** • *n*
restricció *f*

**result** /ɹɪˈzʌlt/ • *n* resultat *m*

**resume** /ɹɪˈzjuːm, ɹɪˈz(j)uːm/ • *n*
resum *m*, sumari *m* • *v*
reprendre

**retire** /ɹəˈtaɪ.ə(ɹ)/ • *v* jubilar **~d** •
*adj* jubilat **~ment** • *n* jubilació
*f*

**retrieve** /ɹɪˈtɹiːv/ • *v* recuperar

**return** /ɹɪˈtɜːn, ɹɪˈtɝn/ • *v* tornar;
restar

**reve|al** /ɹəˈviːl/ • *v* revelar
**~lation** • *n* revelació *f*

**revenge** /ɹɪˈvɛndʒ/ • *n* revenja *m*,
venjança *f* • *v* revenjar-se

**revenue** /ˈɹɛvənjuː, ˈɹɛvəˌn(j)uː/ •
*n* rèdit

**revision** • *n* revisió *f*

**revive** • *v* reviscolar

**revolting** • *adj* repugnant

**revolution** /ˌɹɛvəˈl(j)uːʃən/ • *n*
revolució *f* • *adj*
revolucionari

**reward** /ɹɪˈwɔːd/ • *v*
recompensar

**rhetoric** /ˈɹɛtəɹɪk/ • *n* retòrica *f*

**rhinoceros** /ɹaɪˈnɒsəɹəs,
ɹaɪˈnɑːsəɹəs/ • *n* rinoceront *m*

**rhyme** /ɹaɪm/ • *n* rima *f* • *v*
rimar

**rhythm** /ˈɹɪð(ə)m/ • *n* ritme *m*
**~ic** • *adj* rítmic

**rib** /ɹɪb/ • *n* costella *f*; quaderna
*f*

**ribbon** /ˈɹɪbən/ • *n* cinta *f*, llaç

**rice** /ɹaɪs/ • *n* arròs *m*

**rich** /ɹɪtʃ/ • *adj* ric

**rid** /ˈɹɪd/ • *v* (*sp* rid, *pp* rid)
alliberar

**ridded** (*sp/pp*) ▷ RID

**ridden** (*pp*) ▷ RIDE

**ride** /ɹaɪd/ • *v* (*sp* rode, *pp*
ridden) colcar, muntar,
cavalcar **~r** • *n* genet *m*

**ridge** /ɹɪdʒ/ • *n* serralada *f*;
serra *f*

**ridiculous** /ɹɪˈdɪkjʊləs/ • *adj*
ridícul **~ly** • *adv* ridículament

**rifle** /ˈɹaɪfəl/ • *n* fusell *m*, rifle *m*

**right** /ˈɹaɪt, ɹeɪt/ • *adj* dret • *n*
dret *m*; dreta *f* **~-handed** • *n*
dretà **~ now** • *adv* ara mateix

**ring** /ɹɪŋ/ • *n* cèrcol *m*; anell *m*;
anella; rodanxa; ring; pista;
cercle; corona • *v* (*sp* rang, *pp*
rung) dringar, trucar; fer
sonar

**ripe** /ɹaɪp/ • *adj* madur

**rise** /ɹaɪz, ɹaɪs/ • *v* (*sp* rose, *pp*
risen) pujar

**risen** (*pp*) ▷ RISE

**risk** /ɹɪsk/ • *n* risc *m* • *v* arriscar
~**y** • *adj* riscós, arriscat
**ritual** /ˈɹɪ.tʃu.əl/ • *adj* ritual *f*
**rival** /ˈɹaɪvəl/ • *n* rival ~**ry** • *n*
rivalitat *f*
**river** /ˈɹɪvə, ˈɹɪvɚ/ • *n* riu *m* ~**bed**
• *n* buc *m* ~**side** • *adj* riberenc
*m* • *n* ribera *f*, riba *f*, ribatge *m*
**road** /ɹəʊd, ɹoʊd/ • *n* carretera *f*;
camí
**roast** /ɹəʊst, ɹoʊst/ • *adj* rostit
~**ed** • *adj* rostit
**rob** /ɹɒb, ɹɑb/ • *v* robar, atracar
~**ber** • *n* lladre *f*
**robe** /ɹəʊb, ɹoʊb/ • *n* hàbit *m*,
toga *f*
**robin** /ˈɹɒb.ɪn, ˈɹɑb.ɪn/ • *n* pit-roig
*m*
**robot** /ˈɹəʊbɒt, ˈɹoʊbɑt/ • *n* robot
*m*
**rock** /ɹɒk, ɹɑk/ • *n* quer *m*, roc
*m*, roca *f*, pedra *f*; pedra
preciosa *f*; rock
**rocket** /ˈɹɒkɪt, ˈɹɒkɪt/ • *n* coet *m*
**rod** /ɹɒd, ɹɑd/ • *n* verga *f*
**rode** *(sp)* ▷ RIDE
**rollercoaster** /ˈɹoʊlɚˌkoʊstɚ/ • *n*
muntanyes russes
**romantic** /ɹəʊˈmæntɪk,
ɹoʊˈmæn(t)ɪk/ • *adj* romàntic
**Romania** • *n* Romania *f* ~**n** •
*adj* romanès *m*, romanesa *f*
**Rom|e** • *n* Roma *f* ~**an** • *adj*
romà; romana *f* • *n* romà *m*;
llatí *m* • *n* Romà *m*
**roof** /ɹuːf/ • *n* teulada *f*; sostre
*m*
**room** /ɹuːm, ɹʊm/ • *n* espai *m*,
lloc *m*; cambra *f*, sala *f*,
habitació *f*, peça *f*, aposento

~**mate** • *n* company
d'habitació *m*
**rooster** /ˈɹuːstə, ˈɹustɚ/ • *n* gall *m*
**root** /ɹuːt, ɹʊt/ • *n* arrel *f* • *v*
furgar
**rope** /ɹəʊp, ɹoʊp/ • *n* corda *f*
**rose** /ɹəʊz, ɹoʊz/ • *adj* rosat • *n*
roser *m*; rosa *f* • *(also)* ▷ RISE
**rosemary** • *n* romaní *m*, romer
*m*
**rotten** /ˈɹɑtn̩, ˈɹɒtn̩/ • *adj* podrit
*m*
**rough** /ɹʌf/ • *adj* aspre;
aproximat, quasi; difícil; rude
*f*, tosc *m*
**roulette** • *n* ruleta *f*
**round** /ˈɹaʊnd/ • *adj* rodó • *n*
ronda *f*; volta *f* ~ **up** • *v*
arrodonir ~**about** • *n* rotonda
*f*; carrussel *m*, cavallets
**route** /ɹuːt, ɹuːt/ • *n* ruta *f*
**routine** /ɹuːˈtiːn/ • *adj* rutinari
**row** /ɹəʊ, ɹoʊ/ • *n* fila *f*, filera *f*
• *v* remar
**royal** /ˈɹɔɪəl/ • *adj* reial ~**ty** • *n*
reialesa *f*; drets d'autor
**rub** /ɹʌb/ • *v* fregar
**rubber** /ˈɹʌbə(ɹ), ˈɹʌbɚ/ • *n*
cautxú *m*; goma *f*; condó *m*;
placa del llançador *f*
**ruby** • *n* robí *m*
**rude** /ɹuːd, ɹud/ • *adj* rude *m*,
bast *m*; obscè *m*; robust
**rugby** /ˈɹʌgbi/ • *n* rugbi *m*
**ruin** /ˈɹuːɪn, ˈɹu.ɪn/ • *n* ruïna • *v*
espatllar
**rule** /ɹuːl/ • *n* regla *f*, norma *f* •
*v* manar, governar, regnar ~**r**
• *n* regle *m*; líder *m*,
governant *m*

R

**rumor** /ˈruːmə(ɹ), ˈɹuːməɹ/ • n
rumor m

**rumour** *(British)* ▷ RUMOR

**run** /ɹʌn, ɹʊn/ • n córrer;
recorregut m, ruta f; galopar;
carrera f • v (sp ran, pp run)
fluir, escolar-se; fer fluir;
córrer; fer funcionar;
executar, arrancar; funcionar;
fer córrer **~ away** • v fugir **~
over sb/sth** • v atropellar
**~ner** • n corredor m

**rung** *(pp)* ▷ RING

**rupture** /ˈɹʌptʃə/ • n ruptura

**rural** /ˈɹʊɹəl/ • adj rural

**Russia** • n Rússia f **~n** • adj rus
• n rus m, russa f

**rust** /ɹʌst/ • n rovell m, òxid m •
v rovellar, oxidar **~y** • adj
rovellat

**ruthless** /ˈɹuːθləs/ • adj despietat
m

# S

**sack** /sæk/ • v ensacar;
acomiadar, destituir, despedir

**sacred** /ˈseɪkɹɪd/ • adj sagrat m

**sacrifice** /ˈsækɹɪfaɪs/ • n sacrifici
m • v sacrificar; oferir;
sacrificar-se

**sad** /sæd/ • adj trist m, trista f;
lamentable; deplorable;
patètic **~ly** • adv tristament
**~ness** • n tristesa f

**safe** /seɪf/ • adj segur, salv • n
caixa forta f **~ty** • n
seguretat f

**saffron** /ˈsæfɹən/ • adj safrà • n
safranera f, safrà m

**said** *(sp/pp)* ▷ SAY

**sail** /seɪl/ • n vela f; aspa f • v
navegar **~or** • n marí m,
mariner m

**saint** /seɪnt, sən(t)/ • n sant m,
santa f **~hood** • n santedat f
**for God's ~** • interj per l'amor
de Déu

**salad** /ˈsæləd/ • n amanida f

**salamander** /ˈsæləˌmændə,
ˈsælə.mɑːndə/ • n salamandra f

**salary** /ˈsæləɹi/ • n salari m, sou m

**sale** /seɪl/ • n venda f

**salmon** /ˈsæmən, ˈsælmən/ • n (pl
salmon) salmó m

**salt** /sɔːlt, sɒlt/ • n sal f • v salar
**~y** • adj salat

**same** /seɪm/ • adj mateix • pron
mateix

**Samoa** • n Samoa f

**sample** /ˈsɑːm.pəl, ˈsæm.pəl/ • n
mostra f; tast m

**San Marino** • n San Marino m

**sand** /sænd/ • n sorra f, arena f;
platja f **~y** • adj sorrenc;
vermellós

**sandal** /ˈsændəl/ • n sandàlia f

**sandwich** /ˈsæn(d)wɪdʒ,
ˈsæn.(d)wɪtʃ/ • n entrepà m,
sandvitx m, badall m

**sang** *(sp)* ▷ SING

**sank** *(sp)* ▷ SINK

**sapphire** /ˈsæf.aɪə(ɹ), ˈsæf.aɪɚ/ • n
safir m; colibrí gorjablau m

**sarcas|m** /ˈsɑːɹˌkæzəm/ • n
sarcasme **~tic** • adj sarcàstic

**sardine** /sɑːˈdiːn, sɑɹˈdin/ • *n* sardina *f*

**sat** *(sp/pp)* ▷ SIT

**satellite** /ˈsætəlaɪt/ • *n* satèl·lit *m*

**satire** /ˈsætaɪɹ/ • *n* sàtira *f*

**satisf|y** /ˈsætɪsfaɪ/ • *v* satisfer **~action** • *n* satisfacció *f* **~ied** • *adj* satisfet

**Saturday** • *n* dissabte *m*

**Saturn** • *n* Saturn *m*

**saucepan** /ˈsɔːspæn, ˈsɔːspən/ • *n* cassó *m*

**Saudi Arabia** • *n* Aràbia Saudita *f*

**sausage** /ˈsɒsɪdʒ, ˈsɔːsɪdʒ/ • *n* salsitxa *f*

**save** /seɪv/ • *n* aturada *f* • *v* salvar; desar, guardar; estalviar

**saw** /sɔː, sɔ/ • *n* serra *f* • *v* (*sp* sawed, *pp* sawn) serrar • *(also)* ▷ SEE

**sawed** *(sp/pp)* ▷ SAW

**sawn** *(pp)* ▷ SAW

**saxophone** /ˈsæksəfoʊn/ • *n* saxòfon *m*, saxofon *m*

**say** /seɪ/ • *v* (*sp* said, *pp* said) dir; recitar, declamar

**scaffold** /ˈskæfəld/ • *n* bastida *f* **~ing** • *n* bastida *f*

**scale** /skeɪl/ • *n* escala *f*

**scalp** /skælp/ • *n* cuir cabellut *m*

**scam** /skæm/ • *n* estafa *f*, enredada *f* • *v* estafar **~mer** • *n* estafador *m*

**scan** /skæn/ • *v* escanejar; escorcollar; escandir

**scandal** /ˈskændəl/ • *n* escàndol *m*

**scar** /skɑɹ, skɑː(ɹ)/ • *n* cicatriu *f*

**scarc|e** /skeəs, ˈskɛɚs/ • *adj* escàs **~ity** • *n* escassetat *f*, escassedat *f*, escassesa *f*

**scar|e** /skeə, skɛɚ/ • *v* espantar, espaventar **~y** • *adj* espantós

**scarf** /skɑːf, skɑːɹf/ • *n* (*pl* scarves) bufanda *f*

**scarlet** /ˈskɑːlɪt, ˈskɑːlɪt/ • *n* escarlata

**scarves** *(pl)* ▷ SCARF

**scenario** /sɪˈnɑːɹiːəʊ, sɪˈnɛəɹioʊ/ • *n* escenari *m*

**scene** /siːn/ • *n* escena *f*

**scent** /sɛnt/ • *n* esència *f*; olfacte *m*

**sceptical** *(British)* ▷ SKEPTICAL

**schedule** /ˈʃɛd.juːl, ˈskɛ.dʒʊl/ • *n* horari *m*, programa *m*

**scholarship** /ˈskɒləʃɪp, ˈskɑːləɹʃɪp/ • *n* beca *f*

**school** /skul, skuːl/ • *n* banc *m*, mola de peix *f*; escola *f*

**scien|ce** /ˈsaɪəns/ • *n* ciència *f* **~tific** • *adj* cientific **~tist** • *n* científic *m* **~ce fiction** • *n* ciència-ficció *f*

**scissors** /ˈsɪzəz, ˈsɪzɚz/ • *n* tisores

**score** /skɔː, skɔɹ/ • *n* resultat *m*; partitura *f* • *v* marcar

**scorpion** /ˈskɔː.pi.ən, ˈskɔɹ.pi.ən/ • *n* escorpí *m*

**scramble** /ˈskɹæmbl̩/ • *v* remenar

**scratch** /skɹætʃ/ • *v* rascar, esgarrapar, gratar; arpejar

**scream** /ˈskɹiːm, skɹiːm/ • *v* xisclar, cridar

**screech** /skɹiːtʃ/ • *n* grinyol

**screen** /skɹiːn, skɹiːn/ • *n* pantalla *f*; xarxa *f*

**screw** /skɹuː/ • *n* bis *m*, cargol *m*; hèlice *f* • *v* collar; fotre, follar

S

**~driver** • *n* tornavís *m*, desengramponador

**script** /skɹıpt/ • *n* guió *m*

**scrutinize** /'skɹu:tınaız, 'skɹʌtn̩ˌaız/ • *v* escrutar

**sculpt|or** /skʌlptə/ • *n* escultor *m*, escultora *f* **~ure** • *n* escultura *f*

**sea** /si:/ • *n* mar *f* **~gull** • *n* gavina **~weed** • *n* algues ~ **level** • *n* nivell del mar *m* ~ **lion** • *n* lleó marí *m*

**seal** /si:l/ • *n* foca *f*; segell *m* • *v* segellar

**search** /sɜːtʃ, sɜtʃ/ • *v* inspeccionar, cercar; buscar

**season** /'si:zən, 'sizən/ • *n* estació *f*; temporada *f* • *v* condimentar, amanir **~al** • *adj* estacional

**seat** /si:t/ • *n* seient *m*; escó *m*; seu *f*

**second** /'sɛkənd, 'sɛk.(ə)nd/ • *adj* segon *m* • *n* segona *f*; segon *m*; moment *m*, instant *m* **~ary** • *adj* secundari *m*, secundària *f*

**secre|t** /'si:kɹɪt, 'si:kɹət/ • *adj* secret *m* **~tly** • *adv* secretament, cobertament, en secret **~cy** • *n* secretisme *m*

**section** /'sɛkʃən/ • *n* secció *f*

**sector** /'sɛk.tə/ • *n* sector *m*

**secular** /sɛk.jə.lə(ɹ)/ • *adj* secular, laic

**security** /sɪ'kjʊəɹəti, sə'kjɔɹ.ɪ.ti/ • *n* seguretat *f*

**see** /si:/ • *n* seu *f* • *v* (*sp* saw, *pp* seen) veure

**seed** /si:d/ • *n* llavor *f*

**seem** /si:m/ • *v* semblar, parèixer

**seen** (*pp*) ▷ SEE

**seiz|e** /si:z/ • *v* apoderar-se **~ure** • *n* apropiació *f*; atac *m*

**seldom** /'sɛldəm/ • *adv* rarament

**select** /sɪ'lɛkt/ • *v* seleccionar **~ion** • *n* selecció *f* **~ive** • *adj* selectiu

**self|ish** /'sɛlfɪʃ/ • *adj* egoista **~-esteem** • *n* autoestima *f*

**sell** /sɛl/ • *v* (*sp* sold, *pp* sold) vendre **~er** • *n* venedor *m*

**semantic** /sɪ'mæntɪk/ • *adj* semàntic **~s** • *n* semàntica *f*

**semester** /sɪ'mɛstə, sɪ'mɛstər/ • *n* semestre *m*

**senat|e** /'sɛnɪt/ • *n* senat *m* **~or** • *n* senador *m*, senadora *f*

**send** /sɛnd/ • *v* (*sp* sent, *pp* sent) enviar, trametre

**Senegal** • *n* Senegal *m*

**sensational** • *adj* sensacional **~ist** • *adj* sensacionalista

**sense** /sɛn(t)s, sɪn(t)s/ • *n* sentit *m*; sensació *f*; significat *m*, accepció *f* • *v* sentir

**sensible** /'sɛn.sə.bl̩, 'sɛn.sɪ.bl̩/ • *adj* sensat, assenyat

**sensitivity** • *n* sensibilitat *f*

**sent** (*sp/pp*) ▷ SEND

**sentence** /'sɛntəns/ • *n* sentència *f*; frase *f* • *v* sentenciar

**sentimental** • *adj* sentimental

**separat|e** /'sɛp(ə)ɹət, 'sɛpəɹeɪt/ • *adj* separat • *v* separar **~ion** • *n* separació *f*

**September** • *n* setembre *m*

**sequen|ce** /'sikwəns/ • *n* seqüència *f* **~tial** • *adj* seqüencial

**Serbia** ● *n* Sèrbia *f* **~n** ● *adj* serbi ● *n* serbi *m*, sèrbia *f*

**serene** ● *adj* serè

**series** /ˈsɪə.riːz, ˈsɪriz/ ● *n* (*pl* series) sèrie *f*

**serious** /ˈsɪəri.əs/ ● *adj* seriós **~ly** ● *adv* seriosament **~ness** ● *n* serietat *f*, gravetat *f*

**serv|e** /sɜːv, sɜv/ ● *n* servei *m* ● *v* servir **~ice** ● *n* servei *m* ● *v* servir

**session** /ˈsɛʃən/ ● *n* sessió *f*

**set** /sɛt/ ● *adj* preparat, llest; establert ● *n* set *m*; aparell *m*; joc *m*; conjunt; grup *m*; plató *m* ● *v* (*sp* set, *pp* set) determinar, establir, fixar; parar; introduir; assignar; pondre's; posar; ajustar **~ sb/sth up** ● *v* preparar, muntar

**settle|ment** /ˈset.l.mənt/ ● *n* assentament *m* **~r** ● *n* colon *m*

**seven** /ˈsɛv.ən/ ● *n* set *m* ● *num* set **~teen** ● *num* disset **~th** ● *adj* setè, sèptim ● *n* setè *m*, sèptim *m*; sèptima *f* **~ty** ● *num* setanta

**severely** ● *adv* severament

**sew** /səʊ, soʊ/ ● *v* (*sp* sewed, *pp* sewn) cosir

**sewed** (*sp/pp*) ▷ SEW

**sewn** (*pp*) ▷ SEW

**sex** /sɛks/ ● *n* sexe *m* ● *v* sexar **~ual** ● *adj* sexual **~ually** ● *adv* sexualment

**Seychelles** ● *n* Seychelles

**shade** /ʃeɪd/ ● *n* ombra *f*

**shadow** /ˈʃædoʊ, ˈʃædəʊ/ ● *n* ombra *f*

**shak|e** /ʃeɪk/ ● *n* sacseig *m* **~y** ● *adj* tremolós **~er** ● *n* sacsejador *m*

**shaken** (*pp*) ▷ SHAKE

**shallow** /ˈʃaləʊ, ˈʃæl.oʊ/ ● *adj* pla, poc profund, superficial

**shame** /ʃeɪm/ ● *n* vergonya *f*; llàstima *f* **~less** ● *adj* desvergonyit, pocavergonya

**shampoo** /ʃæmˈpuː, ʃamˈpuː/ ● *n* xampú *m*

**shape** /ʃeɪp/ ● *n* forma *f* ● *v* formar

**share** /ʃɛə, ʃɛɹ/ ● *n* escot *m*; acció *f* ● *v* compartir **~d** ● *adj* compartit **~holder** ● *n* accionista *f*, accionari *m*

**shark** /ʃɑːk, ʃɑːk/ ● *n* tauró *m*

**sharp** /ʃɑːp, ʃɑɹp/ ● *adj* esmolat, agut **~en** ● *v* esmolar

**shat** (*sp*) ▷ SHIT

**shatter** /ˈʃæt.ə(ɹ)/ ● *v* esmicolar-se; esmicolar

**shave** /ʃeɪv/ ● *v* afaitar, rapar; afaitar-se

**she** /ʃiː, ʃi/ ● *pron* ella

**shear** /ʃɪə(ɹ), ʃiɹ/ ● *v* (*sp* sheared, *pp* shorn) esquilar, tondosar; tondre

**sheared** (*sp/pp*) ▷ SHEAR

**shed** /ʃɛd/ ● *n* barraca *f*; carraca *f* ● *v* (*sp* shed, *pp* shed) separar; vessar

**sheep** /ʃip, ʃiːp/ ● *n* (*pl* sheep) ovella *f*

**sheet** /ʃiːt, ʃit/ ● *n* full *m*; escota *f* ● (*also*) ▷ BEDSHEET

**shelf** /ʃɛlf/ ● *n* (*pl* shelves) prestatge *m*, estant *m*, lleixa *f*

**shell** /ʃɛl/ • *n* consola *f*, terminal *m*; closca *f*, clovella *f*; buc *m*; conquilla *f*, conxa *f*

**shelter** /ˈʃɛltə, ˈʃɛltər/ • *n* aixopluc, recer • *v* aixoplugar

**shelves** *(pl)* ▷ SHELF

**sherry** • *n* xerès *m*

**shine** /ʃaɪn/ • *n* brillantor *f*, lluentor *f*, lluïssor *f* • *v* (*sp* shone, *pp* shone) brillar, lluir

**ship** /ʃɪp/ • *n* vaixell *m*, nau

**shirt** /ʃɜt, ʃɜːt/ • *n* camisa *f*

**shit** /ʃɪt/ • *adv* de merda • *interj* merda! • *n* merda; tifa *f*, excrement *m*, caca *f*, femta *f* • *v* (*sp* shit, *pp* shit) cagar; cagar-se

**shitted** *(sp/pp)* ▷ SHIT

**shiver** /ˈʃɪvəɪ, ˈʃɪvə/ • *n* calfred *m*

**shock** /ʃɒk, ʃɑk/ • *n* xoc *m* • *v* xocar

**shod** *(sp/pp)* ▷ SHOE

**shoe** /ʃuː, ʃu/ • *n* sabata *f*, calçat *m* • *v* (*sp* shod, *pp* shod) calçar; ferrar

**shoed** *(sp/pp)* ▷ SHOE

**shone** *(sp)* ▷ SHINE

**shook** *(sp)* ▷ SHAKE

**shoot** /ʃuːt/ • *v* (*sp* shot, *pp* shot) disparar **~ing** • *n* tiroteig *m*, afusellament *m*

**shop** /ʃɒp, ʃɑp/ • *n* botiga *f*, tenda *f*

**shore** /ʃɔː, ʃɔɪ/ • *n* riba *f*, vorera *f*, vora *f*

**shorn** *(pp)* ▷ SHEAR

**short** /ʃɔːt, ʃɔɪt/ • *adj* curt; baix **~ly** • *adv* aviat, en breu; breument; bruscament **in ~** • *phr* en resum

**shot** /ʃɒt, ʃɑt/ • *n* tret *m*; cop *m*, llançament *m* • *(also)* ▷ SHOOT

**shoulder** /ˈʃəʊldə, ˈʃoʊldər/ • *n* espatlla *f*, espatla *f*; muscle *m*; voral *m*, vorera d'emergència *f*

**shout** /ʃaʊt, ʃʌʊt/ • *v* cridar

**shove** /ʃʌv/ • *n* empenta *f* • *v* empentar, empentejar, espitjar, empènyer

**show** /ʃəʊ, ʃoʊ/ • *n* espectacle *m* • *v* (*sp* showed, *pp* shown) mostrar, ensenyar; demostrar

**showed** *(sp/pp)* ▷ SHOW

**shower** /ˈʃaʊ.ə(ɪ), ˈʃaʊ.ər/ • *n* dutxa *f* • *v* dutxar-se

**shown** *(pp)* ▷ SHOW

**shrank** *(sp)* ▷ SHRINK

**shred** /ʃɪɛd/ • *v* (*sp* shred, *pp* shred) trocejar, tallar, triturar, trinxar

**shredded** *(sp/pp)* ▷ SHRED

**shrewd** /ʃɪuːd/ • *adj* astut

**shrimp** /ʃɪɪmp/ • *n* (*pl* shrimp) gamba *f*

**shrink** /ʃɪɪŋk/ • *v* (*sp* shrank, *pp* shrunk) encongir-se; encongir

**shrug** /ʃɪʌg/ • *n* encongiment d'espatlles *m* • *v* arronsar les espatlles

**shrunk** *(sp/pp)* ▷ SHRINK

**shy** /ʃaɪ/ • *adj* vergonyós

**sibling** /ˈsɪblɪŋ/ • *n* germà *m*, germana *f*

**side** /saɪd/ • *n* costat *m* **~walk** • *n* vorera *f*

**sigh** /saɪ/ • *n* sospir *m* • *v* sospirar

**sign** /saɪn/ • *n* senyal

**signal** /ˈsɪgnəl/ • *n* senyal *m*

**signature** /'sɪgnətʃə, 'sɪgnətʃɚ/ • *n* signatura *f*; quadern *m*

**significan|t** /sɪg'nɪ.fɪ.kənt, sɪg'nɪ.fɪ.gənt/ • *adj* significatiu **~ce** • *n* significat *m* **~tly** • *adv* significativament

**silen|t** /'saɪlənt/ • *adj* callar **~tly** • *adv* silenciosament **~ce** • *n* silenci *m*

**silk** /sɪlk/ • *n* seda *f* **~y** • *adj* sedós

**silly** /'sɪli/ • *adj* ximple, ximplet, fava

**silver** /'sɪl.və, 'sɪl.vɚ/ • *adj* platejat, argentat • *n* plata *f*, argent *m*

**similar** /'sɪmələ, 'sɪmələɚ/ • *adj* similar, semblant **~ity** • *n* semblança *f*, similitud *f* **~ly** • *adv* semblantment

**simpl|e** /'sɪmpəl/ • *adj* simple, senzill **~y** • *adv* simplement, senzillament **~icity** • *n* simplicitat *f* **~ify** • *v* simplificar **~ification** • *n* simplificació *f*

**simulat|e** /'sɪmjʊ.leɪt/ • *v* simular **~ion** • *n* simulació *f*; fingiment *m*, teatre *m*, comèdia *f*

**simultaneous** /sɪm.əl'teɪn.i.əs, saɪm.əl'teɪn.i.əs/ • *adj* simultani **~ly** • *adv* simultàniament

**sin** /sɪn/ • *n* pecat *m* • *v* pecar **~ful** • *adj* pecaminós **~ner** • *n* pecador *m*

**since** /sɪn(t)s/ • *conj* des que, des de que; ja que, com que • *prep* des de

**sincer|e** /sɪn'sɪə(ɹ)/ • *adj* sincer **~ely** • *adv* sincerament **~ity** • *n* sinceritat *f*

**sing** /sɪŋ/ • *v* (*sp* sang, *pp* sung) cantar **~er** • *n* cantant *m*, cantor *m*, cantaire *m*

**Singapore** • *n* Singapur

**single** /'sɪŋgl/ • *adj* simple; escàpol • *n* single *m*; batada d'una base *f*

**sink** /sɪŋk/ • *n* pica *f*, lavabo *m*; desaigua *m* • *v* (*sp* sank, *pp* sunk) enfonsar; submergir-se

**sister** /'sɪs.tə, 'sɪs.tɚ/ • *n* germana *f*; sor *f*; infermera *f* **~-in-law** • *n* cunyada *f*

**sit** /sɪt/ • *v* (*sp* sat, *pp* sat) seure; asseure's

**situated** /'sɪtʃueɪtɪd/ • *adj* situat

**six** /sɪks/ • *n* sis *m* • *num* sis; sisena *f* **~teen** • *num* setze **~th** • *adj* sisè, sext • *n* sisè *m*, sext *m*; sexta *f* **~ty** • *num* seixanta

**size** /saɪz/ • *n* mida *f*

**sizzle** /'sɪzəl/ • *v* espurnejar

**skateboard** • *n* monopatí *m*

**skeleton** /'skɛlətən/ • *n* esquelet *m*; estructura *f*

**skeptical** /'skɛptɪkəl/ • *adj* escèptic

**sketch** /skɛtʃ/ • *n* esbós *m*, esbossos; esborrany *m*; esquetx *m*

**ski** /ski:, ʃi:/ • *n* esquí • *v* esquiar **~ing** • *n* esquí *m*

**skill** /skɪl/ • *n* habilitat *f* **~ful** • *adj* hàbil *f*

**skin** /skɪn/ • *n* pell *f* • *v* escorxar **~ny** • *adj* magre

**skirt** /skɜːt, skɝt/ • *n* faldilla *f*

S

**skull** /skʌl/ • *n* crani *m*

**skunk** /skʌŋk/ • *n* mofeta *f*

**sky** /skaɪ/ • *n* cel *m* **~light** • *n* claraboia, lluerna **~scraper** • *n* gratacel *m*

**slam** /slæm/ • *n* esmaixada *f* • *v* tancar de cop; esmaixar

**slap** • *n* bufetada *f*

**slave** /sleɪv/ • *n* esclau *m*, esclava *f* **~ry** • *n* esclavitud *f*, esclavatge *m*

**sleep** /sliːp, slip/ • *n* son *m*; lleganya *f*, llaganya *f* • *v* (*sp* slept, *pp* slept) dormir **~ over** • *v* pernitar **~y** • *adj* somnolent

**sleeve** /sliːv/ • *n* màniga *f*, mànega *f*

**slept** *(sp/pp)* ▷ SLEEP

**slice** /slaɪs/ • *n* llesca *f*

**slid** *(sp/pp)* ▷ SLIDE

**slide** /slaɪd/ • *n* tobogan *m*; diapositiva *f* • *v* (*sp* slid, *pp* slid) lliscar

**slight** /slaɪt/ • *adj* feble, dèbil **~ly** • *adv* lleugerament

**slip** /slɪp/ • *n* engalba *f*; papereta *f*; relliscada *f*; combinació *f* **~pery** • *adj* lliscant

**slipper** • *n* plantofa *f*, sabatilla *f*

**slogan** /ˈsloʊɡən, ˈsloʊɡ(ə)n/ • *n* eslògan *m*

**slot** /slɒt/ • *n* màquina escurabutxaques *f*

**sloth** /slaʊθ, slɔθ/ • *n* accídia *f*, peresa *f*, mandra *f*; peresós *m*

**Slovakia** • *n* Eslovàquia *f*

**Slovenia** • *n* Eslovènia *f*

**slow** /slaʊ, sloʊ/ • *adj* lent **~ly** • *adv* lentament

**small** /smɔːl, smɔl/ • *adj* petit

**smash** /smæʃ/ • *n* esmaixada *f*

**smell** /smɛl/ • *n* olor *f*, flaire *f*; olfacte *m* • *v* (*sp* smelt, *pp* smelt) olorar, odorar, ensumar, flairar; fer olor a

**smelled** *(sp/pp)* ▷ SMELL

**smelly** /ˈsmɛli/ • *adj* pudent

**smelt** *(sp/pp)* ▷ SMELL

**smil|e** /smaɪl/ • *n* somrís *m*, somriure *m* • *v* somriure **~ing** • *adj* somrient

**smoke** /smoʊk, smʊk/ • *n* fum *m* • *v* fumar; fumejar

**smooth** /smuːð/ • *adj* llis • *v* allisar **~ly** • *adv* suaument

**snail** /sneɪl/ • *n* caragol *m*

**snake** /ˈsneɪk/ • *n* serp *f*, serpent *f*

**snap** /snæp/ • *n* esnap *m*

**sneaker** /ˈsnikər/ • *n* vamba *f*, ked *f*, sabatilla

**snow** /snaʊ, snoʊ/ • *n* neu *f* • *v* nevar **~man** • *n* ninot de neu

**so** /saʊ, soʊ/ • *adj* això, açò • *adv* tan; així • *conj* perquè; així que • *interj* així, doncs

**soak** /saʊk, soʊk/ • *v* amarar; penetrar

**soap** /soʊp, saʊp/ • *n* sabó *m* **~ opera** • *n* culebrot *m*, telenovel·la *f*, fulletó *m*

**soccer** /ˈsɒk.ə, ˈsɑk.ər/ • *n* futbol *m*

**socia|l** /ˈsaʊʃəl, ˈsoʊ.ʃəl/ • *adj* social **~lly** • *adv* socialment **~ble** • *adj* sociable **~list** • *adj* socialista • *n* socialista *f* **~lism** • *n* socialisme *m*

**society** /səˈsaɪ.ə.ti/ • *n* societat *f*

**sock** /sɑk, sɒk/ • *n* mitjó *m*

**sodium** /'səʊdɪəm, 'soʊdi.əm/ • *n* sodi *m*

**sofa** /'soʊfə, 'səʊfə/ • *n* sofà *m*

**soft** /sɒft, sɑft/ • *adj* tou; suau; dolç, lleuger **~en** • *v* estovar, ablanir **~ly** • *adv* suaument

**software** /'sɒft,weə, 'sɒft,weɪ/ • *n* programari *m*

**soil** /sɔɪl/ • *n* sòl *m*

**solar** /'soʊlə, 'səʊlə/ • *adj* solar

**sold** *(sp/pp)* ▷ SELL

**soldier** /'səʊldʒə, 'soʊldʒə/ • *n* soldat

**sole** /səʊl, soʊl/ • *adj* sol; solter • *n* planta del peu *f*; sola *f*

**solid** /'sɑlɪd, 'sɒlɪd/ • *adj* sòlid • *n* sòlid *m*

**solidarity** • *n* solidaritat *f*

**sol|ve** /sɒlv, sɑlv/ • *v* resoldre, solucionar **~ution** • *n* solució *f*

**Somali|a** • *n* Somàlia *f* **~** • *adj* somali • *n* somali *m*

**some|body** /'sʌmbədɪ, 'sʌmbʌdi/ • *pron* algú **~one** • *pron* algú, qualcú **~thing** • *pron* alguna cosa, quelcom **~times** • *adv* a vegades, de vegades

**son** /sʌn/ • *n* fill *m* **~-in-law** • *n* gendre *m*

**song** /sɒŋ, sɔŋ/ • *n* cançó *f*

**soon** /suːn/ • *adv* aviat

**sophisticated** • *adj* sofisticat

**sore** /sɔː, sɔɪ/ • *adj* adolorit

**sorry** /'sɔɪi, 'sɒɪi/ • *adj* afligit, perdona; llastimós • *interj* perdó, disculpes

**sort** /sɔːt, sɔɪt/ • *n* tipus *m*, gènere *m*, classe *f*, varietat *f*, mena *f* • *v* classificar; ordenar; arreglar, reparar

**soul** /səʊl, soʊl/ • *n* ànima *f*

**sound** /saʊnd/ • *adj* sa; sòlid • *n* so • *v* sonar **~track** • *n* banda sonora *f*

**soup** /suːp, sup/ • *n* sopa *f*

**sour** /'saʊ(ə)ɪ, 'saʊə/ • *adj* àcid; agre

**source** /sɔɪs, sɔːs/ • *n* font *f*

**south** /saʊθ, sʌʊθ/ • *n* sud *m*, migdia *m*, migjorn *m* **~ern** • *adj* austral, meridional **~west** • *n* sud-oest *m* **~east** • *n* sud-est *m*

**South Africa** • *n* Sud-àfrica *f*, Àfrica del Sud *f*

**South Sudan** • *n* Sudan del Sud *m*

**souvenir** /ˌsuːvəˈnɪə(ɪ)/ • *n* record *m*

**sovereign** /'sɒv.ɪɪn/ • *adj* sobirà • *n* sobirà *m* **~ty** • *n* sobirania *f*

**Soviet** /'səʊ.vi.ət, 'soʊ.vi.ət/ • *adj* soviètic • *n* soviet *m*

**sow** /saʊ/ • *n* truja *f*, porca *f*, verra *f* • *v* *(sp* sowed, *pp* sown) sembrar

**sowed** *(sp/pp)* ▷ SOW

**sown** *(pp)* ▷ SOW

**soy** /sɔɪ/ • *n* soia *f*, soja *f*

**spade** /speɪd/ • *n* pala *f*

**spaghetti** /spəˈɡeti/ • *n* espagueti *m*; laberint *m*

**Spa|in** • *n* Espanya *f* **~nish** • *adj* espanyol; castellà • *n* castellà espanyol

**spam** /spæm/ • *n* correu brossa *m*

**span** /spæn, spæːn/ • *n* pam *m*; període

**spark** /spɑːk, spɑːk/ • *n* espurna *f*, guspira *f*; centella *f* • *v* espurnejar, guspirejar

**sparrow** /ˈspærəʊ, ˈspærəʊ/ • *n* pardal *m*

**spat** *(sp/pp)* ▷ SPIT

**speak** /spiːk, spik/ • *v* (*sp* spoke, *pp* spoken) parlar **~er** • *n* parlant *f*; altaveu *m*

**special** /ˈspeʃəl/ • *adj* especial **~ly** • *adv* especialment **~ty** • *n* especialitat *f* **~ist** • *n* especialista *f*

**species** /ˈspiːʃiːz/ • *n* (*pl* species) espècie *f*

**specif|y** /ˈspesɪfaɪ/ • *v* especificar **~ic** • *adj* específic *m* **~ically** • *adv* específicament **~ication** • *n* especificació *f*

**specimen** /ˈspesɪmɪn/ • *n* espècimen *m*

**specta|cle** /ˈspektəkl/ • *n* espectacle *m* **~cular** • *adj* espectacular **~tor** • *n* espectador *m* **~cles** • *n* ulleres

**spectrum** /ˈspektrəm, ˈspekt(ʃ)rəm/ • *n* espectre *m*

**speculation** • *n* especulació *f*

**sped** *(sp/pp)* ▷ SPEED

**speech** /spiːtʃ/ • *n* parla *f*; discurs *m* **~less** • *adj* bocabadat, emmudit

**speed** /spiːd/ • *n* rapidesa *f*, velocitat *f* **~y** • *adj* ràpid *m*, veloç *m*

**speeded** *(sp/pp)* ▷ SPEED

**spell** /spel/ • *n* encís *m*, conjur *m*, embruixament *m*, encantament *m* • *v* (*sp* spelt, *pp* spelt) lletrejar **~ing** • *n* ortografia *f*

**spelled** *(sp/pp)* ▷ SPELL

**spelt** *(sp/pp)* ▷ SPELL

**spend** /spend/ • *v* (*sp* spent, *pp* spent) gastar; passar

**spent** *(sp/pp)* ▷ SPEND

**spher|e** /sfɪə, sfɪɪ/ • *n* esfera *f* **~ical** • *adj* esfèric

**spicy** • *adj* picant

**spider** /ˈspaɪdə, ˈspaɪdə/ • *n* aranya *f*

**spill** /spɪl/ • *v* (*sp* spilt, *pp* spilt) vessar

**spilled** *(sp/pp)* ▷ SPILL

**spilt** *(sp/pp)* ▷ SPILL

**spin** /spɪn/ • *n* espín *m*; efecte *m*

**spinach** /ˈspɪnɪtʃ/ • *n* espinac *m*

**spine** /spaɪn/ • *n* espinada *f*, raquis *m*; llom *m*; espina *f*

**spirit** /ˈspɪrɪt, ˈspɪrɪt/ • *n* esperit *m* **~ual** • *adj* espiritual

**spit** /spɪt/ • *v* (*sp* spat, *pp* spat) escopir

**spite** /spaɪt/ • *n* despit *m*

**spleen** /spliːn/ • *n* melsa *f*

**splendid** /ˈsplendɪd/ • *adj* esplèndid

**split** /splɪt/ • *n* banyes • *v* (*sp* split, *pp* split) partir, dividir, escindir; repartir; separar

**spoil** /spɔɪl/ • *v* (*sp* spoilt, *pp* spoilt) espoliar; espatllar, fer malbé **~er** • *n* filtració *f*

**spoiled** *(sp/pp)* ▷ SPOIL

**spoilt** *(sp/pp)* ▷ SPOIL

**spoke** *(sp)* ▷ SPEAK

**spokesperson** • *n* portaveu *m*

**sponge** /spʌndʒ/ • *n* esponja *f* • *v* esponjar

**spontane|ously** /spɒnˈteɪ.ni.əs.li, spɑnˈteɪ.ni.əs.li/ • *adv* espontàniament **~ity** • *n* espontaneïtat *f*

**spoon** /spuːn, spun/ • *n* cullera *f* **~ful** • *n* cullerada *f*

**sport** /spɔːt, spɔːt/ • *n* esport *m*, deport *m* **~ing** • *adj* esportiu

**spot** /spɒt, spɑt/ • *n* taca *f* **~light** • *n* focus *m*

**spouse** /spaʊs/ • *n* cònjuge, espòs *m*, esposa *f*

**sprang** *(sp)* ▷ SPRING

**spring** /sprɪŋ/ • *n* primavera *f*; font; molla *f*, ressort *m*

**sprinkle** /'sprɪŋkəl/ • *v* ruixar, arruixar

**sprung** *(pp)* ▷ SPRING

**spun** *(sp/pp)* ▷ SPIN

**spy** /spaɪ/ • *n* espia *f* • *v* espiar

**square** /skweə(ɹ), skwɛɹ/ • *adj* quadrat • *n* quadrat *m*; plaça *f* • *v* arreglar, escairar; elevar al quadrat

**squash** /skwɒʃ, skwɔʃ/ • *n* esquaix *m*

**squeeze** /skwiːz/ • *v* esprémer, estrènyer, serrar, apretar

**squid** /skwɪd/ • *n* (*pl* squid) calamars *m*, calamar *m*

**squirrel** /'skwɪɹl, 'skwɜl/ • *n* esquirol *m*

**Sri Lanka** • *n* Sri Lanka *f* **~n** • *adj* singalès • *n* singalès *m*

**stab** /stæb/ • *n* punyalada, ganivetada • *v* apunyalar, acoltellar

**stab|le** /'steɪ.bəl/ • *adj* estable • *n* estable *m* **~ility** • *n* estabilitat *f* **~ilize** • *v* estabilitzar

**stadium** /'steɪ.di.əm/ • *n* estadi *m*

**staff** /stɑːf, 'stæf/ • *n* bastó *m*; pentagrama *m*; staff *m*, plantilla *f*

**stage** /steɪdʒ/ • *n* pas, estadi, fase, etapa *f*; escena *f*, escenari *m*

**stain** /steɪn/ • *n* taca **~less steel** • *n* acer inoxidable *m*

**staircase** /'stɛɹ.keɪs/ • *n* escala *f*

**stake** /steɪk/ • *n* pal *m*, estaca *f* **at ~** • *phr* en joc

**stall** /stɔːl, stɔl/ • *n* estable *m* • *v* engreixar

**stamp** /stæmp/ • *n* segell *m* • *v* estampar; segellar

**stand** /stænd, æ/ • *v* (*sp* stood, *pp* stood) estar dret; posar-se dret; suportar

**standard** /'stændəd, 'stændəɹd/ • *adj* estàndard; estendard

**staple** /'steɪ.pəl/ • *n* grapa *f* • *v* engrapar, grapar **~r** • *n* engrapadora *f*

**star** /stɑː(ɹ), stɑɹ/ • *n* estrella *f*, estel *m* **~fish** • *n* estrella de mar *f*

**stare** /stɛəɹ, stɛə(ɹ)/ • *v* mirar fixament

**stark** /stɑːk, stɑːk/ • *adj* aspre

**start** /stɑːt, stɑɹt/ • *v* començar; engegar

**state** /steɪt/ • *n* estat *m* • *v* declarar

**station** /'steɪʃən/ • *n* estació *f* • *v* apostar **~ary** • *adj* estacionari; immòbil

**statistics** /stə'tɪstɪks/ • *n* estadística *f*

**statue** /'stæ.tʃuː/ • *n* estàtua *f*

**statute** /'stætʃuːt/ • *n* estatut *m*; estatuts

**stay** /steɪ/ ● *v* quedar-se, restar

**steal** /stiːl/ ● *n* robatori *m* ● *v* (*sp* stole, *pp* stolen) robar

**steam** /stiːm/ ● *n* vapor *m*

**steel** /stiːl/ ● *n* acer *m*

**steep** /stiːp/ ● *adj* escarpat, rost

**steer** /stɪə(ɹ)/ ● *v* guiar; dirigir; manejar, dur; castrar, capar **~ing wheel** ● *n* volant

**stem** /stem/ ● *n* tall *m*; arrel *f*; roda *f*

**step** /step/ ● *n* pas *m*, passa *f*; esglaó *m*; petjada *f*

**stereotyp|e** /ˈsteˌɹɪəˌtaɪp/ ● *n* estereotip *m* **~ical** ● *adj* estereotípic

**stern** /stɜn, stɜːn/ ● *adj* sever ● *n* popa *f*

**stick** /stɪk/ ● *n* garrot *m*, bastó *m*; barra *f*; estic *m* ● *v* (*sp* stuck, *pp* stuck) enganxar, apegar **~y** ● *adj* enganxós, apegalós

**stiff** /stɪf/ ● *adj* rígid; encarcarat **~ness** ● *n* cruiximent *m*

**still** /stɪl/ ● *adj* quiet ● *adv* encara **~ness** ● *n* calma *f*

**stimula|te** /ˈstɪmjʊleɪt/ ● *v* estimular **~nt** ● *n* estimulant *m*; estimulador *m* **~tion** ● *n* estimulació *f*

**stimulating** ● *adj* estimulant

**sting** /stɪŋ/ ● *n* fiblada *f*, picada *f* ● *v* (*sp* stung, *pp* stung) picar, fiblar **~er** ● *n* fibló *m*, agulló *m*

**stingy** /ˈstɪndʒi/ ● *adj* garrepa, aferrat

**stir** /stɜː, stɜ́/ ● *n* avalot *m*, gatzara *f*, cridòria, esvalot *m*,

aldarull *m*, rebombori *m* ● *v* remoure

**stitch** /stɪtʃ/ ● *n* punt *m*

**stock** /stɒk, stɑk/ ● *n* estirp *f*

**Stockholm** ● *n* Estocolm

**stoic** ● *adj* estoic ● *n* estoic *m*; estoica *f*

**stole** (*sp*) ▷ STEAL

**stolen** (*pp*) ▷ STEAL

**stomach** /ˈstʌmək/ ● *n* estómac *m*; panxa *f*

**stone** /stəʊn, stoʊn/ ● *adj* petri, pedrenc ● *n* pedra *f*, roca *f* ● *v* apedregar **~d** ● *adj* col·locat

**stood** (*sp/pp*) ▷ STAND

**stool** /stuːl/ ● *n* tamboret *m*

**stop** /stɒp, stɑp/ ● *n* parada *f*; punt *m* ● *v* parar, aturar; deixar

**stor|e** /stɔɹ, stɔː/ ● *v* emmagatzemar **~age** ● *n* emmagatzematge

**stork** /stɔɹk, stɔːk/ ● *n* cigonya

**storm** /stɔːm, stɔɹm/ ● *n* tempesta *f*, temporal *m*, tempestat *f* **~y** ● *adj* tempestuós

**story** /ˈstɔːˌɹi/ ● *n* història *f*, relat *m*

**stove** /stəʊv, stoʊv/ ● *n* estufa *f*; cuina *f*

**straight** /stɹeɪt/ ● *n* escala *f* **~en** ● *v* adreçar, redreçar

**strain** /stɹeɪn/ ● *v* colar

**strand** /stɹænd/ ● *n* platja *f*; floc *m*

**strange** /ˈstɹeɪndʒ/ ● *adj* estrany **~r** ● *n* desconegut *m*; foraster *m*, forastera *f*, estranger *m*, estrangera *f*

S

**strateg|y** /ˈstɹætədʒi/ • *n*
estratègia *f* **~ic** • *adj*
estratègic

**straw** /stɹɔː, stɹɔ/ • *n* palla *f*

**strawberry** /ˈstɹɔːb(ə)ɹi, ˈstɹɔˌbɛɹi/
• *n* maduixa *f*, fraula *f*;
maduixer *m*, maduixera *f*

**stream** /stɹiːm/ • *n* corrent,
rierol

**street** /stɹiːt, ʃtɹiːt/ • *n* carrer *m*

**strength** /stɹɛŋ(k)θ, stɹɪŋ(k)θ/ • *n*
força *f*; fort *m* **~en** • *v* enfortir

**stress** /stɹɛs/ • *n* tensió *f*; estrès
*m*; accent *m*; èmfasi *m* • *v*
estressar; emfasitzar **~ful** •
*adj* estressant

**stretch** /stɹɛtʃ/ • *v* estirar

**strict** /stɹɪkt/ • *adj* estricte

**strike** /stɹaɪk/ • *n* ple *m*; vaga *f*

**string** /stɹɪŋ/ • *n* corda *f*, cordill,
cordell *m*; seguit *m*, reguitzell
*m* • *v* (*sp* strung, *pp* strung)
enfilar

**striped** /stɹaɪpt/ • *adj* ratllat,
llistat

**stroke** /stɹəʊk, stɹoʊk/ • *n* carícia
*f*; cop *m*

**strong** /stɹɒŋ, ʃtɹɒŋ/ • *adj* fort •
*adv* fort **~ly** • *adv* fort

**struck** (*sp/pp*) ▷ STRIKE

**structur|e** /ˈstɹʌktʃə(ɹ), ˈstɹʌktʃɚ/
• *n* estructura *f* • *v*
estructurar **~al** • *adj*
estructural

**struggle** /ˈstɹʌɡl̩/ • *n* lluita *f*

**strung** (*sp/pp*) ▷ STRING

**stuck** (*sp/pp*) ▷ STICK

**student** /ˈstjuːdənt, ˈstuˌdn̩t/ • *n*
estudiant *f*; alumne *m*;
universitari *m*

**studio** /ˈstuːdioʊ/ • *n* estudi *m*

**study** /ˈstʌdi/ • *n* estudi *m* • *v*
estudiar

**stuff** /stʌf/ • *v* dissecar

**stumble** /ˈstʌmbəl/ • *n*
ensopegada *f* • *v* ensopegar

**stun** /stʌn/ • *v* atordir,
entebenar

**stung** (*sp/pp*) ▷ STING

**stupid** /ˈstjuːpɪd, ˈst(j)upɪd/ • *adj*
toix *m*, estúpid *m*, bèstia *f* **~ly**
• *adv* estúpidament

**sturdy** /ˈstɜː.di/ • *adj* robust

**style** /staɪl/ • *n* estil *m*

**subject** /ˈsʌb.dʒɛkt, ˈsʌb.dʒɪkt/ •
*adj* subjecte • *n* subjecte *m*;
matèria *f*; assignatura *f*;
súbdit *m* • *v* sotmetre **~ive** •
*adj* subjectiu **~ively** • *adv*
subjectivament

**submi|t** /səbˈmɪt/ • *v* sotmetre's;
sotmetre, presentar **~ssion** •
*n* submissió *f*

**subscri|be** /səbˈskɹaɪb/ • *v*
subscriure's **~ber** • *n*
subscriptor *m*, subscriptora *f*
**~ption** • *n* abonament *m*

**subsequent** /ˈsʌbsɪkwənt/ • *adj*
subsegüent **~ly** • *adv*
subseqüentment

**subsid|y** /ˈsʌbsidi/ • *n* subsidi *m*,
subvenció *m* **~iary** • *n* filial *f*

**substance** /ˈsʌbstəns/ • *n*
substància *f*

**substitute** /ˈsʌbstɪtuːt/ • *n*
substitut *m* • *v* substituir;
canviar

**subtitle** /ˈsʌbtaɪtəl/ • *n* subtítol
*m*, subtítols

**subtle** /ˈsʌt(ə)l/ • *adj* subtil **~ty** •
*n* subtilesa *f*

**suburb** /'sʌbɜː(ː)b/ • *n* suburbi *m*, rodalies *f* **~an** • *adj* suburbà

**succeed** /sək'siːd/ • *v* succeir; reeixir; seguir

**success** /sək'sɛs/ • *n* èxit *m*, succés *m* **~ful** • *adj* exitós

**successive** • *adj* successiu

**succinct** /sə(k)'sɪŋkt, sək'sɪŋ(k)t/ • *adj* succint

**such** /sʌʧ/ • *det* tal *m*

**suck** /sʌk, sʊk/ • *v* xuclar

**Sudan** • *n* Sudan *m* **~ese** • *adj* sudanès *m*

**sudden** /'sʌdn̩/ • *adj* sobtat **~ly** • *adv* de sobte, sobtadament, tot d'una **all of a ~** • *adv* de cop, en sec, de sobte, de bursada, d'improvis, tot d'una

**suffer** /'sʌfə, 'sʌfər/ • *v* sofrir, patir; empitjorar **~ing** • *n* patiment *m*

**sufficient** /sə'fɪʃənt/ • *adj* suficient **~ly** • *adv* suficientment

**suffix** /'sʌfɪks/ • *n* sufix *m*

**sugar** /'ʃʊgə(ɪ), 'ʃʊgər/ • *n* sucre *m*; ploma *f*

**suggest** /sə'dʒɛst, səg'dʒɛst/ • *v* suggerir **~ion** • *n* suggeriment *m*; suggestió *f*

**suicide** /'s(j)uːɪˌsaɪd, 's(j)uːɪˌsaɪd/ • *n* suïcidi *m*; suïcida *f*

**suit** /s(j)uːt, s(j)uːt/ • *n* vestit *m* • *v* escaure; convenir

**suitable** /'suːtəbl/ • *adj* apropiat

**sum** /sʌm/ • *n* suma *f*

**summary** /'sʌmərɪ/ • *adj* sumari • *n* resum *m*, sumari *m* **~ize** • *v* resumir; recapitular **in ~y** • *phr* en resum

**summer** /'sʌmə(ɪ), 'sʌmər/ • *n* estiu *m* • *v* estiuejar

**summit** /'sʌmɪt/ • *n* cim *m*; cimera *f*

**summon** /'sʌmən/ • *v* cridar; citar

**sun** /sʌn/ • *n* sol *m* • *n* sol *m* **~ny** • *adj* asolellat; radiant **~glasses** • *n* ulleres de sol

**Sunday** • *n* diumenge *m*

**sung** *(pp)* ▷ SING

**sunk** *(pp)* ▷ SINK

**superb** /suː'pɜːb, sjuː'pɜːb/ • *adj* soberg

**superficial** • *adj* superficial **~ly** • *adv* superficialment **~ity** • *n* superficialitat *f*

**superior** /suː'pɪərɪə(ɪ), suː'pɪːrɪər/ • *adj* superior **~ity** • *n* superioritat *f*

**supermarket** /ˌsuːpəˈmɑːkɪt/ • *n* supermercat *m*

**supernatural** /ˌsuːpəˈnatʃrəl, ˌsuːpəˈnætʃərəl/ • *adj* sobrenatural

**supervise** • *v* supervisar **~or** • *n* supervisor *m*

**supply** /sə'plaɪ/ • *v* fornir, subministrar, proveir; equipar **~ement** • *v* suplementar, complementar

**support** /sə'pɔːt, sə'pɔːrt/ • *v* sostenir; recolzar

**suppose** /sə'pəʊz, sə'poʊz/ • *v* suposar **~d** • *adj* suposat **~dly** • *adv* suposadament

**supreme** /ˌs(j)uː'priːm/ • *adj* suprem **~acy** • *n* supremacia *f*

**sure** /ʃɔː, ʃʊəɪ/ • *adj* segur **~ly** • *adv* segurament **for ~** • *phr* amb tota seguretat

**surf** /sɜːf, sɜf/ • *v* navegar **~ing** •
*n* surf *m*
**surface** /'sɜːfɪs, 'sɜːfɪs/ • *n*
superfície *f*
**surg|ery** /'sɜːdʒəɹi, 'sɜːdʒəɹi/ • *n*
cirurgia *f*, operació *f*;
quiròfan *m* **~eon** • *n* cirurgià,
cirurgiana *f* **~ical** • *adj*
quirúrgic
**Suriname** • *n* Surinam
**surly** /'sɜːli/ • *adj* malcarat,
sorrut
**surplus** /'sɜːplʌs, 'sɜːpləs/ • *n*
superàvit *m*
**surpris|e** /səˈpɹaɪz, səˈpɹaɪz/ • *n*
sorpresa *f* • *v* sorprendre
**~ing** • *adj* sorprenent **~ingly** •
*adv* sorprenentment
**surround** /səˈɹaʊnd/ • *v*
circumdar, rodejar, envoltar,
voltar **~ing** • *adj* circumdant
**surveillance** /səɹˈveɪ.ləns/ • *n*
vigilància *f*
**survey** /'sɜːveɪ, 'sɜveɪ/ • *n*
enquesta *f*; enquestar
**surviv|e** /səˈvaɪv, səˈvaɪv/ • *v*
sobreviure **~al** • *n*
supervivència *f* **~or** • *n*
supervivent *f*
**susp|ect** /'sʌs.pɛkt, səsˈpɛkt/ • *adj*
sospitós • *v* sospitar **~icious** •
*adj* sospitós; suspicaç **~icion** •
*n* sospita *f*
**sustain** /səˈsteɪn/ • *v* sostenir
**~able** • *adj* sostenible **~ability**
• *n* sostenibilitat *f*
**swallow** /'swɒl.əʊ, 'swɑ.loʊ/ • *n*
engoliment; oreneta *f* • *v*
engolir, enviar
**swam** *(sp)* ▷ SWIM
**swan** /swɒn, swɑn/ • *n* cigne *m*

**Swaziland** • *n* Swazilàndia *f*
**swear** /'swɛə, 'swɛə/ • *v (sp*
swore, *pp* sworn) jurar
**sweat** /swɛt/ • *n* suor *f* • *v (sp*
sweat, *pp* sweat) suar
**sweated** *(sp/pp)* ▷ SWEAT
**sweater** /'swɛtə, 'swɛtə/ • *n*
dessuadora *f*; suèter *m*
**Swed|en** • *n* Suècia *f* **~ish** • *adj*
suec • *n* suec *m*
**sweep** /swiːp/ • *v (sp* swept, *pp*
swept) escombrar
**sweet** /swiːt, swit/ • *adj* dolç;
ensucrat *m* • *adv* dolçament •
*n* dolç *m*, llaminadura *f* **~ corn**
• *n* blat de moro dolç *m* **~**
**potato** • *n* batata *f*,
moniatera; moniato *m* **~en** • *v*
endolcir **~ener** • *n* edulcorant
*m* **~ly** • *adv* dolçament
**swell** /swɛl/ • *adj* excel·lent *f* •
*v (sp* swelled, *pp* swollen)
inflar-se, rebotir, unflar-se
**swelled** *(sp/pp)* ▷ SWELL
**swept** *(sp/pp)* ▷ SWEEP
**swift** /swɪft/ • *adj* ràpid • *n*
falciot *m*
**swim** /swɪm/ • *v (sp* swam, *pp*
swum) nedar **~ming** • *n*
natació *f* **~suit** • *n* vestit de
bany *m*, banyador *m* **~ming**
**pool** • *n* piscina *f*
**swing** /swɪŋ/ • *n* gronxador *m* •
*v (sp* swung, *pp* swung)
engronsar, balancejar
**switch** /swɪtʃ/ • *n* interruptor *m*;
agulla *f*; opció *f* **~ sth off** • *v*
apagar
**Swi|tzerland** • *n* Suïssa *f* **~ss** •
*adj* suís *m*, suïssa *f* • *n* suís *m*
**swollen** *(pp)* ▷ SWELL

**sword** /sɔːd, sɔːd/ ● *n* espasa *f*

**swore** *(sp)* ▷ SWEAR

**sworn** *(pp)* ▷ SWEAR

**swum** *(pp)* ▷ SWIM

**swung** *(sp/pp)* ▷ SWING

**syllable** /'sɪləbəl/ ● *n* síl·laba *f*

**symbol** /'sɪmbəl/ ● *n* símbol *m* **~ic** ● *adj* simbòlic **~ism** ● *n* simbolisme *m*

**symmetr|y** /'sɪmɪtrɪ/ ● *n* simetria *f* **~ical** ● *adj* simètric

**sympath|y** /'sɪmpəθɪ/ ● *n* compassió *f*; empatia *f*; simpatia *f* **~etic** ● *adj* simpàtic

**symptom** /'sɪm(p)təm/ ● *n* símptoma *m* **~atic** ● *adj* simptomàtic

**synagogue** /'sɪnəgɑg/ ● *n* sinagoga *f*

**syndrome** /'sɪndrəʊm, 'sɪndroʊm/ ● *n* síndrome *f*

**synthesis** /'sɪnθəsɪs/ ● *n* síntesi *f*

**Syria** ● *n* Síria *f* **~n** ● *adj* sirià; siríac, sirí ● *n* Modern Syria sirià, siriana, siria *f*

**syrup** /'sɪrəp/ ● *n* xarop *m*

**system** /'sɪstəm/ ● *n* sistema *m* **~atic** ● *adj* sistemàtic

# T

**T-shirt** ● *n* samarreta *f*

**table** /'teɪbəl/ ● *n* taula *f* **~spoon** ● *n* cullera de sopa *f*; cullerada *f*

**tablet computer** ● *n* tauleta tàctil *f*

**tabloid** ● *n* tabloide *m*

**tackle** /'tækəl/ ● *n* entrada *f*; placatge *m* ● *v* placar

**tact** ● *n* tacte *m* **~ful** ● *adj* discret **~less** ● *adj* indiscret

**tactic** /'tæktɪk/ ● *n* tàctica *f* **~al** ● *adj* tàctic

**tadpole** /'tædpoʊl/ ● *n* capgròs *m*, cullerot *m*

**tag** /tæg, teɪg/ ● *n* etiqueta *f*; tocar i parar ● *v* etiquetar

**tail** /teɪl/ ● *n* cua *f*; natja *f*

**tailor** /'teɪlə, 'teɪlə/ ● *n* sastre *m*, sastressa *f*

**Taiwan** ● *n* Taiwan **~ese** ● *adj* taiwanès ● *n* taiwanès *m*, taiwanesa *f*

**Tajikistan** ● *n* Tadjikistan *m*

**take** /teɪk/ ● *n* presa *f* ● *v* (*sp* took, *pp* taken) prendre; agafar; portar; escollir; violar, forçar

**taken** *(pp)* ▷ TAKE

**tale** /teɪl/ ● *n* conte *m*, faula *f*

**talent** /'tælənt, 'talənt/ ● *n* talent *m* **~ed** ● *adj* talentós

**talk** /tɔːk, tɔk/ ● *v* parlar, conversar

**tall** /tɔːl, tɔl/ ● *adj* alt

**tank** /tæŋk/ ● *n* tanc *m*, dipòsit *m*

**Tanzania** ● *n* Tanzània *f*

**tap** /tæp/ ● *n* tap *m*; aixeta *f*, canella *f*

**tarantula** /təˈræntʃələ/ ● *n* taràntula *f*

**target** /'tɑːgɪt, tɑːgɪt/ ● *n* blanc *m*

**tart** /tɑːt, tɑːt/ ● *n* pastís; puta, bagassa, bandarra; marcolfa, marfanta

**task** /tɑːsk, tæsk/ • *n* tasca *f*

**taste** /teɪst/ • *n* gust, sabor, tast • *v* tastar, gustar

**taught** *(sp/pp)* ▷ TEACH

**tax** /tæks/ • *n* impost *m*, taxa *f* **~payer** • *n* contribuent *f*

**taxi** /ˈtæk.si/ • *n* taxi *m* **~ driver** • *n* taxista *f*

**tea** /ti, tiː/ • *n* te *m*

**teach** /tiːtʃ/ • *v* (*sp* taught, *pp* taught) ensenyar **~er** • *n* ensenyant *m* **~ing** • *n* ensenyament *m*

**team** /tiːm/ • *n* equip *m*

**tear** /teə, teər/ • *n* llàgrima *f* • *v* (*sp* tore, *pp* torn) estripar, esquinçar; esgarrar

**tease** /tiːz/ • *v* pentinar

**technic|al** /ˈtɛk.nɪk.əl/ • *adj* tècnic **~ally** • *adv* tècnicament **~ian** • *n* tècnic *m*

**technique** /tɛkˈniːk/ • *n* tècnica *f*

**technolog|y** /tɛkˈnɒlədʒi, tɛkˈnɑlədʒi/ • *n* tecnologia *f* **~ical** • *adj* tecnològic

**teeth** *(pl)* ▷ TOOTH

**telephone** /ˈtɛlɪfəʊn, ˈtɛləfoʊn/ • *n* telèfon *m* • *v* telefonar, trucar, cridar

**telescope** /ˈtɛlɪskəʊp, ˈtɛləˌskoʊp/ • *n* telescopi *m*

**television** /ˈtɛlɪˌvɪʒən/ • *n* televisió *f*; televisor *m*

**tell** /tɛl/ • *v* (*sp* told, *pp* told) dir, explicar

**temperature** /ˈtɛmp(ə)rətʃə(r)/ • *n* temperatura *f*; febre *f*

**template** /ˈtɛmplɪt/ • *n* plantilla *f*

**temple** /ˈtɛmp(ə)l/ • *n* temple *m*

**temporar|y** /ˈtɛmpərəri, ˈtɛmpəˌreri/ • *adj* temporal • *n*

eventual **~ily** • *adv* temporalment

**tempt** /tɛmpt/ • *v* temptar

**ten** /tɛn, tɪn/ • *n* deu, 2, 3)

**tenant** /ˈtɛ.nənt/ • *n* llogater

**tend** /tɛnd/ • *v* tendir **~ency** • *n* tendència *f*

**tender** /ˈtɛn.də(ɹ), ˈtɛn.dər/ • *adj* tendre

**tennis** /ˈtɛ.nɪs/ • *n* tennis *m* **~ player** • *n* tennista *f*, tenista *f*

**tense** /tɛns/ • *adj* tens • *n* temps • *v* tesar

**tent** /tɛnt, tɪnt/ • *n* tenda *f*

**term** /tɜːm, tɝm/ • *n* terme *m* **~inology** • *n* terminologia *f*

**terminal** /ˈtɜːmɪnəl/ • *adj* terminal • *n* terminal

**termination** /tɜːmɪˈneɪʃən/ • *n* terminació *f*

**terrain** /ˈtɛreɪn/ • *n* terreny *m*

**terribl|e** /ˈtɛ.ɹə.bl/ • *adv* terrible **~y** • *adv* terriblement

**terrify** /ˈtɛɹɪfaɪ/ • *v* aterrir

**territor|y** /ˈtɛɹɪˌtɔɹi, ˈtɛɹɪt(ə)ɹi/ • *n* territori *m* **~ial** • *adj* territorial

**terror** /ˈtɛɹə, ˈtɛɹə/ • *n* terror *f* **~ism** • *n* terrorisme *m* **~ist** • *adj* terrorista • *n* terrorista *f*

**test** /tɛst, tɛst/ • *n* prova *f*, test *m*; examen *m* • *v* provar

**text** /tɛkst/ • *n* text *m* **~book** • *n* llibre de text *m*, llibre de classe *m*

**texture** /ˈtɛkstʃə(ɹ)/ • *n* textura *f*

**Thai|land** • *n* Tailàndia *f* **~** • *adj* tailandès • *n* tailandès *m*, tailandesa *f*; thai *m*, tai *m*

**than** /ðæn, ðən/ • *prep* que

**thank** /θæŋk/ • *v* agrair **~ful** • *adj* agraït **~s** • *interj* gràcies, mercès

**that** /ˈðæt, ˈðet/ • *conj* que • *det* aqueix *m*, aqueixa *f* • *pron* (*pl* those) açò, això, allò

**the** /ðiː, ði/ • *art* el, es

**theat|er** /ˈθi(ə)tɚ, ˈθi.eɪ.tɚ/ • *n* teatre *m* **~rical** • *adj* teatral

**theatre** *(British)* ▷ THEATER

**theft** /θɛft/ • *n* furt *m*

**their** /ðɛə(ɹ), ðɛɚ/ • *det* llur

**them** /ðɛm, ðəm/ • *pron* els *m*, les *f* **~selves** • *pron* es; mateix

**then** /ðɛn, ðen/ • *adv* llavors; després; mentrestant, al mateix temps

**theolog|y** /θiˈɒ.lə.dʒi/ • *n* teologia *f* **~ical** • *adj* teològic

**theor|y** /ˈθɪəɹi, ˈθiːəɹi/ • *n* teoria *f* **~etical** • *adj* teòric

**therap|y** /ˈθɛɹ.ə.pi/ • *n* teràpia *f* **~eutic** • *adj* terapèutic **~ist** • *n* terapeuta *f*

**there** /ðɛə(ɹ), ðɛɚ/ • *adv* allà, allí **~fore** • *adv* per tant, per això

**thesaurus** /θɪˈsɔːɹəs/ • *n* diccionari de sinònims; tesaurus *m*

**thesis** /ˈθiːsɪs/ • *n* tesi *f*; tesi doctoral *f*

**they** /ðeɪ/ • *pron* ells, elles

**thick** /θɪk, θɪk/ • *adj* espès

**thief** /θiːf/ • *n* lladre *m*

**thigh** /θaɪ/ • *n* cuixa *f*

**thin** /ˈθɪn/ • *adj* clar • *v* aprimar; aprimar-se

**thing** /θɪŋ/ • *n* cosa *f*

**think** /θɪŋk/ • *v* pensar

**third** /θɜːd, θɝd/ • *adj* tercer; tercera *f*

**thirst** /θɜːst, θɝst/ • *n* set *f*; ambició *f* **~y** • *adj* assedegat

**thirteen** /ˈθɜː.tiːn, ˈθɝ(t).tin/ • *num* tretze

**thirty** /ˈθɜːti, ˈθɝti/ • *num* trenta

**this** /ðɪs/ • *det* aquest, est, este • *pron* (*pl* these) això *n*, aquest *m*, aquesta *f*

**thorough** /ˈθʌ.ɹə, ˈθʌ.ɹoʊ/ • *adj* minuciós **~ly** • *adv* completament, exhaustivament

**thought** /θɔːt, θɑt/ • *n* pensament *m* **~ful** • *adj* pensarós; atent

**thousand** /ˈθaʊz(ə)nd/ • *num* mil ; miler or milenar (approximately, or a set of a size numbered in the thousands)

**thread** /θɹɛd/ • *n* fil *m*; fil conductor *m*; tema *m* • *v* enfilar

**threat** /θɹɛt/ • *n* amenaça *f* **~en** • *v* amenaçar

**three** /θɹiː, θɹi/ • *n* tres *m* • *num* tres

**threshold** /ˈθɹɛʃ(h)əʊld, ˈθɹɛʃ(h)oʊld/ • *n* llindar *m*

**threw** *(sp)* ▷ THROW

**thrifty** /ˈθɹɪfti/ • *adj* estalviador

**throat** /ˈθɹəʊt, ˈθɹoʊt/ • *n* gola *f*

**through** /θɹuː, θɹu/ • *prep* mitjançant **~out** • *prep* al llarg de

**throw** /θɹəʊ, θɹoʊ/ • *v* (*sp* threw, *pp* thrown) llançar, tirar **~ sth away** • *v* llençar

**thrown** *(pp)* ▷ THROW

**thumb** /θʌm/ • *n* polze *m*

**thunder** /'θʌndə, 'θʌndər/ • *n* tro
*m* • *v* tronar
**Thursday** • *n* dijous *m*
**thus** /'ðʌs/ • *adv* aixì
**thyme** /taɪm/ • *n* farigola *f*
**tick** /tɪk/ • *n* paparra *f*
**ticket** /'tɪkɪt/ • *n* bitllet *m*
**tide** /taɪd, ta:d/ • *n* marea *f*
**tidy** /'taɪdi/ • *adj* endreçat
**tie** /taɪ/ • *n* empat *m*; lligam *m*;
lligadura *f* • *v* fermar, lligar,
ennuar • *(also)* ▷ NECKTIE
**tiger** /'taɪgə, 'taɪgər/ • *n* tigre *m*
**tile** /taɪl/ • *n* teula *f*, rajola *f* • *v*
enrajolar, teular
**till** /tɪl/ • *n* caixa *f*
**timber** /'tɪmbə, 'tɪmbər/ • *n* biga *f*
**time** /taɪm, taem/ • *n* temps *m*;
pena *f*; hora *f*; vegada *f*, cop
*m* **~ly** • *adj* oportú **at a ~** •
*phr* a la vegada
**timid** /'tɪmɪd/ • *adj* tímid
**tin** /tɪn/ • *n* estany *m*
**tiny** /'taɪni/ • *adj* minúscul
**tip** /tɪp/ • *n* punta *f*, punxa *f*;
propina *f*; indici *m*
**tire** /'taɪə(ɹ), 'taɪər/ • *v* cansar-se,
fatigar-se; cansar, fatigar;
avorrir-se; adornar, guarnir
**~d** • *adj* cansat *m*, cansada *f*
**tissue** /'tɪʃu, 'tɪʃjuː/ • *n* teixit *m*
**title** /'taɪtl/ • *n* títol *m*
**to** /tuː, tu/ • *part* -ar ; -er, -r, -re ;
-ir • *prep* a, cap a
**toad** /toʊd, təʊd/ • *n* gripau *m*
**toast** /təʊst, toʊst/ • *n* torrada *f*;
brindis *m* • *v* torrar; brindar
**~er** • *n* torradora *f*
**tobacco** /təˈbækoʊ/ • *n* tabac *m*
**today** /təˈdeɪ/ • *adv* avui; avui en
dia, avui dia • *n* avui, hui *m*

**toddler** • *n* nen *m*
**toe** /təʊ, toʊ/ • *n* dit del peu *m*;
dit *m*
**together** /tʊˈgɛð.ə(ɹ), tʊˈgɛðər/ •
*adv* junt
**Togo** • *n* Togo
**toilet** /'tɔɪ.lət/ • *n* bany *m*, servei
*m*, servici *m*, vàter *m*; escusat
*m*, lavabo *m* **~ paper** • *n*
paper higiènic *m*
**Tokyo** • *n* Tòquio *m*
**told** *(sp/pp)* ▷ TELL
**tolera|te** /'tɑl.ə.ɹeɪt, 'tɒl.əˌɹeɪt/ • *v*
tolerar **~nce** • *n* tolerància *f*
**~nt** • *adj* tolerant
**toll** /təʊl, toʊl/ • *n* peatge *m*
**tomato** /təˈmæto:, təˈmɑːtəʊ/ • *n*
tomaquera *f*; tomàquet *m*
**tomorrow** /təˈmɑɹoʊ, təˈmɒɹəʊ/ •
*adv* demà • *n* demà *m*
**tone** /təʊn, toʊn/ • *n* to *m*
**Tonga** • *n* Tonga
**tongue** /tʌŋ, tʌŋ/ • *n* llengua *f*
**tonight** /təˈnaɪt/ • *adv* anit;
aquesta nit • *n* anit
**too** /tuː, tu/ • *adv* també; massa
**took** *(sp)* ▷ TAKE
**tool** /tuːl/ • *n* eina *f*; equipar
**tooth** /tuːθ, tʊθ/ • *n* (*pl* teeth)
dent *f* **~brush** • *n* raspall de
dents *m*, raspallet *m*, raspallet
de les dents *m*
**top** /tɒp, tɑp/ • *n* baldufa *f*; cofa
*f*
**torch** /tɔːtʃ, tɔɹtʃ/ • *n* teia *f*, torxa
*f*
**tore** *(sp)* ▷ TEAR
**torn** *(pp)* ▷ TEAR
**torture** /'tɔɹtʃər, 'tɔːtʃə(ɹ)/ • *n*
tortura *f* • *v* torturar

**total** /'təʊ.təl, 'toʊ.təl/ • *n* total *m*; suma *f* • *v* totalitzar **~ly** • *adv* totalment

**touch** /tʌʧ/ • *v* tocar **in ~** • *phr* en contacte

**touris|t** /'tʊərɪst, 'tʊɹ.ɪst/ • *n* turista *f* **~m** • *n* turisme *m*

**tournament** /'tʊənəmənt, 'tʊməmɪnt/ • *n* torneig *m*

**toward** /tə'wɔːd, tʊ'wɔːrd/ • *prep* cap a; sobre, en relació a, envers, vers; per, per a

**towel** /taʊl/ • *n* tovallola *f*

**tower** /'taʊ.ə(ɹ), 'taʊɚ/ • *n* torre *f*; la torre, casa de déu

**town** /taʊn/ • *n* poble *m*

**toxic** /'tɒk.sɪk, 'tɑk.sɪk/ • *adj* tòxic, verinós

**toy** /tɔɪ/ • *n* joguina *f*

**trace** /tɹeɪs/ • *v* traçar

**track** /tɹæk/ • *n* rastre *m*, traça *f*; petjada *f*

**tradition** /tɹə'dɪʃən/ • *n* tradició *f* **~al** • *adj* tradicional **~ally** • *adv* tradicionalment

**traffic** /'tɹæfɪk/ • *n* tràfic *m* **~ jam** • *n* embotellament **~ light** • *n* semàfor *m*

**trag|edy** /'tɹædʒɪdi/ • *n* tragèdia *f* **~ic** • *adj* tràgic

**trail** /tɹeɪl/ • *n* rastre *m*; pista *f*; corriol *m* • *v* arrossegar

**train** /tɹeɪn/ • *n* tren *m* • *v* entrenar **~er** • *n* entrenador *m* **~ing** • *n* entrenament *m*

**trait** /tɹeɪ, tɹeɪt/ • *n* tret *m*

**tranquil** /'tɹæŋ.kwɪl/ • *adj* tranquil **~lity** • *n* tranquil·litat *f*

**transcription** /tɹæn'skɹɪpʃən/ • *n* transcripció *f*

**transform** /tɹænz'fɔːm, tɹænz'fɔɹm/ • *v* transformar **~ation** • *n* transformació *f*

**transit** /'tɹæn.zɪt, 'tɹæn.zət/ • *n* trànsit *m* **~ion** • *n* transició *f*

**translat|e** /tɹɑːnz'leɪt, 'tɹænzleɪt/ • *v* traduir **~ion** • *n* traducció *f* **~or** • *n* traductor *m*, traductora *f*

**translucent** /tɹænz'luː.sənt/ • *adj* translúcid

**transparen|t** /tɹæn(t)s'pɛɹənt, tɹæn(t)s'pɛɹənt/ • *adj* transparent **~cy** • *n* transparència *f*

**transport** /tɹænz'pɔːt, tɹænz'pɔɹt/ • *n* transport *m*; deportat *m* • *v* transportar; deportar

**trap** /tɹæp/ • *n* parany *m*

**traumatic** • *adj* traumàtic

**travel** /'tɹævəl/ • *n* viatge *m* • *v* viatjar; transitar; fer passes **~ler** • *n* viatger *m*

**tray** /tɹeɪ/ • *n* safata *f*

**tread** /tɹɛd/ • *n* trepitjada *f*; dibuix *f* • *v* (*sp* trod, *pp* trodden) trepitjar

**treasure** /'tɹɛʒə, 'tɹɛʒɚ/ • *n* tresor *m*, tesor *m*

**treat** /tɹiːt/ • *v* tractar **~ment** • *n* tractament *m*

**tree** /tɹiː, tɹi/ • *n* arbre *m*

**trekking** • *n* tresc *m*

**trial** /'tɹaɪəl/ • *n* prova *f*; procés *m*, judici *m*

**triangle** /'tɹaɪəŋɡəl, 'tɹaɪ.æŋɡəl/ • *n* triangle *m*

**trib|e** /tɹaɪb/ • *n* tribu *f* **~al** • *adj* tribal

**trick** /tɹɪk/ • *n* basa *f* • *v* enganyar

**trigger** /ˈtrɪgə/ • *n* gallet *m*
**trillion** /ˈtrɪljən/ • *num* billó; trilió
**trilogy** • *n* trilogia *f*
**trinity** • *n* trinitat *f*, trio *m*
**trip** /trɪp/ • *n* traveta *f* • *v*
    entrebancar-se; fer una
    traveta
**triple** /ˈtrɪpəl/ • *adj* triple; ternari
    • *n* batada triple *f*; terna • *v*
    triplicar
**triumph** /ˈtraɪʌmf, ˈtraɪʌmpf/ • *n*
    triomf *m*
**trod** *(sp)* ▷ TREAD
**trodden** *(pp)* ▷ TREAD
**trombone** /ˌtrɒmˈbəʊn,
    ˌtrɑmˈboʊn/ • *n* trombó *m*
**troop** /truːp/ • *n* colla *f*, tropa *f*;
    soldats *m*
**trophy** /ˈtroʊfi/ • *n* trofeu *m*
**trousers** • *n* PANTS
**trout** /traʊt, trʌʊt/ • *n* truita *f*
**truck** /trʌk/ • *n* camió *m*
**tru|e** /truː, tru/ • *adj* veritable
    **~ly** • *adv* veritablement
**trumpet** /ˈtrʌmpɪt/ • *n* trompeta
    *f*
**trunk** /trʌŋk/ • *n* tronc *m*;
    trompa *f*; portaequipatge *m*,
    maleter *m*
**trust** /trʌst/ • *n* confiança *f* • *v*
    fiar, confiar **~worthy** • *adj*
    fidedigne
**truth** /truːθ/ • *n* veritat *f*
**try** /traɪ/ • *n* assaig *m* • *v*
    intentar, tractar de; provar;
    esforçar-se; tastar; jutjar **~ sth
    out** • *v* provar
**tsunami** /suːˈnɑːmi, suˈnɑmi/ • *n*
    tsunami *m*
**tube** /tjuːb, tuːb/ • *n* tub *m*
**Tuesday** • *n* dimarts *m*

**tumor** /tjuːˌmə, tuːˌmər/ • *n*
    tumor *m*
**tuna** /tjuːˌnə, ˈtuˌnə/ • *n* (*pl* tuna)
    tonyina *f*
**tune** /tjuːn, t(j)un/ • *n* melodia *f*;
    tonada *f* • *v* afinar
**Tunisia** • *n* Tunísia *f* **~n** • *adj*
    tunisià • *n* tunisià *m*,
    tunisiana *f*
**turkey** /ˈtɜːki, ˈtɜːki/ • *n* gall dindi
    *m*, indiot *m*, polla d'índia *f*
**Turk|ey** /ˈtɜːki, ˈtɜːki/ • *n* Turquia
    *f* **~ish** • *adj* turc *m*
**Turkmenistan** • *n* Turkmenistan
    *m*
**turn** /tɜːn, tɜn/ • *n* torn *m* • *v*
    girar **~ sth down** • *v* rebutjar,
    refusar; abaixar, disminuir,
    reduir **~ sth off** • *v* apagar;
    tancar **~ sth on** • *v* obrir;
    encendre, engegar
**turnover** • *n* pèrdua de
    possessió *f*
**turtle** /ˈtɜːtəl, ˈtɜtəl/ • *n* tortuga *f*
**TV** • *n* TV
**twelve** /twɛlv/ • *num* dotze
**twent|y** /ˈtwɛnti, ˈtwʌnti/ • *num*
    vint **~ieth** • *adj* vintè, vigèsim
    • *n* vintè *m*
**twice** /twaɪs/ • *adv* dos cops,
    dues vegades
**twin** /twɪn/ • *adj* bessó • *n*
    bessó *m*
**twisted** /ˈtwɪstɪd/ • *adj* tort
**two** /tuː, tu/ • *n* dos *m* • *num*
    dues *f*
**type** /taɪp/ • *n* tipus *m*, mena *f*,
    classe *f* • *v* mecanografiar;
    teclejar **~writer** • *n* màquina
    d'escriure *f*

**typical** /ˈtɪpɪkəl/ ● *adj* típic **~ly** ●
*adv* típicament

**typography** /taɪˈpɒɡɹəfi,
taɪˈpɑːɡɹəfi/ ● *n* tipografia *f*

**tyre** /taɪə(ɹ)/ ● *n* neumàtic *m*,
pneumàtic *m*

**UAE** *(abbr)* ▷ UNITED ARAB
EMIRATES

**UFO** ● *n (abbr* Unidentified
Flying Object) ovni *m*

**Uganda** ● *n* Uganda

**ugl|y** /ˈʌɡli/ ● *adj* lleig **~iness** ●
*n* lletgesa *f*, lletjor *f*

**UK** *(abbr)* ▷ UNITED KINGDOM

**Ukrain|e** ● *n* Ucraïna *f* **~ian** ●
*adj* ucraïnès *m*, ucraïnesa *f*

**ultimately** /ˈʌltɪmətli/ ● *adv*
finalment

**ultimatum** /ˌʌl.tɪˈmeɪ.təm/ ● *n (pl*
ultimata) ultimàtum *m*

**umbrella** /ʌmˈbɹelə/ ● *n* paraigua
*m*, para-sol *m*, ombrel·la *f*

**unable** /ʌnˈeɪbəl/ ● *adj* incapaç

**unacceptable** /ˌʌn.æk.ˈsep.tə.bl̩/ ●
*adj* inacceptable

**unbelievable** /ˌʌnbəˈliːvəbl/ ● *adj*
increïble

**uncertain** /ʌnˈsɜːtən/ ● *adj* incert
**~ty** ● *n* incertesa *f*

**uncle** /ˈʌŋ.kəl/ ● *n* oncle *m*, tio *m*

**uncomfortabl|e**
/ʌnˈkʌm.fɚ.tə.bəl,
ʌnˈkʌmf.tə.bəl/ ● *adj* incòmode
**~y** ● *adv* incòmodament

**unconscious** /ˌʌnˈkɒnʃəs/ ● *adj*
inconscient ● *n* inconscient *m*
**~ly** ● *adv* inconscientment

**under** /ˈʌndə(ɹ), ˈʌndɚ/ ● *adv* sota

**undergo** ● *v* suportar

**underground** ● *adj* subterrani

**underlying** ● *adj* subjacent

**undermine** /ʌndəˈmaɪn/ ● *v*
soscavar

**understand** /(ˌ)ʌndəˈstænd,
ˌʌndɚˈstænd/ ● *v* entendre,
comprendre **~ing** ● *adj*
comprensiu

**undertake** /ʌndəˈteɪk/ ● *v*
emprendre

**underwear** /ˈʌndəwɛɹ, ˈʌndəwɛə/
● *n* roba interior *f*

**undoubtedly** /ʌnˈdaʊtɪdli/ ● *adv*
indubtablement

**unemploy|ed** ● *adj* desocupat,
aturat **~ment** ● *n* atur *m*,
parada forçosa *f*, manca de
treball *f*

**unequal** ● *adj* desigual

**uneven** /ʌnˈiːvən/ ● *adj* desigual;
rugós

**unexpected** /ʌnɪkˈspektɪd/ ● *adj*
inesperat **~ly** ● *adv*
inesperadament

**unfair** /ʌnˈfɛə(ɹ), ʌnˈfɛɚ/ ● *adj*
injust

**unfortunate** /ʌnˈfɔːtʃənət,
ʌnˈfɔɪtʃənɪt/ ● *adj* desafortunat
**~ly** ● *adv* malauradament,
desgraciadament

**unfriendly** /ʌnˈfɹɛn(d)li/ ● *adj*
antipàtic; hostil

**unhappy** /ʌnˈhæpi/ ● *adj* infeliç

**uniform** /ˈjuːnɪfɔːm, ˈjunəfɔɹm/ ●
*adj* uniforme ● *n* uniforme *m*

**unif|y** /'juːnɪfaɪ/ • v unificar; unificar-se **~ication** • n unificació f

**unintentional** • adj involuntari **~ly** • adv involuntàriament

**union** /'juːnjən/ • n unió f

**unique** /juːˈniːk, juˈniːk/ • adj únic

**unit** /'juːnɪt/ • n unitat f

**unit|e** /juˈnaɪt/ • v unir **~y** • n unitat f

**United Arab Emirates** • n Emirats Àrabs Units

**United Kingdom** • n Regne Unit m, Regne Unit de la Gran Bretanya i Irlanda del Nord m

**United States** • n Estats Units

**universe** /'juːnɪˌvɜːs, 'juːnəˌvɜrs/ • n univers m

**university** /juːnɪˈvɜːsətiː, juniˈvɜrsəti/ • n universitat f

**unknown** /ʌnˈnəʊn, ʌnˈnoʊn/ • adj desconegut

**unless** /ənˈlɛs/ • conj a menys que, llevat que, tret que, fora que

**unlike** /ʌnˈlaɪk/ • prep a diferència de **~ly** • adj improbable

**unnecessary** /ʌnˈnɛsəsˌsərɪ, ʌnˈnɛsˌsɛˌri/ • adj innecessari

**unpleasant** /ʌnˈplɛzənt/ • adj desagradable

**unpopular** • adj impopular

**unpredictable** • adj imprevisible

**unstable** /ʌnˈsteɪbəl/ • adj inestable

**until** /ʌnˈtɪl/ • prep fins

**unusual** /ʌnˈjuːʒʊəl/ • adj inusual

**unveil** /ʌnˈveɪl/ • v desvelar

**unwilling** /ʌnˈwɪlɪŋ/ • adj reaci

**up** /ʌp, ap/ • adv amunt • prep dalt

**update** /'ʌp.deɪt, əpˈdeɪt/ • n actualització f • v actualitzar

**upper** /'ʌpə, 'ʌpər/ • adj superior; alt

**upset** /'ʌpsɛt, ʌpˈsɛt/ • adj molest, trasbalsat, disgustat • n trastorn m • v trastornar; bolcar

**Uranus** • n Urà m

**urban** /'ɜːbən, 'ɜrbən/ • adj urbà

**urgen|t** /'ɜːdʒənt, 'ɜrdʒənt/ • adj urgent **~tly** • adv urgentment **~cy** • n urgència f

**Uruguay** • n Uruguai m **~an** • adj uruguaià • n uruguaià m, uruguaiana f

**USA** (abbr) ▷ UNITED STATES

**use** /juːs, juːz/ • n ús m • v fer servir, usar, utilitzar **~ful** • adj útil **~less** • adj inútil f **~r** • n usuari m **~d to** • adj acostumat

**usual** /'juːʒʊəl/ • adj usual **~ly** • adv normalment

**utility** /juːˈtɪl.ɪ.ti/ • adj utilitat f

**utterly** ▷ COMPLETELY

U
V

**vacation** /vəˈkeɪʃ(ə)n, veɪˈkeɪʃən/ • v fer vacances

**vaccin|e** /ˈvæksiːn/ • n vacuna f, vaccí m **~ate** • v vacunar, vaccinar **~ation** • n vacunació f

**vacuum** /'væ.kju:m/ • *n* buit *m* ~ **cleaner** • *n* aspiradora *f*

**vague** /veɪg, væg/ • *adj* vague

**valid** • *adj* vàlid ~**ity** • *n* validesa *f*, validitat *f*

**valley** /'væli/ • *n* vall *f*

**valu|e** /'vælju:, 'vælju/ • *n* valor ~**able** • *adj* valuós

**van** /væn/ • *n* furgoneta *f*

**vanish** /'vænɪʃ/ • *v* esvanir-se, desaparèixer

**varnish** • *n* vernís *m*

**vari|able** /'vɛəɹ.i.ə.bl̩, 'væɹ.i.ə.bl̩/ • *adj* variable • *n* variable *f* ~**ation** • *n* variació *f* ~**ety** • *n* varietat *f* ~**ous** • *adj* varis

**vast** /vɑːst, væst/ • *adj* vast

**Vatican City** • *n* Ciutat del Vaticà *f*, Vaticà *m*

**vegetable** /'vɛdʒtəbəl, 'vɛdʒətəbəl/ • *adj* vegetal • *n* vegetal *m*; verdura *f*, hortalissa *f*, llegum *m*

**vehicle** /'viː.ɹ.kəl, 'vi.ə.kəl/ • *n* vehicle *m*; mitjà *m*

**vein** /veɪn/ • *n* vena *f*

**vendor** • *n* venedor *m*, venedora *f*

**Venezuela** • *n* Veneçuela *f* ~**n** • *adj* veneçolà • *n* veneçolà *m*, veneçolana *f*

**venture** /'vɛn.tʃɚ, 'vɛn.tʃə/ • *n* aventura *f* • *v* aventurar; arriscar

**venue** /'vɛnju:/ • *n* local *m*, seu *f*; escena, jurisdicció *f*

**Venus** • *n* Venus *f*

**verb** /vɜb, vɜːb/ • *n* verb ~**al** • *adj* verbal

**verdict** /'vɜ.dɪkt/ • *n* veredicte *m*; parer *m*

**verification** • *n* verificació *f*

**versatil|e** /'vɜsətl̩, 'vɜːsətaɪl/ • *adj* versàtil ~**ity** • *n* versatilitat *f*

**version** /'vɜʒən, 'vɜːʒən/ • *n* versió *f*

**versus** /'vɜːsəs, 'vɜsəs/ • *prep* en comparació amb

**vertical** /'vɜːtɪkəl, 'vɜːtɪkəl/ • *adj* vertical ~**ly** • *adv* verticalment

**very** /'vɛɹi/ • *adv* molt

**vessel** /'vɛs.əl/ • *n* vaixell

**vet** ▷ VETERINARIAN

**veteran** /'vɛ.tə.ɹən/ • *n* veterà *m*

**veterinarian** /ˌvɛt(ə)ɹəˈnɛɹi.ən/ • *n* veterinari *m*

**viable** /'vaɪəbəl/ • *adj* viable

**vice** /vaɪs/ • *n* vici *m*

**victim** /'vɪktɪm, 'vɪktəm/ • *n* víctima *f*

**victor|y** /'vɪkt(ə)ɹi/ • *n* victòria *f* ~**ious** • *adj* victoriós

**Vienna** • *n* Viena

**Vietnam** • *n* Vietnam *m* ~**ese** • *adj* vietnamita • *n* vietnamita *f*

**view** /vju:/ • *n* vista *f*; parer *m* • *v* veure

**vigilant** /'vɪdʒɪlənt/ • *adj* vigilant

**village** /'vɪlɪdʒ/ • *n* poble *m*

**vinegar** /'vɪnəgɚ/ • *n* vinagre *m*

**vineyard** /'vɪn.jɑːd/ • *n* vinya *f*

**vinyl** /'vaɪ.nəl/ • *n* vinil *m*

**viola** /vi'əʊ.lə, vi'oʊ.lə/ • *n* viola *f*

**violen|t** /vaɪ(ə)lənt/ • *adj* violent ~**tly** • *adv* violentament ~**ce** • *n* violència *f*

**violin** /ˌvaɪəˈlɪn, ˌvaɪˈlən/ • *n* violí *m*

**virtual** /'vɜːtʃuəl, 'vɜːtʃuəl/ • *adj* virtual ~**ly** • *adv* virtualment ~ **reality** • *n* realitat virtual

**virtu|e** /'vɜ:.tju:/ • *n* virtut *f*
  **~ous** • *adj* virtuós
**virus** /'vaɪ(ə)ɹɪs/ • *n* virus *m*
**visa** /'vi:zə/ • *n* visat *m*
**visib|le** /'vɪzəb(ə)l/ • *adj* visible
  **~ility** • *n* visibilitat *f*
**visit** /'vɪzɪt/ • *n* visita *f* • *v* visitar
**vis|ual** /'vɪʒʊəl, 'vɪʒuəl/ • *adj*
  visual **~ion** • *n* vista *f*, visió *f*
**vital** /'vaɪtəl, 'vaɪt̬əl/ • *adj* vital *f*
  **~ity** • *n* vitalitat *f*
**vitamin** /'vɪt.ə.mɪn, 'vaɪ.tə.mɪn/ •
  *n* vitamina *f*
**vivacious** /vaɪˈveɪʃəs/ • *adj* vivaç
  *f*
**vivid** /'vɪvɪd/ • *adj* vívid
**vocabulary** /vəʊˈkabjʊlənɪ,
  voʊˈkæbjələɹɪ/ • *n* vocabulari *m*
**vocal** /'vəʊ.kəl, 'voʊ.kəl/ • *adj*
  vocal
**voice** /vɔɪs/ • *n* veu *f*; sonor *m*;
  vot *m*
**volcan|o** /vɒlˈkeɪnəʊ, vɑlˈkeɪnoʊ/
  • *n* volcà *m* **~ic** • *adj* volcànic
**volleyball** /'vɒlɪbɔ(:)l/ • *n*
  voleibol *m*, vòlei *m*
**volume** /'vɒl.ju:m, 'vɑl.jum/ • *n*
  volum *m*
**voluntar|y** /'vɒ.lən.tɹɪ,
  'vɑ.lən.tɛ.ɹi/ • *adj* voluntari **~ily**
  • *adv* voluntàriament
**vot|e** /vəʊt, voʊt/ • *n* vot *m* • *v*
  votar **~er** • *n* votant *f* **~ing** •
  *n* votació *f*
**vow** /vaʊ/ • *n* vot *m* • *v* jurar,
  prometre solemnement
**vulnerab|le** /'vʌln(ə)ɹəbl,
  'vʌnəɹəbl/ • *adj* vulnerable
  **~ility** • *n* vulnerabilitat *f*
**vulture** /'vʌltʃə, 'vʌltʃɚ/ • *n*
  voltor *m*

**wage** /weɪdʒ/ • *n* salari *m*, sou
  *m*, paga *f*, honorari *m*,
  estipendi *m*, remuneració *f*,
  retribució *f*
**wagon** /'wæg(ə)n, 'wægən/ • *n*
  carro *m*, cotxe *m*; cotxet *m*
**waist** /weɪst/ • *n* cintura *f* **~coat**
  • *n* armilla *f*
**wait** /weɪt/ • *v* esperar,
  esperar-se
**wait|er** /'weɪtə, 'weɪt̬ɚ/ • *n*
  cambrer *m* **~ress** • *n* cambrera
**wake up** • *v* despertar-se;
  despertar
**walk** /wɔ:k, wɔk/ • *n* passejada
  *m*; passeig *m* • *v* caminar
**wall** /wɔ:l, wɔl/ • *n* mur *m*;
  muralla *f*; paret *f*, envà *m* • *v*
  emmurallar, murar
**walnut** /'wɔlnət, 'wɔ:lnʌt/ • *n*
  noguera *f*
**wander** /'wɒndə, 'wɒndɚ/ • *v*
  vagar, deambular **~er** • *n*
  rodamón *m*, nòmada *f*
**want** /wɒnt, wɑnt/ • *n* desig *m* •
  *v* voler
**war** /wɔ:, wɔɹ/ • *n* guerra *f* • *v*
  guerrejar **~rior** • *n* guerrer *m*,
  guerrera *f*
**wardrobe** /'wɔːdɹəʊb, 'wɔɹdɹoʊb/
  • *n* armari *m*
**warehouse** • *n* magatzem
**warm** /wɔːm, wɔɹm/ • *adj* calent,
  càlid

**warn** /wɔːn, wɔɪn/ • v advertir, avisar **~ing** • n advertència f, advertiment m, avís m

**Warsaw** • n Varsòvia f

**wary** /weərɪi/ • adj cautelós

**was** (sp) ▷ BE

**wash** /wɒʃ, wɒʃ/ • v rentar, llavar **~ing machine** • n rentadora f **~basin** • n lavabo m, pica f

**wasp** /wɒsp, wɑsp/ • n vespa f

**waste** /weɪst/ • n malbaratament m, pèrdua f

**watch** /wɒtʃ, wɔtʃ/ • n rellotge; guarda f, guardià m; guàrdia f • v mirar; vigilar, anar amb compte; vetllar

**water** /wɔːtə, wɒtə/ • n aigua f; aigües • v regar; donar aigua a **~melon** • n sindriera f; síndria f

**wave** /weɪv/ • n ona f; onada f • v saludar

**wax** /wæks/ • adj cerós • n cera f • v encerar; tornar-se; créixer

**way** /weɪ/ • n via f, camí m; mitjà m; manera f **by the ~** • phr per cert

**we** /wiː, wi/ • pron nosaltres

**weak** /wiːk/ • adj feble, dèbil **~ly** • adv dèbilment, feblement **~en** • v debilitar, afeblir; debilitar-se, afeblir-se **~ness** • n debilitat f, feblesa f

**wealth** /wɛlθ/ • n patrimoni m, riquesa f; abundància f **~y** • adj adinerat, ric

**weapon** /ˈwɛpən/ • n arma f

**wear** /weə, weə(ɪ)/ • v (sp wore, pp worn) portar

**weasel** /ˈwiːz(ə)l, ˈwizəl/ • n mostela f

**weather** /ˈwɛðə, ˈwɛðɚ/ • n temps m

**weave** /wiːv/ • v (sp wove, pp woven) teixir

**web** /wɛb/ • n xarxa f; membrana f **~site** • n pàgina web f, lloc web m

**wedding** /ˈwɛdɪŋ/ • n boda f, casament m

**Wednesday** • n dimecres m

**weed** /wiːd/ • n mala herba f

**week** /wik, wiːk/ • n setmana f **~end** • n cap de setmana m **~ly** • adj setmanal • adv setmanalment, setmanal; cada setmana

**weep** /wiːp/ • v (sp wept, pp wept) plorar

**weigh** /weɪ/ • v pesar **~t**; pes m

**weird** /wɪəd, ˈwiɚd/ • adj rar, estrany

**welcome** /ˈwɛlkəm/ • adj benvingut • interj benvingut m, benvinguda f, benvinguts, benvingudes • v donar la benvinguda, acollir

**welfare** /ˈwɛlˌfɛə, ˈwɛlˌfɛɚ/ • n benestar m

**well** /wɛl/ • adv bé, ben • interj bé • n pou m **~-being** • n benestar m, benanança f

**went** (sp) ▷ GO

**wept** (sp/pp) ▷ WEEP

**were** (sp) ▷ BE

**west** /wɛst/ • n oest m, ponent m, occident **~ern** • adj occidental

**wet** /wɛt/ • adj moll • v (sp wet, pp wet) mullar; mullar-se

**wetted** *(sp/pp)* ▷ WET
**whale** /weɪl, ʍeɪl/ • *n* balena *f*
**what** /wɔt, ʍɒt/ • *adv* que •
*interj* com, i ara • *pron* què
**whatever** /ʍɒt'ɛvə, wʌt'ɛvə/ •
*det* qualsevol • *interj* el que tu
diguis
**wheat** /wiːt, ʍiːt/ • *n* blat *m*
**wheel** /wiːl/ • *n* roda *f*; roda de
timó *f*; peix gros *m* • *v* rodar;
voltar **~barrow** • *n* carretó *m*
**~chair** • *n* cadira de rodes *f*
**when** /ʍɛn, ʍɪn/ • *adv* quan
**where** /ʍɛə(ɹ), ʍɛə/ • *adv* on
**~ver** • *adv* onsevulla • *conj*
onsevulga, onsevol
**which** /wɪtʃ, ʍɪtʃ/ • *det* quin •
*pron* quin; que, el qual, cosa
que
**while** /ʍaɪl/ • *conj* mentre;
malgrat • *n* estona *f* **~st** •
*conj* mentre que
**whip** /wɪp, ʍɪp/ • *n* fuet *m* • *v*
assotar, fuetejar
**whisk** /(h)wɪsk/ • *n* batedora *f*
**whiskey** /'wɪski, 'ʍɪski/ • *n*
whisky *m*
**whisper** /'(h)wɪspə, '(h)wɪspə/ • *n*
xiuxiueig • *v* xiuxiuejar
**whistle** /wɪsl̩/ • *n* xiulet *m*; xiulo
*m*; xiulada *f* • *v* xiular
**white** /waɪt, ʍaɪt/ • *adj* blanc •
*n* blanc *m*
**who** /huː/ • *pron* qui **~se** • *det*
de qui; el subjecte del qual
**whole** /həʊl, hoʊl/ • *adj* tot *m*;
integral • *n* tot, totalitat
**why** /ʍaɪ/ • *adv* per què • *n*
perquè *m*
**wide** /waɪd, wɑed/ • *adj* ample

**widow** /'wɪ.dəʊ, 'wɪ.doʊ/ • *n* vidu
*f* **~er** • *n* vidu *m*
**wife** /waɪf/ • *n* (*pl* wives) dona *f*,
muller *f*
**wig** /wɪg/ • *n* perruca *f*
**wild** /waɪld/ • *adj* salvatge ~
**boar** • *n* senglar *m*, porc
senglar *m*
**will** /wɪl/ • *n* voluntat *f*;
testament *m* • *v* llegar;
desitjar **~ing** • *adj* disposat
**win** /wɪn/ • *v* (*sp*
won, *pp* won) guanyar,
vèncer; conquerir **~ner** • *n*
guanyador *m*, guanyadora *f*
**wind** /wɪnd, waɪnd/ • *n* vent *m*
**~y** • *adj* ventós; va **~mill** • *n*
molí de vent *m*
**window** /'wɪndəʊ, 'wɪndoʊ/ • *n*
finestra *f*
**wine** /waɪn/ • *n* vi *m*
**wing** /wɪŋ/ • *n* ala *f*; banda *f*;
aler *m*, lateral
**winter** /'wɪntə, 'wɪntə/ • *n* hivern
*m* • *v* hivernar
**wipe** /waɪp/ • *v* eixugar
**wire** /waɪə(ɹ), 'waɪə/ • *n* filferro
*m*, fil d'aram *m*; cable *m* **~less**
• *adj* sense fil • *n* ràdio *f*
**wise** /waɪz/ • *adj* savi **~dom** • *n*
saviesa *f*
**wish** /wɪʃ/ • *n* desig *m* • *v*
desitjar
**wit** /wɪt/ • *n* ment *f*, enteniment
*m*; divertit
**with** /wɪð, wɪθ/ • *prep* amb **~in**
• *prep* en, dins; d'aquí a **~out** •
*prep* sense
**withdraw** /wɪð'drɔː/ • *v* retirar;
retirar-se

W

**witness** /'wɪtnəs/ • *n* testimoni *m*; prova *f*, evidència *f*; testimoniatge *m*, atestat *m* • *v* testificar; provar; veure, contemplar

**wives** *(pl)* ▷ WIFE

**wolf** /wʊlf, wʌlf/ • *n (pl* wolves) llop *m*

**woman** /'wʊmən/ • *n (pl* women) dona *f*

**womb** /wu:m/ • *n* úter *m*, matriu *f*

**women** *(pl)* ▷ WOMAN

**won** *(sp/pp)* ▷ WIN

**wonder** /'wʌndə, 'wʌndər/ • *n* meravella *f* • *v* sorprendre's, quedar-se estorat; preguntar-se ~**ful** • *adj* meravellós

**wood** /wʊd/ • *n* fusta *f*; bosc *m*; llenya *f* ~**en** • *adj* ligni *m* ~**pecker** • *n* picot *m*

**wool** /wʊl/ • *n* llana *f*

**word** /wɜ:d, wɜd/ • *n* paraula *f*, mot *m* • *v* redactar

**wore** *(sp)* ▷ WEAR

**work** /wɜ:k, wɜk/ • *n* treball *m* • *v* treballar ~**er** • *n* treballador *m*, treballadora *f*, obrer *m* ~**force** • *n* mà d'obra *f* ~**shop** • *n* taller *m*; seminari *m*

**world** /wɜ:ld, wɜld/ • *n* món *m*; terra *f* ~**wide** • *adj* mundial • *adv* mundialment

**worm** /wɜ:m, wɜm/ • *n* cuc *m*

**worn** *(pp)* ▷ WEAR

**worr|y** /'wʌɹi, 'wʊɹi/ • *n* preocupació, angoixa • *v* preocupar-se, amoïnar-se; preocupar, amoïnar, neguitejar ~**ying** • *adj* preocupant, inquietant ~**ied** • *adj* preocupat

**worse** /wɜ:s, wɜs/ • *adj* pitjor • *(also)* ▷ GOOD

**worship** /'wɜ:ʃɪp, 'wɜʃɪp/ • *n* adoració *f*, culte *m*, veneració *f* • *v* adorar, venerar

**worth** /wɜ:θ, wɜθ/ • *n* valor *m* ~**y** • *adj* digne

**would** /wʊd, wəd/ • *v* 'Use the conditional tense

**wound** /wu:nd, wund/ • *n* ferida; lesió • *v* ferir • *(also)* ▷ WIND

**wove** *(sp)* ▷ WEAVE

**woven** *(pp)* ▷ WEAVE

**wrap** /ɹæp/ • *v* embolicar

**wreck** /ɹɛk/ • *n* ruïna *f*

**wrestl|e** • *v* lluitar ~**ing** • *n* lluita

**wrist** /ɹɪst/ • *n* canell *m*

**writ|e** /ɹaɪt/ • *v (sp* wrote, *pp* written) escriure ~**er** • *n* escriptor *m*, escriptora *f* ~**ing** • *n* escriptura *f*

**written** /ɹɪtn̩/ • *adj* escrit • *(also)* ▷ WRITE

**wrong** /ɹɒŋ, ɹɔŋ/ • *adj* incorrecte, erroni, equivocat

**wrote** *(sp)* ▷ WRITE

# X

**X-ray** • *n* raig X *m*; radiografia *f*

**xenophobia** /zɛnəˈfəʊbɪə/ • *n* xenofòbia *f*

**xerox** /ˈzɛ.ɹɒks, ˈzi:(ə)ɹɑks/ • *v* fotocopiar

**xylophone** /ˈzaɪ.lə.ˌfəʊn, ˈzaɪləˌfoʊn/ • *n* xilòfon *m*

**yacht** /jɒt, jɑt/ • *n* iot *m*

**yard** /jɑ:d, jɑɹd/ • *n* iarda *f*

**yeah** /jɛə̯/ • *part* sí

**year** /jɪə, jɪɹ/ • *n* any *m* ~**ly** • *adj* anual • *adv* anualment

**yearn** /jɜ:n, jɜ̃n/ • *v* anhelar, ansiejar

**yeast** /ji:st, i:st/ • *n* llevat *m*

**yellow** /ˈjɛl.əʊ, ˈjɛl.oʊ/ • *adj* groc; covard • *n* groc *m*

**Yemen** • *n* Iemen *m* ~**i** • *adj* iemenita • *n* iemenita *f*

**yes** /jɛs/ • *part* sí

**yesterday** /ˈjɛstədeɪ, ˈjɛstɚdeɪ/ • *adv* ahir; dia d'ahir *m*

**yet** /jɛt/ • *adv* encara • *conj* tanmateix, no obstant això

**yield** /ji:ld/ • *v* cedir

**yoga** /ˈjoʊɡə/ • *n* ioga *m*

**yogurt** /ˈjɒɡət, ˈjoʊɡɚt/ • *n* iogurt *m*

**yolk** /jəʊk, joʊk/ • *n* rovell *m*

**you** /ju:, ju/ • *pron* vosaltres, vostès, vós; tu, vostè; hom, u

**young** /jʌŋ/ • *adj* jove *f* • *n* jovent *m*

**your** /jɔ:, jɔ:ɹ/ • *det* el teu, la teva; el vostre *m*, la vostra *f* ~**self** • *pron* et; mateix

**youth** /ju:θ, juθ/ • *n* joventut *f*, abril *m*; jove *f*; jovent *m*

**Yugoslavia** • *n* Iugoslàvia *f* ~**n** • *adj* iugoslau • *n* iuguslau

**Zambian** • *adj* zambià

**zeal** /zi:l/ • *n* zel *m*

**zebra** /ˈzɛbɹə, ˈzi:bɹə/ • *n* zebra *f*

**zero** /ˈzɪəɹəʊ, ˈzɪɹ(ˌ)oʊ/ • *n* zero; res; zero a l'esquerra • *num* zero • *v* posar a zero

**Zimbabwe** • *n* Zimbabue

**zinc** /zɪŋk/ • *n* zinc

**zip** /zɪp/ • *n* codi postal *m*

**zombie** /ˈzɒmbi, ˈzɑmbi/ • *n* zombi *f*

**zone** /zoʊn, zəʊn/ • *n* zona *f*

**zoo** /zu:/ • *n* zoològic *m*

# Catalan-English

## A

**a** • *prep* at, to
**àbac** • *n* chessboard
**abaixar** • *v* lower, turn down
**abandó** • *n* abandonment
**abandonar** • *v* abandon, forsake
**abans** • *adv* before
**abarrotat** • *adj* crowded
**abast** • *n* range, reach
**abastar** • *v* reach
**abdomen** • *n* belly
**abella** • *n* bee
**abellir** • *v* appeal
**abjecte** • *adj* base
**ablanir** • *v* soften
**abocar** • *v* lean, pour
**abolició** • *n* abolition
**abolir** • *v* abolish
**abonament** • *n* subscription

**abraçada** • *n* embrace, hug
**abraçar** • *v* embrace, hug
**abric** • *n* coat
**abril** • *n* April • *n* youth
**absència** • *n* absence
**absent** • *adj* absent
**absentar** • *v* absent
**absolut** • *adj* absolute
**absolutament** • *adv* absolutely
**absorbent** • *adj* absorbent
**absorbir** • *v* absorb
**absort** • *adj* engrossed
**abstracció** • *n* abstract, abstraction
**abstracte** • *adj* abstract
**absurd** • *adj* absurd
**abundància** • *n* abundance, wealth
**abundant** • *adj* abundant
**abús** • *n* abuse
**abusar** • *v* abuse
**abusiu** • *adj* abusive
**acabar** • *v* end, end up, finish
**acabat** • *adv* after

A

**acadèmia** • *n* academy
**acadèmic** • *adj* academic
**acampar** • *v* camp
**acaronar** • *v* cuddle
**acceleració** • *n* acceleration
**accelera|r** • *v* accelerate, hurry ~**dor** • *n* accelerator
**accent** • *n* accent, stress
**accentuar** • *v* accent
**accepció** • *n* sense
**accepta|r** • *v* accept ~**ble** • *adj* acceptable
**accés** • *n* entry
**accessibilitat** • *n* accessibility
**accessible** • *adj* accessible
**accessori** • *adj* accessory
**accident** • *n* accident, accidental
**accidental** • *adj* accidental ~**ment** • *adv* accidentally
**accídia** • *n* sloth
**acció** • *n* action, share
**accionari** • *n* shareholder
**accionista** • *n* shareholder
**acer** • *n* steel
**ací** • *adv* here
**àcid** • *adj* acid, acidic, sour
**acidesa** • *n* acidity
**aclaparador** • *adj* overwhelming
**aclari|r** • *v* clarify ~**ment** • *n* clarification
**açò** • *adj* so • *pron* that
**acoblar** • *v* couple
**acollir** • *v* welcome
**acolorir** • *v* color
**acoltellar** • *v* knife, stab
**acomiada|r** • *v* dismiss, fire, sack ~**ment** • *n* notice
**acomodació** • *n* accommodation

**acompanya|r** • *v* accompany ~**nt** • *n* companion ~**ment** • *n* accompaniment
**acompli|r** • *v* achieve ~**ment** • *n* feat
**aconseguir** • *v* achieve, attain, get
**aconsella|r** • *v* advise ~**ble** • *adj* advisable
**acord** • *n* agreement, arrangement
**acordió** • *n* accordion
**acostumat** • *adj* used to
**acre** • *n* acre
**acrobàcia** • *n* acrobatics
**acròbata** • *n* acrobat
**acta** • *n* deed, minute
**acte** • *n* act, deed
**actitud** • *n* attitude
**actiu** • *adj* active
**activació** • *n* activation
**activa|r** • *v* activate ~**ment** • *adv* actively
**activista** • *n* activist
**activitat** • *n* activity
**actor** • *n* actor
**actriu** • *n* actor, actress
**actuació** • *n* acting, performance
**actual** • *adj* current, present ~**ment** • *adv* currently, nowadays
**actualització** • *n* update
**actualitzar** • *v* update
**actuar** • *v* act, perform, play
**acuar** • *v* rat
**acudit** • *n* joke
**acumulació** • *n* accumulation
**acumular** • *v* accumulate
**acuradament** • *adv* accurately, carefully

**acurat** • *adj* painstaking
**acusació** • *n* accusation
**acusada** • *n* accused
**acusar** • *v* accuse, charge
**acusat** • *n* accused
**acusatiu** • *adj* accusative
**acústic** • *adj* acoustic
**acústica** • *n* acoustics
**adaptació** • *n* adaptation
**adaptar** • *v* adapt
**addicció** • *n* addiction
**addició** • *n* addition
**addicional** • *adj* additional
~**ment** • *adv* additionally
**addictiu** • *adj* addictive
**additiu** • *n* additive
**adequadament** • *adv* adequately
**adequat** • *adj* adequate, appropriate, fit, proper
**adéu** • *interj* bye, goodbye
**adherir** • *v* adhere
**àdhuc** • *adv* even
**adinerat** • *adj* wealthy
**adjacent** • *adj* adjacent
**adjectiu** • *adj* adjective
**admetre** • *v* grant
**administració** • *n* administration, management
**administra|r** • *v* administer ~**dor** • *n* administrator ~**dora** • *n* administrator
**administratiu** • *adj* administrative
**admiració** • *n* admiration
**admira|r** • *v* admire ~**ble** • *adj* admirable
**admissió** • *n* admission
**ADN** • *n* DNA
**adob** • *n* fertilizer
**adolescència** • *n* adolescence

**adolescent** • *adj* adolescent
**adolorit** • *adj* sore
**adopció** • *n* adoption
**adoptar** • *v* adopt
**adoptiu** • *adj* adoptive
**adoració** • *n* adoration, worship
**adora|r** • *v* worship ~**ble** • *adj* adorable
**adormit** • *adj* asleep
**adornar** • *v* tire
**adquirir** • *v* acquire
**adquisició** • *n* acquisition
**adreça** • *n* address
**adreçar** • *v* address, direct, straighten
**adrogueria** • *n* grocery
**adult** • *adj* adult
**adulteri** • *n* adultery
**adverbi** • *n* adverb
**advers** • *adj* adverse
**adversari** • *n* adversary
**advertència** • *n* warning
**adverti|r** • *v* mark, warn ~**ment** • *n* warning
**advocada** • *n* lawyer
**advocar** • *v* advocate
**advocat** • *n* advocate, attorney, lawyer
**aeri** • *adj* aerial
**aeròbic** • *adj* aerobic
**aerolínia** • *n* airline
**aeronau** • *n* aircraft
**aeroport** • *n* airport
**aerosfera** • *n* atmosphere
**afaitar** • *v* shave
**afamat** • *adj* hungry
**afany** • *n* eagerness
**afanyar** • *v* hurry up
**afavorir** • *v* favor
**afeblir** • *v* weaken
**afecció** • *n* affection

**A**

**afectar** • *v* affect
**afecte** • *n* affect, affection
**afectuós** • *adj* affectionate
**afegir** • *v* add
**afer** • *n* affair
**aferrat** • *adj* stingy
**aficionat** • *n* fan
**afinar** • *v* tune
**afirmació** • *n* assertion
**afligit** • *adj* sorry
**afluixar** • *v* loose, relax
**afores** • *n* outskirts
**afortunadament** • *adv* fortunately, happily, luckily
**afortunat** • *adj* happy, lucky
**africà** • *adj* African
**Àfrica** • *n* Africa
**africana** • *n* African
**afrontament** • *n* confrontation
**afusellament** • *n* shooting
**agafa|r** • *v* grip, take ~dor • *n* grab ~ment • *n* grab
**agència** • *n* agency
**agenda** • *n* agenda, calendar, planner
**agent** • *n* agent
**àgil** • *adj* agile
**agilitat** • *n* agility
**agobiar** • *v* overwhelm
**agosarat** • *adj* bold
**agost** • *n* August
**agrada|r** • *v* appeal, like, love, please, pleasure ~ble • *adj* agreeable, pleasant
**agraïment** • *n* acknowledgment
**agrair** • *v* appreciate, thank
**agraït** • *adj* grateful, thankful
**agre** • *adj* sour
**agredolç** • *adj* bittersweet
**agressió** • *n* aggression
**agressiu** • *adj* aggressive

**agressivitat** • *n* aggressiveness
**agrícola** • *adj* agricultural
**agricultura** • *n* agriculture
**agrupar** • *v* collect
**aguantar** • *v* endure, hold
**àguila** • *n* eagle
**agulla** • *n* agility, hand, needle, switch
**agulló** • *n* stinger
**agut** • *adj* acute, sharp
**ahir** • *adv* yesterday
**aidar** • *v* help
**aigua** • *n* water
**aiguat** • *n* flood
**aigües** • *n* water
**aïlla|r** • *v* isolate ~ment • *n* isolation
**aïllat** • *adj* isolated
**airbag** • *n* airbag
**aire** • *n* air
**airejar** • *v* air
**airejós** • *adj* breezy
**airós** • *adj* breezy
**aixafar** • *v* crush
**aixecar** • *v* heighten
**aixella** • *n* armpit
**aixeta** • *n* tap
**així** • *adv* so, thus
**això** • *adj* so • *pron* that, this
**aixopluc** • *n* shelter
**aixoplugar** • *v* shelter
**ajornar** • *v* postpone
**ajuda** • *n* help
**ajuda|r** • *v* help ~dor • *n* helper ~nt • *n* helper
**ajunta|r** • *v* collect ~ment • *n* city hall
**ajust** • *n* adjustment
**ajusta|r** • *v* adjust, set ~ment • *n* adjustment
**ala** • *n* forward, wing

**A**

**alabança** • *n* praise
**alarma** • *n* alarm
**alarma|r** • *v* alarm ~**nt** • *adj* alarming
**alba** • *n* dawn
**albada** • *n* dawn
**albanès** • *adj* Albanian • *n* Albanian
**albanesa** • *n* Albanian
**Albània** • *n* Albania
**albatros** • *n* albatross
**albercoc** • *n* apricot
**albercoquer** • *n* apricot
**albergínia** • *n* eggplant
**alberginiera** • *n* eggplant
**albors** • *n* dawn
**àlbum** • *n* book
**alçada** • *n* height
**alcalde** • *n* mayor
**alcaldessa** • *n* mayor
**alçar** • *v* lift, raise
**alçat** • *n* elevation
**alcohol** • *n* alcohol
**alcohòlic** • *adj* alcoholic
**alcoholisme** • *n* alcoholism
**aldarull** • *n* stir
**alè** • *n* breath
**aleatori** • *adj* random
**aleatòriament** • *adv* randomly
**alegre** • *adj* glad, happy ~**ment** • *adv* happily
**alegria** • *n* joy
**Alemània** • *n* Germany
**alemany** • *adj* German
**alemanya** • *n* German
**Alemanya** • *n* Germany
**alenar** • *v* breathe
**aler** • *n* forward, wing
**alerta** • *n* alert
**alertar** • *v* alert
**aleví** • *n* fry

**alfàbega** • *n* basil
**alfabet** • *adj* literate
**alfabetisme** • *n* literacy
**alfàbrega** • *n* basil
**alfil** • *n* bishop
**Algèria** • *n* Algeria
**algú** • *pron* anyone, somebody, someone
**algues** • *n* seaweed
**algun** • *det* any
**aliança** • *n* alliance
**alié** • *adj* alien
**aliè** • *adj* alien
**alienació** • *n* alienation
**alienar** • *v* alienate
**alienígena** • *adj* alien
**àliga** • *n* eagle
**aliment** • *n* food
**alimenta|r** • *v* feed ~**dor** • *adj* nutritious
**alimentós** • *adj* nutritious
**all** • *n* garlic
**allà** • *adv* there
**allargar** • *v* lengthen
**allejar** • *v* garlic
**alleta|r** • *v* breastfeed, nurse ~**ment** • *n* breastfeeding
**alleujament** • *n* relief
**alleujat** • *adj* relieved
**allí** • *adv* there
**alliberació** • *n* liberation
**allibera|r** • *v* free, liberate, loose, release, rid ~**ment** • *n* liberation, release
**alliberat** • *n* release
**alligar** • *v* league
**allisar** • *v* smooth
**allistar** • *v* list
**allò** • *pron* that
**allotja|r** • *v* host, house ~**ment** • *n* housing

**almenys** ● *phr* at least
**alpinis|me** ● *n* mountaineering
~**ta** ● *n* mountaineer
**alt** ● *adj* high, loud, tall, upper
**altament** ● *adv* highly
**altaveu** ● *n* speaker
**alterar** ● *v* alter
**alternar** ● *v* alternate
**alternatiu** ● *adj* alternative
**alternativament** ● *adv*
alternatively
**altrament** ● *adv* otherwise
**altre** ● *adj* else
**altres** ● *n* others
**altura** ● *n* height
**alumini** ● *n* aluminium
**alumna** ● *n* pupil
**alumne** ● *n* pupil, student
**alvocat** ● *n* avocado
**alvocater** ● *n* avocado
**amable** ● *adj* kind, lovable
~**ment** ● *adv* kindly
**amagar** ● *v* conceal, hide
**amagat** ● *adj* hidden
**amagatall** ● *n* corner
**amanida** ● *n* salad
**amanir** ● *v* season
**amant** ● *n* lover
**amarar** ● *v* soak
**amarg** ● *adj* bitter
**amb** ● *prep* with
**ambaixada** ● *n* embassy
**ambaixador** ● *n* ambassador
**ambdós** ● *det* both
**ambició** ● *n* ambition, thirst
**ambiciós** ● *adj* ambitious
**ambient** ● *n* atmosphere,
environment
**ambiental** ● *adj* environmental
**ambigu** ● *adj* ambiguous
**ambigüitat** ● *n* ambiguity

**àmbit** ● *n* compass, range
**ambulància** ● *n* ambulance
**amenaça** ● *n* threat
**amenaçar** ● *v* threaten
**americà** ● *adj* American
**americana** ● *n* American
**ametlla** ● *n* almond
**ametller** ● *n* almond
**amfitrió** ● *n* host
**amfitriona** ● *n* host, hostess
**amic** ● *n* boyfriend, friend
**amidar** ● *v* measure
**amiga** ● *n* friend, girlfriend
**amigable** ● *adj* amicable
**amistançada** ● *n* mistress
**amistançat** ● *n* lover
**amistat** ● *n* friendship
**amistós** ● *adj* friendly
**amistosament** ● *adv* friendly
**amo** ● *n* landlord
**amoïnar** ● *v* worry
**amollar** ● *v* release
**amor** ● *n* love
**amorós** ● *adj* loving
**amorosament** ● *adv* lovingly
**ample** ● *adj* wide
**amplitud** ● *n* range
**ampolla** ● *n* bottle
**amprar** ● *v* borrow
**Amsterdam** ● *n* Amsterdam
**amulet** ● *n* charm
**amunt** ● *adv* up
**analfabet** ● *adj* illiterate
**analgèsic** ● *n* painkiller
**anàlisi** ● *n* analysis
**analitzar** ● *v* analyze
**analogia** ● *n* analogy
**ananàs** ● *n* pineapple
**anar** ● *v* do, go
**ancestral** ● *adj* ancestral
**ancià** ● *adj* elderly

**ancian** • *n* elder
**àncora** • *n* anchor
**ancorar** • *v* anchor
**andana** • *n* platform
**Andorra** • *n* Andorra
**ànec** • *n* duck
**anell** • *n* ring
**anella** • *n* ring
**anet** • *n* dill
**àngel** • *n* angel
**angèlic** • *adj* angelic
**angelical** • *adj* angelic
**angle** • *n* angle
**anglès** • *adj* English • *n* English
**anglesa** • *n* English
**angoixa** • *n* worry
**Angola** • *n* Angola
**angost** • *adj* narrow
**anguila** • *n* eel
**anhelar** • *v* yearn
**ànim** • *n* mood
**ànima** • *n* soul
**animació** • *n* animation
**animal** • *adj* animal
**animar** • *v* animate
**animat** • *adj* animate, animated
**anit** • *adv* tonight
**anivellar** • *v* level
**anivellat** • *adj* level
**aniversari** • *n* anniversary, birthday
**anomenar** • *v* name
**anònim** • *adj* anonymous
**anorac** • *n* anorak
**anormal** • *adj* abnormal
**anotació** • *n* observation
**anotar** • *v* book
**ànsia** • *n* eagerness
**ansiejar** • *v* yearn
**ansietat** • *n* anxiety
**ansiós** • *adj* anxious

**ansiosament** • *adv* anxiously
**ant** • *n* moose
**antagonis|me** • *n* antagonism
  **~ta** • *n* antagonist
**Antàrtida** • *n* Antarctica
**antecedents** • *n* background
**antecessor** • *n* predecessor
**antena** • *n* aerial, antenna
**anterior** • *adj* previous **~ment** •
  *adv* formerly, previously
**antibales** • *adj* bulletproof
**antic** • *adj* ancient, old
**anticipar** • *v* anticipate
**antílop** • *n* antelope
**antipàtic** • *adj* unfriendly
**antítesi** • *n* antithesis
**antologia** • *n* anthology
**antull** • *n* impulse
**anual** • *adj* annual, yearly
  **~ment** • *adv* annually, yearly
**anuari** • *n* annual
**anunci** • *n* advertisement,
  commercial, notice
**anunciar** • *v* announce
**any** • *n* year
**anyal** • *adj* annual
**anyell** • *n* lamb
**apagar** • *v* put out, switch off,
  turn off
**apagat** • *adj* off
**apaïsat** • *n* landscape
**aparèixer** • *v* appear
**aparell** • *n* bond, set
**aparença** • *n* appearance
**aparent** • *adj* apparent **~ment**
  • *adv* apparently
**aparició** • *n* appearance
**apassionadament** • *adv*
  passionately
**apassionat** • *adj* passionate
**àpat** • *n* meal

**apedaçar** ● *v* patch
**apedregar** ● *v* stone
**apegalós** ● *adj* sticky
**apegar** ● *v* stick
**apetit** ● *n* appetite
**api** ● *n* celery
**aplaudi|r** ● *v* applaud **~ment** ● *n* applause
**aplegar** ● *v* collect
**aplicable** ● *adj* applicable
**aplicat** ● *adj* applied
**apologètic** ● *adj* apologetic
**apologia** ● *n* apology
**apologitzar** ● *v* apologize
**aposento** ● *n* room
**aposta** ● *n* bet
**apostar** ● *v* bet, station
**apreciable** ● *adj* considerable
**aprehendre** ● *v* apprehend
**aprendre** ● *v* learn
**aprenent** ● *n* learner
**aprenentatge** ● *n* learning
**aprensiu** ● *adj* apprehensive
**apressar** ● *v* hurry
**apretar** ● *v* squeeze
**aprimar** ● *v* thin
**aprofundir** ● *v* elaborate
**apropa|r** ● *v* near **~ment** ● *n* approach
**apropiació** ● *n* seizure
**apropiadament** ● *adv* accordingly, appropriately
**apropiat** ● *adj* appropriate, suitable
**aprovació** ● *n* go
**aprovar** ● *v* approve, pass
**aproximació** ● *n* approach
**aproximadament** ● *adv* approximately
**aproximar** ● *v* near

**aproximat** ● *adj* approximate, rough
**apte** ● *adj* fit
**apuntar** ● *v* aim, point out, prompt
**apunyalar** ● *v* fist, knife, stab
**apunyegar** ● *v* punch
**aqüeducte** ● *n* aqueduct
**aqueix** ● *det* that
**aqueixa** ● *det* that
**aquest** ● *det* this
**aquesta** ● *pron* this
**aquí** ● *adv* here
**ara** ● *adv* now ● *interj* now
**àrab** ● *adj* Arab
**aram** ● *n* copper
**aranger** ● *n* grapefruit
**aranja** ● *n* grapefruit
**aranya** ● *n* spider
**arbitrari** ● *adj* arbitrary
**arbitràriament** ● *adv* arbitrarily
**àrbitre** ● *n* judge, referee
**arbre** ● *n* tree
**arbust** ● *n* bush
**arc** ● *n* arch, bow
**arca** ● *n* chest
**ardent** ● *adj* burning
**àrea** ● *n* area, compass
**arena** ● *n* arena, sand
**areng** ● *n* herring
**argamassa** ● *n* plaster
**argent** ● *n* silver
**argentat** ● *adj* silver
**Argentina** ● *n* Argentina
**argila** ● *n* clay
**arguïble** ● *adj* arguable
**argüir** ● *v* argue
**argument** ● *n* argument, plot
**argumentació** ● *n* argument
**argumentar** ● *v* argue
**aritmètica** ● *n* arithmetic

**arma** • *n* arm, weapon
**armadillo** • *n* armadillo
**armadura** • *n* armour
**armar** • *v* arm
**armari** • *n* cabinet, cupboard, locker, wardrobe
**armat** • *adj* armed
**armeni** • *adj* Armenian • *n* Armenian
**armènia** • *n* Armenian
**Armènia** • *n* Armenia
**armilla** • *n* waistcoat
**arna** • *n* beehive, moth
**arnès** • *n* armour
**arpa** • *n* claw, harp
**arpejar** • *v* scratch
**arquejar** • *v* arch
**arquer** • *n* archer
**arquitecte** • *n* architect
**arquitectònic** • *adj* architectural
**arquitectura** • *n* architecture
**arraconar** • *v* corner
**arrambador** • *n* banister
**arrancar** • *v* execute, run
**arrangement** • *n* arrangement
**arrebossar** • *v* batter, bread, plaster
**arreglada** • *n* arrangement
**arreglar** • *v* arrange, array, clean, fix, sort, square
**arrel** • *n* race, root, stem
**arrencar** • *v* execute
**arrenjar** • *v* arrange
**arreplegar** • *v* collect
**arrest** • *n* arrest
**arribada** • *n* arrival
**arribar** • *v* arrive, get
**arriscar** • *v* risk, venture
**arriscat** • *adj* risky
**arrissat** • *adj* curly, fuzzy
**arrodonir** • *v* round up

**arrogància** • *n* arrogance
**arrogant** • *adj* arrogant, proud
~**ment** • *adv* arrogantly
**arròs** • *n* rice
**arrossegar** • *v* drag, trail
**arruixar** • *v* sprinkle
**arsenal** • *n* magazine
**artefacte** • *n* artifact
**artell** • *n* knuckle
**artesà** • *n* craftsman
**article** • *n* article, paper
**articulació** • *n* articulation, joint
**articulat** • *adj* articulate
**artificial** • *adj* artificial, false
~**ment** • *adv* artificially
**artista** • *n* artist
**artístic** • *adv* artistic
**arxiu** • *n* archive, file
**ascendència** • *n* ancestry
**ascensió** • *n* climb
**ascensor** • *n* lift
**ase** • *n* donkey
**asfalt** • *n* asphalt
**Àsia** • *n* Asia
**asiàtic** • *adj* Asian
**asiàtica** • *n* Asian
**asil** • *n* asylum, home
**asimètric** • *adj* asymmetrical
**asolellat** • *adj* sunny
**aspa** • *n* sail
**aspiració** • *n* aspiration
**aspiradora** • *n* vacuum cleaner
**aspirar** • *v* aspire
**aspre** • *adj* harsh, rough, stark
**assaig** • *n* rehearsal, try
**assajar** • *v* rehearse
**assassí** • *n* assassin, murderer
**assassinar** • *v* assassinate, kill, murder
**assassinat** • *n* assassination, kill, murder

**assecadora** • *n* dryer, tumble dryer
**assecar** • *v* dry
**assedegat** • *adj* thirsty
**assegurança** • *n* insurance
**assemblea** • *n* assembly
**assentament** • *n* settlement
**assenyalar** • *v* point out
**assenyat** • *adj* sensible
**asserció** • *n* assertion
**assertiu** • *adj* assertive
**assessor** • *n* advisor
**assignar** • *v* set
**assignatura** • *n* subject
**assistència** • *n* assist, assistance
**assistente** • *n* assistant
**assistir** • *v* attend
**associació** • *n* association
**associar** • *v* associate
**associat** • *n* associate
**assoliment** • *n* achievement
**assossegat** • *adj* peaceful
**assotar** • *v* whip
**assumpció** • *n* assumption
**asticot** • *n* maggot
**astrònom** • *n* astronomer
**astrònoma** • *n* astronomer
**astronomia** • *n* astronomy
**astut** • *adj* shrewd
**atac** • *n* attack, seizure
**ataca|r** • *v* attack ~**nt** • *n* attacker, forward
**ataronjat** • *adj* orange
**atemorit** • *adj* frightened
**atenció** • *n* attention, notice
**atendre** • *v* attend
**Atenes** • *n* Athens
**atent** • *adj* attentive, thoughtful
**aterrar** • *v* land
**aterratge** • *n* landing

**aterrir** • *v* terrify
**atestat** • *n* witness
**àtic** • *n* attic
**atípic** • *adj* atypical
**atles** • *n* atlas
**atleta** • *n* athlete
**atlètic** • *adj* athletic
**atmosfera** • *n* atmosphere
**atordir** • *v* stun
**atracar** • *v* land, rob
**atracció** • *n* attraction
**atractiu** • *n* appeal • *adj* attractive
**atreure** • *v* attract
**atroç** • *adj* atrocious
**atrocitat** • *n* atrocity, outrage
**atropellar** • *v* run over
**atur** • *n* unemployment
**aturada** • *n* save
**aturar** • *adj* quit • *v* stop
**aturat** • *adj* unemployed
**atzabegenc** • *n* jet
**atzabeja** • *n* jet
**atzar** • *n* chance
**atzarós** • *adj* hazardous
**au** • *n* bird
**audaç** • *adj* brave
**audàcia** • *n* bottle
**àudio** • *adj* audio
**auditoria** • *n* audit
**augment** • *n* increase
**augmentar** • *v* increase
**auriculars** • *n* headphones
**aurora** • *n* dawn
**austral** • *adj* southern
**australià** • *adj* Australian
**Austràlia** • *n* Australia
**Àustria** • *n* Austria
**austríac** • *adj* Austrian
**autèntic** • *adj* authentic
**autenticitat** • *n* authenticity

A
B

**auto** • *n* machine
**autobiografia** • *n* autobiography
**autobús** • *n* bus
**autocar** • *n* coach
**autoestima** • *n* self-esteem
**automàtic** • *adj* automatic
**automàticament** • *adv* automatically
**automatització** • *n* automation
**automatitzar** • *v* automate
**automòbil** • *n* automobile, car, machine
**autònom** • *adj* autonomous
**autonomia** • *n* autonomy
**autonomy** • *n* autonomy
**autor** • *n* author ~**itat** • *n* authority
**autora** • *n* author
**autorització** • *n* authorization, permission
**autoritzar** • *v* authorize
**auxili** • *interj* help
**auxiliar** • *adj* assistant
**avall** • *adv* down
**avalot** • *n* stir
**avaluar** • *v* assess, evaluate
**avantatge** • *n* advantage
**avantatjós** • *adj* advantageous
**avantpassat** • *n* ancestor
**avar** • *adj* greedy
**avaria** • *n* breakdown, flat
**avarícia** • *n* greed
**avariciós** • *adj* greedy
**avenç** • *n* breakthrough
**avenir** • *n* future
**aventura** • *n* adventure, fling, venture
**aventurar** • *v* venture
**aventurer** • *adj* adventurous
**avergonyida** • *adj* embarrassed

**avergonyiment** • *n* embarrassment
**avergonyit** • *adj* ashamed, embarrassed
**avi** • *n* grandfather
**àvia** • *n* grandmother
**aviat** • *adv* early, shortly, soon
**àvid** • *adj* greedy
**avió** • *n* airplane
**avís** • *n* notice, warning
**avisar** • *v* warn
**avorrit** • *adj* bored, boring
**avort** • *n* abortion
**avorta|r** • *v* abort ~**ment** • *n* abort, abortion
**avui** • *adv* today
**axis** • *n* axis
**Azerbaidjan** • *n* Azerbaijan

**babaiana** • *n* butterfly
**babor** • *n* port
**bac** • *n* ferry
**bacallà** • *n* cod
**badall** • *n* crack, sandwich
**badia** • *n* bay
**bàdminton** • *n* badminton
**bagassa** • *n* tart
**bagatge** • *n* background, luggage
**Bahames** • *n* Bahamas
**Bahrain** • *n* Bahrain
**bai** • *n* bay
**baia** • *n* berry

B

**baix** • *adj* base, down, low, short

**baixa** • *n* casualty

**baixada** • *n* descent, download

**baixar** • *v* download, lower

**bajanada** • *n* nonsense

**bala** • *n* bullet, marble

**balanç** • *n* balance

**balança** • *n* balance

**balancejar** • *v* swing

**balcó** • *n* balcony

**balda** • *n* bolt

**baldufa** • *n* top

**balena** • *n* whale

**ball** • *n* dance

**balla|r** • *v* dance **~dor** • *n* dancer

**ballarí** • *n* dancer

**ballet** • *n* ballet

**baló** • *n* balloon

**balustre** • *n* banister

**ban** • *n* ban

**banana** • *n* banana

**banc** • *n* bank, bench, school

**banda** • *n* bend, crew, wing

**bandarra** • *n* tart

**bandeja|r** • *v* exile **~ment** • *n* exile

**bandejat** • *n* exile

**bandera** • *n* banner, flag

**banderola** • *n* banner

**Bangladesh** • *n* Bangladesh

**banner** • *n* banner

**banquer** • *n* banker

**banquera** • *n* banker

**banquet** • *n* dinner

**banqueta** • *n* bench

**bany** • *n* bath, bathroom, toilet

**banya** • *n* horn

**banyador** • *n* swimsuit

**banyegar** • *v* gore

**banyes** • *n* split

**bar** • *n* pub

**baralla** • *n* deck, quarrel

**barat** • *adj* cheap, inexpensive

**barba** • *n* beard

**Barbados** • *n* Barbados

**barbar** • *v* beard

**bàrbar** • *adj* barbarian

**barber** • *n* barber

**baríton** • *n* baritone

**barra** • *n* bar, stick

**barraca** • *n* shed

**barral** • *n* barrel

**barratgina** • *n* dragonfly

**barreja** • *n* mixture

**barrejar** • *v* mix

**barrera** • *n* barrier

**barret** • *n* hat

**barri** • *n* neighborhood

**barril** • *n* barrel, drum

**barroer** • *adj* clumsy

**basa** • *n* trick **~ment** • *n* base

**basa|r** • *v* base **~ment** • *n* base

**basarda** • *n* fear

**base** • *n* base

**bàsic** • *adj* basic • *n* primary

**bàsicament** • *adv* basically

**bàsquet** • *n* basket, basketball

**basquetbol** • *n* basketball

**bassa** • *n* pond

**bassal** • *n* pool

**bast** • *adj* rude

**bastant** • *adv* quite, rather

**bastida** • *n* scaffold, scaffolding

**bastó** • *n* club, staff, stick

**bastonejar** • *v* club

**bat** • *n* bat

**bata** • *n* dressing gown

**batalla** • *n* battle, combat

**batallar** • *v* battle

**batata** • *n* sweet potato

**batec** • *n* beat
**batedor** • *n* batter ~a • *n* mixer, whisk
**bategar** • *v* beat
**bateria** • *n* battery
**batí** • *n* dressing gown
**batlle** • *n* mayor
**batllessa** • *n* mayor
**batre** • *v* hit, knock
**batut** • *n* batter
**baula** • *n* link
**be** • *n* bee
**bé** • *adv* well
**bear** • *n* bear
**bebè** • *n* baby
**bec** • *n* bill
**beca** • *n* scholarship
**becaina** • *n* nap
**beguda** • *n* drink
**begut** • *adj* drunk
**beisbol** • *n* baseball
**belga** • *adj* Belgian
**Bèlgica** • *n* Belgium
**Belize** • *n* Belize
**bell** • *adj* beautiful, fair
**bella** • *adj* beautiful ~ment • *adv* beautifully
**bellesa** • *n* beauty
**bemoll** • *n* flat
**ben** • *adv* well
**bena** • *n* bandage, blindfold
**benanança** • *n* well-being
**benefici** • *n* advantage, benefit, profit
**beneficiar** • *v* benefit
**beneficiari** • *n* beneficiary
**beneficiós** • *adj* beneficial
**beneir** • *v* bless
**beneit** • *n* fool
**benestar** • *n* comfort, welfare, well-being

**benfactor** • *n* benefactor
**benigne** • *adj* benign
**Benín** • *n* Benin
**benjamí** • *n* baby
**béns** • *n* estate, goods
**benvinguda** • *interj* welcome
**benvingudes** • *interj* welcome
**benvingut** • *adj* welcome
**benvinguts** • *interj* welcome
**benvolgut** • *adj* dear
**benzina** • *n* gasoline, oil
**Berlín** • *n* Berlin
**Berna** • *n* Bern
**bes** • *n* kiss
**besada** • *n* kiss
**besar** • *v* kiss
**bessó** • *n* essence, meat, twin
**bèstia** • *n* animal, beast • *adj* stupid
**bestiar** • *n* cattle
**bestiesa** • *n* nonsense
**beure** • *v* drink
**biaix** • *n* angle, bias
**Bíblia** • *n* Bible
**bibliografia** • *n* bibliography
**biblioteca** • *n* library
**bibliotecari** • *n* librarian
**bici** • *n* bike
**bicicleta** • *n* bicycle
**bicoca** • *n* bargain
**Bielarús** • *n* Belarus
**Bielorússia** • *n* Belarus
**bifurcació** • *n* fork
**bifurcar** • *v* fork
**biga** • *n* timber
**bilió** • *n* billion • *num* trillion
**biodegradable** • *adj* biodegradable
**biodiversitat** • *n* biodiversity
**biografia** • *n* biography
**biogràfic** • *adj* biographical

**B**

biòleg • *n* biologist
biòloga • *n* biologist
biologia • *n* biology
biològic • *n* biological
biquini • *n* bikini
birra • *n* beer
bis • *n* screw
bisbe • *n* bishop
bitllar • *v* boost
bitlles • *n* bowling
bitllet • *n* ticket
blanc • *n* target, white
blat • *n* wheat
blau • *adj* blue
ble • *n* lock
blincar • *v* bow
bloc • *n* block
blocar • *v* block
blog • *n* blog
bloqueig • *n* block
bloquejar • *v* block, hang
bo • *adj* good • *n* good
boc • *n* buck
boca • *n* mouth
bocabadat • *adj* speechless
bocí • *n* mouthful
bocoi • *n* barrel
boda • *n* marriage, wedding
bòfia • *n* heat
bogeria • *n* insanity
Bogotà • *n* Bogota
boig • *adj* certifiable, crazy, mad • *n* fool
boira • *n* fog, mist
boix • *n* box
boja • *adj* mad
bol • *n* bowl
bola • *n* ball
bolcar • *v* upset
bolet • *n* mushroom
bolígraf • *n* pen

Bolívia • *n* Bolivia
bomba • *n* bomb, pump
bombar • *v* pump
bombardejar • *v* bomb
bomber • *n* firefighter
bombera • *n* firefighter
bombeta • *n* light bulb
bombó • *n* chocolate
bombolla • *n* bubble
bon • *adj* good
bona • *n* good
bondat • *n* goodness, kindness
bonesa • *n* goodness
bonic • *adj* beautiful, pretty
bonica • *adj* beautiful
boom • *n* boom
bord • *n* board
borinot • *n* bumblebee
borratxo • *adj* drunk
borrós • *adj* fuzzy
bosc • *n* forest, wood
bosnià • *adj* Bosnian
Bòsnia • *n* Bosnia
bosniana • *adj* Bosnian
bossa • *n* bag
bota • *n* boot
bóta • *n* barrel
botella • *n* bottle
botí • *n* prize
botiga • *n* shop
botó • *n* button
botonar • *v* button
botre • *v* bounce
Botswana • *n* Botswana
bou • *n* ox
boxar • *v* box
boxejar • *v* box
braç • *n* arm
braçalet • *n* bracelet
bragues • *n* pants
bragueta • *n* fly

**branca** • *n* branch
**brandi** • *n* brandy
**brasa** • *n* coal
**Brasil** • *n* Brazil
**breu** • *adj* brief ~ment • *adv* briefly, shortly
**bridge** • *n* bridge
**brillantor** • *n* shine
**brilla|r** • *v* shine ~nt • *adj* bright, brilliant
**brindar** • *v* toast
**brindis** • *n* toast
**brisa** • *n* breeze
**britànic** • *adj* British
**broc** • *n* neck
**bròcoli** • *n* broccoli
**broma** • *n* joke
**bronze** • *adj* bronze
**brou** • *n* broth
**bruixa** • *n* cow
**brúixola** • *n* compass
**Brunei** • *n* Brunei
**bruscament** • *adv* shortly
**brut** • *adj* dirty, nasty
**brutal** • *adj* brutal
**buc** • *n* bed, beehive, belly, body, riverbed, shell
**bucal** • *adj* oral
**bucle** • *n* loop
**budell** • *n* intestine
**bufanda** • *n* scarf
**bufar** • *v* blow
**bufeta** • *n* bladder
**bufetada** • *n* slap
**bufó** • *adj* cute
**bugada** • *n* laundry
**bugaderia** • *n* launderette
**buidar** • *v* empty
**buidesa** • *n* emptiness
**buidor** • *n* emptiness
**buit** • *adj* empty • *n* vacuum

**bulb** • *n* bulb
**búlgar** • *adj* Bulgarian
**búlgara** • *n* Bulgarian
**Bulgària** • *n* Bulgaria
**bullent** • *adj* boiling
**bullir** • *v* boil
**burilla** • *n* butt
**burocràcia** • *n* bureaucracy
**burra** • *n* donkey
**burro** • *n* donkey
**Burundi** • *n* Burundi
**bus** • *n* bus, diver
**busca** • *n* hand
**buscar** • *v* look, look for, search
**bust** • *n* bust
**bústia** • *n* mailbox
**butaca** • *n* armchair
**butlla** • *n* bull
**butxaca** • *n* pocket
**butza** • *n* chicken

**ca** • *n* dog
**cabal** • *n* flow
**cabana** • *n* hut
**cabanya** • *n* hut
**cabell** • *n* hair
**cabellera** • *n* coma
**cabina** • *n* car
**cable** • *n* cable, cord, wire
**cablejar** • *v* cable
**cabota** • *n* head
**cabotejar** • *v* head
**cabra** • *n* crab, goat
**cabrejar** • *v* anger

**cabreria** • *n* dairy
**cabrit** • *n* kid
**caca** • *n* shit
**caça** • *n* fighter, game, hunt, hunting
**caça|r** • *v* hunt ~**dor** • *n* hunter
**cacauet** • *n* peanut
**cacera** • *n* hunt
**cactus** • *n* cactus
**cada** • *det* each, every
**cadascú** • *pron* everyone
**cadàver** • *n* body
**cadena** • *n* chain
**cadenat** • *n* lock
**cadira** • *n* chair
**cafè** • *n* café, coffee
**cafeteria** • *n* café
**cagar** • *v* shit
**cagondena** • *interj* damn
**caiguda** • *n* borrow, decline, fall
**Caire** • *n* Cairo
**caixa** • *n* box, case, till
**caixer** • *n* cashier
**calabós** • *n* cell
**calaix** • *n* drawer
**calaixera** • *n* cupboard
**calamar** • *n* squid
**calamars** • *n* squid
**calamarsa** • *n* hail
**calamarsejar** • *v* hail
**calat** • *n* draft
**calb** • *adj* bald
**calç** • *n* lime
**calçar** • *v* shoe
**calçat** • *n* shoe
**calces** • *n* panties
**calçons** • *n* pants, panties
**calçotets** • *n* pants
**càlcul** • *n* calculation

**calcula|r** • *v* calculate ~**dor** • *n* computer ~**dora** • *n* calculator
**caldre** • *v* need
**calefacció** • *n* heating
**calendari** • *n* calendar, forecast
**calendàriu** • *n* calendar
**calent** • *adj* hot, warm
**calfred** • *n* shiver
**càlid** • *adj* warm
**call** • *n* corn, ghetto
**callar** • *adj* silent
**calm** • *adj* calm
**calma** • *n* calm, stillness
**calmar** • *v* calm, quiet
**calmat** • *adj* easygoing
**calor** • *n* heat
**cama** • *n* leg
**camaleó** • *n* chameleon
**camarada** • *n* comrade
**Cambodja** • *n* Cambodia
**cambra** • *n* bedroom, chamber, room
**cambrer** • *n* waiter
**cambrera** • *n* waitress
**camell** • *n* camel
**càmera** • *n* camera
**cameràman** • *n* cameraman
**Camerun** • *n* Cameroon
**camí** • *n* path, road, way
**caminada** • *n* hike
**caminar** • *v* walk
**camió** • *n* truck
**camisa** • *n* shirt
**camp** • *n* country, field, ground
**campament** • *n* camp
**campana** • *n* bell
**campanya** • *n* campaign
**camperol** • *n* peasant
**campestre** • *adj* country
**càmping** • *n* camp

**campió** • *n* champion
**campionat** • *n* championship
**campus** • *n* campus
**Canadà** • *n* Canada
**canadenc** • *adj* Canadian
**canadenca** • *n* Canadian
**canal** • *n* canal, channel, gutter
**canaladura** • *n* flute
**canalitzar** • *v* channel
**canari** • *n* canary
**Canberra** • *n* Canberra
**canceller** • *n* chancellor
**càncer** • *n* cancer
**cançó** • *n* song
**candela** • *n* candle
**càndid** • *adj* naive
**candidat** • *n* candidate
**canell** • *n* wrist
**canella** • *adj* cinnamon • *n* tap
**caneller** • *n* cinnamon
**cànem** • *n* cannabis
**cangur** • *n* kangaroo
**cànnabis** • *n* cannabis
**canó** • *n* barrel, gun
**canoa** • *n* canoe
**canonada** • *n* pipe
**cansada** • *adj* tired
**cansalada** • *n* bacon
**cansar** • *v* tire
**cansat** • *adj* tired
**cantaire** • *n* singer
**canta|r** • *v* sing ~**nt** • *n* singer
**canterano** • *n* cupboard
**cantonada** • *n* angle, corner
**cantor** • *n* singer
**canvi** • *n* change
**canviar** • *v* change, substitute
**canyella** • *adj* cinnamon
**canyeller** • *n* cinnamon
**caos** • *n* chaos
**caòtic** • *adj* chaotic

**cap** • *n* chief, head • *det* no • *pron* none
**capa** • *n* bed, cloak, layer
**capaç** • *adj* able, capable, proficient
**capacitat** • *n* ability, capacity
**capar** • *v* steer
**capça** • *n* head
**capçada** • *n* crown, head
**capçal** • *n* head
**capçalera** • *n* head
**capcinejar** • *v* nod
**capejada** • *n* nod
**capejar** • *v* nod
**capell** • *n* hat
**capellà** • *n* plaice, priest
**capgròs** • *n* tadpole
**capità** • *n* captain
**capital** • *adj* capital
**capitalis|me** • *n* capitalism ~**ta** • *adj* capitalist
**capitanejar** • *v* captain
**capitell** • *n* capital
**capítol** • *n* chapter, episode
**caplletra** • *n* initial
**caprici** • *n* impulse
**capritx** • *n* impulse
**capsa** • *n* box, case
**captaire** • *n* beggar
**captura** • *n* capture
**capturar** • *v* capture
**car** • *conj* because • *adj* expensive ~**itat** • *n* charity
**cara** • *n* face, front
**carabassa** • *adj* orange • *n* pumpkin
**carabassera** • *n* pumpkin
**carabassó** • *n* courgette
**caràcter** • *n* character, letter
**característic** • *adj* characteristic
**característica** • *n* characteristic

caracteritzar • v characterize
caragol • n snail
caramel • n candy
carapulla • n ice cream
carbassa • n pumpkin
carbassera • n pumpkin
carbó • n carbon, coal
carbohidrat • n carbohydrate
carboni • n carbon
carburant • n fuel
cardar • v fuck
càrdigan • n cardigan
careta • n mask
carga • n burden
cargol • n screw
caricatura • n cartoon
carícia • n stroke
carmanyola • n lunchbox
carn • n flesh, meat
carnisser • n butcher
carnissera • n butcher
carpa • n carp
carpí • n goldfish
carraca • n shed
carranc • n crab
càrrec • n office
càrrega • n burden, cargo, charge
carrega|r • v load ~dor • n charger, magazine
carrer • n street
carrera • n career, ladder, run
carreró • n alley
carret • n cart
carreta • n cart
carretera • n road
carretó • n cart, wheelbarrow
carril • n lane, rail
carro • n wagon
carrossa • n float
carrosseria • n body

carrossí • n gig
carruatge • n carriage
carrussel • n roundabout
carta • n letter, menu
cartell • n poster
carter • n mailman
cartó • n cartoon
carxofa • n artichoke
carxofera • n artichoke
cas • n case
casa • n home, house ~ment • n marriage, wedding
casaca • n coat
casa|r • v marry ~ment • n marriage, wedding
casat • adj married
casc • n helmet
casera • n beehive
caserna • n base
casino • n casino
casolà • adj homemade
casolana • adj homemade
cassó • n saucepan
castany • adj chestnut
castanya • n chestnut
castell • n castle
castellà • n lord • adj Spanish
càstig • n penalty, punishment
castigar • v punish
castor • n beaver
castrar • v steer
casual • adj casual
catàleg • n catalogue
càtedra • n chair
catedral • n cathedral
categoria • n category
catifa • n carpet
catòlic • adj Catholic
catorze • num fourteen
catúfol • n bucket
cau • n joint

**caure** • v fall
**causa** • n case, cause
**causal** • adj causal
**causar** • v prompt
**càustic** • adj caustic
**caut** • adj cautious
**cautelós** • adj careful, cautious, wary
**cautxú** • n rubber
**cavalcar** • v ride
**cavall** • n horse
**cavaller** • n gentleman
**cavalleresc** • adj chivalrous
**cavallerós** • adj chivalrous
**cavallets** • n roundabout
**cavar** • v dig
**ceba** • n onion
**cec** • adj blind
**cedir** • v give in, yield
**cegar** • v blind
**ceguesa** • n blindness
**cel** • n heaven, sky
**celebració** • n celebration
**celebrar** • v celebrate
**cèlebre** • adj famous
**celebritat** • n celebrity
**celiandre** • n coriander
**cella** • n eyebrow
**cementiri** • n graveyard
**cendra** • n ash
**cendre** • n ash
**censor** • n censor
**censurar** • v censor
**cent** • num hundred
**centau** • n cent
**centella** • n spark
**cèntim** • n cent
**centímetre** • n inch
**central** • n center, headquarters • adj central
**centre** • n center

**centúria** • n century
**cera** • n wax
**ceràmic** • adj ceramic
**ceràmica** • n ceramic, ceramics
**cercar** • v look, look up, look for, search
**cercle** • n circle, ring
**cèrcol** • n ring
**cereal** • n cereal, grain
**cereals** • n cereal
**cerimònia** • n ceremony
**cerimonial** • adj ceremonial
**cerós** • adj wax
**cert** • adj certain
**certament** • adv certainly, indeed
**certesa** • n certainty
**certificable** • adj certifiable
**certificació** • n certification
**certificat** • n certificate
**cervell** • n brain, noodle
**cervesa** • n beer
**cérvol** • n buck, deer
**cessar** • v cease
**cicatriu** • n scar
**cicle** • n cycle, loop
**ciclisme** • n cycling
**ciència** • n science
**científic** • adj scientific • n scientist
**cigarret** • n cigarette
**cigne** • n swan
**cigonya** • n stork
**cigró** • n chickpea
**cigronera** • n chickpea
**cilindre** • n cylinder
**cim** • n peak, summit
**cimera** • n summit
**cinc** • n five
**cineasta** • n filmmaker
**cinema** • n cinema, picture

**cinquanta** • *num* fifty
**cinquè** • *adj* fifth
**cinta** • *n* ribbon
**cintura** • *n* middle, waist
**cinturó** • *n* belt
**circ** • *n* circus
**circuit** • *n* circuit
**circular** • *adj* circular
**circumda|r** • *v* surround **~nt** • *adj* surrounding
**circumscripció** • *n* constituency
**circumspecte** • *adj* circumspect
**circumstància** • *n* circumstance
**cirera** • *n* cherry
**cirerer** • *n* cherry
**cirurgia** • *n* surgery
**cirurgià** • *n* surgeon
**cirurgiana** • *n* surgeon
**cisell** • *n* chisel
**cistell** • *n* basket
**cistella** • *n* basket
**cita** • *n* appointment, date
**citació** • *n* quote
**citar** • *v* summon
**ciuró** • *n* chickpea
**ciutadà** • *n* citizen
**ciutadania** • *n* citizenship
**ciutat** • *n* city
**civada** • *n* oat
**cívic** • *adj* civic
**civil** • *adj* civil **~itat** • *n* civilization
**civilització** • *n* civilization
**clar** • *adj* bright, brilliant, clear, light, thin
**claraboia** • *n* skylight
**clarament** • *adv* clearly
**claredat** • *n* clarity
**clarejar** • *v* dawn
**clarinet** • *n* clarinet
**classe** • *n* class, kind, sort, type

**clàssic** • *adj* classic
**classificació** • *n* classification
**classificar** • *v* sort
**clau** • *n* cock, code, fuck, key, nail
**clauer** • *n* keyring
**clàusula** • *n* clause
**clausura** • *n* closure
**clavar** • *v* hammer, nail
**clavecí** • *n* harpsichord
**clavicèmbal** • *n* harpsichord
**clavilla** • *n* plug
**clàxon** • *n* horn
**clergue** • *n* clerk
**clic** • *n* click
**clicar** • *v* click
**client** • *n* client, customer
**clientela** • *n* clientele
**clima** • *n* climate
**clínic** • *adj* clinical
**clínica** • *n* clinic
**clissar** • *v* get
**cloïssa** • *n* clam
**closca** • *n* head, shell
**cloure** • *v* close
**clovella** • *n* shell
**club** • *n* club
**coartada** • *n* alibi
**cobaia** • *n* guinea pig
**cobdícia** • *n* greed
**cobdiciós** • *adj* greedy
**cobejós** • *adj* greedy
**cobert** • *adj* covered
**coberta** • *n* deck **~ment** • *adv* secretly
**cobertura** • *n* coat
**cobrar** • *v* earn
**cobrir** • *v* coat
**coca** • *n* cookie
**coça** • *n* kick
**cocaïna** • *n* cocaine

**coco** • *n* coconut
**cocodril** • *n* crocodile
**còctel** • *n* cocktail
**codi** • *n* code, language
**codony** • *n* quince
**codonyer** • *n* quince
**coet** • *n* rocket
**cofa** • *n* top
**cofre** • *n* chest
**cognitiu** • *adj* cognitive
**cogombre** • *n* cucumber
**cogombrera** • *n* cucumber
**cogombret** • *n* gherkin
**coherència** • *n* coherence
**coherent** • *adj* coherent
**cohort** • *n* cohort
**coincidir** • *v* coincide, match
**coix** • *adj* lame
**coixí** • *n* bag, cushion, pillow
**col** • *n* cabbage
**colar** • *v* strain
**colcar** • *v* ride
**còlera** • *n* anger
**colesterol** • *n* cholesterol
**coliflor** • *n* cauliflower
**coll** • *n* collar, neck
**colla** • *n* bunch, crew, troop
**collage** • *n* collage
**collar** • *n* collar • *v* screw
**collera** • *n* collar
**collir** • *v* harvest
**collita** • *n* harvest
**colliter** • *n* harvester
**colló** • *n* ball
**colom** • *n* cock, dove, pigeon
**colombià** • *adj* Colombian
**Colòmbia** • *n* Colombia
**colombiana** • *n* Colombian
**colon** • *n* settler
**còlon** • *n* colon
**colònia** • *n* colony

**colonial** • *adj* colonial
**color** • *n* color
**coloret** • *n* blush
**colossal** • *adj* colossal
**colpejar** • *v* hit, knock
**coltell** • *n* knife
**columna** • *n* column, file
**columnista** • *n* columnist
**colze** • *n* elbow
**com** • *conj* as • *prep* like • *adv* how • *part* like • *interj* what
**coma** • *n* coma, comma
**comanda** • *n* order
**comanda|r** • *v* head ~nt • *n* commander
**comarca** • *n* county, district
**combat** • *n* combat, fight
**combatent** • *n* combatant
**combatiu** • *adj* combative
**combatre** • *v* battle, combat, fight
**combinació** • *n* combination, slip
**combregar** • *v* communicate
**combustible** • *n* fuel
**comèdia** • *n* comedy, simulation
**comença|r** • *v* begin, commence, start ~ment • *n* beginning
**comentar** • *v* comment
**comentari** • *n* comment, commentary, observation
**comerç** • *n* commerce
**comercial** • *adj* commercial
**comerciar** • *v* deal
**cometre** • *v* commit
**comí** • *n* cumin
**comiat** • *n* leave
**còmic** • *adj* comic
**comissaria** • *n* police station**

**comissió** • *n* commission
**comissionar** • *v* commission
**comissionat** • *n* commissioner
**comitè** • *n* committee
**commovedor** • *adj* moving
**còmode** • *adj* comfortable
**comoditat** • *n* comfort
**Comores** • *n* Comoros
**company** • *n* buddy, colleague
**companyia** • *n* company
**comparació** • *n* comparison
**compara|r** • *v* check, compare
~**ble** • *adj* comparable
**comparatiu** • *adj* comparative
**compartir** • *v* share
**compartit** • *adj* shared
**compassió** • *n* compassion,
sympathy
**compassiu** • *adj* compassionate
**compensació** • *n* compensation
**compensar** • *v* balance
**competència** • *n* competition,
competence, proficiency
**competent** • *adj* able,
competent
**competició** • *n* competition,
contest
**competir** • *v* compete
**competitiu** • *adj* competitive
**compilació** • *n* compilation
**complaure** • *v* please
**complementar** • *v* complement,
supplement
**complementari** • *adj*
complementary
**complet** • *adj* complete, full
**completa** • *adj* complete ~**ment**
• *adv* altogether, completely,
fully, quite, thoroughly
**complex** • *adj* complex ~**itat** • *n*
complexity

**complicació** • *n* complication
**complicar** • *v* complicate
**complicat** • *adj* complicated,
hard
**complir** • *v* complete, fulfill
**complot** • *n* plot
**compondre** • *v* compose
**comporta|r** • *v* act ~**ment** • *n*
behavior
**compositor** • *n* composer
**compositora** • *n* composer
**compost** • *adj* compound
**compra|r** • *v* buy, deal ~**dor** • *n*
buyer
**comprendre** • *v* grasp,
understand
**comprensió** • *n* comprehension
**comprensiu** • *adj*
understanding
**comprometre** • *v* commit
**compromís** • *n* appointment,
commitment, compromise,
obligation
**comprovar** • *v* check
**comptaquilòmetres** • *n* clock
**compta|r** • *v* count, number
~**dor** • *n* counter, meter ~**ble**
• *n* accountant
**comptatge** • *n* count
**comptavoltes** • *n* counter
**compte** • *n* bill, care, check,
count
**computa|r** • *v* compute ~**dor** •
*n* computer
**comtat** • *n* county
**comte** • *n* count
**comú** • *adj* common
**comuna** • *adj* common ~**ment** •
*adv* commonly
**comunicació** • *n*
communication

**comunicar** • *adj* engaged
**comunis|me** • *n* communism
~**ta** • *adj* communist
**comunitat** • *n* community
**con** • *n* cone
**concebre** • *v* beget, conceive
**concentració** • *n* concentration
**concentrar** • *v* concentrate
**concepció** • *n* conception
**concepte** • *n* concept
**conceptual** • *adj* conceptual
**concert** • *n* concert
**concís** • *adj* brief
**concloure** • *v* conclude
**conclusió** • *n* conclusion
**concordança** • *n* agreement
**concordar** • *v* match
**concret** • *adj* concrete
**concurs** • *n* contest
**concursant** • *n* contestant
**condemnar** • *v* condemn, convict
**condescendent** • *adj* condescending
**condició** • *n* condition
**condicional** • *adj* conditional
**condicionar** • *v* condition
**condimentar** • *v* season
**condó** • *n* condom, rubber
**condom** • *n* condom
**condret** • *adj* correct
**conducta** • *n* behavior, conduct
**conductor** • *n* driver
**conduir** • *v* drive, lead
**coneguda** • *n* friend
**conegut** • *n* acquaintance, friend • *adv* AKA
**coneixement** • *n* judgment, knowledge
**coneixements** • *n* knowledge
**conèixer** • *v* meet

**confessar** • *v* confess
**confessió** • *n* confession
**confiança** • *n* confidence, trust
**confiar** • *v* commit, trust
**confiat** • *adj* confident
**configuració** • *n* configuration
**confinament** • *n* confinement
**confirmació** • *n* confirmation
**confirmar** • *v* confirm
**conflicte** • *n* conflict
**confondre** • *v* confuse
**confort** • *n* comfort
**confortar** • *v* comfort
**confrontació** • *n* confrontation
**confrontament** • *n* confrontation
**confús** • *adj* confused, confusing
**confusió** • *n* confusion
**congela|r** • *v* freeze ~**dor** • *n* freezer
**congregació** • *n* congregation
**congregar** • *v* congregate
**conill** • *n* rabbit
**conillet** • *n* beaver
**conjetura** • *n* guess
**cònjuge** • *n* spouse
**conjunció** • *n* conjunction
**conjunt** • *adj* joint • *n* set
**conjuntament** • *adv* jointly
**conjur** • *n* spell
**connotació** • *n* connotation
**conquerir** • *v* conquer, win
**conquilla** • *n* shell
**conquistar** • *v* conquer
**conrear** • *v* cultivate
**consagrar** • *v* devote
**consciència** • *n* awareness, conscience
**conscient** • *adj* aware, conscious

**consecució** ● *n* achievement, feat

**consecutiu** ● *adj* consecutive

**consell** ● *n* advice, council

**conseller** ● *n* advisor

**consenti|r** ● *v* consent ~ment ● *n* consent

**conseqüència** ● *n* consequence

**conseqüentment** ● *adv* consequently

**conserge** ● *n* caretaker

**conservació** ● *n* conservation

**conserva|r** ● *v* conserve, preserve ~dor ● *adj* conservative

**considera|r** ● *v* consider ~ble ● *adj* considerable ~blement ● *adv* considerably

**considerat** ● *adj* considerate

**consignar** ● *v* commit

**consistència** ● *n* consistency

**consistent** ● *adj* consistent ~ment ● *adv* consistently

**consistir** ● *v* consist

**consol** ● *n* comfort, relief

**consola** ● *n* shell

**consolar** ● *v* comfort

**consolidar** ● *v* consolidate

**conspiració** ● *n* conspiracy, plot

**conspirar** ● *v* plot

**constant** ● *adj* constant ~ment ● *adv* constantly

**consternació** ● *n* concern

**constipat** ● *n* cold

**constitució** ● *n* constitution, frame

**constitucional** ● *adj* constitutional

**constituent** ● *adj* constituent

**construcció** ● *n* building, construction

**construir** ● *v* build, construct

**consulta** ● *n* appointment, consultation

**consultar** ● *v* consult

**consum** ● *n* consumption

**consumidor** ● *n* consumer

**contagiar** ● *v* infect

**contaminació** ● *n* pollution

**conte** ● *n* tale

**contemplar** ● *v* witness

**contemporani** ● *adj* contemporary

**contenidor** ● *n* container

**contenir** ● *v* contain

**content** ● *adj* content, happy, pleased

**context** ● *n* context

**contextualitzar** ● *v* frame

**continent** ● *n* continent, mainland

**contingut** ● *n* content

**continu** ● *adj* continuous

**continuadament** ● *adv* continually

**continuar** ● *v* continue, keep

**contra** ● *prep* against

**contracció** ● *n* contraction

**contractar** ● *v* hire

**contracte** ● *n* agreement, contract

**contradicció** ● *n* contradiction

**contradictori** ● *adj* contradictory

**contradir** ● *v* contradict

**contrari** ● *n* opposite

**contràriament** ● *phr* on the contrary

**contrasenya** ● *n* password

**contrast** ● *n* contrast

**contreure** ● *v* contract

**contribució** ● *n* contribution

**contribuent** • *n* taxpayer
**contribuir** • *v* contribute
**control** • *n* control
**controlar** • *v* control
**controvertit** • *adj* controversial
**convèncer** • *v* convince
**convenció** • *n* convention
**convencional** • *adj* conventional, formal
**convençut** • *adj* convinced
**conveni** • *n* agreement
**conveniència** • *n* convenience
**convenient** • *adj* convenient
**convenir** • *v* suit
**conversa** • *n* conversation
**conversació** • *n* conversation
**conversar** • *v* talk
**convertir** • *v* convert
**convicció** • *n* conviction
**convidar** • *v* invite
**convidat** • *n* guest
**convincent** • *adj* compelling, convincing
**conxa** • *n* shell
**conyac** • *n* brandy
**cooperació** • *n* cooperation
**cooperar** • *v* cooperate
**cooperatiu** • *adj* cooperative
**cooperativa** • *n* cooperative
**coordinador** • *n* coordinator
**cop** • *n* belt, blow, knock, shot, stroke, time • *adj* hit
**copa** • *n* cup
**copçar** • *v* devise
**còpia** • *n* copy, mirror
**copiar** • *v* copy, mirror
**copsar** • *v* get
**cor** • *n* choir, heart
**coratge** • *n* backbone, bottle, courage

**coratjós** • *adj* brave, courageous
**corb** • *n* crow, raven
**corba** • *n* bow, curve
**corbar** • *v* bow
**corbata** • *n* necktie
**corbatí** • *n* bowtie
**corbes** • *n* curve
**corda** • *n* cord, rope, string
**cordell** • *n* string
**corder** • *n* lamb
**cordill** • *n* cord, string
**Corea** • *n* Korea
**coreà** • *adj* Korean
**coreana** • *n* Korean
**coreògraf** • *n* choreographer
**coreografia** • *n* choreography
**coriandre** • *n* coriander
**corn** • *n* horn
**corona** • *n* crown, ring
**coronar** • *v* king
**corporal** • *adj* bodily, personal
**corpori** • *adj* bodily
**corpus** • *n* corpus
**correcció** • *n* correction, remedy
**correctament** • *adv* correctly
**correcte** • *adj* correct
**correctiu** • *n* remedy
**corredor** • *n* aisle, corridor, runner
**corregir** • *v* correct
**correlació** • *n* correlation
**corrent** • *n* current, draft, stream
**correntia** • *n* draft
**corrents** • *adv* quick
**córrer** • *n* run
**correspondència** • *n* correspondence
**correspondre** • *v* correspond, match

**corresponent** • *adj* corresponding

**corresponsal** • *n* correspondent

**corretja** • *n* belt

**corriol** • *n* trail

**corrompre** • *v* corrupt

**corrupte** • *adj* corrupt

**cort** • *n* court

**cortejar** • *v* court

**cortès** • *adj* courteous, polite

**cortesia** • *n* courtesy, kindness

**cortina** • *n* curtain

**còrvid** • *n* crow

**cos** • *n* body, field

**cosa** • *n* thing

**cosí** • *n* cousin

**cosina** • *n* cousin

**cosir** • *v* sew

**cost** • *n* charge, cost

**costa** • *n* coast

**costal** • *adj* coastal

**costaner** • *adj* coastal

**costar** • *v* cost

**costat** • *n* side

**costella** • *n* rib

**coster** • *adj* coastal

**costós** • *adj* costly

**costum** • *n* custom, habit

**costura** • *n* cut

**cotó** • *n* cotton

**cotxe** • *n* car, carriage, wagon

**cotxet** • *n* wagon

**coure** • *v* cook, fire • *n* copper

**courenc** • *adj* copper

**cova** • *n* cave

**covard** • *n* coward • *adj* cowardly, yellow

**covardament** • *adv* cowardly

**cranc** • *n* crab

**crani** • *n* skull

**creació** • *n* creation

**crea|r** • *v* create ~dor • *n* creator

**creatiu** • *adj* creative

**creativitat** • *n* creativity

**credibilitat** • *n* credibility

**crèdul** • *adj* credulous

**creença** • *n* belief

**creïble** • *adj* believable, credible

**creient** • *n* believer

**creixement** • *n* growth

**creixent** • *adj* growing, increasing

**créixer** • *v* grow, grow up, wax

**crema** • *n* cream

**cremada** • *n* burn

**cremar** • *v* burn

**cremós** • *adj* creamy

**creta** • *n* chalk

**creu** • *n* cross

**creuer** • *n* cruise

**creure** • *v* believe

**criar** • *v* breed, foster, raise

**crida** • *n* call

**cridaner** • *adj* loud

**cridar** • *v* call, cry, scream, shout, summon, telephone

**cridòria** • *n* stir

**crim** • *n* crime

**criminal** • *adj* criminal

**criquet** • *n* cricket

**crisi** • *n* crisis

**cristall** • *n* crystal

**cristià** • *adj* Christian

**cristiana** • *n* Christian

**cristianisme** • *n* Christianity

**crit** • *n* call, cry

**criteri** • *n* criterion

**crític** • *n* critic • *adj* critical

**crítica** • *n* critique ~ment • *adv* critically

**criticar** • *v* criticize, harsh

**Croàcia** • *n* Croatia
**croat** • *adj* Croatian
**croata** • *n* Croatian
**crònic** • *adj* chronic
**cronologia** • *n* chronology
**cronometrar** • *v* clock
**crostó** • *n* heel
**cru** • *adj* crude, rare, raw
**crucial** • *adj* crucial
**cruel** • *adj* cruel, outrageous
**crueltat** • *n* cruelty
**cruïlla** • *n* crossroads
**cruiximent** • *n* stiffness
**cu** • *n* cue
**cua** • *n* queue, tail
**cub** • *n* block, cube
**Cuba** • *n* Cuba
**cubà** • *adj* Cuban
**cubell** • *n* bucket
**cubellada** • *n* bucket
**cubicar** • *v* cube
**cuc** • *n* worm
**cuca** • *n* bug
**cucaburra** • *n* kookaburra
**cucut** • *n* cuckoo
**cuina** • *n* kitchen, stove
**cuinar** • *v* cook
**cuiner** • *n* cook
**cuir** • *n* leather
**cuitar** • *v* hurry
**cuixa** • *n* thigh
**cul** • *n* ass, bottom
**culebrot** • *n* soap opera
**cullera** • *n* spoon
**cullerada** • *n* spoonful, tablespoon
**cullerot** • *n* tadpole
**culpa** • *n* blame, fault, guilt
**culpabilitat** • *n* guilt
**culpa|r** • *v* blame ~**ble** • *adj* guilty

**culte** • *n* worship
**cultiu** • *n* culture
**cultivar** • *v* cultivate, foster, grow
**cultura** • *n* culture
**cultural** • *adj* cultural
**culturista** • *n* bodybuilder
**cuneta** • *n* gutter
**cunyada** • *n* sister-in-law
**cunyat** • *n* brother-in-law
**cupcake** • *n* cupcake
**cura** • *n* care
**curar** • *v* heal
**curiós** • *adj* curious
**curiosa** • *adj* curious
**curiositat** • *n* curiosity
**curós** • *adj* careful
**curs** • *n* class, course
**cursa** • *n* race
**cursar** • *v* course
**curt** • *adj* short
**custòdia** • *n* custody
**cutxu** • *n* dog
**cv** • *n* CV

# D

**dades** • *n* data
**daga** • *n* knife
**dalt** • *adv* above • *prep* up
**damunt** • *prep* above
**danès** • *adj* Danish
**dansa** • *n* dance
**dansar** • *v* dance
**dany** • *n* damage, harm
**danyar** • *v* damage

**darrer** • *adj* last
**darrerament** • *adv* recently
**darrere** • *adv* behind
**darreries** • *n* dessert
**data** • *n* date
**dàtil** • *n* date
**dau** • *n* die
**daurada** • *adj* golden
**daurar** • *v* gild
**daurat** • *adj* gold, golden
**davant** • *prep* against, before
**davantal** • *n* apron
**davanter** • *n* forward
**de** • *prep* about, from, of
**deambular** • *v* wander
**debat** • *n* debate
**debatre** • *v* debate, discuss
**dèbil** • *adj* faint, feeble, slight, weak ~ment • *adv* weakly
**debilitar** • *v* weaken
**debilitat** • *n* weakness
**debut** • *n* debut
**debutar** • *v* debut
**dècada** • *n* decade
**decalatge** • *n* offset
**decalatges** • *n* offset
**decebedor** • *adj* deceptive
**decebre** • *v* deceive, disappoint
**decebut** • *adj* disappointed
**decència** • *n* decency
**decenni** • *n* decade
**decepció** • *n* disappointment
**deceptiu** • *adj* deceptive
**decididament** • *adv* definitely
**decidir** • *v* decide
**decisió** • *n* decision
**decisiu** • *adj* decisive
**declamar** • *v* say
**declaració** • *n* declaration
**declarar** • *v* declare, state
**declinació** • *n* declension

**declinar** • *v* decline
**declivi** • *n* decline
**decoració** • *n* decoration
**decorar** • *v* decorate
**decoratiu** • *adj* decorative
**decreixença** • *n* decrease
**decréixer** • *v* decrease
**decretar** • *v* award
**dedicar** • *v* dedicate
**dedicatòria** • *n* dedication
**defecte** • *n* bug, defect, fault
**defectiu** • *adj* defective
**defectuós** • *adj* defective
**defendre** • *v* defend
**defensa** • *n* defense
**defensar** • *v* defend
**defensor** • *n* defender
**deficiència** • *n* deficiency
**deficient** • *adj* deficient
**dèficit** • *n* deficiency, deficit
**definició** • *n* definition
**definir** • *v* define
**definit** • *adj* definite
**definitiu** • *adj* definitive
**definitivament** • *adv* definitely
**deformar** • *v* distort
**degà** • *n* dean
**deixar** • *v* abandon, allow, depart, leave, let, stop • *adj* quit
**dejuna|r** • *v* fast ~dor • *n* faster ~dora • *n* faster
**delatar** • *v* rat
**delegada** • *n* delegate
**delegat** • *n* delegate
**deliberació** • *n* deliberation
**deliberadament** • *adv* deliberately
**deliberat** • *adj* deliberate
**delicat** • *adj* delicate
**deliciós** • *adj* delicious

**deliciosament** ● *adv* deliciously

**delicte** ● *n* crime

**delit** ● *n* delight

**demà** ● *adv* tomorrow

**demanar** ● *v* ask, order, request

**democràcia** ● *n* democracy

**democràtic** ● *adj* democratic

**demogràfic** ● *adj* demographic

**demoníac** ● *adj* demonic

**demora** ● *n* delay

**demorar** ● *v* delay

**demostrar** ● *v* demonstrate, prove, show

**demostratiu** ● *adj* demonstrative

**denegar** ● *v* forbid

**denominar** ● *v* name

**dens** ● *adj* dense ~itat ● *n* density

**dent** ● *n* tooth

**dentista** ● *n* dentist

**denunciar** ● *v* denounce

**departir** ● *v* depart

**dependència** ● *n* dependence

**dependent** ● *adj* dependent

**dependre** ● *v* depend

**deplorable** ● *adj* sad

**deport** ● *n* sport

**deportar** ● *v* transport

**deportat** ● *n* transport

**depressió** ● *n* depression

**depressiu** ● *adj* depressive

**depriment** ● *adj* depressing

**deprimir** ● *v* depress

**deprimit** ● *adj* depressed, down

**derivació** ● *n* derivation

**derivar** ● *v* derive

**derrota** ● *n* defeat

**desacord** ● *n* disagreement

**desactivar** ● *v* deactivate

**desafia|r** ● *v* challenge ~dor ● *adj* challenging ~ment ● *n* challenge

**desafortunat** ● *adj* unfortunate

**desagrada|r** ● *v* dislike ~ble ● *adj* unpleasant

**desaigua** ● *n* sink

**desallotjar** ● *v* displace

**desaparèixer** ● *v* disappear, go, vanish

**desaparició** ● *n* disappearance

**desar** ● *v* keep, save

**desastre** ● *n* disaster

**desastrós** ● *adj* disastrous

**desavantatge** ● *n* disadvantage

**descalç** ● *adj* barefoot

**descans** ● *n* rest

**descansar** ● *v* rest

**descarat** ● *adj* cheeky

**descarregar** ● *v* download

**descendent** ● *n* descendant

**descendir** ● *v* descend

**descloure** ● *v* open

**descobri|r** ● *v* discover ~ment ● *n* discovery

**descompte** ● *n* discount

**desconcertat** ● *adj* confused

**desconegut** ● *n* stranger ● *adj* unknown

**descongelar** ● *v* defrost

**desconnectar** ● *v* disconnect

**descordar** ● *v* loose

**descripció** ● *n* description

**descriptiu** ● *adj* descriptive

**descriure** ● *v* describe

**desembocadura** ● *n* mouth

**desembre** ● *n* December

**desempolsar** ● *v* dust

**desencaminar** ● *v* mislead

**desengramponador** ● *n* screwdriver**

D

**desenvolupa|r** • *v* develop, evolve **~dor** • *n* developer **~ment** • *n* development

**desert** • *adj* desert

**desertar** • *v* desert

**desertor** • *n* deserter

**desesperació** • *n* despair, desperation

**desesperadament** • *adv* desperately

**desesperat** • *adj* desperate, hopeless

**desfilada** • *n* parade

**desforestació** • *n* deforestation

**desgelar** • *v* defrost

**desglaçar** • *v* defrost

**desgraciadament** • *adv* unfortunately

**desgraciat** • *adj* miserable

**desguàs** • *n* outlet

**deshonest** • *adj* dishonest

**desig** • *n* desire, want, wish

**desigual** • *adj* unequal, uneven

**desigualtat** • *n* inequality

**desitja|r** • *v* desire, will, wish **~ble** • *adj* desirable

**deslligar** • *v* loose

**desmai** • *n* faint

**desmentiment** • *n* denial

**desmoralitzar** • *v* demoralize

**desnerit** • *adj* puny

**desnivell** • *n* inclination

**desnonar** • *v* displace

**desocupat** • *adj* free, unemployed

**desordre** • *n* disorder, disruption

**desossar** • *v* bone

**despedir** • *v* dismiss, sack

**despert** • *adj* awake

**desperta|r** • *v* awake, wake up **~dor** • *n* alarm

**despesa** • *n* expenditure

**despietat** • *adj* merciless, ruthless

**despit** • *n* spite

**desplaça|r** • *v* displace **~ment** • *n* displacement

**després** • *adv* after, afterwards, later, then

**despullat** • *adj* naked

**dessagnar** • *v* bleed

**dessuadora** • *n* sweater

**destacat** • *adj* outstanding

**desterra|r** • *v* exile **~ment** • *n* exile

**destí** • *n* destiny, fate, fortune

**destinació** • *n* destination

**destinar** • *v* dedicate

**destituir** • *v* cashier, dismiss, sack

**destrucció** • *n* destruction

**destructiu** • *adj* destructive

**destruir** • *v* destroy, go

**desvelar** • *v* unveil

**desvergonyit** • *adj* shameless

**desvetllat** • *adj* restless

**desviar** • *v* divert

**detall** • *n* detail

**detallar** • *v* detail

**detallat** • *adj* detailed

**detecció** • *n* detection

**detectar** • *v* detect

**detectiu** • *n* detective

**detenir** • *v* detain

**determinar** • *v* ascertain, determine, set

**determinat** • *adj* determined

**detindre** • *v* detain

**deu** • *n* ten

**déu** • *n* god

**Déu** • *n* God

**deure** • *n* duty • *v* must, owe

**deures** • *n* homework

**deute** • *n* debt

**devasta|r** • *v* devastate **~dor** • *adj* devastating

**devesa** • *n* range

**devoció** • *n* devotion

**dia** • *n* day

**diabetis** • *n* diabetes

**diable** • *n* demon, devil

**diables** • *phr* on earth

**diagnosi** • *n* diagnosis

**diagnòstic** • *n* diagnosis

**diagnosticar** • *v* diagnose

**diagrama** • *n* diagram

**diàleg** • *n* dialogue

**dialogar** • *v* dialogue

**diamant** • *n* diamond

**diapositiva** • *n* slide

**diari** • *adj* daily • *n* diary, journal, news, newspaper

**diàriament** • *adv* daily

**dibuix** • *n* drawing, tread

**dibuixar** • *v* draw

**diccionari** • *n* dictionary

**dictadura** • *n* dictatorship

**didàctic** • *adj* didactic, educational

**dieta** • *n* diet

**diferència** • *n* difference

**diferent** • *adj* different **~ment** • *adv* differently

**diferir** • *v* differ

**difícil** • *adj* difficult, hard, rough

**dificultat** • *n* difficulty

**difús** • *adj* diffuse

**difusió** • *n* diffusion

**digerir** • *v* digest

**digestiu** • *adj* digestive

**digital** • *adj* digital **~ment** • *adv* digitally

**digne** • *adj* dignified, worthy

**dignitat** • *n* dignity

**digui** • *interj* hello

**dijous** • *n* Thursday

**dilema** • *n* dilemma

**diligent** • *adj* diligent **~ment** • *adv* diligently

**dilluns** • *n* Monday

**dimarts** • *n* Tuesday

**dimecres** • *n* Wednesday

**dimensió** • *n* dimension

**diminut** • *adj* minute

**dimissió** • *n* notice

**dimitir** • *v* resign

**dimoni** • *n* demon, devil, monster

**dimonis** • *phr* on earth

**Dinamarca** • *n* Denmark

**dinàmic** • *adj* dynamic

**dinàmica** • *n* dynamic, dynamics

**dinar** • *n* dinner, lunch

**diner** • *n* money

**dinosaure** • *n* dinosaur

**dinou** • *num* nineteen

**dins** • *adv* in, inside • *prep* within • *adj* inside

**diploma** • *n* degree, diploma

**diplomàcia** • *n* diplomacy

**diplomàtic** • *n* diplomat • *adj* diplomatic

**diplomàtica** • *n* diplomat

**dipòsit** • *n* deposit, tank

**dipositar** • *v* deposit, leave

**dir** • *v* go, say, tell

**direcció** • *n* direction, management

**directament** • *adv* directly

**directe** • *adj* direct

**director** • *n* director, head, principal

**directora** • *n* director, head, principal

**dirigent** • *n* leader

**dirigir** • *v* cast, direct, head, lead, steer

**disc** • *n* circle, disk

**discapacitat** • *adj* disabled

**disciplina** • *n* discipline

**disciplinar** • *v* discipline

**discret** • *adj* discrete, tactful

**discriminació** • *n* discrimination

**discriminar** • *v* discriminate

**disculpa** • *n* apology

**disculpes** • *interj* sorry

**discurs** • *n* speech

**discussió** • *n* discussion

**discutible** • *adj* arguable, debatable

**discutir** • *v* argue, discuss, quarrel

**disfressa** • *n* disguise

**disfressar** • *v* disguise

**disgustat** • *adj* upset

**disminució** • *n* decrease

**disminuir** • *v* decrease, diminish, lower, turn down

**disparar** • *v* fire, gun, shoot

**disponibilitat** • *n* availability

**disponible** • *adj* available, disposable, out

**disposat** • *adj* prepared, ready, willing

**dispositiu** • *n* device

**disputa** • *n* argument

**disputar** • *v* dispute

**dissabte** • *n* Saturday

**dissecar** • *v* stuff

**disseny** • *n* design

**dissenya|r** • *v* design ~dor • *n* designer

**disset** • *num* seventeen

**distància** • *n* distance, range

**distant** • *adj* distant

**distinció** • *n* distinction

**distingir** • *v* distinguish

**distingit** • *adj* distinguished

**distint** • *adj* distinct

**distintiu** • *n* badge • *adj* distinctive

**distorsió** • *n* distortion

**distorsionar** • *v* distort

**distracció** • *n* distraction

**distreure** • *v* amuse, distract, entertain

**distribució** • *n* distribution

**districte** • *n* district

**dit** • *adv* AKA • *n* digit, finger, toe

**diumenge** • *n* Sunday

**divendres** • *n* Friday

**divers** • *adj* diverse ~itat • *n* diversity

**diversificar** • *v* diversify

**diversió** • *n* fun

**divertir** • *v* amuse, entertain

**divertit** • *adj* amusing, entertaining, fun, funny • *n* wit

**diví** • *adj* divine

**dividend** • *n* dividend

**dividir** • *v* divide, split

**divisar** • *v* devise

**divisió** • *n* chapter, division

**divorci** • *n* divorce

**divorciar** • *v* divorce

**divorciat** • *adj* divorced

**divuit** • *num* eighteen

**divulgar** • *v* disclose

**do** • *n* do, gift

**doblar** • *v* double, dub
**doblatge** • *n* dubbing
**doble** • *adj* double, dual
**doblec** • *n* lap
**doblegar** • *v* bow, fold
**doctorat** • *n* doctorate
**doctrina** • *n* doctrine
**document** • *n* document
**documentació** • *n* documentation
**documental** • *adj* documentary
**documentar** • *v* document
**dofí** • *n* dolphin
**dòlar** • *n* dollar
**dolç** • *adj* soft, sweet
**dolçamara** • *n* bittersweet
**dolçament** • *adv* sweet, sweetly
**doldre** • *v* hurt
**dolent** • *adj* bad, evil, off
**doler** • *v* hurt
**dolor** • *n* pain
**dolorós** • *adj* painful
**domèstic** • *adj* domestic
**domesticar** • *v* domesticate
**domicili** • *n* residence
**dominar** • *v* dominate
**domini** • *n* realm
**dona** • *n* wife, woman
**donació** • *n* donation
**dona|r** • *v* give **~dor** • *n* donor **~dora** • *n* donor **~nt** • *n* donor
**donatiu** • *n* donation
**doncs** • *interj* so
**dormir** • *v* sleep
**dormitori** • *n* bedroom, dormitory
**dos** • *n* two
**dosi** • *n* dose
**dot** • *n* gift
**dotor** • *adj* nosy

**dotze** • *num* twelve
**dotzena** • *n* dozen
**drac** • *n* dragon
**drama** • *n* drama
**dramàtic** • *adj* dramatic
**dramàticament** • *adv* dramatically
**drap** • *n* cloth
**drenatge** • *n* drainage
**dret** • *n* law, right
**dreta** • *n* right
**dretà** • *n* right-handed
**dringar** • *v* ring
**droga** • *n* drug
**drogat** • *adj* high
**dual** • *adj* dual
**Dublín** • *n* Dublin
**dubtar** • *v* doubt, hesitate
**dubte** • *n* doubt
**dubtós** • *adj* doubtful, problematic
**dues** • *num* two
**duplicar** • *v* mirror
**dur** • *adj* hard • *v* steer
**dura** • *adj* hard
**duració** • *n* duration
**durada** • *n* duration
**durant** • *prep* during
**dutxa** • *n* shower

**eco** • *n* echo
**ecologia** • *n* ecology
**ecològic** • *adj* ecological
**economia** • *n* economy, economics

**econòmic** • *adj* economic
**econòmicament** • *adv* economically
**economista** • *n* economist
**ecosistema** • *n* ecosystem
**edat** • *n* age
**edició** • *n* edit, edition
**edificar** • *v* build
**edifici** • *n* building
**Edimburg** • *n* Edinburgh
**editar** • *v* edit
**editor** • *n* editor, publisher
**editora** • *n* editor
**editorial** • *adj* editorial • *n* publisher
**educació** • *n* education
**educar** • *v* educate
**educat** • *adj* educated
**educatiu** • *adj* educational
**edulcorant** • *n* sweetener
**efecte** • *n* effect, spin
**efectiu** • *n* cash • *adj* effective
**efectivament** • *adv* indeed
**efectuar** • *v* effect
**eficaç** • *adj* effective
**eficàcia** • *n* effectiveness
**eficiència** • *n* efficiency
**eficient** • *adj* efficient ~ment • *adv* efficiently
**egipci** • *adj* Egyptian • *n* Egyptian
**Egipte** • *n* Egypt
**ego** • *n* ego
**egoista** • *adj* selfish
**egua** • *n* mare
**eh** • *interj* hey
**ei** • *interj* hey
**eina** • *n* tool
**eix** • *n* axis
**eixida** • *n* exit
**eixir** • *v* exit • *adj* quit

**eixugar** • *v* dry, wipe
**eixut** • *adj* dry
**el** • *art* the
**elàstic** • *adj* elastic
**elasticitat** • *n* elasticity
**elecció** • *n* election
**electoral** • *adj* electoral
**elèctric** • *adj* electric, electrical
**electricista** • *n* electrician
**electricitat** • *n* electricity
**electrònic** • *adj* electronic
**electrònica** • *n* electronics
**elefant** • *n* elephant
**elegant** • *adj* elegant ~ment • *adv* elegantly
**elegible** • *adj* eligible
**elegir** • *v* choose
**elevació** • *n* elevation
**elevat** • *adj* high
**eliminació** • *n* out, put out
**eliminar** • *v* eliminate
**elit** • *n* elite
**ell** • *det* he
**ella** • *pron* she
**elles** • *pron* they
**ells** • *pron* they
**elm** • *n* helmet
**els** • *pron* them
**eludir** • *v* escape
**em** • *pron* me, myself
**embadalir** • *v* entrance
**embaràs** • *n* pregnancy
**embarassat** • *adj* pregnant
**embarcar** • *v* board, embark, get on
**embenar** • *v* bandage
**embenat** • *n* bandage
**embocadura** • *n* mouth
**emboçar** • *v* cloak
**embolic** • *n* mess
**embolicar** • *v* wrap

**embotella|r** • v bottle **~ment** • n traffic jam

**embriac** • adj drunk

**embruixament** • n spell

**embrutar** • v dirty

**embutxacar** • v pocket

**emergència** • n emergence, emergency

**emergir** • v emerge

**emetre** • v broadcast, emit

**èmfasi** • n emphasis, stress

**emfasitzar** • v highlight, stress

**emfatitzar** • v emphasize

**eminència** • n eminence

**emissió** • n broadcast, emission

**emmagatzemar** • v store

**emmagatzematge** • n storage

**emmarcar** • v frame

**emmascarar** • v mask

**emmetzinar** • v poison

**emmudit** • adj speechless

**emmurallar** • v wall

**emoció** • n emotion

**emocional** • adj emotional **~ment** • adv emotionally

**emocionar** • v move

**emocionat** • adj excited

**empaitar** • v chase

**empaperar** • v paper

**empaquetar** • v box, case, package

**empaquetatge** • n package

**empastar** • v fill

**empat** • n tie

**empatar** • v draw

**empatia** • n sympathy

**empenta** • n push, shove

**empentar** • v push, shove

**empentejar** • v shove

**empènyer** • v boost, push, shove

**empenyorar** • v pledge

**emperador** • n emperor

**emperadriu** • n empress

**empitjorar** • v suffer

**empleat** • n employee

**empolsar** • v dust

**emprendre** • v undertake

**emprenedor** • n entrepreneur

**emprenedoria** • n entrepreneurship

**empresa** • n enterprise

**empresona|r** • v commit, imprison **~ment** • n imprisonment

**empunyar** • v grip

**en** • prep in, within

**enamorat** • phr in love

**enboirat** • adj foggy

**ençà** • adv far

**encalçar** • v chase

**encallar** • v hang

**encant** • n charm

**encanta|r** • v entrance **~dor** • adj charming, delightful, lovely **~ment** • n spell

**encantat** • adj delighted

**encapçalar** • v head, lead

**encapsar** • v box

**encara** • adv even, still, yet

**encarar** • v face, look

**encarcarat** • adj stiff

**encàrrec** • n charge, commission

**encarregar** • v commission

**encastar** • v embed

**encendre** • v light, turn on

**encerar** • v wax

**encertar** • v hit

**enciam** • n lettuce

**enciclopèdia** • n encyclopedia

**encinta** • adj pregnant

**encís** • *n* spell
**encisador** • *adj* charming
**encistellada** • *n* basket
**encolar** • *v* glue
**encongir** • *v* shrink
**encontre** • *n* encounter
**encoratja|r** • *v* encourage **~dor**
  • *adj* encouraging
**encreuament** • *n* crossroads
**encuny** • *n* die
**encunyar** • *v* coin, mint
**endarrere** • *adv* backwards
**endarreri|r** • *v* delay **~ment** • *n*
  delay
**endemés** • *adv* furthermore
**endevinar** • *v* guess
**endolcir** • *v* sweeten
**endoll** • *n* plug
**endollar** • *v* plug in
**endreçat** • *adj* tidy
**enemic** • *adj* enemy
**energètic** • *adj* energetic
**energia** • *n* energy
**enèrgic** • *adj* energetic
**enfadar** • *v* anger
**enfadat** • *adj* angry
**enfadós** • *v* annoying
**enfangar** • *v* mud
**enfarinar** • *v* flour
**enfat** • *n* anger
**enfiladissa** • *n* climber
**enfilar** • *v* string, thread
**enfocar** • *v* focus
**enfonsar** • *v* sink
**enfortir** • *v* strengthen
**enfrontament** • *n*
  confrontation
**engabiar** • *v* cage
**engalba** • *n* slip
**enganar** • *v* fool
**enganxar** • *v* hook, paste, stick

**enganxós** • *adj* sticky
**engany** • *n* deception
**enganyar** • *v* cheat, deceive,
  mislead, trick
**enganyós** • *adj* deceptive
**engegar** • *v* start, turn on
**engendrar** • *v* beget, breed
**enginyer** • *n* engineer
**enginyeria** • *n* engineering
**enginyós** • *adj* inventive, neat
**engoli|r** • *v* swallow **~ment** • *n*
  swallow
**engrapadora** • *n* stapler
**engrapar** • *v* staple
**engreixar** • *v* stall
**engronsar** • *v* swing
**enguixat** • *n* cast
**enhorabona** • *interj*
  congratulations
**enjogassat** • *adj* playful
**enllà** • *adv* far
**enllaç** • *n* anchor, link
**enllaçar** • *v* link
**enllaunar** • *v* can
**enlloc** • *adv* nowhere
**enllotar** • *v* mud
**enlluernador** • *adj* dazzling
**enllumenat** • *n* lighting
**ennuar** • *v* tie
**ennuvolat** • *adj* cloudy
**enorme** • *adj* enormous, great,
  huge
**enquadrar** • *v* frame
**enquesta** • *n* poll, survey
**enquestar** • *n* survey
**enrajolar** • *v* tile
**enredada** • *n* scam
**enrere** • *adv* backwards
**enriqui|r** • *v* enrich **~ment** • *n*
  enrichment
**enrocar** • *v* castle

**enrolar** • *v* enroll

**enrossir** • *v* brown

**ens** • *pron* ourselves

**ensacar** • *v* sack

**ensenya|r** • *v* show, teach **~nt** • *n* teacher **~ment** • *n* teaching

**ensopegada** • *n* stumble

**ensopegar** • *v* stumble

**ensordidor** • *adj* deafening

**ensota** • *adv* below

**ensucrat** • *adj* sweet

**ensumar** • *v* smell

**entallament** • *n* carving

**entebenar** • *v* stun

**entendre** • *v* understand

**enteniment** • *n* wit

**enter** • *adj* entire

**enterament** • *adv* entirely

**enteresa** • *n* integrity

**enterra|r** • *v* bury **~ment** • *n* burial

**entès** • *adj* knowledgeable

**entonació** • *n* intonation

**entorn** • *n* environment

**entrada** • *n* break, entrance, entry, tackle

**entrar** • *v* enter

**entre** • *prep* among, between

**entrega** • *n* delivery

**entregar** • *v* deliver

**entremaliat** • *adj* naughty

**entrena|r** • *v* train **~dor** • *n* coach, trainer **~dora** • *n* coach **~ment** • *n* training

**entrepà** • *n* sandwich

**entretant** • *adv* meanwhile

**entreteni|r** • *v* amuse, entertain **~ment** • *n* entertainment

**entretingut** • *adj* amusing

**entrevista** • *n* interview

**entrevista|r** • *v* interview **~dor** • *n* interviewer

**entusiasmat** • *adj* excited

**entusiasme** • *n* enthusiasm

**entusiasta** • *n* enthusiast • *adj* keen

**entusiàstic** • *adj* enthusiastic

**enuig** • *n* anger

**enutjar** • *v* anger

**enutjat** • *adj* angry

**enutjós** • *v* annoying

**envà** • *n* wall

**envair** • *v* invade

**envant** • *adv* forth

**enveja** • *n* envy

**envejar** • *v* envy

**envejós** • *adj* envious

**envellir** • *v* age, get on

**enverina|r** • *v* poison **~ment** • *n* poisoning

**envers** • *prep* toward

**envescada** • *n* lime

**enviar** • *v* send, swallow

**envoltar** • *v* surround

**enyorança** • *n* longing

**enyorar** • *v* long, miss

**enyorat** • *adj* homesick

**ep** • *interj* hey

**èpic** • *adj* epic

**epidèmia** • *n* epidemic

**epidèmic** • *adj* epidemic

**episodi** • *n* episode

**època** • *n* era

**epopeia** • *n* epic

**equació** • *n* equation

**Equador** • *n* Ecuador

**eqüestre** • *adj* equestrian

**equilibrar** • *v* balance

**equilibri** • *n* balance

**equilibrista** • *n* acrobat

**equip** • *n* crew, equipment, team

**equipa|r** • *v* supply, tool ~**ment** • *n* equipment

**equipatge** • *n* equipment, luggage

**equitatiu** • *adj* fair

**equivaldra** • *v* equal

**equivocat** • *adj* wrong

**era** • *n* era

**erecció** • *n* erection

**erecte** • *adj* erect

**erèctil** • *adj* erectile

**eriçó** • *n* hedgehog

**Eritrea** • *n* Eritrea

**erosió** • *n* erosion

**errada** • *n* error, fault

**erroni** • *adj* wrong

**error** • *n* bug, error, fault

**erudit** • *adj* knowledgeable

**eruga** • *n* caterpillar

**erupció** • *n* eruption

**es** • *pron* herself, himself, itself, themselves • *art* the

**esbalaïdor** • *adj* awesome

**esbarzer** • *n* blackberry

**esbiaixat** • *adj* biased

**esborrany** • *n* draft, sketch

**esborrar** • *v* delete, erase

**esborronador** • *adj* creepy

**esbós** • *n* draft, sketch

**esbossos** • *n* sketch

**esbudellar** • *v* gut

**escacs** • *n* chess

**escairar** • *v* square

**escala** • *n* ladder, scale, staircase, straight

**escalafó** • *n* ladder

**escalar** • *v* climb

**escaldar** • *v* poach

**escalfa|r** • *v* heat ~**ment** • *n* heating

**escamarlà** • *n* lobster

**escandalós** • *adj* boisterous, outrageous

**escandir** • *v* scan

**escàndol** • *n* scandal

**escanejar** • *v* scan

**escapada** • *n* break

**escapar** • *v* escape

**escàpol** • *phr* at large • *adj* single

**escarabat** • *n* beetle, cockroach

**escarlata** • *n* scarlet

**escarpat** • *adj* steep

**escarransit** • *adj* puny

**escàs** • *adj* scarce

**escassedat** • *n* scarcity

**escassesa** • *n* scarcity

**escassetat** • *n* scarcity

**escaure** • *v* become, suit

**escena** • *n* scene, stage, venue

**escenari** • *n* backdrop, scenario, stage

**escèptic** • *adj* skeptical

**escindir** • *v* split

**esclatar** • *v* break out, explode

**esclau** • *n* slave

**esclava** • *n* slave

**esclavatge** • *n* slavery

**esclavitud** • *n* slavery

**esclavitzar** • *v* enslave

**escletxa** • *n* crack

**escó** • *n* seat

**escola** • *n* school

**escollir** • *v* choose, name, take

**escoltar** • *v* listen

**escombrar** • *v* sweep

**escopeta** • *n* gun

**escopir** • *v* spit

**escorcollar** • *v* scan

escorpí • *n* scorpion
escorta • *n* guard
escorxar • *v* skin
escot • *n* cleavage, share
escota • *n* sheet
escriptor • *n* writer
escriptora • *n* writer
escriptori • *n* desktop
escriptura • *n* deed, writing
escrit • *adj* written
escriure • *v* write
escrutar • *v* scrutinize
escultor • *n* sculptor
escultora • *n* sculptor
escultura • *n* sculpture
escusat • *n* toilet
esdeveni|r • *v* become, get
~ment • *n* event
esència • *n* scent
esfera • *n* sphere
esfèric • *adj* spherical
esforç • *n* effort, endeavor
esgarrapar • *v* claw, scratch
esgarrar • *v* tear
esgarrifar • *v* frighten
esgarrifós • *adj* chilling, horrible
esglaó • *n* step
església • *n* church
esgrimir • *v* fence
eslògan • *n* slogan
Eslovàquia • *n* Slovakia
Eslovènia • *n* Slovenia
esma • *n* judgment
esmaixada • *n* jam, slam, smash
esmaixar • *v* slam
esmena • *n* amendment
esmenar • *v* amend
esmentar • *v* mention
esmicolar • *v* shatter
esmolar • *v* sharpen
esmolat • *adj* sharp

esmorzar • *n* breakfast
esnap • *n* snap
espagueti • *n* spaghetti
espai • *n* room
espantar • *v* frighten, scare
espantós • *adj* eerie, scary
Espanya • *n* Spain
espanyol • *adj* Spanish
esparreguera • *n* asparagus
espasa • *n* sword
espatla • *n* shoulder
espatlla • *n* shoulder
espatllar • *v* ruin, spoil
espatllat • *adj* broken
espaventar • *v* frighten, scare
especial • *adj* special ~ment •
*adv* especially, specially ~itat •
*n* specialty
especialista • *n* specialist
espècie • *n* species
específic • *adj* specific
especificació • *n* specification
específicament • *adv* specifically
especificar • *v* name, specify
espècimen • *n* specimen
espectacle • *n* display, show,
spectacle
espectacular • *adj* spectacular
espectador • *n* spectator
espectre • *n* spectrum
especulació • *n* speculation
espelma • *n* candle
esperança • *n* hope
esperar • *v* await, hope, wait
esperit • *n* spirit
espès • *adj* thick
espia • *n* spy
espiadimonis • *n* dragonfly
espiar • *v* spy
espiell • *n* peephole
espiera • *n* peephole

**espiga** • *n* ear
**espigar** • *v* ear
**espiguejar** • *v* ear
**espill** • *n* mirror
**espín** • *n* spin
**espina** • *n* spine
**espinac** • *n* spinach
**espinada** • *n* backbone, spine
**espinós** • *adj* prickly
**espiritual** • *adj* spiritual
**espitjar** • *v* shove
**espitllera** • *n* loophole
**esplèndid** • *adj* splendid
**esplèndit** • *adj* gorgeous
**espoliar** • *v* spoil
**espolsar** • *v* dust
**esponja** • *n* sponge
**esponjar** • *v* sponge
**espontaneïtat** • *n* spontaneity
**espontàniament** • *adv* spontaneously
**esporgar** • *v* prune
**esport** • *n* sport
**esportiu** • *adj* sporting
**esporuguir** • *v* frighten
**espòs** • *n* spouse
**esposa** • *n* spouse
**esprémer** • *v* squeeze
**espurna** • *n* spark
**espurnejar** • *v* sizzle, spark
**esquaix** • *n* squash
**esquelet** • *n* skeleton
**esquena** • *n* back
**esquerda** • *n* crack
**esquerdar** • *v* crack
**esquerra** • *n* left
**esquerrà** • *adj* left • *n* left-handed
**esquerre** • *adj* left
**esquetx** • *n* sketch
**esquí** • *n* ski, skiing

**esquiar** • *v* ski
**esquilar** • *v* shear
**esquinçar** • *v* tear
**esquirol** • *n* squirrel
**essencial** • *adj* essential
**ésser** • *v* be • *n* being
**est** • *n* east • *det* this
**estabilitat** • *n* stability
**estabilitzar** • *v* stabilize
**establert** • *adj* set
**establi|r** • *v* ascertain, establish, set ~ment • *n* establishment
**estaca** • *n* stake
**estació** • *n* season, station
**estacional** • *adj* seasonal
**estacionari** • *adj* stationary
**estadi** • *n* stadium, stage
**estadística** • *n* statistics
**estafa** • *n* scam
**estafa|r** • *v* scam ~dor • *n* scammer
**estalonar** • *v* heel
**estalvia|r** • *v* save ~dor • *adj* thrifty
**estampar** • *v* stamp
**estàndard** • *adj* standard
**estany** • *n* tin
**esta|r** • *v* be ~nt • *n* shelf ~ble • *adj* stable • *n* stall
**estat** • *n* nation, state
**estàtua** • *n* statue
**estatunidenc** • *adj* American
**estatura** • *n* height
**estatut** • *n* statute
**estatuts** • *n* statute
**este** • *det* this
**estel** • *n* kite, star
**estendard** • *n* banner, standard
**estereotip** • *n* stereotype
**estereotípic** • *adj* stereotypical
**estètic** • *adj* aesthetic

estètica • *n* aesthetics ~ment • *adv* aesthetically
estic • *n* stick
estil • *n* style
estimació • *n* estimation
estimada • *adj* beloved
estimar • *v* love
estimat • *adj* beloved, dear
estímul • *n* cue
estimulació • *n* stimulation
estimula|r • *v* stimulate ~dor • *n* stimulant ~nt • *n* stimulant • *adj* stimulating
estipendi • *n* wage
estirabot • *n* nonsense
estirada • *n* dive
estirar • *v* stretch
estirp • *n* stock
estiu • *n* summer
estiuejar • *v* summer
Estocolm • *n* Stockholm
estoic • *adj* stoic
estoica • *n* stoic
estol • *n* fleet
estómac • *n* stomach
estona • *n* while
estonià • *adj* Estonian
Estònia • *n* Estonia
estoniana • *adj* Estonian
estorament • *n* astonishment
estovar • *v* soften
estrafolari • *adj* bizarre
estranger • *n* abroad, stranger • *adj* foreign
estrangera • *adj* foreign • *n* foreigner, stranger
estrany • *n* alien • *adj* bizarre, foreign, odd, strange, weird
estranya • *n* alien • *adj* foreign
estratègia • *n* strategy
estratègic • *adj* strategic

estrella • *n* star
estrena • *n* premiere, release
estrenar • *v* premiere, release
estrènyer • *v* squeeze
estrès • *n* stress
estressa|r • *v* stress ~nt • *adj* stressful
estret • *adj* narrow
estreta • *adj* narrow
estria • *n* flute
estricte • *adj* strict
estrident • *adj* loud
estripar • *v* gut, tear
estruç • *n* ostrich
estructura • *n* frame, skeleton, structure
estructural • *adj* structural
estructurar • *v* structure
estudi • *n* studio, study
estudia|r • *v* learn, read, study ~nt • *n* student
estufa • *n* stove
estúpid • *adj* dumb, stupid
estúpidament • *adv* stupidly
esvalot • *n* stir
et • *pron* yourself
etapa • *n* stage
etern • *adj* eternal ~itat • *n* eternity, lifetime
eternal • *adj* eternal
ètic • *adj* ethical
ètica • *n* ethics
Etiòpia • *n* Ethiopia
etiqueta • *n* label, tag
etiquetar • *v* label, tag
etiquetatge • *n* labeling
ètnic • *adj* ethnic
euga • *n* horse, mare
euro • *n* euro
Europa • *n* Europe
europea • *adj* European

**europeu** ● *adj* European
**evacuació** ● *n* evacuation
**evacuar** ● *v* evacuate
**evasió** ● *n* evasion
**evasiu** ● *adj* evasive
**eventual** ● *n* temporary
**evidència** ● *n* witness
**evidenciar** ● *v* get across
**evident** ● *adj* evident **~ment** ●
  *adv* evidently
**evitar** ● *v* avoid
**evocar** ● *v* evoke, recall
**evolució** ● *n* evolution
**evolutiu** ● *adj* evolutionary
**exactament** ● *adv* accurately,
  exactly
**exacte** ● *adj* accurate, exact
**exactitud** ● *n* accuracy
**exageració** ● *n* exaggeration
**exagerar** ● *v* exaggerate
**examen** ● *n* examination, test
**excavació** ● *n* dig
**excavar** ● *v* dig
**excedir** ● *v* exceed
**excepció** ● *n* exception
**excepcional** ● *adj* exceptional,
  outstanding
**excepte** ● *conj* but ● *prep*
  except
**excés** ● *n* excess
**excessiu** ● *adj* excessive
**excitant** ● *adj* exciting
**excitat** ● *adj* excited
**exclamar** ● *v* exclaim
**excloure** ● *v* exclude
**exclusió** ● *n* exclusion
**exclusiu** ● *adj* exclusive
**exclusivament** ● *adv* exclusively
**excrement** ● *n* shit
**excursionista** ● *n* hiker
**excusa** ● *n* excuse

**excusar** ● *v* excuse
**execució** ● *n* execution,
  performance
**executar** ● *v* execute, run
**exemplar** ● *n* copy
**exemple** ● *n* example
**exercici** ● *n* exercise
**exercir** ● *v* exercise
**exèrcit** ● *n* army, military
**exercitar** ● *v* exercise
**exhaust** ● *adj* exhausted
**exhaustivament** ● *adv*
  thoroughly
**exhibir** ● *v* display, exhibit
**exigència** ● *n* requirement
**exigent** ● *adj* demanding, picky
**exigir** ● *v* demand
**exili** ● *n* exile
**exiliada** ● *n* exile
**exiliar** ● *v* exile
**exiliat** ● *n* exile
**existència** ● *n* existence
**existent** ● *adj* existing
**existir** ● *v* exist
**èxit** ● *adj* hit ● *n* success
**exitós** ● *adj* successful
**exòtic** ● *adj* exotic
**expectativa** ● *n* expectation
**experiència** ● *n* experience
**experimental** ● *adj*
  experimental
**experimentar** ● *v* experience
**expert** ● *adj* expert
**explicació** ● *n* explanation
**explicar** ● *v* explain, narrate, tell
**explícit** ● *adj* explicit
**explícitament** ● *adv* explicitly
**exploració** ● *n* exploration
**explora|r** ● *v* explore **~dor** ● *n*
  explorer
**explosió** ● *n* explosion

**explosiu** • *adj* explosive
**explotació** • *n* exploitation
**explotar** • *v* explode, exploit
**exporta|r** • *v* export **~dor** • *n* exporter
**exposar** • *v* exhibit
**expressar** • *v* express
**expressió** • *n* expression
**expressiu** • *adj* expressive
**extendre** • *v* extend
**extens** • *adj* extensive
**extensament** • *adv* extensively
**extensió** • *n* extension
**extern** • *adj* external
**externa** • *adj* external
**extinció** • *n* extinction
**extint** • *adj* extinct
**extraordinari** • *adj* extraordinary
**extraordinàriament** • *adv* extraordinarily
**extraradi** • *n* outskirts
**extraterrestre** • *adj* alien
**extrem** • *adj* extreme, far
**extremadament** • *adv* extremely
**extremista** • *adj* extremist
**extreure** • *v* extract

**fa** • *adv* ago
**fabricant** • *n* maker
**fabulós** • *adj* great
**fabulosament** • *adv* fabulously
**faç** • *n* face

**façana** • *n* facade
**facció** • *n* faction
**faceta** • *n* face
**facial** • *adj* facial
**fàcil** • *adj* easy, effortless **~ment** • *adv* easily
**factura** • *n* bill, invoice
**faedor** • *n* maker
**fagot** • *n* bassoon
**faisà** • *n* pheasant
**falciot** • *n* swift
**falcó** • *n* falcon, hawk, kestrel
**falda** • *n* lap
**faldilla** • *n* skirt
**falla** • *n* fault
**fallar** • *v* award, miss
**fals** • *adj* artificial, false
**falsejar** • *v* fake
**falta** • *n* fault, lack
**faltar** • *v* lack
**fam** • *n* hunger
**fama** • *n* fame
**família** • *n* family, people
**familiar** • *n* family • *adj* familiar
**familiars** • *n* household
**famós** • *adj* famous
**fan** • *n* fan
**fanàtic** • *adj* fanatic
**fang** • *n* clay, mud
**fangós** • *adj* muddy
**fantasia** • *n* fancy, fantasy
**fantàstic** • *adj* awesome, fantastic
**far** • *n* lighthouse
**farga** • *n* forge
**farigola** • *n* thyme
**farina** • *n* flour
**farmacèutic** • *adj* pharmaceutical • *n* pharmacist
**farmàcia** • *n* pharmacy

**farola** • *n* lamppost
**farsi** • *n* Persian
**fascinació** • *n* fascination
**fascina|r** • *v* fascinate ~**dor** • *adj* fascinating ~**nt** • *adj* fascinating
**fase** • *n* phase, stage
**fastiguejar** • *v* harass
**fastijós** • *v* annoying
**fat** • *adj* dull
**fatal** • *adj* fatal
**fatiga** • *n* fatigue
**fatigar** • *v* fatigue, tire
**fatxada** • *n* facade
**faula** • *n* fable, tale
**fava** • *n* head • *adj* silly
**favor** • *n* favor
**favorable** • *adj* favourable
**favorit** • *adj* favourite
**fe** • *n* faith
**feble** • *adj* faint, feeble, puny, slight, weak ~**ment** • *adv* weakly
**feblesa** • *n* weakness
**febre** • *n* bug, fever, temperature
**febrer** • *n* February
**febril** • *adj* feverish
**federal** • *adj* federal
**feina** • *n* job
**feliç** • *adj* happy ~**ment** • *adv* fortunately, happily
**felicitat** • *n* happiness
**felicitats** • *interj* congratulations
**femella** • *adj* female
**femení** • *adj* female • *n* feminine
**femenina** • *adj* female
**feminis|me** • *n* feminism ~**ta** • *adj* feminist

**femta** • *n* shit
**fenc** • *n* hay
**fenomen** • *n* phenomenon
**fer** • *v* be, do, go, make, pack, prepare
**fera** • *n* beast
**ferida** • *n* injury, wound
**ferir** • *v* hurt, injure, wound
**ferit** • *adj* hurt
**ferm** • *adj* fast, firm
**ferma|r** • *v* tie ~**ment** • *adv* fast, firmly
**feroç** • *adj* fierce
**ferotge** • *adj* ferocious, fierce
**ferramenta** • *n* hardware
**ferrar** • *v* shoe
**ferreteria** • *n* hardware
**ferro** • *n* iron
**fèrtil** • *adj* fertile
**fertilitat** • *n* fertility
**fervent** • *adj* fervent
**fesol** • *n* bean
**festa** • *n* holiday, party
**festivitat** • *n* festivity
**fet** • *n* deed, fact
**feta** • *n* feat
**fetge** • *n* liver
**fi** • *n* end, ending, finish
**fiabilitat** • *n* reliability
**fiança** • *n* bail
**fiar** • *v* trust
**fiblada** • *n* sting
**fiblar** • *v* sting
**fibló** • *n* stinger
**fibra** • *n* fibre
**ficar** • *v* put
**ficció** • *n* fiction
**ficcional** • *adj* fictional
**fidedigne** • *adj* trustworthy
**fidel** • *adj* faithful ~**ment** • *adv* faithfully

fideu • *n* noodle
figa • *n* fig
figuera • *n* fig
figura • *n* figure
Fiji • *n* Fiji
fil • *n* thread
fila • *n* queue, rank, row
filera • *n* row
filferro • *n* wire
filial • *n* subsidiary
Filipines • *n* Philippines
fill • *n* son
filla • *n* daughter
film • *n* movie
filmar • *v* film
filòsof • *n* philosopher
filòsofa • *n* philosopher
filosofia • *n* philosophy
filosòfic • *adj* philosophical
filtració • *n* spoiler
filtrar • *v* filter
filtre • *n* filter
final • *n* end, ending, final
~ment • *adv* eventually,
finally, ultimately
finalitzar • *v* finish
finançament • *n* funding
financer • *adj* financial
financerament • *adv* financially
finances • *n* finance
finès • *adj* Finnish
finestra • *n* window
fingi|r • *v* pretend ~ment • *n*
simulation
finir • *v* finish
finlandès • *adj* Finnish
Finlàndia • *n* Finland
fins • *prep* until
fira • *n* fair
fiscal • *adj* fiscal • *n* prosecutor
físic • *adj* physical • *n* physicist

física • *n* physics ~ment • *adv*
physically
fita • *n* exploit, feat, finish
fitxa • *n* counter
fitxer • *n* file
fix • *adj* fixed
fixar • *v* fix, set
flairar • *v* smell
flaire • *n* smell
flaix • *n* flash
flama • *n* flame, light
flamant • *adj* flamboyant
flamenc • *n* flamingo
flauta • *n* flute
fleca • *n* bakery
fletxa • *n* arrow
flexibilitat • *n* flexibility
flexible • *adj* flexible
flirtar • *v* flirt
flirtejar • *v* flirt
floc • *n* lock, strand
flor • *n* flower
florir • *v* flower
florista • *n* florist
flota • *n* fleet
flotar • *v* float
fluid • *n* fluid
fluir • *v* flow, run
flux • *n* flow
foc • *n* fire
foca • *n* cow, seal
focus • *n* focus, spotlight
fogó • *n* range
follar • *v* fuck, screw
folrar • *v* line
fon • *n* phone
fonament • *n* base
fonamental • *adj* fundamental
• *n* primary
fonaments • *n* foundation
fondo • *adj* deep

**fondre** • *v* cast, melt
**fonedor** • *n* founder
**fonètic** • *adj* phonetic
**fonètica** • *n* phonetics
**fong** • *n* mushroom
**fonoll** • *n* fennel
**fons** • *n* background, bottom, ground
**font** • *n* source, spring
**fora** • *adv* outside
**foradar** • *v* drill, hole
**foraster** • *n* alien, foreigner, stranger • *adj* foreign
**forastera** • *n* alien, foreigner, stranger • *adj* foreign
**forat** • *n* hole
**forca** • *n* fork
**força** • *adv* fairly, pretty, rather • *n* force, strength
**forçar** • *v* take
**forest** • *n* forest
**forja** • *n* forge
**forjar** • *v* forge
**forma** • *n* form, shape
**formal** • *adj* formal ~**ment** • *adv* formally ~**itat** • *n* formality
**formalisme** • *n* formality
**formar** • *v* form, shape
**format** • *n* format
**formatar** • *v* format
**formatge** • *n* cheese
**formiga** • *n* ant
**formigó** • *n* concrete
**formós** • *adj* beautiful
**formósa** • *adj* beautiful
**fórmula** • *n* formula
**formulació** • *n* formulation
**formular** • *v* formulate
**formulari** • *n* form
**forn** • *n* bakery, oven
**fornejar** • *v* bake

**forner** • *n* baker
**fornir** • *v* supply
**forquilla** • *n* fork
**fort** • *n* fort, strength • *adj* loud, strong • *adv* strongly
**fortuna** • *n* fortune
**fòrum** • *n* forum
**fosc** • *adj* black, dark
**fosca** • *n* night
**foscant** • *n* night
**foscor** • *n* dark, darkness
**fòssil** • *n* fossil
**foto** • *n* photograph, picture
**fotocopiar** • *v* xerox
**fotògraf** • *n* photographer
**fotografia** • *n* photograph, photography, picture
**fotografiar** • *v* photograph
**fotre** • *v* fuck, screw
**fracàs** • *n* failure
**fracassar** • *v* fail
**fracció** • *n* fraction
**fràgil** • *adj* fragile
**fragilitat** • *n* fragility
**fragment** • *n* fragment
**fragmentar** • *v* fragment
**franc** • *adj* frank
**França** • *n* France
**francament** • *adv* fairly
**francès** • *adj* French
**frase** • *n* phrase, sentence
**fraternitat** • *n* brotherhood
**frau** • *n* fraud
**fraula** • *n* strawberry
**fre** • *n* brake
**fred** • *adj* cold, cool
**freda** • *adj* cool
**fregar** • *v* rub
**fregir** • *v* fry
**frenar** • *v* brake
**freqüència** • *n* frequency

**freqüentar** • *v* frequent
**freqüentment** • *adv* frequently
**fresc** • *adj* cool, fresh, recent
**fresca** • *adj* fresh
**frigorífic** • *n* refrigerator
**front** • *n* forehead, front
**frontera** • *n* border, boundary, facade, frontier
**fronterer** • *adj* frontier
**fruit** • *n* fruit
**fruita** • *n* fruit
**frustració** • *n* frustration
**frustrar** • *v* frustrate
**frustrat** • *adj* frustrated
**fuet** • *n* whip
**fuetejar** • *v* whip
**fuga** • *n* flight
**fugida** • *n* flight
**fugir** • *v* flee, fly, run away
**fuita** • *n* escape
**fulano** • *n* random
**full** • *n* leaf, sheet
**fulla** • *n* leaf
**fulletó** • *n* soap opera
**fum** • *n* smoke
**fumar** • *v* smoke
**fumejar** • *v* smoke
**funció** • *n* function
**funcionar** • *v* function, go, run
**funcionari** • *n* official
**fundació** • *n* foundation
**funda|r** • *v* found **~dor** • *n* founder
**funeral** • *n* funeral
**funerals** • *n* funeral
**furgar** • *v* root
**furgoneta** • *n* van
**furiós** • *adj* furious
**furt** • *n* theft
**fusell** • *n* rifle
**fusta** • *n* wood

**fuster** • *n* carpenter
**fustera** • *n* carpenter
**futbol** • *n* football, soccer
**futur** • *adj* future, later

# G

**gàbia** • *n* cage
**gabinet** • *n* cabinet
**gai** • *adj* gay
**gaia** • *adj* gay
**gaieta** • *n* jet
**gaig** • *n* jay
**gairebé** • *adv* almost, nearly, practically
**gaita** • *n* pipe
**galàxia** • *n* galaxy
**galeria** • *n* gallery
**galeta** • *n* biscuit, cookie
**gall** • *n* chicken, rooster
**galleda** • *n* bucket
**gallet** • *n* trigger
**gallina** • *n* chicken, hen
**galó** • *n* gallon
**galopar** • *n* run
**galta** • *n* cheek
**gamba** • *n* shrimp
**Gàmbia** • *n* Gambia
**gamma** • *n* range
**gana** • *n* appetite, hunger
**gandulejar** • *v* loaf
**ganga** • *n* bargain
**ganivet** • *n* knife
**ganivetada** • *n* stab
**ganxo** • *n* hook
**ganyota** • *n* mop

**garantia** • *n* guarantee, pledge
**garantir** • *v* guarantee
**garatge** • *n* garage
**garbuix** • *n* mess
**garfi** • *n* claw, hook
**garfir** • *v* claw
**garita** • *n* box
**garjola** • *n* pokey
**garrepa** • *adj* stingy
**garrot** • *n* stick
**gas** • *n* gas
**gasela** • *n* gazelle
**gaseta** • *n* journal
**gasolina** • *n* gasoline
**gasolinera** • *n* gas station
**gastar** • *v* spend
**gata** • *n* queen
**gatejar** • *v* crawl
**gatzara** • *n* stir
**gaudir** • *v* enjoy
**gavina** • *n* seagull
**gegant** • *adj* giant
**gegantesc** • *adj* gigantic
**gegantí** • *adj* giant, gigantic
**gel** • *n* ice
**gelada** • *n* freeze
**gelar** • *v* freeze
**gelat** • *adj* frozen • *n* ice cream
**gelatina** • *n* jelly
**gelós** • *adj* jealous
**gelosia** • *n* jealousy
**gemec** • *n* moan
**gemegar** • *v* moan
**gemma** • *n* jewel
**gen** • *n* gene
**gendre** • *n* son-in-law
**gener** • *n* January
**generació** • *n* generation
**generacional** • *adj* generational
**general** • *adj* general **~ment** •
 *adv* generally

**generalització** • *n*
 generalization
**generalitzar** • *v* generalize
**gènere** • *n* gender, genre, kind,
 sort
**genèric** • *adj* generic
**generós** • *adj* generous
**generosament** • *adv* generously
**genet** • *n* rider
**genètic** • *adj* genetic
**geni** • *n* genius
**genial** • *adj* great
**genitor** • *n* parent
**geniva** • *n* gum
**genocidi** • *n* genocide
**genoll** • *n* knee
**gens** • *det* no
**gent** • *n* people
**gentada** • *n* crowd
**gentalla** • *n* rabble
**gentilesa** • *n* kindness
**gentola** • *n* rabble
**genuí** • *adj* genuine
**geografia** • *n* geography
**geogràfic** • *adj* geographic
**geometria** • *n* geometry
**geomètric** • *adj* geometric
**Geòrgia** • *n* Georgia
**gerència** • *n* management
**germà** • *n* brother, sibling
**germana** • *n* sibling, sister
**germànic** • *n* German
**germanor** • *n* brotherhood
**gernació** • *n* crowd
**gerra** • *n* jug, pitcher
**gespa** • *n* lawn
**gest** • *n* face, gesture
**gesta** • *n* exploit, feat
**gestió** • *n* management
**getó** • *n* counter
**gimnàs** • *n* gymnasium

**gimnasta** • *n* gymnast
**gimnàstica** • *n* gymnastics
**gin** • *n* gin
**ginebra** • *n* gin
**ginecologia** • *n* gynecology
**ginecològic** • *adj* gynecological
**gingebre** • *n* ginger
**girafa** • *n* giraffe
**girar** • *v* turn
**glaçada** • *n* freeze
**glaça|r** • *v* freeze ~**dor** • *adj* chilling
**global** • *adj* global
**globular** • *adj* global
**globus** • *n* balloon, globe
**glop** • *n* drink
**glòria** • *n* glory
**gloriós** • *adj* glorious
**glossari** • *n* glossary
**go** • *n* go
**gol** • *n* goal
**gola** • *n* throat
**golafre** • *n* pig
**golf** • *n* golf
**golfes** • *n* attic
**golfista** • *n* golfer
**goma** • *n* eraser, rubber
**gomfaró** • *n* banner
**gorg** • *n* pool
**gorra** • *n* cap
**gos** • *n* dog
**gosar** • *v* dare
**gossa** • *n* dog
**got** • *n* glass
**gota** • *n* drop
**govern** • *n* government
**governa|r** • *v* govern, rule ~**dor** • *n* governor ~**nt** • *n* ruler
**gra** • *n* grain
**gràcia** • *n* grace
**gràcies** • *interj* thanks

**graciosament** • *adv* gracefully
**gradual** • *adj* gradual ~**ment** • *adv* gradually
**graella** • *n* grill
**gràfic** • *adj* graphic
**gràfica** • *n* plot
**gràfics** • *n* graphic
**gralla** • *n* jackdaw
**gram** • *n* gram
**gran** • *adj* big, great, old
**grandiloqüent** • *adj* grandiloquent
**grandiós** • *adj* grandiose
**granger** • *n* farmer
**granja** • *n* farm
**granota** • *n* frog
**grans** • *n* elder
**grapa** • *n* staple
**grapar** • *v* staple
**grapat** • *n* bunch, handful
**gras** • *adj* fat
**gratacel** • *n* skyscraper
**gratar** • *v* scratch
**gratis** • *adv* free
**gratuïtament** • *adv* free
**grau** • *n* degree
**gravar** • *v* engrave
**gravat** • *n* engraving
**gravetat** • *n* gravity, seriousness
**gràvid** • *adj* pregnant
**grec** • *adj* Greek
**Grècia** • *n* Greece
**grega** • *n* Greek
**gregari** • *adj* gregarious
**greixar** • *v* grease, oil
**greixós** • *adj* greasy
**greu** • *adj* deep, grave, heavy
**grill** • *n* cricket
**grinyol** • *n* screech
**gripau** • *n* toad
**gris** • *adj* gray

G

**groc** • *adj* yellow
**groller** • *adj* crude, filthy
**gronxador** • *n* swing
**grop** • *n* knot
**gros** • *adj* big
**grossa** • *n* gross
**gruix** • *n* bulk
**grup** • *n* group, set
**guai** • *adj* cool
**gual** • *n* dip
**guant** • *n* glove
**guany** • *n* gain
**guanya|r** • *v* earn, win ~**dor** • *n* winner ~**dora** • *n* winner
**guarda** • *n* guard, watch
**guardaespatlles** • *n* bodyguard
**guardar** • *v* keep, save
**guardià** • *n* guardian, watch
**guàrdia** • *n* guard, guardian, watch
**guardó** • *n* award
**guardonar** • *v* award
**guarir** • *v* heal
**guarnició** • *n* garnish
**guarni|r** • *v* garnish, tire ~**ment** • *n* garnish
**Guatemala** • *n* Guatemala
**guatlla** • *n* quail
**guerra** • *n* war
**guerrejar** • *v* war
**guerrer** • *n* warrior
**guerrera** • *n* warrior
**guerrilla** • *n* guerrilla
**gueto** • *n* ghetto
**guia** • *n* guide
**guiar** • *v* guide, steer
**guilla** • *n* fox
**guineu** • *n* fox
**guió** • *n* script
**guitarra** • *n* guitar
**guitarrista** • *n* guitarist

**guitza** • *n* kick
**guix** • *n* chalk
**guspira** • *n* spark
**guspirejar** • *v* spark
**gust** • *n* flavor, taste
**gustar** • *v* taste
**gustós** • *adj* delicious
**gustosament** • *adv* gladly
**Guyana** • *n* Guyana

**ha** • *interj* ha
**hàbil** • *adj* skillful
**habilitar** • *v* enable
**habilitat** • *n* ability, proficiency, skill
**hàbit** • *n* habit, robe
**habitació** • *n* room
**habitant** • *n* inhabitant
**hàbitat** • *n* habitat, range
**habitatge** • *n* housing
**habitual** • *adj* habitual
**Haití** • *n* Haiti
**hàmster** • *n* hamster
**handbol** • *n* handball
**hangar** • *n* hangar
**harmonia** • *n* harmony
**harmònic** • *adj* harmonious
**harmònica** • *n* harmonica
**Hawai** • *n* Hawaii
**Hawaii** • *n* Hawaii
**he** • *n* he
**hectàrea** • *n* hectare
**hèlice** • *n* screw
**helicòpter** • *n* helicopter

**herba** • *n* grass, herb
**heretar** • *v* inherit
**hereu** • *n* heir
**heroi** • *n* hero
**heroic** • *adj* heroic
**heroïna** • *n* hero, heroin, heroine
**hesitació** • *n* hesitation
**hesitar** • *v* hesitate
**hidrogen** • *n* hydrogen
**hiena** • *n* hyena
**hilarant** • *adj* hilarious
**hipèrbole** • *n* hyperbole
**hipoteca** • *n* mortgage
**hipotecar** • *v* mortgage
**hipòtesi** • *n* hypothesis
**hipotètic** • *adj* hypothetical
**histèric** • *adj* hysterical
**història** • *n* history, story
**historiador** • *n* historian
**historial** • *n* history
**històric** • *adj* historic, historical
**històricament** • *adv* historically
**hivern** • *n* winter
**hivernacle** • *n* greenhouse
**hivernar** • *v* winter
**hola** • *interj* hello, hi
**Holanda** • *n* Netherlands
**holandès** • *adj* Dutch, Netherlands
**holandesa** • *n* Dutch
**hom** • *pron* one, you
**home** • *n* boy, man
**homenatge** • *n* keep
**Hondures** • *n* Honduras
**honest** • *adj* honest
**honestament** • *adv* honestly
**honestedat** • *n* honesty
**hongarès** • *adj* Hungarian
**hongaresa** • *n* Hungarian
**Hongria** • *n* Hungary

**honor** • *n* honor
**honorable** • *adj* honorable
**honorari** • *n* wage
**honradesa** • *n* honesty
**hoquei** • *n* hockey
**hora** • *n* hour, time
**horabaixa** • *n* afternoon
**horari** • *n* schedule
**horitzó** • *n* horizon
**horitzontal** • *adj* horizontal
**hormona** • *n* hormone
**hormonal** • *adj* hormonal
**horrible** • *adj* horrible, lousy
**hòrrid** • *adj* horrible
**horror** • *n* horror
**horrorós** • *adj* awful
**hortalissa** • *n* vegetable
**hospital** • *n* hospital ~itat • *n* hospitality
**hospitalització** • *n* hospitalization
**hospitalitzar** • *v* hospitalize
**host** • *n* army
**hoste** • *n* guest
**hostessa** • *n* flight attendant
**hostil** • *adj* hostile, unfriendly ~itat • *n* hostility
**hotel** • *n* hotel
**hui** • *n* today
**humà** • *adj* human, humane • *n* human being, man
**humanitari** • *adj* humanitarian
**humanitària** • *adj* humanitarian
**humanitat** • *n* humanity
**humil** • *adj* humble ~ment • *adv* humbly
**humiliar** • *v* humble
**humit** • *adj* damp
**humitat** • *n* damp
**humor** • *n* humour, mood
**huracà** • *n* hurricane

i • *conj* and
iaia • *n* grandmother
iarda • *n* yard
icona • *n* icon
icònic • *adj* iconic
idea • *n* idea
ideal • *adj* ideal
idealis|me • *n* idealism ~ta • *n*
    idealist • *adj* idealistic
idèntic • *adj* identical
identificació • *n* identification
identificar • *v* identify
identitat • *n* identity
ideologia • *n* ideology
ideològic • *adj* ideological
ideològica • *adj* ideological
idioma • *n* language
idiota • *n* fool, idiot, moron •
    *adj* idiotic
Iemen • *n* Yemen
iemenita • *adj* Yemeni
ignorància • *n* ignorance
ignora|r • *v* ignore ~nt • *adj*
    ignorant
igual • *adj* equal, even ~ment •
    *adv* equally
igualtat • *n* equality
iguana • *n* iguana
illa • *n* block, island
illetrat • *adj* illiterate
illusió • *n* illusion
imaginació • *n* imagination
imaginar • *v* imagine
imaginari • *adj* imaginary
imaginatiu • *adj* imaginative
imant • *n* magnet

imatge • *n* image
imatgeria • *n* imagery
imbècil • *n* moron
immadur • *adj* immature
immaduresa • *n* immaturity
immediat • *adj* immediate
immediatament • *adv*
    immediately
immens • *adj* immense ~itat • *n*
    immensity
immensament • *adv* immensely
immersió • *n* plunge
immigració • *n* immigration
immigrant • *n* immigrant
imminent • *adj* imminent
immòbil • *adj* stationary
immoble • *n* property
immoral • *adj* base, outrageous
immundícia • *n* filth
immune • *adj* immune
impaciència • *n* impatience
impacient • *adj* impatient
    ~ment • *adv* impatiently
impactar • *v* impact
imparcial • *adj* impartial ~itat •
    *n* impartiality
imparell • *adj* odd
impedir • *v* prevent
imperi • *n* empire
impermeable • *n* raincoat
impersonal • *adj* impersonal
implementació • *n*
    implementation
implicar • *v* entail, imply
impopular • *adj* unpopular
importància • *n* importance
importa|r • *v* import, matter
    ~nt • *adj* important ~ntment
    • *adv* importantly
impossibilitat • *n* impossibility

**impossible** • *adj* impossible • *interj* no way
**impost** • *n* tax
**imprès** • *adj* impressed
**impressió** • *n* impression
**impressionant** • *adj* impressive
**impressionat** • *adj* impressed
**impressora** • *n* press, printer
**imprevisible** • *adj* unpredictable
**imprimir** • *v* print
**improbable** • *adj* unlikely
**imprudent** • *adj* careless
**impuls** • *n* boost, impulse, momentum
**impulsió** • *n* impulse
**impulsiu** • *adj* impulsive
**impur** • *adj* filthy
**inacabable** • *adj* endless
**inacceptable** • *adj* unacceptable
**inactiu** • *adj* inactive
**inactivitat** • *n* inactivity
**inadequat** • *adj* inadequate
**inapropiat** • *adj* inappropriate
**inaugurar** • *v* dedicate
**incapaç** • *adj* unable
**incendi** • *n* fire
**incentiu** • *n* incentive
**incert** • *adj* problematic, uncertain
**incertesa** • *n* uncertainty
**incisiu** • *adj* incisive
**incitar** • *v* prompt
**inclinació** • *n* bow, inclination
**inclinar** • *v* lean
**incloure** • *v* include
**inclusió** • *n* inclusion
**incòmodament** • *adv* uncomfortably
**incòmode** • *adj* uncomfortable
**incompetent** • *adj* incompetent

**inconscient** • *adj* unconscious ~ment • *adv* unconsciously
**inconsiderat** • *adj* inconsiderate
**inconsistència** • *n* inconsistency
**inconsistent** • *adj* inconsistent
**incorporar** • *v* incorporate
**incorrecte** • *adj* false, incorrect, wrong
**incórrer** • *v* incur
**increïble** • *adj* incredible, unbelievable ~ment • *adv* incredibly
**inculpar** • *v* charge
**indagació** • *n* inquiry
**indefens** • *adj* defenseless, helpless
**independència** • *n* independence
**independent** • *adj* independent ~ment • *adv* independently
**índex** • *n* index
**indexar** • *v* index
**indi** • *adj* Indian
**índia** • *n* Indian
**Índia** • *n* India
**indicar** • *v* indicate, point out
**indicatiu** • *adj* indicative
**indici** • *n* tip
**indígena** • *adj* indigenous
**indignació** • *n* outrage
**indignar** • *v* outrage
**indigne** • *adj* base
**indiot** • *n* turkey
**indirectament** • *adv* indirectly
**indirecte** • *adj* indirect
**indiscret** • *adj* indiscreet, tactless
**individu** • *n* individual
**individual** • *adj* individual ~ment • *adv* individually

**individualis|me** ● *n*
individualism **~ta** ● *n*
individualist
**indolent** ● *adj* indolent
**indolor** ● *adj* painless
**indonesi** ● *adj* Indonesian
**indonèsia** ● *n* Indonesian
**Indonèsia** ● *n* Indonesia
**indret** ● *n* place
**indubtablement** ● *adv*
undoubtedly
**induir** ● *v* induce
**indulgent** ● *adj* indulgent
**indústria** ● *n* industry
**industrial** ● *adj* industrial
**inesperadament** ● *adv*
unexpectedly
**inesperat** ● *adj* unexpected
**inestabilitat** ● *n* instability
**inestable** ● *adj* unstable
**inevitable** ● *adj* inevitable
**~ment** ● *adv* inevitably
**infame** ● *adj* infamous
**infància** ● *n* childhood
**infanteria** ● *n* infantry
**infantesa** ● *n* childhood
**infecció** ● *n* infection
**infecciós** ● *adj* infectious
**infectar** ● *v* infect
**infeliç** ● *adj* unhappy
**inferioritat** ● *n* inferiority
**infermer** ● *n* nurse
**infermera** ● *n* sister
**infermeria** ● *n* nursing
**infern** ● *n* hell
**inflació** ● *n* inflation
**inflament** ● *n* inflation
**infligir** ● *v* inflict
**influència** ● *n* influence
**influenciar** ● *v* influence
**influir** ● *v* influence

**informació** ● *n* data,
information
**informal** ● *adj* casual, informal
**~ment** ● *adv* informally **~itat** ●
*n* informality
**informar** ● *v* report
**informatiu** ● *adj* informative ● *n*
news
**informe** ● *n* report
**infraestructura** ● *n* framework,
infrastructure
**ingenu** ● *adj* naive
**ingredient** ● *n* ingredient
**inherent** ● *adj* inherent
**inhibició** ● *n* inhibition
**inhibir** ● *v* inhibit
**inici** ● *n* beginning
**inicial** ● *adj* initial
**inicials** ● *n* initial
**iniciar** ● *v* begin
**iniciativa** ● *n* initiative
**injecció** ● *n* injection
**injectar** ● *v* inject
**injúria** ● *n* injury
**injust** ● *adj* unfair
**injustícia** ● *n* injustice
**innecessari** ● *adj* needless,
unnecessary
**innoble** ● *adj* base
**innocència** ● *n* innocence
**innocent** ● *adj* innocent
**innovació** ● *n* innovation
**innova|r** ● *v* innovate **~dor** ●
*adj* innovative
**inofensiu** ● *adj* harmless
**inquiet** ● *adj* restless
**inquietant** ● *adj* worrying
**insanitat** ● *n* insanity
**inscriure** ● *v* enroll
**insecte** ● *n* insect
**insecticida** ● *n* insecticide

**insensible** • *adj* insensitive
**inserció** • *n* insertion
**insígnia** • *n* badge, button
**insinuar** • *v* imply
**insistència** • *n* insistence
**insistir** • *v* insist
**inspecció** • *n* check, inspection
**inspeccionar** • *v* inspect, search
**inspirador** • *adj* inspiring
**instant** • *n* moment, second
**instantàniament** • *adv* instantly
**instint** • *n* instinct
**instintiu** • *adj* instinctive
**institució** • *n* institution
**institucionalització** • *n* institutionalization
**institucionalitzar** • *v* institutionalize
**instituir** • *v* institute
**institut** • *n* institute
**instrucció** • *n* instruction
**instructor** • *n* instructor
**instruir** • *v* educate, instruct
**instrument** • *n* instrument
**instrumental** • *adj* instrumental
**insuficient** • *adj* insufficient
**insuls** • *adj* dull
**insult** • *n* insult, offense
**insulta|r** • *v* insult ~nt • *adj* insulting
**insuportable** • *adj* impossible
**intacte** • *adj* intact
**integral** • *adj* whole
**integrar** • *v* integrate
**integritat** • *n* integrity
**intenció** • *n* intention
**intencionadament** • *adv* intentionally
**intencionalment** • *adv* intentionally
**intencionat** • *adj* intentional

**intens** • *adj* deep, intense ~itat • *n* intensity
**intensament** • *adv* intensely
**intensificar** • *v* intensify
**intensiu** • *adj* intensive
**intent** • *n* down, go
**intentar** • *v* try
**interacció** • *n* interaction
**interactiu** • *adj* interactive
**interactuar** • *v* interact
**intercanvi** • *n* exchange
**intercanviar** • *v* exchange
**interdicció** • *n* prohibition
**interès** • *n* interest
**interessant** • *adj* interesting
**interessat** • *adj* interested
**interferència** • *n* interference
**interferir** • *v* interfere
**interfície** • *n* interface
**interí** • *adj* interim
**interior** • *adj* domestic, inner, interior • *n* inside ~ment • *adv* internally
**interjecció** • *n* interjection
**intermedi** • *adj* intermediate
**interminable** • *adj* endless
**intern** • *n* inmate • *adj* internal
**internacional** • *adj* international ~ment • *adv* internationally
**internament** • *adv* internally
**internat** • *n* inmate
**Internet** • *n* Internet
**intèrpret** • *n* interpreter
**interpretació** • *n* interpretation
**interpretar** • *v* interpret
**interroga|r** • *v* interrogate, question ~nt • *n* question mark
**interrogatori** • *n* interrogation
**interrompre** • *v* interrupt

**interrupció** • *n* disruption
**interruptor** • *n* switch
**interval** • *n* range
**intervenció** • *n* intervention
**intervenir** • *v* intervene
**interviu** • *n* interview
**intestí** • *n* intestine
**íntim** • *adj* intimate
**intimitat** • *n* intimacy
**intolerant** • *adj* intolerant
**intranquil** • *adj* restless
**intriga** • *n* intrigue
**intriga|r** • *v* intrigue **~nt** • *adj* intriguing
**introducció** • *n* introduction
**introductori** • *adj* introductory
**introduir** • *v* introduce, set
**intuïció** • *n* intuition
**intuïtiu** • *adj* intuitive
**inundació** • *n* flood
**inusual** • *adj* unusual
**inútil** • *adj* useless
**invàlid** • *adj* disabled
**invasió** • *n* invasion
**invasor** • *n* invader
**invenció** • *n* invention
**invent** • *n* invention
**inventar** • *v* invent
**inventari** • *n* inventory
**inventariar** • *v* inventory
**inventiu** • *adj* inventive
**inventiva** • *n* invention
**inversió** • *n* investment
**invertir** • *v* invest
**investigació** • *n* investigation
**investiga|r** • *v* investigate **~dor** • *n* investigator, researcher
**investir** • *v* invest
**invisible** • *adj* invisible
**invitació** • *n* invite
**invitar** • *v* invite

**invitat** • *n* guest
**invocar** • *v* invoke
**involuntari** • *adj* unintentional
**involuntàriament** • *adv* unintentionally
**iode** • *n* iodine
**ioga** • *n* yoga
**iogurt** • *n* yogurt
**iot** • *n* yacht
**ira** • *n* anger
**Iran** • *n* Iran
**iranià** • *adj* Iranian
**Iraq** • *n* Iraq
**iraquià** • *adj* Iraqi
**Irlanda** • *n* Ireland
**irlandès** • *adj* Irish
**irlandesos** • *n* Irish
**ironia** • *n* irony
**irònic** • *adj* ironic
**irònicament** • *adv* ironically
**irrellevant** • *adj* irrelevant
**irresistible** • *adj* irresistible
**irritació** • *n* irritation
**irritant** • *adj* irritating
**irrompre** • *v* break in
**islam** • *n* Islam
**islàmic** • *adj* Islamic
**islàmica** • *adj* Islamic
**islamisme** • *n* Islam
**Islàndia** • *n* Iceland
**isolació** • *n* isolation
**isola|r** • *v* isolate **~ment** • *n* isolation
**Israel** • *n* Israel
**israelià** • *adj* Israeli
**Istanbul** • *n* Istanbul
**italià** • *adj* Italian
**Itàlia** • *n* Italy
**italiana** • *n* Italian
**itinerari** • *n* course
**iugoslau** • *adj* Yugoslavian

**Iugoslàvia** • *n* Yugoslavia
**iuguslau** • *n* Yugoslavian

**ja** • *adv* already • *interj* now
**jaç** • *n* bed
**jaciment** • *n* deposit
**Jamaica** • *n* Jamaica
**jamaicà** • *adj* Jamaican
**jamaicana** • *n* Jamaican
**Japó** • *n* Japan
**japonès** • *adj* Japanese
**japonesa** • *n* Japanese
**jaqueta** • *n* jacket
**jardí** • *n* garden
**jardiner** • *n* gardener
**jardinera** • *n* gardener
**jardineria** • *n* gardening
**jazz** • *n* jazz
**jerarquia** • *n* hierarchy
**jeràrquic** • *adj* hierarchical
**jeure** • *v* lie
**jo** • *n* ego • *pron* I
**joc** • *n* game, play, set
**joguina** • *n* toy
**joia** • *n* jewel, joy
**joier** • *n* jeweler
**joiós** • *adj* joyful
**Jordà** • *n* Jordan
**Jordània** • *n* Jordan
**jorn** • *n* day
**jornada** • *n* day
**jota** • *n* jay
**jou** • *n* collar
**jove** • *adj* young • *n* youth

**jovent** • *n* young, youth
**joventut** • *n* youth
**jubilació** • *n* retirement
**jubilar** • *v* retire
**jubilat** • *adj* retired
**judici** • *n* judgment, trial
**judicial** • *adj* judicial
**judiciari** • *adj* judicial
**judo** • *n* judo
**jueria** • *n* ghetto
**jueu** • *n* Jew • *adj* Jewish
**jueva** • *n* Jew
**jugada** • *n* play
**juganer** • *adj* playful
**juga|r** • *v* play ~dor • *n* gambler, player
**juguesca** • *n* bet
**juliol** • *n* July
**julivert** • *n* parsley
**jungla** • *n* jungle
**junt** • *adv* together
**junta** • *n* board
**juntura** • *n* joint
**juny** • *n* June
**Júpiter** • *n* Jupiter
**jura|r** • *v* swear, vow ~ment • *n* pledge
**jurat** • *n* jury, juror
**jurídic** • *adj* legal
**jurisdicció** • *n* venue
**just** • *adj* fair, just
**justament** • *adv* fairly
**justesa** • *n* justice
**justícia** • *n* justice
**justificació** • *n* justification
**justificar** • *v* justify
**jutge** • *n* judge
**jutja|r** • *v* judge, try ~ment • *n* judgment

**Kazakhstan** • *n* Kazakhstan
**ked** • *n* sneaker
**kilòmetre** • *n* kilometre
**Kirguizistan** • *n* Kyrgyzstan
**kiwi** • *n* kiwi
**Kosovo** • *n* Kosovo
**kuwaitià** • *adj* Kuwaiti

**laberint** • *n* spaghetti
**laboratori** • *n* laboratory
**laca** • *n* lake
**lactis** • *n* dairy
**laic** • *adj* lay, secular
**lamentable** • *adv* pitiful • *adj* sad
**làmina** • *n* plate
**làmpada** • *n* lamp
**Laos** • *n* Laos
**larva** • *n* larva
**làser** • *n* laser
**lateral** • *n* wing
**lavabo** • *n* sink, toilet, washbasin
**lector** • *n* reader
**legal** • *adj* legal ~**ment** • *adv* legally ~**itat** • *n* legality
**legalització** • *n* legalization
**legislació** • *n* legislation

**legisla|r** • *v* legislate ~**dor** • *n* legislator
**legislatiu** • *adj* legislative
**legítim** • *adj* legitimate
**lent** • *n* lens • *adj* slow
**lentament** • *adv* slowly
**les** • *pron* them
**lesbià** • *adj* lesbian
**lesbiana** • *adj* lesbian
**lesió** • *n* wound
**Lesotho** • *n* Lesotho
**letal** • *adj* deadly, lethal
**letargia** • *n* lethargy
**letàrgic** • *adj* lethargic
**letó** • *adj* Latvian
**letona** • *n* Latvian
**Letònia** • *n* Latvia
**Líban** • *n* Lebanon
**libanès** • *adj* Lebanese
**liberal** • *adj* liberal
**liberalisme** • *n* liberalism
**Libèria** • *n* Liberia
**Líbia** • *n* Libya
**líder** • *n* head, leader, ruler
**liderar** • *v* head
**lideratge** • *n* leadership
**Liechtenstein** • *n* Liechtenstein
**light** • *adj* light
**ligni** • *adj* wooden
**límit** • *n* bound, limit
**limitar** • *v* limit
**línia** • *n* line
**link** • *n* link
**linx** • *n* lynx
**líquid** • *adj* liquid
**Lisboa** • *n* Lisbon
**literal** • *adj* literal ~**ment** • *adv* literally
**literari** • *adj* literary
**literatura** • *n* literature
**litigi** • *n* lawsuit

**litre** • *n* litre
**lituà** • *adj* Lithuanian
**Lituània** • *n* Lithuania
**llac** • *n* lake
**llaç** • *n* ribbon
**lladre** • *n* robber, thief
**llaganya** • *n* sleep
**llagosta** • *n* grasshopper, lobster
**llàgrima** • *n* tear
**llama** • *n* llama
**llamàntol** • *n* lobster
**llambregada** • *n* glance
**llambregar** • *v* glance
**llaminadura** • *n* candy, sweet
**llamp** • *n* lightning
**llampant** • *adj* gleaming, loud
**llampec** • *n* bolt, lightning
**llana** • *n* wool
**llança|r** • *v* launch, pitch, release, throw **~dor** • *n* pitcher **~ment** • *n* cast, launch, pitch, shot
**llangardaix** • *n* lizard
**llanxa** • *n* launch
**llapis** • *n* pencil
**llar** • *n* home
**llard** • *n* lard
**llarg** • *adj* large
**llàstima** • *n* pity, shame
**llastimós** • *adj* sorry
**llatí** • *adj* Latin • *n* Roman
**llatina** • *adj* Latin
**llauna** • *n* can
**llautó** • *n* brass
**llavar** • *v* wash
**llavi** • *n* lip
**llavor** • *n* seed
**llavors** • *adv* then
**llebre** • *n* hare
**lleganya** • *n* sleep

**llegar** • *v* will
**llegat** • *n* legacy
**llegenda** • *n* legend
**llegendari** • *adj* legendary
**llegir** • *v* read
**llegua** • *n* league
**llegum** • *n* legume, vegetable
**llei** • *n* law
**lleial** • *adj* faithful, loyal **~ment** • *adv* loyally
**lleialtat** • *n* loyalty
**lleig** • *adj* ugly
**lleixa** • *n* shelf
**llenç** • *n* canvas
**llençar** • *v* cast, throw away
**llenceria** • *n* lingerie
**llençol** • *n* bedsheet
**llengua** • *n* language, tongue
**llenguatge** • *n* language
**llentilla** • *n* lentil
**llenya** • *n* wood
**lleó** • *n* lion
**lleona** • *n* lioness
**lleopard** • *n* leopard
**llepar** • *v* blow
**llesca** • *n* slice
**llest** • *adj* clever, ready, set
**llestesa** • *n* intelligence
**llet** • *n* milk
**lleteria** • *n* dairy
**lletgesa** • *n* ugliness
**lletjor** • *n* ugliness
**lletós** • *adj* milky
**lletra** • *n* letter, lyrics
**lletrat** • *adj* literate
**lletrejar** • *v* spell
**lletuga** • *n* lettuce
**lleuger** • *adj* light, soft
**lleugerament** • *adv* lightly, slightly
**lleure** • *n* leisure

**llevadora** • *n* midwife
**llevant** • *n* east • *adj* eastern
**llevat** • *adj* awake • *prep* except • *n* yeast
**lli** • *n* linen
**llibertat** • *n* freedom, liberty
**llibre** • *n* book
**llibres** • *n* book
**llibreta** • *n* notebook
**llicència** • *n* license
**lliçó** • *n* lesson
**lliga** • *n* league
**lligadura** • *n* tie
**lligam** • *n* tie
**lligar** • *v* bind, cable, link, tie
**llima** • *n* file
**llimona** • *n* lemon
**llimoner** • *n* lemon
**llimonera** • *n* lemon
**llinatge** • *n* ancestry
**llindar** • *n* threshold
**llis** • *adj* smooth
**llisca|r** • *v* slide ~**nt** • *adj* slippery
**llista** • *n* list, range
**llistar** • *v* list
**llistat** • *adj* striped
**llit** • *n* bed
**lliura** • *n* pound ~**ment** • *n* delivery
**lliura|r** • *v* deliver, issue ~**ment** • *n* delivery
**lliure** • *adj* free, open ~**ment** • *adv* freely
**llivell** • *n* level
**lloança** • *n* praise
**lloar** • *v* praise
**lloc** • *n* place, room
**llogar** • *v* hire, rent
**llogater** • *n* tenant
**lloguer** • *n* rent

**llom** • *n* spine
**llombrígol** • *n* navel
**llong** • *adj* long
**llop** • *n* wolf
**lloro** • *n* parrot
**llot** • *n* mud
**llotja** • *n* box
**lluç** • *n* hake
**llúdria** • *n* otter
**llúdriga** • *n* otter
**lluentor** • *n* shine
**lluerna** • *n* skylight
**lluir** • *v* shine
**lluïssor** • *n* shine
**lluita** • *n* fight, struggle, wrestling
**lluitar** • *v* fight, wrestle
**llum** • *n* highlight, light
**lluna** • *n* moon
**lluny** • *adv* far
**llunyà** • *adj* far, long
**llunyania** • *n* distance
**llur** • *det* their
**lobby** • *n* lobby
**local** • *adj* local • *n* venue ~**ment** • *adv* locally
**localitzar** • *v* localize
**lògic** • *adj* logical
**lògica** • *n* logic ~**ment** • *adv* logically
**logístic** • *adj* logistical
**lona** • *n* canvas
**Londres** • *n* London
**longitud** • *n* length
**loteria** • *n* lottery
**lupa** • *n* magnifying glass
**Luxemburg** • *n* Luxembourg
**luxós** • *adj* luxurious
**luxúria** • *n* lust
**luxuriós** • *adj* luxurious

**mà** • *n* hand
**macedoni** • *adj* Macedonian
**macedònia** • *n* Macedonian
**Macedònia** • *n* Macedonia
**macedònic** • *adj* Macedonian
**macedònica** • *n* Macedonian
**maco** • *adj* cute, kind
**Madagascar** • *n* Madagascar
**Madrid** • *n* Madrid
**maduixa** • *n* strawberry
**maduixer** • *n* strawberry
**maduixera** • *n* strawberry
**madur** • *adj* mature, ripe
**madurar** • *v* mature
**maduresa** • *n* maturity
**magatzem** • *n* warehouse
**màgia** • *n* magic
**màgic** • *adj* magic, magical
**magnèsia** • *n* chalk
**magnètic** • *adj* magnetic
**magnífic** • *adj* gorgeous, magnificent
**magre** • *adj* lean, skinny
**mai** • *adv* never
**maig** • *n* May
**maionesa** • *n* mayonnaise
**maixella** • *n* jaw
**major** • *adj* major
**majoria** • *n* majority
**majúscula** • *adj* capital
**mal** • *adv* badly • *n* evil
**malaïdament** • *adv* damn
**malaisi** • *adj* Malaysian
**Malàisia** • *n* Malaysia
**malalt** • *adj* ill
**malaltia** • *n* disease, illness

**malament** • *adv* badly
**malauradament** • *adv* unfortunately
**Malawi** • *n* Malawi
**malbaratament** • *n* waste
**malcarat** • *adj* surly
**maldecap** • *n* headache
**maldestre** • *adj* awkward, clumsy
**Maldives** • *n* Maldives
**malèfic** • *adj* evil
**maleir** • *v* damn
**maleït** • *adj* bloody, damn
**maleta** • *n* case
**maleter** • *n* trunk
**malgrat** • *n* despite • *conj* while
**malhumorós** • *adj* prickly
**maliciós** • *adj* evil
**malla** • *n* net
**malson** • *n* nightmare
**Malta** • *n* Malta
**maltès** • *adj* Maltese
**maltesa** • *adj* Maltese
**maluc** • *n* hip
**malvat** • *adj* evil
**mama** • *n* breast, mum
**mamella** • *n* breast
**mamut** • *n* mammoth
**manar** • *v* command, rule
**manat** • *n* command
**manca** • *n* lack
**mancar** • *v* lack
**mandat** • *n* mandate
**mandíbula** • *n* jaw
**mandolina** • *n* mandolin
**mandonguilla** • *n* meatball
**mandra** • *n* sloth
**mandrós** • *adj* lazy
**mànec** • *n* handle
**mànega** • *n* sleeve
**maneig** • *n* management

manejar • v steer
manera • n manner, way
maneres • n manner
maneta • n hand, handle
mangosta • n mongoose
mania • n bug
manifest • adj manifest
manifestació • n march, rally
manifesta|r • v manifest ~nt • n protester
màniga • n sleeve
manilles • n handcuffs
manipulació • n handling
manipula|r • v manipulate ~dor • adj manipulative
manllevar • v borrow
manta • n blanket
mantega • n butter
mantell • n cloak
manteni|r • v maintain ~ment • n maintenance
manualment • adv manually
manuscrit • adj manuscript
manyà • n locksmith
maó • n brick
mapa • n map
maqueta • n model
maquillatge • n makeup
màquina • n machine
maquinari • n hardware
maquinària • n machinery
mar • n sea
marató • n marathon
marbre • n marble
marc • n frame, mark
març • n March
marca • n brand, march, mark
marcapassos • n pacemaker
marcar • v highlight, mark, plot, score
marcial • adj martial

marcolfa • n tart
mare • n mother, parent
marea • n tide
marejat • adj dizzy
marfanta • n tart
marge • n margin
marginal • adj marginal
marí • adj marine • n sailor
maricó • n fruit
marieta • adj family • n fruit, ladybird, queen
mariner • n sailor
marineria • n crew
marit • n husband
marjal • n plot
marmota • n marmot
màrqueting • n marketing
marrà • n hog
marró • adj brown, chestnut, coffee • n cow
Marroc • n Morocco
marroquí • adj Moroccan
Mart • n Mars
martell • n hammer
martellejar • v hammer
marxa • n march
marxar • v march
màscara • n mask
mascarada • n mask
mascla • adj male
mascle • n cock, male
mascota • n pet
masculí • adj male
masculina • adj male
massa • n dough, earth, mass • adv too
massacrar • v massacre
massacre • n massacre
massiu • adj bulk, massive
mastegar • v chew
masticar • v chew

**mastodòntic** • *adj* mammoth
**matalàs** • *n* mattress
**matar** • *v* kill
**mateix** • *pron* herself, himself, itself, myself, ourselves, same, themselves, yourself • *adj* one, own
**matemàtic** • *adj* mathematical
**matemàtica** • *n* mathematics
**matemàtiques** • *n* mathematics
**matèria** • *n* subject
**material** • *adj* material
**materialis|me** • *n* materialism ~**ta** • *adj* materialistic
**materialitzar** • *v* materialize
**maternal** • *adj* maternal
**matí** • *n* morning
**matinada** • *n* morning
**matrícula** • *n* plate
**matricular** • *v* enroll
**matrimoni** • *n* marriage
**matriu** • *n* matrix, womb
**matx** • *n* match
**matxo** • *n* mule
**Mauritània** • *n* Mauritania
**màxim** • *adj* maximum
**maximitzar** • *v* maximize
**me** • *pron* me
**mecànic** • *adj* mechanical
**mecanisme** • *n* device, mechanism
**mecanografiar** • *v* type
**medalla** • *n* award, medal
**medi** • *n* environment, medium
**mediambiental** • *adj* environmental
**mèdic** • *adj* medical
**medicament** • *n* medicine, medication
**medicina** • *n* medicine
**medieval** • *adj* medieval

**meditació** • *n* meditation
**meditar** • *v* meditate
**mèdium** • *n* medium
**medusa** • *n* jellyfish
**meitat** • *n* half
**mel** • *n* honey
**melic** • *n* navel
**melmelada** • *n* jam, jelly
**meló** • *n* melon
**melodia** • *n* melody, tune
**melòdic** • *adj* melodic
**melsa** • *n* spleen
**membrana** • *n* web
**membre** • *n* limb, member
**memorable** • *adj* memorable
**memòria** • *n* memory, remembrance
**memoritzar** • *v* memorize
**mena** • *n* sort, type
**mencionar** • *v* mention
**mendica|r** • *v* beg ~**nt** • *n* beggar
**menester** • *n* requirement
**menja|r** • *n* dinner, food • *v* eat ~**dor** • *n* dining room, eater
**menor** • *n* minor
**mensual** • *adj* monthly ~**ment** • *adv* monthly
**mènsula** • *n* bracket
**ment** • *n* mind, wit
**menta** • *adj* mint
**mental** • *adj* mental ~**ment** • *adv* mentally
**mentida** • *n* lie
**mentider** • *n* liar
**mentir** • *v* cheat, lie
**mentó** • *n* chin
**mentre** • *conj* while
**mentrestant** • *adv* meanwhile, then

M

**menú** • *n* menu
**menut** • *adj* minute
**menys** • *conj* but • *det* fewer • *adj* less • *prep* less
**menyspreable** • *adj* nasty
**mer** • *adj* mere
**merament** • *adv* merely
**meravella** • *n* wonder
**meravellós** • *adj* wonderful
**mercader** • *n* merchant
**mercat** • *n* market
**mercès** • *interj* thanks
**Mercuri** • *n* Mercury
**mercurial** • *adj* mercurial
**merda** • *n* shit
**merèixer** • *v* deserve, merit
**meridional** • *adj* southern
**mèrit** • *n* merit
**meritar** • *v* deserve
**merla** • *n* blackbird
**mes** • *n* month
**més** • *adv* any more, more • *adj* else, plus • *det* more • *prep* plus
**mesa** • *n* board
**mescla** • *n* blend, mixture
**mesclar** • *v* mix
**mesquita** • *n* mosque
**mestre** • *n* master
**mestressa** • *n* landlord, mistress
**mesura** • *n* measure
**mesurar** • *v* measure
**meta** • *n* finish, goal, home
**metàfora** • *n* metaphor
**metafòric** • *adj* metaphorical
**metal** • *n* metal
**metall** • *n* brass, metal
**meteorit** • *n* meteorite
**meteoròleg** • *n* meteorologist
**meteorologia** • *n* meteorology
**metge** • *n* physician

**metgessa** • *n* physician
**meticulós** • *adj* meticulous
**mètode** • *n* method
**metòdic** • *adj* methodical
**metodologia** • *n* methodology
**metre** • *v* put
**metropolità** • *adj* metropolitan
**metxa** • *n* light
**metzina** • *n* poison
**meu** • *det* my
**Mèxic** • *n* Mexico
**mexicà** • *adj* Mexican
**mexicana** • *adj* Mexican
**mi** • *pron* me
**mica** • *n* bit • *adj* quiet
**mico** • *n* monkey
**Micronèsia** • *n* Micronesia
**microona** • *n* microwave
**mida** • *n* size
**mig** • *adj* half, mean • *n* middle
**migdia** • *n* south
**migdiada** • *n* nap
**migjorn** • *n* south
**migració** • *n* migration
**migratori** • *adj* migratory
**milà** • *n* kite
**miliard** • *n* billion
**milió** • *num* million
**militar** • *adj* military
**milla** • *n* mile
**millor** • *adj* better
**millora** • *n* improvement
**millorar** • *v* better, improve
**milotxa** • *n* kite
**milpeu** • *n* millipede
**mina** • *n* mine
**minaire** • *n* miner
**minar** • *v* mine
**miner** • *n* miner
**mineral** • *adj* mineral
**mineria** • *n* mining

M

**minifaldilla** • *n* miniskirt
**mínim** • *adj* minimal • *n* minimum
**minimalis|me** • *n* minimalism ~**ta** • *adj* minimal, minimalist
**minimitzar** • *v* minimize
**ministeri** • *n* ministry
**ministre** • *n* minister
**minoria** • *n* minority
**minoritat** • *n* minority
**minuciós** • *adj* meticulous, thorough
**minúscul** • *adj* minute, tiny
**minusvàlid** • *adj* disabled
**minut** • *n* minute
**minyó** • *n* boy
**miracle** • *n* miracle
**miraculós** • *adj* miraculous
**mirada** • *n* look
**mirall** • *n* mirror
**mirar** • *v* look, watch
**miserable** • *adv* pitiful
**misèria** • *n* misery
**misericòrdia** • *n* mercy
**missa** • *n* mass
**missatge** • *n* message
**míssil** • *n* missile
**missió** • *n* mission
**missioner** • *n* missionary
**misteri** • *n* mystery
**misteriós** • *adj* eerie, mysterious
**misto** • *n* match
**mite** • *n* myth
**mites** • *n* myth
**mític** • *adj* mythical
**mitigar** • *v* alleviate
**mitjà** • *adj* medium, middle • *n* vehicle, way
**mitjana** • *n* average, mean
**mitjançant** • *prep* through
**mitjancer** • *n* middleman

**mitjanit** • *n* midnight
**mitjó** • *n* sock
**mitologia** • *n* mythology
**mitològic** • *adj* mythological
**mixtura** • *n* mixture
**mòbil** • *adj* mobile
**mobilitat** • *n* mobility
**Moçambic** • *n* Mozambique
**moció** • *n* motion
**moda** • *n* mode
**model** • *n* model, pattern
**moderació** • *n* moderation
**modera|r** • *v* moderate ~**dor** • *n* moderator
**moderat** • *adj* moderate
**modern** • *adj* modern ~**itat** • *n* modernity
**modernisme** • *n* modernism
**modernitzar** • *v* modernize
**modest** • *adj* modest
**modèstia** • *n* modesty
**modificació** • *n* edit
**modificar** • *v* change, modify
**mofeta** • *n* skunk
**moix** • *adj* down
**mol** • *n* mole
**Moldàvia** • *n* Moldova
**moldre** • *v* grind, mill
**molècula** • *n* molecule
**molecular** • *adj* molecular
**molest** • *v* annoying • *adj* upset
**molestar** • *v* annoy, bother, disturb, harass
**molèstia** • *n* annoyance
**molí** • *n* mill
**moll** • *adj* wet
**molla** • *n* spring
**molt** • *det* many, much • *adv* very
**mòlt** • *adj* ground
**moltes** • *det* many

M

**moment** • *n* minute, moment, second
**món** • *n* world
**Mònaco** • *n* Monaco
**moneda** • *n* coin, currency
**moneder** • *n* purse
**mongeta** • *n* bean
**mongol** • *adj* Mongolian
**Mongòlia** • *n* Mongolia
**moniatera** • *n* sweet potato
**moniato** • *n* sweet potato
**monitor** • *n* display, monitor
**monjo** • *n* monk
**monòleg** • *n* monologue
**monopatí** • *n* skateboard
**monopoli** • *n* monopoly
**monstre** • *n* monster
**monstruós** • *adj* monster
**Montenegro** • *n* Montenegro
**monument** • *n* bomb, monument
**monumental** • *adj* monumental
**moqueta** • *n* carpet
**móra** • *n* blackberry
**moral** • *adj* moral **~ment** • *adv* morally **~itat** • *n* moral, morality
**mòrbid** • *adj* morbid
**mòrbida** • *adj* morbid
**mordaç** • *adj* cutting
**morir** • *v* die
**mort** • *adj* dead • *n* death, kill
**mortal** • *adj* deadly, lethal, mortal **~itat** • *n* mortality
**mortífer** • *adj* deadly
**morts** • *n* dead
**mos** • *n* bit, mouthful
**mosaic** • *n* mosaic
**mosca** • *n* fly
**Moscou** • *n* Moscow
**mossegada** • *n* bite, mouthful

**mossegar** • *v* bite
**most** • *n* must
**mostassa** • *n* mustard
**mostela** • *n* weasel
**mostra** • *n* pattern, sample
**mostrar** • *v* show
**mot** • *n* word
**motel** • *n* motel
**motiu** • *n* motive
**motivació** • *n* motivation
**motivar** • *v* motivate
**motlle** • *n* cast
**moto** • *n* bike, motorcycle
**motocicleta** • *n* motorcycle
**motor** • *n* engine, motor
**motorista** • *n* motorist
**motxilla** • *n* backpack
**moure** • *v* move
**moviment** • *n* motion, movement
**muda** • *n* mute **~ment** • *n* move
**mudança** • *n* move
**muda|r** • *v* move **~ment** • *n* move
**mugró** • *n* nipple
**mul** • *n* mule
**mula** • *n* mule
**mullar** • *v* wet
**muller** • *n* wife
**multa** • *n* fine
**multar** • *v* fine
**múltiple** • *adj* multiple
**multiplicació** • *n* multiplication
**multiplicar** • *v* multiply
**multitud** • *n* crowd
**mundial** • *adj* global, worldwide **~ment** • *adv* worldwide
**municipal** • *adj* municipal
**municipi** • *n* municipality
**munt** • *n* mountain

M

muntanya • *n* mountain
muntanyós • *adj* mountainous
muntar • *v* assemble, get on, ride, set up
munyir • *v* milk
mur • *n* wall
muralla • *n* wall
murar • *v* wall
muricec • *n* bat
muscle • *n* shoulder
musclo • *n* mussel
múscul • *n* muscle
muscular • *adj* muscular
musculós • *adj* muscular
museu • *n* museum
músic • *n* musician
música • *n* music
musical • *adj* musical
mussol • *n* owl
musulmà • *adj* Muslim
mut • *adj* mute
mutu • *adj* mutual
Myanmar • *n* Myanmar

nabiu • *n* cranberry
nació • *n* nation
nacional • *adj* national
Nadal • *n* Christmas
nadó • *n* baby
naïf • *adj* naive
naixença • *n* birth
Namíbia • *n* Namibia
nansa • *n* handle
nariu • *n* nostril

narració • *n* narrative
narra|r • *v* narrate ~dor • *n* narrator
narratiu • *adj* narrative
narrativa • *n* narrative
nas • *n* nose
nat • *adj* born
nata • *n* cream
natació • *n* swimming
natalici • *n* birthday
natja • *n* butt, tail
natura • *n* nature
natural • *n* nature • *adj* natural, plain ~ment • *adv* naturally
nau • *n* aisle, ship
Nauru • *n* Nauru
nàutica • *n* navigation
naval • *adj* naval
navegació • *n* navigation
navegar • *v* navigate, sail, surf
nebulós • *adj* cloudy
necessari • *adj* necessary
necessàriament • *adv* necessarily
necessitar • *v* need
necessitat • *n* necessity, need
nectarina • *n* nectarine
nedar • *v* swim
neerlandès • *adj* Dutch
neerlandesa • *n* Dutch
negar • *v* deny
negatiu • *adj* negative
negativa • *n* no
negativitat • *n* negativity
negligència • *n* neglect
negligent • *adj* careless
negligir • *v* neglect
negoci • *n* business
negociació • *n* negotiation
negociar • *v* negotiate
negra • *n* black

M
N

**negre** • *adj* black
**negreta** • *adj* bold
**negror** • *n* darkness
**neguitejar** • *v* worry
**néixer** • *v* dawn
**nen** • *n* child, toddler
**nena** • *n* girl
**neozelandès** • *n* New Zealander
**Nepal** • *n* Nepal
**nepalès** • *adj* Nepali • *n* Nepali
**nepalesa** • *adj* Nepali • *n* Nepali
**Neptú** • *n* Neptune
**nervi** • *n* nerve
**nerviós** • *adj* nervous
**net** • *adj* clean, neat, net, plain
**nét** • *n* grandchild, grandson
**néta** • *n* grandchild, granddaughter
**neteja|r** • *v* clean, clean up ~dor • *n* cleaner
**neu** • *n* snow
**neumàtic** • *n* tyre
**neutral** • *adj* neutral ~itat • *n* neutrality
**neutre** • *adj* neutral
**nevar** • *v* snow
**Nicaragua** • *n* Nicaragua
**nicaragüenc** • *adj* Nicaraguan
**nicaragüenca** • *n* Nicaraguan
**nigerià** • *adj* Nigerian
**Nigèria** • *n* Nigeria
**nimfa** • *n* nymph
**nina** • *n* doll
**ningú** • *pron* anyone, no one • *n* nobody
**nínxol** • *n* niche
**nit** • *n* night
**niu** • *n* nest
**nivell** • *n* level
**no** • *det* no • *part* no • *adv* not

**noble** • *adj* noble
**noblesa** • *n* nobility
**noció** • *n* notion
**nociu** • *adj* harmful
**nogensmenys** • *adv* however, nevertheless, nonetheless
**noguera** • *n* walnut
**noi** • *n* boy
**noia** • *n* bird, girl
**noliejar** • *v* charter
**nom** • *n* name
**nòmada** • *n* wanderer
**nombre** • *n* number
**nombrós** • *adj* numerous
**nomenament** • *n* appointment
**només** • *adv* alone, just, only
**nominar** • *v* nominate
**nora** • *n* daughter-in-law
**noranta** • *num* ninety
**nord** • *n* north
**nordista** • *n* northerner
**norma** • *n* rule
**normal** • *adj* normal ~ment • *adv* normally, usually ~itat • *n* normality
**noruec** • *adj* Norwegian
**noruega** • *adj* Norwegian
**Noruega** • *n* Norway
**nosaltres** • *pron* we
**nostre** • *det* our
**nota** • *n* mark, note, notice
**nota|r** • *v* note, notice ~ble • *adj* notable ~blement • *adv* importantly, notably
**notícia** • *n* message
**notícies** • *n* news
**notificació** • *n* notification
**notificar** • *v* report
**notori** • *adj* notorious
**notòriament** • *adv* notoriously
**notorietat** • *n* notoriety

**nou** ● *adj* new ● *n* nine, nut
**noucasada** ● *n* newlywed
**noucasat** ● *adj* newlywed
**nounada** ● *n* newborn
**nounat** ● *adj* new, newborn
**novaiorquès** ● *adj* New York
**novament** ● *adv* newly, once again
**novè** ● *adj* ninth
**novell** ● *adj* new
**novembre** ● *n* November
**novena** ● *num* nine ● *n* ninth
**nòvia** ● *n* girlfriend
**nòvio** ● *n* boyfriend
**nu** ● *adj* naked
**nuclear** ● *adj* nuclear
**nucli** ● *n* nucleus
**nuesa** ● *n* nakedness
**numeral** ● *n* numeral
**numerar** ● *v* number
**numèric** ● *adj* numerical
**número** ● *n* number, numeral
**nus** ● *n* knot, knuckle
**nutrici** ● *adj* nutritious
**nutricional** ● *adj* nutritional
**nutrient** ● *adj* nutritious
**nutritiu** ● *adj* nutritional, nutritious
**nuvi** ● *n* bridegroom
**núvia** ● *n* bride
**núvol** ● *n* cloud
**nuvolós** ● *adj* cloudy
**nyanyo** ● *n* bump

**o** ● *conj* or
**obediència** ● *n* obedience
**obedient** ● *adj* obedient
**obeir** ● *v* obey
**obert** ● *adj* open
**obertament** ● *adv* openly
**obertura** ● *n* initial, opening
**obès** ● *adj* obese
**obesitat** ● *n* obesity
**objecció** ● *n* objection
**objecte** ● *n* object
**objectiu** ● *n* goal, objective
**objectivitat** ● *n* objectivity
**oblidadís** ● *adj* forgetful
**oblidar** ● *v* forget
**oblidós** ● *adj* forgetful
**obligació** ● *n* duty, obligation
**obligar** ● *v* oblige
**obligatori** ● *adj* compulsory, mandatory
**oblit** ● *n* oversight
**oboè** ● *n* oboe
**obra** ● *n* play
**obrer** ● *n* worker
**obrir** ● *v* open, turn on
**obscè** ● *adj* filthy, rude
**obscur** ● *adj* dark ~**itat** ● *n* dark, night
**observació** ● *n* observation
**observa|r** ● *v* mark, observe ~**dor** ● *n* observer
**observatori** ● *n* observatory
**obsessió** ● *n* obsession
**obsessionat** ● *adj* obsessed
**obsessiu** ● *adj* obsessive
**obstacle** ● *n* obstacle
**obtenir** ● *v* achieve, get, guess, obtain
**obús** ● *n* gun
**obvi** ● *adj* obvious
**òbviament** ● *adv* obviously

N

O

oca • *n* goose

ocasional • *adj* casual, occasional ~ment • *adv* occasionally

occident • *n* west

occidental • *adj* western

oceà • *n* ocean

Oceania • *n* Oceania

oceànic • *adj* oceanic

ocell • *n* bird

oci • *n* leisure

ocórrer • *v* happen, occur

octava • *n* octave

octubre • *n* October

ocultar • *v* conceal

ocupació • *n* occupation

ocupar • *v* occupy

ocupat • *adj* busy

oda • *n* poem

odi • *n* hatred

odiar • *v* hate

odiós • *adj* hateful

odorar • *v* smell

oest • *n* west

ofegar • *v* drown

ofendre • *v* offend

ofensa • *n* offense

ofensiu • *adj* offensive

ofensiva • *adj* offensive

oferi|r • *v* offer, sacrifice ~ment • *n* offering

oferta • *n* offer

ofès • *adj* hurt

ofici • *n* office, profession

oficial • *adj* official ~ment • *adv* officially

oficina • *n* office

oficinista • *n* clerk

ofrenar • *v* offer

oïda • *n* hearing

oir • *v* hear

olfacte • *n* scent, smell

oli • *n* oil

òliba • *n* owl

olimpíada • *n* Olympics

olimpíades • *n* Olympics

olímpic • *adj* Olympic

oliva • *n* olive

olivera • *n* olive tree

olla • *n* pot

olor • *n* smell

olorar • *v* smell

ombra • *n* shade, shadow

on • *adv* where

ona • *n* wave

onada • *n* wave

oncle • *n* uncle

onejar • *v* fly

ONG • *n* NGO

onsevol • *conj* wherever

onsevulga • *adv* anywhere • *conj* wherever

onsevulla • *adv* wherever

onze • *num* eleven

opció • *n* option, switch

opcional • *adj* optional

open • *n* open

òpera • *n* opera

operació • *n* operation, surgery

operatiu • *adj* operational

opinió • *n* opinion

oportú • *adj* timely

oportunitat • *n* chance, opportunity

oposar • *v* oppose

oposat • *adj* opposite

oposició • *n* opposition

òptic • *adj* optical • *n* optician

optimis|me • *n* optimism ~ta • *adj* optimistic

oració • *n* prayer

oral • *adj* oral

**orb** • *adj* blind
**òrbita** • *n* orbit
**orbitar** • *v* orbit
**orde** • *n* order
**ordenar** • *v* clean, command, order, sort
**ordinador** • *n* computer
**ordinari** • *adj* ordinary
**ordinàriament** • *adv* ordinarily
**ordre** • *n* command, order
**orella** • *n* ear
**oreneta** • *n* swallow
**orenga** • *n* oregano
**òrgan** • *n* organ
**orgànic** • *adj* organic
**organisme** • *n* organism
**organització** • *n* organization
**organitza|r** • *v* arrange, organize **~dor** • *n* organizer
**organitzat** • *adj* organized
**orgue** • *n* organ
**orgull** • *n* pride
**orgullós** • *adj* proud
**orient** • *n* east
**orientació** • *n* orientation
**oriental** • *adj* eastern
**origen** • *n* origin
**original** • *n* manuscript
**originàriament** • *adv* originally
**orla** • *n* border
**ornitorinc** • *n* platypus
**orquestra** • *n* orchestra
**orquestral** • *adj* orchestral
**ortografia** • *n* spelling
**os** • *n* bone
**ós** • *n* bear
**Oslo** • *n* Oslo
**ostatge** • *n* hostage
**ostentós** • *adj* ostentatious, pretentious
**ostra** • *n* oyster

**OTAN** • *n* NATO
**ou** • *n* egg, nut
**ous** • *n* plum
**ovella** • *n* sheep
**ovni** • *n* UFO
**òvul** • *n* egg
**òxid** • *n* rust
**oxidar** • *v* rust
**oxigen** • *n* oxygen
**oxímoron** • *n* oxymoron
**ozó** • *n* ozone

**pa** • *n* bread
**paciència** • *n* patience
**pacient** • *adj* patient **~ment** • *adv* patiently
**pacífic** • *adj* peaceful
**pacíficament** • *adv* peacefully
**pacte** • *n* agreement
**paella** • *n* frying pan
**paga** • *n* wage **~ment** • *n* payment
**pagà** • *adj* ethnic
**paga|r** • *v* pay **~ment** • *n* payment
**pagès** • *n* peasant
**pàgina** • *n* page
**paio** • *n* dude, guy
**país** • *n* country
**paisatge** • *n* landscape
**Pakistan** • *n* Pakistan
**pakistanès** • *adj* Pakistani
**pal** • *n* pale, stake
**pala** • *n* spade

O
P

**palau** • *n* palace
**Palau** • *n* Palau
**palestí** • *adj* Palestinian
**Palestina** • *n* Palestine
**palestinenc** • *adj* Palestinian
**paleta** • *n* bricklayer
**palla** • *n* straw
**palmell** • *n* palm
**palmito** • *n* fan
**paloma** • *n* butterfly
**palometa** • *n* butterfly
**pam** • *n* span
**pana** • *n* breakdown
**Panamà** • *n* Panama
**panameny** • *adj* Panamanian
**panamenya** • *n* Panamanian
**pancarta** • *n* banner
**panda** • *n* panda
**panel** • *n* panel
**panell** • *n* panel
**panerola** • *n* cockroach
**pànic** • *n* panic
**pansa** • *n* raisin
**pantalla** • *n* screen
**pantaló** • *n* pants
**pantalons** • *n* pants
**panteixar** • *v* pant
**panxa** • *n* belly, stomach
**panxell** • *n* calf
**paó** • *n* peacock
**pap** • *n* crop
**papa** • *n* dad, pop
**papagai** • *n* parrot
**papaió** • *n* butterfly
**papalló** • *n* butterfly
**papallona** • *n* butterfly
**paparra** • *n* tick
**paper** • *n* paper
**paperada** • *n* paperwork
**paperassa** • *n* paperwork
**papereta** • *n* slip

**papi** • *n* pop
**paquet** • *n* package
**paràbola** • *n* parable
**paracaigudes** • *n* parachute
**parada** • *n* stop
**paraigua** • *n* umbrella
**paràmetre** • *n* parameter
**parany** • *n* trap
**par|ar** • *v* set, stop **~ent** • *n* relative
**paraula** • *n* word
**parc** • *n* garden, park
**parcial** • *adj* biased, partial **~ment** • *adv* partially
**pardal** • *n* sparrow
**pare** • *n* father, parent
**parèixer** • *v* seem
**parell** • *adj* even • *n* pair
**parella** • *n* couple, pair, partner
**parenta** • *n* relative
**parèntesi** • *n* parenthesis
**parer** • *n* verdict, view
**pares** • *n* parent
**paret** • *n* wall
**Paris** • *n* Paris
**París** • *n* Paris
**parla** • *n* speech **~ment** • *n* parliament
**parlamentari** • *adj* parliamentary
**parla|r** • *v* speak, talk **~nt** • *n* speaker **~ment** • *n* parliament
**paròdia** • *n* parody
**parodiar** • *v* parody
**parpella** • *n* eyelid
**parroquià** • *n* parishioner
**parròquia** • *n* parish
**part** • *n* birth, part, party
**participar** • *v* participate, play
**partícula** • *n* particle

**partida** • *n* game
**partir** • *v* leave, split
**partit** • *n* match
**partitura** • *n* score
**pas** • *n* march, pace, stage, step
**passa** • *n* pace, step
**passada** • *n* passing
**passadís** • *n* aisle, corridor
**passaport** • *n* passport
**passa|r** • *v* happen, pass, spend ~nt • *prep* around
**passat** • *adj* off, past
**passatemps** • *n* pastime
**passatge** • *n* passage
**passatger** • *n* passenger • *adj* passing
**passeig** • *n* walk
**passejada** • *n* walk
**passió** • *n* passion
**passiu** • *adj* passive
**passivament** • *adv* passively
**pasta** • *n* brass, dough, pasta
**pastanaga** • *n* carrot
**pastís** • *n* cake, pie, tart
**pastor** • *n* pastor
**patacada** • *n* crash
**patata** • *n* potato
**patent** • *adj* patent
**patentar** • *v* patent
**patentitzar** • *v* get across
**patern** • *adj* paternal
**patètic** • *adj* sad
**patge** • *n* page
**pati** • *n* court ~ment • *n* suffering
**pati|r** • *v* suffer ~ment • *n* suffering
**pàtria** • *n* homeland
**patrimoni** • *n* wealth
**patró** • *n* boss, pattern
**patrulla** • *n* patrol

**patrullar** • *v* patrol
**pau** • *n* peace
**paüra** • *n* fear
**pausa** • *n* pause
**peatge** • *n* toll
**pebre** • *n* pepper
**pebrot** • *n* pepper
**pebrotera** • *n* pepper
**peça** • *n* piece, room
**pecaminós** • *adj* sinful
**peca|r** • *v* sin ~dor • *n* sinner
**pecat** • *n* sin
**peculiar** • *adj* peculiar
**pedaç** • *n* patch
**pedra** • *n* cow, rock, stone
**pedrenc** • *adj* stone
**pegar** • *v* hit, marry
**peix** • *n* fish
**pèl** • *n* hair
**pelat** • *adj* broke
**pelicà** • *n* pelican
**pell** • *n* skin
**pena** • *n* pain, time
**pendent** • *adj* outstanding, pending
**pèndol** • *n* pendulum
**penetració** • *n* penetration
**penetrar** • *v* penetrate, soak
**penis** • *n* penis
**penjar** • *v* hang, hang up
**pensa|r** • *v* think ~ment • *n* thought
**pensarós** • *adj* thoughtful
**pensatiu** • *adj* pensive
**pensió** • *n* pension
**pentagrama** • *n* staff
**pentinar** • *v* comb, tease
**penyora** • *n* pledge
**penyorar** • *v* pledge
**Pequín** • *n* Beijing
**per** • *prep* by, for, per, toward

**pera** • *n* pear
**perca** • *n* perch
**percebre** • *v* perceive
**percentatge** • *n* percentage
**percepció** • *n* perception
**perdiu** • *n* partridge
**perdó** • *interj* sorry
**perdona** • *adj* sorry
**perdonar** • *v* forgive
**perdre** • *v* lose
**pèrdua** • *n* loss, waste
**perdut** • *adj* lost
**perepunyetes** • *adj* fussy
**perera** • *n* pear
**peresa** • *n* sloth
**peresós** • *adj* lazy • *n* sloth
**perfecció** • *n* perfection
**perfeccionar** • *v* perfect
**perfectament** • *adv* flawlessly,
  perfectly
**perfecte** • *adj* flawless, perfect
**perfet** • *adj* perfect
**perforar** • *v* drill, punch
**perill** • *n* danger, hazard
**perillós** • *adj* dangerous
**període** • *n* era, period, span
**periòdic** • *n* newspaper • *adj*
  periodic
**periòdicament** • *adv*
  periodically
**periodis|me** • *n* journalism **~ta**
  • *n* journalist
**periquito** • *n* parakeet
**perista** • *n* fence
**perit** • *adj* professional,
  proficient
**perjudicial** • *adj* damaging
**permanència** • *n* permanence
**permanent** • *adj* permanent
  **~ment** • *adv* permanently
**permetre** • *v* let

**permís** • *n* leave, license,
  permission
**pernil** • *n* ham
**pernitar** • *v* sleep over
**però** • *conj* albeit, but
**perquè** • *conj* because, so • *n*
  why
**perquisició** • *n* inquiry
**perruca** • *n* wig
**perruquer** • *n* hairdresser
**persa** • *adj* Persian
**persà** • *adj* Persian
**persana** • *adj* Persian
**persecució** • *n* chase
**persegui|r** • *v* chase, prosecute
  **~ment** • *n* pursuit
**perseverança** • *n* perseverance
**perseverància** • *n* pluck
**perseverar** • *v* persevere
**persiana** • *n* blind
**persistència** • *n* persistence
**persistent** • *adj* persistent
**persistir** • *v* persist
**persona** • *n* person
**personal** • *adj* personal, private
  **~ment** • *adv* personally **~itat**
  • *n* personality
**personalització** • *n*
  personalization
**personalitzar** • *v* personalize
**personalitzat** • *adj* custom
**personatge** • *n* character
**perspectiva** • *n* perspective
**persuadir** • *v* persuade
**persuasió** • *n* persuasion
**persuasiu** • *adj* persuasive
**pertànyer** • *v* belong
**pertinença** • *n* property
**pertinent** • *adj* relevant
**pertot** • *adv* everywhere
**Perú** • *n* Peru

**peruà** • *adj* Peruvian
**peruana** • *n* Peruvian
**perviure** • *v* linger
**pes** • *n* weight
**pesar** • *v* weigh
**pesat** • *adj* heavy
**pesca** • *n* fishing
**pesca|r** • *v* fish **~dor** • *n* fisherman **~dora** • *n* fisherman
**pèsol** • *n* pea
**pesolera** • *n* pea
**pessic** • *n* pinch
**pessigar** • *v* pinch
**pèssim** • *adj* lousy
**pesta** • *n* plague
**pestanya** • *n* eyelash
**pesticida** • *n* pesticide
**peta** • *n* blunt
**petar** • *v* burst
**petge** • *n* leg
**petició** • *n* petition, request
**petit** • *adj* little, small
**petjada** • *n* step, track
**petó** • *n* kiss
**petonejar** • *v* kiss
**petri** • *adj* stone
**petroli** • *n* oil
**peu** • *n* foot
**peülla** • *n* hoof
**pi** • *n* pine
**pianista** • *n* pianist
**piano** • *n* piano
**pic** • *n* peak, pick
**pica** • *n* pike, sink, washbasin
**picada** • *n* sting
**pica|r** • *adj* itchy • *v* sting **~nt** • *adj* spicy
**picot** • *n* woodpecker
**pidolar** • *v* beg
**piga** • *n* freckle, mole

**pila** • *n* cell, pile
**pilot** • *adj* pilot
**pilota** • *n* ball, football
**pilotar** • *v* captain, fly, pilot
**piloteig** • *n* rally
**pilotes** • *n* ball, plum
**pinça** • *n* claw
**píndola** • *n* pill
**pingüí** • *n* penguin
**pinsà** • *n* finch
**pinso** • *n* feed
**pinta** • *n* comb
**pintallavis** • *n* lipstick
**pintar** • *v* paint
**pintor** • *n* painter
**pintura** • *n* paint, painting
**pinya** • *n* cone, pineapple
**pinyol** • *n* pit
**pinzell** • *n* paintbrush
**pioner** • *n* pioneer
**pionera** • *n* pioneer
**pipada** • *n* drag
**piràmide** • *n* pyramid
**piranya** • *n* piranha
**pirata** • *n* pirate
**piratejar** • *v* pirate
**pirateria** • *n* piracy
**pis** • *n* apartment
**piscina** • *n* swimming pool
**pispar** • *v* pinch
**pissarra** • *n* blackboard
**pista** • *n* ring, trail
**pistola** • *n* gun, pistol
**pit** • *n* breast, chest
**pitjor** • *adj* worse
**pitó** • *n* python
**pitrera** • *n* jug, rack
**pivot** • *n* center, post
**pizza** • *n* pizza
**pla** • *adj* even, flat, shallow • *n* plan, plane

P

**placa** • *n* plate
**plaça** • *n* square
**placar** • *v* tackle
**placatge** • *n* tackle
**plàcid** • *adj* placid
**plaent** • *adj* pleasant
**plaer** • *n* delight, pleasure
**plagi** • *n* plagiarism
**plaguicida** • *n* pesticide
**plana** • *n* plain
**planejar** • *v* plan, plot
**planeta** • *n* destiny, fate, planet
**planetari** • *n* planetarium
**planícia** • *n* plain
**planificació** • *n* planning
**planificar** • *v* arrange
**plànol** • *n* map
**planta** • *n* plant
**plantar** • *v* plant
**plantilla** • *n* staff, template
**plantofa** • *n* slipper
**planura** • *n* plain
**planxa** • *n* iron, plate
**planxar** • *v* iron
**plàstic** • *adj* plastic
**plat** • *n* course, dish, plate
**plata** • *n* silver
**plataforma** • *n* platform
**plàtan** • *n* banana
**platejat** • *adj* silver
**platerets** • *n* cymbal
**platja** • *n* beach, sand, strand
**plató** • *n* set
**plaure** • *v* please
**ple** • *adj* full • *n* strike
**plec** • *n* fold
**plega|r** • *v* collapse, fold ~**dor** • *adj* folding ~**ble** • *adj* folding ~**ment** • *n* fold
**plegatge** • *n* folding
**plenament** • *adv* fully

**plet** • *n* lawsuit
**plom** • *n* lead
**ploma** • *n* feather, sugar
**plomissol** • *n* down
**plor** • *n* cry
**plorar** • *v* cry, weep
**ploure** • *v* rain
**pluja** • *n* rain
**plujós** • *adj* rainy
**PMF** • *n* FAQ
**pneumàtic** • *n* tyre
**població** • *n* population
**poblar** • *v* people
**poble** • *n* people, town, village
**pobre** • *adj* poor
**pobres** • *n* poor
**pobresa** • *n* poverty
**poc** • *det* few, little • *adj* quiet
**pocavergonya** • *adj* shameless
**podar** • *v* prune
**poder** • *v* can, may • *n* power
**poderós** • *adj* mighty, powerful
**podrit** • *adj* rotten
**poema** • *n* poem
**poesia** • *n* poem, poetry
**poeta** • *n* poet
**poètic** • *adj* poetic
**poeticitat** • *n* poetry
**poguer** • *v* can
**pol** • *n* pole
**polèmic** • *adj* controversial
**policia** • *n* police
**polir** • *v* polish
**pòlissa** • *n* policy
**polític** • *adj* political • *n* politician
**política** • *n* policy, politician • *v* politics ~**ment** • *adv* politically
**poll** • *n* louse
**pollastre** • *n* chicken
**pollós** • *adj* lousy

**polo** • *n* polo
**polonès** • *adj* Polish
**Polònia** • *n* Poland
**pols** • *n* dust, powder, pulse
**polseguera** • *n* cloud
**poltre** • *n* rack
**pólvora** • *n* gunpowder
**polzada** • *n* inch
**polze** • *n* thumb
**poma** • *n* apple
**poncella** • *n* button
**ponent** • *adj* latter • *n* west
**poni** • *n* pony
**pont** • *n* bridge
**ponx** • *n* punch
**pop** • *n* octopus
**popa** • *n* jug, stern
**popular** • *adj* popular ~itat • *n* popularity
**pòquer** • *n* poker
**poquet** • *n* bit
**por** • *n* fear
**porc** • *n* pig
**porca** • *n* sow
**porcellana** • *n* porcelain
**porció** • *n* portion
**porpra** • *adj* purple
**porqueria** • *n* filth
**porret** • *n* joint
**porro** • *n* blunt, leek
**port** • *n* harbor, port
**porta** • *n* door, gate
**portaequipatge** • *n* trunk
**porta|r** • *v* act, bear, bring, carry, lead, take, wear ~dor • *n* carrier ~dora • *n* carrier
**portàtil** • *n* laptop
**portaveu** • *n* spokesperson
**porteria** • *n* goal
**Portugal** • *n* Portugal
**portugalès** • *adj* Portuguese

**portugalesa** • *n* Portuguese
**portuguès** • *adj* Portuguese
**portuguesa** • *n* Portuguese
**posar** • *v* put, set
**posició** • *n* position
**positiu** • *adj* plus, positive
**positura** • *n* attitude
**posposar** • *v* postpone
**posseïr** • *v* possess
**possessió** • *n* ownership, possession, property
**possessiu** • *adj* possessive
**possibilitat** • *n* possibility
**possible** • *adj* possible ~ment • *adv* perhaps, possibly
**post** • *n* board
**pòster** • *n* poster
**posteriorment** • *adv* later
**postís** • *adj* false
**postres** • *n* dessert
**pota** • *n* foot
**potència** • *n* power
**potencial** • *adj* potential ~ment • *adv* potentially
**potent** • *adj* powerful
**potser** • *adv* maybe, perhaps
**pou** • *n* well
**pràctic** • *adj* handy, practical
**pràctica** • *n* practice ~ment • *adv* practically
**practicar** • *v* practise
**precedent** • *n* precedent
**precedir** • *v* precede
**preciós** • *adj* lovely, precious
**precís** • *adj* accurate, exact, precise
**precisa|r** • *v* name ~ment • *adv* accurately, precisely
**precisió** • *n* accuracy, precision
**predicció** • *n* prediction
**predir** • *v* predict

P

**predominant** ● *adj* predominant **~ment** ● *adv* predominantly
**prefaci** ● *n* preface
**preferència** ● *n* preference
**preferències** ● *n* like
**preferiblement** ● *adv* preferably, rather
**preferir** ● *v* prefer
**preferit** ● *adj* favourite
**prefix** ● *n* prefix
**pregar** ● *v* beg, beseech, pray
**pregària** ● *n* prayer
**pregon** ● *adj* deep
**pregunta** ● *n* question
**preguntar** ● *v* ask
**prejudici** ● *n* prejudice
**preliminar** ● *adj* preliminary
**prematur** ● *adj* previous
**prémer** ● *v* press
**premi** ● *n* award, prize
**premiar** ● *v* award
**premsa** ● *n* press
**prendre** ● *v* take
**prenyat** ● *adj* pregnant ● *n* pregnancy
**preocupació** ● *n* concern, worry
**preocupa|r** ● *v* concern, worry **~nt** ● *adj* worrying
**preocupat** ● *adj* worried
**preparar** ● *v* fix, prepare, set up
**preparat** ● *adj* prepared, set
**preposició** ● *n* preposition
**pres** ● *n* prisoner
**presa** ● *n* dam, hurry, prey, take
**presència** ● *n* presence
**present** ● *adj* present
**presentació** ● *n* introduction
**presenta|r** ● *v* present, submit **~dor** ● *n* presenter
**preservació** ● *n* preservation

**preservar** ● *v* preserve
**preservatiu** ● *n* condom
**presidència** ● *n* presidency
**presidencial** ● *adj* presidential
**president** ● *n* president
**presidenta** ● *n* president
**presidir** ● *v* chair
**presó** ● *n* prison
**presoner** ● *n* prisoner
**préssec** ● *n* peach
**presseguer** ● *n* peach
**pressió** ● *n* pressure
**pressionar** ● *v* pressure
**pressupost** ● *n* budget
**prestar** ● *v* loan
**prestatge** ● *n* shelf
**préstec** ● *n* loan
**prestigi** ● *n* prestige
**prestigiós** ● *adj* prestigious
**presumiblement** ● *adv* presumably
**presumptament** ● *adv* allegedly
**presumpte** ● *adj* alleged
**presumptuós** ● *adj* conceited
**pretendre** ● *v* mean
**pretensió** ● *n* claim
**pretensiós** ● *adj* pretentious
**preu** ● *n* charge, price
**prevenció** ● *n* prevention
**preventiu** ● *adj* preventive
**preveure** ● *v* anticipate, devise
**previ** ● *adj* former, previous
**prèviament** ● *adv* previously
**prima** ● *n* premium
**primari** ● *adj* primary
**primària** ● *adj* primary **~ment** ● *adv* primarily
**primavera** ● *n* spring
**primer** ● *adj* first, prime ● *n* first
**primerament** ● *adv* firstly
**príncep** ● *n* prince

**princesa** ● *n* princess
**principal** ● *adj* chief, main
  **~ment** ● *adv* mainly
**principi** ● *n* base, beginning,
  principle
**prior** ● *n* prior **~itat** ● *n* priority
**prioritzar** ● *v* prioritize
**privacitat** ● *n* privacy
**privadament** ● *adv* privately
**privadesa** ● *n* privacy
**privat** ● *adj* private
**privatització** ● *n* privatization
**privilegi** ● *n* privilege
**pro** ● *n* pro
**proa** ● *n* bow
**probabilitat** ● *n* chance,
  likelihood, probability
**probable** ● *adj* probable **~ment**
  ● *adv* probably
**problema** ● *n* problem
**problemàtic** ● *adj* problematic
**procediment** ● *n* procedure
**procedimental** ● *adj* procedural
**procés** ● *n* process, trial
**processador** ● *n* processor
**processament** ● *n* processing
**proclamació** ● *n* proclamation
**producció** ● *n* production
**producte** ● *n* product
**productiu** ● *adj* productive
**productivitat** ● *n* productivity
**productor** ● *n* producer
**productora** ● *n* producer
**produir** ● *v* produce
**proesa** ● *n* exploit, feat
**profà** ● *adj* lay
**professió** ● *n* profession
**professional** ● *adj* professional
**professor** ● *n* professor
**professora** ● *n* professor
**profilàctic** ● *adj* preventive

**profitós** ● *adj* profitable
**profund** ● *adj* deep **~itat** ● *n*
  depth
**profundament** ● *adv* deeply
**progenitor** ● *n* parent
**programa** ● *n* broadcast,
  platform, program, schedule
**programador** ● *n* programmer
**programari** ● *n* software
**progrés** ● *n* breakthrough,
  progress
**progressar** ● *v* evolve, get on
**progressió** ● *n* progression
**progressista** ● *adj* progressive
**progressiu** ● *adj* progressive
**progressivament** ● *adv*
  progressively
**prohibició** ● *n* prohibition
**prohibir** ● *v* prohibit
**prohibit** ● *det* no
**proïsme** ● *n* neighbour
**projecte** ● *n* project
**projectil** ● *n* missile
**projector** ● *n* projector
**pròleg** ● *n* prologue
**promès** ● *adj* engaged
**promesa** ● *n* pledge, promise
**prometedor** ● *adj* promising
**prometre** ● *v* pledge, promise
**prominència** ● *n* prominence
**prominent** ● *adj* prominent
**promoció** ● *n* class
**pronom** ● *n* pronoun
**pronúncia** ● *n* pronunciation
**pronunciació** ● *n* pronunciation
**pronunciar** ● *v* pronounce
**propaganda** ● *n* propaganda
**proper** ● *adj* next
**propi** ● *adj* own
**propietari** ● *n* owner

P

propietat • *n* estate, ownership, possession, property
propina • *n* tip
proporció • *n* proportion
proporcional • *adj* proportional
proposar • *v* propose
proposta • *n* proposal
prora • *n* bow
prosa • *n* prose
prospeccions • *n* prospect
prospectar • *v* prospect
prosperitat • *n* prosperity
prostituta • *n* hooker
protagonista • *n* protagonist
protecció • *n* protection
protegir • *v* protect
proteïna • *n* protein
protesta • *n* protest
protesta|r • *v* protest ~nt • *n* protester, Protestant
prou • *adv* enough • *pron* enough
prova • *n* evidence, proof, test, trial, witness
provar • *v* pilot, prove, test, try, try out, witness
proveir • *v* provide, supply
província • *n* province
provincial • *adj* provincial
provisional • *adj* provisional
provisori • *adj* provisional
provoca|r • *v* provoke ~dor • *adj* provocative
provocatiu • *adj* provocative
pròxim • *adj* close, immediate
prudència • *n* prudence
prudentment • *adv* deliberately
pruna • *adj* plum
pruner • *n* plum
prunera • *n* plum

pseudònim • *n* pseudonym
psicòleg • *n* psychologist
psicologia • *n* psychology
psicològic • *adj* psychological
psiquiatre • *n* psychiatrist
psiquiatria • *n* psychiatry
psiquiàtric • *adj* psychiatric
públic • *n* audience • *adj* public
publicació • *n* publication
públicament • *adv* publicly
publicar • *v* publish, release
publicitat • *n* publicity
puça • *n* flea
pudent • *adj* smelly
puig • *n* hill
puix • *conj* because
pujada • *n* climb
pujar • *v* board, get on, rise
pulcre • *adj* neat
pulmó • *n* lung
pulsació • *n* pulse
punició • *n* punishment
puni|r • *v* punish ~ment • *n* punishment
punt • *n* dot, point, stitch, stop
punta • *n* butt, head, peak, tip
puntada • *n* kick
puntuació • *n* punctuation
puntual • *adj* prompt, punctual ~itat • *n* punctuality
puntuar • *v* mark
punxa • *n* tip
punxada • *n* flat
punxegut • *adj* pointed
puny • *n* cuff, fist
punyal • *n* knife
punyalada • *n* stab
pupil • *n* pupil
pur • *adj* clean, neat, pure
púrpura • *n* purple
purpuri • *adj* purple

**puta** • *n* tart

**Qatar** • *n* Qatar
**quadern** • *n* notebook, signature
**quaderna** • *n* rib
**quadrat** • *adj* square
**quadre** • *n* painting
**quadrícula** • *n* grid
**qualcú** • *pron* someone
**qualificació** • *n* qualification
**qualificat** • *adj* qualified
**qualitat** • *n* quality
**quality** • *n* quality
**qualque** • *pron* any
**qualsevol** • *det* any, whatever • *pron* anyone
**qualssevol** • *det* any
**quan** • *adv* when
**quantitat** • *n* amount, quantity
**quaranta** • *num* forty
**quart** • *n* barrel, quarter • *adj* fourth
**quarter** • *n* quarter
**quasi** • *adv* almost, nearly • *adj* rough
**quatre** • *n* four
**que** • *adv* how, what • *prep* than • *conj* that • *pron* which
**què** • *pron* what
**quedar** • *v* date, meet
**queixa** • *n* complaint, quarrel
**quelcom** • *pron* anything, something

**quer** • *n* rock
**qüern** • *num* four
**qüestió** • *n* question
**qüestionar** • *v* question
**qüestionari** • *n* questionnaire
**queviures** • *n* groceries
**qui** • *pron* who
**quiet** • *adj* quiet, still
**quilo** • *n* kilo
**quilòmetre** • *n* kilometre
**químic** • *adj* chemical • *n* chemist
**química** • *n* chemistry, chemist
**quin** • *det* which
**quint** • *adj* fifth
**quinta** • *n* fifth
**quinze** • *num* fifteen
**quinzena** • *adv* fortnight
**quiròfan** • *n* surgery
**quirúrgic** • *adj* surgical

**rabí** • *n* rabbi
**ràbia** • *n* anger, outrage, rage
**rabosa** • *n* fox
**raça** • *n* breed, race
**racial** • *adj* racial
**racional** • *adj* rational ~**ment** • *adv* rationally ~**itat** • *n* rationality
**racionalitzar** • *v* rationalize
**racis|me** • *n* racism ~**ta** • *adj* racist
**racó** • *n* angle, corner
**radar** • *n* radar

**radi** • *n* radius
**radiació** • *n* radiation
**radiant** • *adj* radiant, sunny
**radical** • *adj* radical
**ràdio** • *n* radio, wireless
**radioactiu** • *adj* radioactive
**radioactivitat** • *n* radioactivity
**radiografia** • *n* X-ray
**rai** • *n* ferry
**raig** • *n* jet, ray
**raïm** • *n* bunch, grape
**rajada** • *n* ray
**rajola** • *n* tile
**ranci** • *adj* rank
**rang** • *n* range, rank
**rànquing** • *n* ranking
**ranxo** • *n* ranch
**raó** • *n* reason
**raona|r** • *v* reason **~ble** • *adj* reasonable **~blement** • *adv* reasonably **~ment** • *n* reasoning
**raonat** • *adj* mature
**rapar** • *v* shave
**ràpid** • *adj* fast, prompt, rapid, speedy, swift • *n* rapid
**ràpidament** • *adv* fast, quickly, rapidly
**rapidesa** • *n* speed
**raptar** • *v* kidnap
**rapte** • *n* kidnap
**raquis** • *n* spine
**rar** • *adj* rare, weird
**rarament** • *adv* rarely, seldom
**rascar** • *v* scratch
**raspall** • *n* brush
**raspallar** • *n* brush
**raspallet** • *n* toothbrush
**rastre** • *n* track, trail
**rat** • *n* rat
**rata** • *n* rat

**ratapinyada** • *n* bat
**ratllat** • *adj* striped
**ratolí** • *n* mouse
**ratpenat** • *n* bat
**rave** • *n* radish
**ravenera** • *n* radish
**reacció** • *n* reaction
**reaci** • *adj* unwilling
**real** • *adj* actual **~ment** • *adv* really **~itat** • *n* reality
**realis|me** • *n* realism **~ta** • *adj* realistic
**realitzar** • *v* perform
**rebaixa** • *n* discount
**rebeca** • *n* cardigan
**rebel** • *n* rebel
**rebentar** • *v* burst
**rebombori** • *n* stir
**rebotir** • *v* swell
**rebre** • *v* get, receive
**rebuda** • *n* receipt
**rebuig** • *n* refuse, rejection
**rebut** • *n* receipt
**rebutjar** • *v* clear, dismiss, refuse, reject, turn down
**recambra** • *n* chamber
**recapitular** • *v* summarize
**recent** • *adj* recent **~ment** • *adv* recently
**recepció** • *n* receipt
**recepcionista** • *n* receptionist
**recepta** • *n* prescription, receipt, recipe
**receptiu** • *adj* receptive
**recer** • *n* shelter
**recerca** • *n* research
**reciclar** • *v* recycle
**reciclatge** • *n* recycling
**recitar** • *v* say
**recluta|r** • *v* recruit **~ment** • *n* recruitment

**recollir** • *v* collect, gather
**recolzar** • *v* support
**recomanació** • *n* recommendation
**recomanar** • *v* recommend
**recompensar** • *v* reward
**reconciliació** • *n* reconciliation
**reconeixement** • *n* acknowledgment • *v* credit
**reconèixer** • *v* recognize
**reconquerir** • *v* regain
**reconstruir** • *v* rebuild
**recopilació** • *n* compilation
**record** • *n* memory, reminder, souvenir
**recordar** • *v* recall, remember, remind
**recordatori** • *n* remembrance, reminder
**recorregut** • *n* course, run
**recórrer** • *v* course
**recta** • *n* line
**recular** • *v* back
**recuperació** • *n* recovery
**recuperar** • *v* retrieve
**redacció** • *n* essay
**redactar** • *v* word
**rèdit** • *n* revenue
**redreçar** • *v* straighten
**reducció** • *n* reduction
**reduir** • *v* lower, reduce, turn down
**redundància** • *n* redundancy
**redundant** • *adj* redundant
**reeixir** • *v* succeed
**reemplaça|r** • *v* fill in, replace ~ment • *n* replacement
**referència** • *n* reference
**referenciar** • *v* reference
**referèndum** • *n* referendum
**referir** • *v* refer

**reflectant** • *adj* reflective
**reflector** • *adj* reflective
**reflex** • *n* reflection
**reflexió** • *n* reflection
**reforç** • *n* reinforcement
**reforçament** • *n* reinforcement
**reforma** • *n* reform
**reformar** • *v* reform
**refredat** • *n* cold
**refrescant** • *adj* chilling
**refugi** • *n* harbor, refuge
**refugiada** • *n* refugee
**refugiar** • *v* harbor
**refugiat** • *n* refugee
**refús** • *n* rejection
**refusar** • *v* decline, refuse, reject, turn down
**regal** • *n* gift
**regalar** • *v* gift
**regar** • *v* water
**règim** • *n* regime
**regió** • *n* belt, region
**regional** • *adj* regional
**registre** • *n* observation
**regla** • *n* rule
**regle** • *n* ruler
**regnar** • *v* reign, rule
**regnat** • *n* reign
**regne** • *n* kingdom
**reguitzell** • *n* string
**regulador** • *n* governor, regulator
**regularment** • *adv* regularly
**rehabilitació** • *n* rehabilitation
**rei** • *n* king
**reial** • *adj* royal
**reialesa** • *n* royalty
**reina** • *n* queen
**reïna** • *n* pitch
**reixat** • *n* gate
**relació** • *n* relationship

R

relat • *n* story
relatiu • *adj* relative
relativament • *adv* relatively
relaxació • *n* relaxation
relaxa|r • *v* relax ~nt • *adj* relaxing
relaxat • *adj* easygoing, relaxed
religió • *n* religion
religiós • *adj* religious
relíquia • *n* relic
rellamp • *n* lightning
relleu • *n* relief
rellevància • *n* relevance
rellevant • *adj* relevant
relliscada • *n* slip
rellotge • *n* clock, watch
reluctància • *n* reluctance
remar • *v* row
remarca|r • *v* highlight ~ble • *adj* remarkable
remei • *n* remedy
remeiar • *v* remedy
rememorar • *v* remember
remenar • *v* scramble
remot • *adj* remote
remotament • *adv* remotely
remoure • *v* stir
remuneració • *n* wage
ren • *n* reindeer
renda • *n* income
rendible • *adj* profitable
rendi|r • *v* give up ~ment • *n* efficiency
renovació • *n* renewal
renova|r • *v* renew ~ble • *adj* renewable
rentadora • *n* washing machine
rentaplats • *n* dishwasher
rentar • *v* wash
reparar • *v* repair, sort

reparti|r • *v* deal, split ~ment • *n* cast
repetició • *n* repetition
repetidament • *adv* repeatedly
repetir • *v* repeat
replà • *n* landing
replegar • *v* collect
reporter • *n* reporter
repòs • *n* rest
reposar • *v* rest
reprendre • *v* resume
representació • *n* depiction, performance, representation
representar • *v* represent
reproducció • *n* reproduction
reproduir • *v* rehearse, reproduce
reprovable • *adj* guilty
repte • *n* challenge
republicà • *adj* conservative, republican, Republican
república • *n* republic
republicana • *n* republican
repugnant • *adj* revolting
repulsiu • *adj* repulsive
reputació • *n* name, reputation
requerir • *v* need
requisat • *adj* impressed
requisit • *n* requirement
rerefons • *n* background
rerequart • *n* quarterback
res • *pron* anything, nothing • *n* love, zero
rés • *n* prayer
resar • *v* pray
rescat • *n* rescue
rescatar • *v* rescue
resclosa • *n* lock
reservar • *v* book
reservat • *adj* reserved
residència • *n* residence

**residencial** • *adj* residential
**resident** • *n* inmate
**residir** • *v* reside
**residu** • *n* remainder, residue
**resistència** • *n* resistance
**resistent** • *adj* resistant
**resistir** • *v* resist
**resoldre** • *v* resolve, solve
**resolució** • *n* resolve
**resolut** • *adj* resolute
**respectar** • *v* fear, respect
**respecte** • *n* fear, respect
**respectiu** • *adj* respective
**respectivament** • *adv* respectively
**respectuós** • *adj* respectful
**respiració** • *n* breath
**respirar** • *v* breathe
**respondre** • *v* answer, respond
**responsabilitat** • *n* accountability, liability, responsibility
**responsable** • *adj* liable, responsible
**resposta** • *n* answer, feedback, reply, response
**ressaca** • *n* hangover
**ressaltar** • *v* highlight
**ressenya** • *n* notice
**ressort** • *n* spring
**resta** • *n* remainder, rest
**resta|r** • *v* remain, return, stay ~nt • *adj* remaining
**restaurant** • *n* restaurant
**restes** • *n* debris, remains
**restricció** • *n* constraint, restriction
**restrictiu** • *adj* restrictive
**restringir** • *v* restrict
**resultat** • *n* outcome, result, score

**resum** • *n* abstract, resume, summary
**resumir** • *v* summarize
**retallar** • *v* cut
**retard** • *n* delay
**retardat** • *n* moron
**retirar** • *v* withdraw
**retòrica** • *n* rhetoric
**retrat** • *n* portrait
**retret** • *adj* awkward
**retribució** • *n* wage
**reunió** • *n* meeting
**reunir** • *v* collect, meet
**revelació** • *n* revelation
**revelar** • *v* disclose, reveal
**revenja** • *n* revenge
**reverència** • *n* bow
**reviscolar** • *v* revive
**revisió** • *n* revision
**revista** • *n* magazine
**revolt** • *n* curve
**revolució** • *n* revolution
**revolucionari** • *adj* revolutionary
**rialla** • *n* laughter
**riba** • *n* bank, riverside, shore
**ribatge** • *n* riverside
**ribera** • *n* riverside
**riberenc** • *adj* riverside
**ribot** • *n* plane
**ric** • *adj* rich, wealthy
**rictus** • *n* face
**ridícul** • *adj* ridiculous
**ridículament** • *adv* ridiculously
**rierol** • *n* stream
**rifle** • *n* rifle
**rígid** • *adj* stiff
**rima** • *n* rhyme
**rimar** • *v* rhyme
**ring** • *n* ring
**rinoceront** • *n* rhinoceros

R

**riquesa** • *n* wealth
**risc** • *n* hazard, risk
**riscós** • *adj* risky
**ritme** • *n* pace, rhythm
**rítmic** • *adj* rhythmic
**ritual** • *adj* ritual
**riu** • *n* current, river
**riure** • *n* laugh, laughter
**rival** • *n* rival ~**itat** • *n* rivalry
**roba** • *n* clothes, clothing
**robar** • *v* rob, steal
**robatori** • *n* steal
**robí** • *n* ruby
**robot** • *n* robot
**robust** • *adj* rude, sturdy
**roc** • *n* rock
**roca** • *n* rock, stone
**rock** • *n* rock
**roda** • *n* stem, wheel
**rodalies** • *n* suburb
**rodamón** • *n* wanderer
**rodanxa** • *n* ring
**rodar** • *v* wheel
**rodejar** • *v* surround
**rodó** • *adj* round
**roí** • *adj* evil
**roig** • *adj* red
**roja** • *n* red
**rom** • *adj* blunt
**Roma** • *n* Rome
**romà** • *adj* Latin, Roman
**Romà** • *n* Roman
**romana** • *adj* Roman
**romandre** • *v* linger
**romanent** • *adj* remaining
**romanès** • *adj* Romanian
**romanesa** • *adj* Romanian
**romaní** • *n* rosemary
**Romania** • *n* Romania
**romàntic** • *adj* romantic
**romer** • *n* rosemary

**ronc** • *adj* husky
**roncar** • *v* purr
**ronda** • *n* round
**rondinaire** • *adj* grumpy
**ronronejar** • *v* purr
**ronyó** • *n* kidney
**ros** • *n* blond
**rosa** • *adj* pink • *n* rose
**rosat** • *adj* rose
**rosegar** • *v* gnaw
**rosella** • *n* poppy
**roser** • *n* rose
**rossinyol** • *n* nightingale
**rost** • *adj* steep
**rostit** • *adj* roast, roasted
**rotonda** • *n* roundabout
**roure** • *n* oak
**rovell** • *n* rust, yolk
**rovellar** • *v* rust
**rovellat** • *adj* rusty
**ruc** • *n* donkey
**ruca** • *n* donkey
**rude** • *adj* rough, rude
**rugbi** • *n* rugby
**rugós** • *adj* uneven
**ruïna** • *n* ruin, wreck
**ruixar** • *v* sprinkle
**ruleta** • *n* roulette
**rumb** • *n* course
**rumiar** • *v* linger
**rumor** • *n* rumor
**ruptura** • *n* rupture
**rural** • *adj* rural
**rus** • *adj* Russian
**rusc** • *n* beehive
**russa** • *n* Russian
**Rússia** • *n* Russia
**ruta** • *n* course, path, route, run
**rutinari** • *adj* routine

R

sa • *adj* clean, sound
sabata • *n* shoe
sabatilla • *n* slipper, sneaker
saber • *v* know
sabó • *n* soap
sabor • *n* flavor, taste
saborós • *adj* delicious
sacerdot • *n* priest
sacrificar • *v* sacrifice
sacrifici • *n* sacrifice
sacseig • *n* shake
sacsejador • *n* shaker
safanòria • *n* carrot
safata • *n* tray
safir • *n* sapphire
safrà • *adj* saffron
safranera • *n* saffron
sageta • *n* arrow
sagna|r • *v* bleed ~nt • *adj*
 bloody
sagrada • *adj* holy
sagrat • *adj* holy, sacred
sal • *n* salt
sala • *n* room
salamandra • *n* salamander
salar • *v* salt
salari • *n* salary, wage
salat • *adj* salty
salivar • *v* drool
salmó • *n* salmon
salsitxa • *n* sausage
salt • *n* jump, leap
saltamartí • *n* grasshopper
saltar • *v* jump, leap
salts • *n* diving
salubre • *adj* healthy

saludar • *v* greet, wave
salut • *n* greeting, health
salv • *adj* safe
salvar • *v* save
salvatge • *adj* wild
samarreta • *n* T-shirt
Samoa • *n* Samoa
sandàlia • *n* sandal
sandvitx • *n* sandwich
sanefa • *n* border
sang • *n* blood
sanitat • *n* health
sant • *adj* holy • *n* saint
santa • *adj* holy • *n* saint
santedat • *n* sainthood
sapastre • *adj* clumsy
sarau • *n* party
sarcasme • *n* sarcasm
sarcàstic • *adj* sarcastic
sardina • *n* sardine
sargantana • *n* lizard
sastre • *n* tailor
sastressa • *n* tailor
sàtira • *n* satire
satisfacció • *n* satisfaction
satisfer • *v* satisfy
satisfet • *adj* happy, satisfied
Saturn • *n* Saturn
saüc • *n* elder
savi • *adj* wise
saviesa • *n* wisdom
saxofon • *n* saxophone
saxòfon • *n* saxophone
sec • *adj* dry
séc • *n* fold
seca • *n* drought, mint
secada • *n* drought
secció • *n* section
secret • *adj* secret
secretament • *adv* secretly
secretisme • *n* secrecy

**sector** ● *n* sector
**secular** ● *adj* secular
**secundari** ● *adj* secondary
**secundària** ● *adj* secondary
**seda** ● *n* silk
**sedós** ● *adj* silky
**segar** ● *v* harvest, mow
**segell** ● *n* bull, seal, stamp
**segellar** ● *v* seal, stamp
**segle** ● *n* century
**segon** ● *adj* latter, second ● *n* minute
**segona** ● *n* accompaniment, second
**segons** ● *prep* according to, per
**segrest** ● *n* kidnap
**segrestar** ● *v* kidnap
**següent** ● *adj* following, next
**seguici** ● *n* household
**seguidor** ● *n* follower
**seguir** ● *v* follow, keep, observe, succeed
**seguit** ● *n* string
**segur** ● *adj* safe, sure
**segurament** ● *adv* surely
**seguretat** ● *n* safety, security
**seient** ● *n* seat
**seixanta** ● *num* sixty
**selecció** ● *n* selection
**seleccionar** ● *v* select
**selectiu** ● *adj* selective
**selva** ● *n* forest
**semàfor** ● *n* traffic light
**semàntic** ● *adj* semantic
**semàntica** ● *n* semantics
**semblança** ● *n* resemblance, similarity
**sembla|r** ● *v* appear, look, resemble, seem **~nt** ● *adj* like, similar **~ntment** ● *adv* similarly
**sembrar** ● *v* sow

**semestre** ● *n* semester
**seminari** ● *n* workshop
**semirecta** ● *n* ray
**sempre** ● *adv* always
**sena|r** ● *adj* odd **~dor** ● *n* senator **~dora** ● *n* senator
**senat** ● *n* senate
**sencer** ● *adj* full
**sender** ● *n* path
**sendera** ● *n* path
**senderisme** ● *n* hiking
**Senegal** ● *n* Senegal
**senglar** ● *n* wild boar
**sensació** ● *n* feeling, sense
**sensacional** ● *adj* sensational
**sensacionalista** ● *adj* sensationalist
**sensat** ● *adj* sensible
**sense** ● *prep* without
**sensellar** ● *adj* homeless
**sensesostre** ● *adj* homeless
**sensibilitat** ● *n* sensitivity
**sentència** ● *n* sentence
**sentenciar** ● *v* award, sentence
**sentimental** ● *adj* sentimental
**senti|r** ● *v* hear, read, sense **~ment** ● *n* feeling
**sentit** ● *n* meaning, sense
**seny** ● *n* head, intelligence, judgment
**senyal** ● *n* sign, signal
**senyor** ● *n* lord
**senyora** ● *n* lady
**senyorejar** ● *v* lord
**senzill** ● *adj* plain, simple
**senzillament** ● *adv* simply
**separació** ● *n* separation
**separar** ● *v* separate, shed, split
**separat** ● *adj* divorced, separate
**septentrió** ● *n* north

septentrional • *adj* northern •
  *n* northerner
sèptim • *adj* seventh
sèptima • *n* seventh
sepulcre • *n* grave
seqüència • *n* sequence
seqüencial • *adj* sequential
sequera • *n* drought
ser • *v* be, get
serbi • *adj* Serbian
sèrbia • *n* Serbian
Sèrbia • *n* Serbia
serè • *adj* serene
sèrie • *n* series
serietat • *n* seriousness
seriós • *adj* earnest, grave,
  serious
seriosament • *adv* seriously
serp • *n* snake
serpent • *n* snake
serra • *n* ridge, saw
serralada • *n* range, ridge
serrar • *v* saw, squeeze
serrell • *n* bang
servei • *n* duty, serve, service,
  toilet
servici • *n* toilet
servir • *v* serve, service
sessió • *n* session
set • *n* set, seven, thirst
setanta • *num* seventy
setè • *adj* seventh
setembre • *n* September
setmana • *n* week
setmanal • *adj* weekly ~ment •
  *adv* weekly
setze • *num* sixteen
seu • *n* base, headquarters,
  seat, see, venue • *det* her, his,
  its
seure • *v* sit

seva • *det* her
sever • *adj* harsh, stern
severa • *adj* harsh ~ment • *adv*
  severely
sexar • *v* sex
sexe • *n* gender, sex
sext • *adj* sixth
sexta • *n* sixth
sexual • *adj* sexual ~ment • *adv*
  sexually
Seychelles • *n* Seychelles
si • *n* heart • *interj* hello • *conj*
  if
sí • *part* yeah, yes
sida • *n* AIDS
SIDA • *n* AIDS
sidra • *n* cider
signar • *v* ink
signatura • *n* signature
significar • *v* mean
significat • *n* meaning, sense,
  significance
significatiu • *adj* meaningful,
  significant
significativament • *adv*
  significantly
silenci • *n* silence
silenciós • *adj* quiet
silenciosament • *adv* quietly,
  silently
símbol • *n* symbol
simbòlic • *adj* symbolic
simbolisme • *n* symbolism
simetria • *n* symmetry
simètric • *adj* symmetrical
similar • *adj* similar
similitud • *n* similarity
simpatia • *n* sympathy
simpàtic • *adj* sympathetic

S

**simple** • *adj* plain, simple, single
~**ment** • *adv* just, merely,
simply
**simplicitat** • *n* simplicity
**simplificació** • *n* simplification
**simplificar** • *v* simplify
**símptoma** • *n* symptom
**simptomàtic** • *adj* symptomatic
**simulació** • *n* simulation
**simular** • *v* simulate
**simultani** • *adj* simultaneous
**simultàniament** • *adv*
simultaneously
**sina** • *n* breast
**sinagoga** • *n* synagogue
**sincer** • *adj* honest, sincere ~**itat**
• *n* sincerity
**sincerament** • *adv* sincerely
**síndria** • *n* watermelon
**sindriera** • *n* watermelon
**síndrome** • *n* syndrome
**singalès** • *adj* Sri Lankan
**Singapur** • *n* Singapore
**single** • *n* single
**sintagma** • *n* phrase
**síntesi** • *n* synthesis
**sirí** • *adj* Syrian
**siria** • *n* Syrian
**Síria** • *n* Syria
**siriana** • *n* Syrian
**sis** • *n* six
**sisè** • *adj* sixth
**sisena** • *num* six
**sisme** • *n* earthquake
**sistema** • *n* system
**sistemàtic** • *adj* systematic
**situació** • *n* lie
**situat** • *adj* situated
**so** • *n* sound
**soberg** • *adj* superb
**sobirà** • *adj* sovereign

**sobirania** • *n* sovereignty
**sobre** • *prep* about, on, toward
• *n* envelope
**sobrenatural** • *adj* supernatural
**sobrer** • *adj* remaining
**sobresalt** • *n* jump
**sobresaltar** • *v* jump
**sobresortint** • *adj* outstanding
**sobretaula** • *n* desktop
**sobretot** • *phr* above all • *adv*
especially, mostly
**sobreviure** • *v* survive
**sobtadament** • *adv* suddenly
**sobtat** • *adj* sudden
**sociable** • *adj* sociable
**social** • *adj* social ~**ment** • *adv*
socially
**socialis|me** • *n* socialism ~**ta** •
*adj* socialist
**societat** • *n* society
**socorrista** • *n* lifeguard
**socors** • *interj* help
**sodi** • *n* sodium
**sofà** • *n* couch, sofa
**sofisticat** • *adj* sophisticated
**sofrir** • *v* suffer
**sogra** • *n* mother-in-law
**sogre** • *n* father-in-law
**soia** • *n* soy
**soja** • *n* soy
**sol** • *adj* alone, neat, sole • *n*
sun
**sòl** • *n* earth, floor, ground, soil
**sola** • *n* sole ~**ment** • *adv* only
**sola|r** • *n* plot • *adj* solar
~**ment** • *adv* only
**soldat** • *n* soldier
**soldats** • *n* troop
**solemne** • *adj* formal
**sòlid** • *adj* solid, sound
**solidaritat** • *n* solidarity

**solitari** • *adj* lonely • *n* patience
**sols** • *adv* just, only
**solter** • *adj* sole
**solució** • *n* solution
**solucionar** • *v* resolve, solve
**somali** • *adj* Somali
**Somàlia** • *n* Somalia
**somera** • *n* donkey
**somiar** • *v* dream
**somni** • *n* dream
**somnolent** • *adj* sleepy
**somrient** • *adj* smiling
**somrís** • *n* smile
**somriure** • *n* smile
**son** • *n* sleep
**sonar** • *v* sound
**sonor** • *n* voice
**sonso** • *adj* lame
**sopa** • *n* soup
**sopar** • *v* dine • *n* dinner
**sor** • *n* sister
**sord** • *adj* deaf
**sorgir** • *v* emerge
**soroll** • *n* noise
**sorollós** • *adj* boisterous, loud, noisy
**sorollosament** • *adv* loudly
**sorprendre** • *v* surprise
**sorprenent** • *adj* astonishing, surprising ~ment • *adv* surprisingly
**sorpresa** • *n* astonishment, surprise
**sorra** • *n* sand
**sorrenc** • *adj* sandy
**sorrut** • *adj* surly
**sort** • *n* luck
**sortida** • *n* exit, outlet
**sortint** • *adj* outgoing
**sortir** • *v* appear, date, exit, go out, leave, log out • *adj* quit

**soscavar** • *v* undermine
**sospir** • *n* sigh
**sospirar** • *v* sigh
**sospita** • *n* suspicion
**sospitar** • *v* suspect
**sospitós** • *adj* suspect, suspicious
**sostenibilitat** • *n* sustainability
**sostenible** • *adj* sustainable
**sostenidors** • *n* bra
**sostenir** • *v* hold, support, sustain
**sostre** • *n* ceiling, roof
**sot** • *n* pit
**sota** • *adv* below, beneath, under
**soterrani** • *n* basement
**sotmetre** • *v* subject, submit
**sotrac** • *n* bump
**sou** • *n* salary, wage
**soviet** • *n* Soviet
**soviètic** • *adj* Soviet
**sovint** • *adv* often
**staff** • *n* staff
**suar** • *v* sweat
**suau** • *adj* mild, soft ~ment • *adv* gently, smoothly, softly
**súbdit** • *n* subject
**subhasta** • *n* auction
**subhastar** • *v* auction
**subjacent** • *adj* underlying
**subjecte** • *adj* liable, subject
**subjectiu** • *adj* subjective
**subjectivament** • *adv* subjectively
**submergir** • *v* drown, plunge
**subministrar** • *v* supply
**submissió** • *n* submission
**subnormal** • *n* moron
**subratllar** • *v* highlight
**subscriptor** • *n* subscriber

subscriptora • n subscriber
subsegüent • adj subsequent
subseqüentment • adv
  subsequently
subsidi • n subsidy
substància • n substance
substantiu • n noun
substituir • v substitute
substitut • n replacement,
  substitute
subterrani • adj underground
subtil • adj subtle
subtilesa • n subtlety
subtítol • n subtitle
subtítols • n subtitle
suburbà • adj suburban
suburbi • n suburb
subvenció • n subsidy
suc • n juice
sucar • v dip
succeir • v happen, succeed
succés • n success
successiu • adj successive
succint • adj succinct
sucós • adj juicy
sucre • n sugar
sucursal • n branch
sud • n south
Sudan • n Sudan
sudanès • adj Sudanese
suec • adj Swedish
Suècia • n Sweden
suèter • n sweater
suficient • det enough • adj
  sufficient ~ment • adv
  enough, sufficiently
sufix • n suffix
suggeri|r • v suggest ~ment •
  n suggestion
suggestió • n suggestion
suïcida • n suicide

suïcidi • n suicide
suid • n hog
suís • adj Swiss
suïssa • adj Swiss
Suïssa • n Switzerland
suma • n sum, total
sumar • v add, number
sumari • n resume, summary
suor • n sweat
superar • v overwhelm
superàvit • n surplus
superficial • adj shallow,
  superficial ~ment • adv
  superficially ~itat • n
  superficiality
superfície • n surface
superior • adj superior, upper
  ~itat • n superiority
supermercat • n supermarket
supervisar • v supervise
supervisió • n oversight
supervisor • n supervisor
supervivència • n survival
supervivent • n survivor
suplantar • v displace
suplementar • v supplement
súplica • n plea
suplicar • v beg
suportar • v bear, stand,
  undergo
suposadament • adv
  supposedly
suposar • v guess, suppose
suposat • adj supposed
suprem • adj supreme
supremacia • n supremacy
suprimir • v abolish
surf • n surfing
Surinam • n Suriname
suro • n cork
suspicaç • adj suspicious

**Swazilàndia** • *n* Swaziland

**tabac** • *n* tobacco
**tabloide** • *n* tabloid
**tac** • *n* cue
**taca** • *n* spot, stain
**tacany** • *n* hog
**tacar** • *v* mark
**tacte** • *n* tact
**tàctic** • *adj* tactical
**tàctica** • *n* tactic
**Tadjikistan** • *n* Tajikistan
**tafaner** • *n* gossip
**tai** • *n* Thai
**tailandès** • *adj* Thai
**tailandesa** • *n* Thai
**Tailàndia** • *n* Thailand
**Taiwan** • *n* Taiwan
**taiwanès** • *adj* Taiwanese
**taiwanesa** • *n* Taiwanese
**tal** • *det* such
**talent** • *n* talent
**talentós** • *adj* talented
**tall** • *n* stem
**tallanassos** • *n* dragonfly
**tallar** • *v* carve, cut, shred
**tallat** • *adj* light, off
**taller** • *n* workshop
**taló** • *n* heel
**taloja** • *n* float
**talonador** • *n* hooker
**talp** • *n* mole
**també** • *adv* also, too
**tambor** • *n* drum

**tamboret** • *n* stool
**tamborinejar** • *v* drum
**tampoc** • *adv* either
**tan** • *adv* so
**tanc** • *n* tank
**tanca** • *n* fence
**tancar** • *v* close, commit, turn off
**tancat** • *adj* acute, closed, off
**tanmateix** • *conj* albeit, yet • *adv* however, nevertheless
**Tanzània** • *n* Tanzania
**tap** • *n* cork, tap
**tapa** • *n* cover, lid
**tàpera** • *n* caper
**taperera** • *n* caper
**taquilla** • *n* box office, gate
**tarannà** • *n* character
**taràntula** • *n* tarantula
**tard** • *adj* late
**tarda** • *n* afternoon, evening
**tardor** • *n* autumn
**targeta** • *n* card
**tarifa** • *n* fare
**tarima** • *n* platform
**taronger** • *n* orange
**taronja** • *n* orange
**tartana** • *n* bomb
**tasca** • *n* task
**tassa** • *n* cup
**tast** • *n* sample, taste
**tastar** • *v* taste, try
**tatuar** • *v* ink
**taula** • *n* table
**taulell** • *n* counter
**tauler** • *n* board
**tauró** • *n* shark
**taverna** • *n* pub
**taxa** • *n* duty, tax
**taxi** • *n* taxi
**taxista** • *n* taxi driver**

S
T

te • *n* tea
teatral • *adj* theatrical
teatre • *n* simulation, theater
tecla • *n* key
teclat • *n* keyboard
teclejar • *v* keyboard, type
tècnic • *adj* technical • *n* technician
tècnica • *n* technique ~ment • *adv* technically
tecnologia • *n* technology
tecnològic • *adj* technological
teia • *n* torch
teixidor • *n* dragonfly
teixir • *v* weave
teixit • *n* tissue
tela • *n* canvas, cloth, fabric
telèfon • *n* telephone
telefonada • *n* call
telefonar • *v* call, phone, telephone
telenotícies • *n* news
teler • *n* loom
telescopi • *n* telescope
televisió • *n* television
televisor • *n* television
teló • *n* curtain
tema • *n* thread
témer • *v* dread, fear
temerari • *adj* daredevil
temor • *n* fear
temperatura • *n* temperature
tempesta • *n* storm
tempestat • *n* storm
tempestuós • *adj* stormy
temple • *n* temple
temporada • *n* season
temporal • *n* storm • *adj* temporary ~ment • *adv* temporarily
temps • *n* tense, time, weather

temptar • *v* tempt
temptativa • *n* attempt, go
tenda • *n* shop, tent
tendència • *n* tendency
tendenciós • *adj* biased
tendir • *v* tend
tendre • *adj* tender
tenebres • *n* darkness
tenir • *v* be, have
tenista • *n* tennis player
tennis • *n* tennis
tennista • *n* tennis player
tens • *adj* tense
tensió • *n* stress
tènue • *adj* faint
teologia • *n* theology
teològic • *adj* theological
teoria • *n* theory
teòric • *adj* theoretical
terapeuta • *n* therapist
terapèutic • *adj* therapeutic
teràpia • *n* therapy
tercer • *adj* third
tercera • *n* third
tergiversar • *v* distort
terme • *n* term
terminació • *n* termination
terminal • *n* shell, terminal
terminar • *v* finish
terminologia • *n* terminology
terna • *n* triple
ternari • *adj* triple
terra • *n* deck, dirt, earth, floor, ground, land, world
terratrèmol • *n* earthquake
terreny • *n* field, land, plot, terrain
terrible • *adv* terrible ~ment • *adv* terribly
terrissa • *n* pottery
territori • *n* territory

**territorial** • *adj* territorial
**terror** • *n* horror, terror
**terroris|me** • *n* terrorism **~ta** • *adj* terrorist
**tesar** • *v* tense
**tesaurus** • *n* thesaurus
**tesi** • *n* thesis
**tesor** • *n* treasure
**test** • *n* test
**testa** • *n* head **~ment** • *n* will
**testificar** • *v* witness
**testimoni** • *n* witness
**testimoniatge** • *n* witness
**teta** • *n* breast
**teula** • *n* tile
**teulada** • *n* roof
**teular** • *v* tile
**texans** • *n* jeans
**text** • *n* text
**textura** • *n* texture
**thai** • *n* Thai
**tia** • *n* aunt
**tifa** • *n* shit
**tigre** • *n* tiger
**timbre** • *n* doorbell
**tímid** • *adj* timid
**tindre** • *v* be
**tinta** • *n* ink
**tintar** • *v* ink
**tio** • *n* dude, uncle
**tip** • *adj* full
**típic** • *adj* typical
**típicament** • *adv* typically
**tipografia** • *n* typography
**tipus** • *n* kind, sort, type
**tira|r** • *v* loose, pull, throw **~dor** • *n* handle
**tiro** • *n* draft
**tiroteig** • *n* shooting
**tisores** • *n* scissors
**titlla** • *n* accent

**títol** • *n* degree, diploma, title
**titubejar** • *v* hesitate
**to** • *n* tone
**tobogan** • *n* slide
**tocar** • *v* call, play, touch
**toga** • *n* robe
**Togo** • *n* Togo
**toix** • *adj* stupid
**tolerància** • *n* tolerance
**tolera|r** • *v* tolerate **~nt** • *adj* tolerant
**toll** • *n* pool
**tomaquera** • *n* tomato
**tomàquet** • *n* tomato
**tonada** • *n* tune
**tondosar** • *v* shear
**tondre** • *v* shear
**Tonga** • *n* Tonga
**tonyina** • *n* tuna
**Tòquio** • *n* Tokyo
**tòrax** • *n* chest
**torcaboques** • *n* napkin
**torn** • *n* go, turn
**tornar** • *v* return
**tornavís** • *n* screwdriver
**torneig** • *n* tournament
**toro** • *n* bull
**torrada** • *n* toast
**torradora** • *n* toaster
**torrar** • *v* toast
**torre** • *n* tower
**tort** • *adj* bent, crooked, twisted
**tortuga** • *n* turtle
**tortuós** • *adj* crooked
**tortura** • *n* torture
**torturar** • *v* torture
**torxa** • *n* link, torch
**tos** • *n* cough
**tosc** • *adj* rough
**tossar** • *v* butt

**tossir** • *v* cough

**tot** • *det* all • *n* whole • *pron* anything, everything • *adj* whole

**tota** • *det* all

**total** • *adj* full • *n* total ~**ment** • *adv* altogether, completely, entirely, quite, totally ~**itat** • *n* whole

**totalitzar** • *v* total

**totes** • *det* all

**tothom** • *pron* anyone, everybody, everyone

**tots** • *det* all

**tou** • *n* mountain • *adj* soft

**tovalló** • *n* napkin

**tovallola** • *n* towel

**tòxic** • *adj* poisonous, toxic

**traça** • *n* track

**traçada** • *n* plot

**traçar** • *v* plot, trace

**tracta|r** • *v* deal, treat ~**ble** • *adj* agreeable ~**ment** • *n* treatment

**tracte** • *n* deal

**tradició** • *n* tradition

**tradicional** • *adj* traditional ~**ment** • *adv* traditionally

**traducció** • *n* translation

**traductor** • *n* translator

**traductora** • *n* translator

**traduir** • *v* render, translate

**tràfic** • *n* traffic

**tragèdia** • *n* tragedy

**tràgic** • *adj* tragic

**trair** • *v* betray

**trajectòria** • *n* course, path

**trama** • *n* plot

**trametre** • *v* send

**trampejar** • *v* cheat

**trampós** • *n* cheat

**tranqui** • *adj* cool

**tranquil** • *adj* easygoing, quiet, tranquil

**transcripció** • *n* transcription

**transferència** • *n* commit

**transformació** • *n* conversion, transformation

**transformar** • *v* transform

**transició** • *n* transition

**trànsit** • *n* transit

**transitar** • *v* travel

**translúcid** • *adj* translucent

**transmetre** • *v* broadcast

**transparència** • *n* transparency

**transparent** • *adj* transparent

**transport** • *n* transport

**transportar** • *v* transport

**trapella** • *adj* naughty

**trasbalsat** • *adj* upset

**traslladar** • *v* move

**trastorn** • *n* disorder, upset

**trastornar** • *v* upset

**traumàtic** • *adj* traumatic

**traveta** • *n* trip

**treball** • *n* job, work

**treballa|r** • *v* work ~**dor** • *n* worker ~**dora** • *n* worker

**tremolós** • *adj* shaky

**tren** • *n* train

**trencaclosques** • *n* puzzle

**trenca|r** • *v* break ~**ble** • *adj* breakable

**trencat** • *adj* broken

**trenta** • *num* thirty

**trepant** • *n* drill

**trepitjada** • *n* tread

**trepitjar** • *v* tread

**tres** • *n* three

**tresc** • *n* trekking

**tresor** • *n* treasure

**tret** • *n* feature, shot, trait

**tretze** • *num* thirteen
**treure** • *v* remove
**trèvol** • *n* club
**tria** • *n* choice
**triangle** • *n* triangle
**triar** • *v* choose
**tribal** • *adj* tribal
**tribu** • *n* tribe
**tribunal** • *n* court
**trilió** • *num* trillion
**trilogia** • *n* trilogy
**trinitat** • *n* trinity
**trinxar** • *v* shred
**trio** • *n* trinity
**triomf** • *n* triumph
**triple** • *adj* triple
**triplicar** • *v* triple
**tripulació** • *n* crew
**tripulant** • *n* crew
**trist** • *adj* miserable, sad
**trista** • *adj* sad ~ment • *adv* sadly
**tristesa** • *n* sadness
**triturar** • *v* grind, shred
**tro** • *n* thunder
**trobada** • *n* encounter, meeting
**trobar** • *v* find
**trocejar** • *v* shred
**trofeu** • *n* award, trophy
**trombó** • *n* trombone
**trompa** • *n* trunk
**trompeta** • *n* trumpet
**tronar** • *v* thunder
**tronc** • *n* trunk
**tronera** • *n* pocket
**tropa** • *n* troop
**tros** • *n* piece
**truc** • *n* cheat
**trucada** • *n* call
**trucar** • *v* call, phone, ring, telephone

**truita** • *n* omelette, trout
**truja** • *n* sow
**tsunami** • *n* tsunami
**tu** • *pron* you
**tub** • *n* pipe, tube
**tumor** • *n* tumor
**túnel** • *n* nutmeg
**tunisià** • *adj* Tunisian
**Tunísia** • *n* Tunisia
**tunisiana** • *n* Tunisian
**turc** • *adj* Turkish
**turis|me** • *n* tourism ~ta • *n* tourist
**Turkmenistan** • *n* Turkmenistan
**turmell** • *n* ankle
**turó** • *n* hill
**Turquia** • *n* Turkey
**tustar** • *v* knock
**tutor** • *n* guardian
**TV** • *n* TV
**Txad** • *n* Chad
**txec** • *adj* Czech
**txeca** • *n* Czech
**Txèquia** • *n* Czech Republic

# U

**u** • *adj* one • *pron* you
**ubicació** • *n* location
**Ucraïna** • *n* Ukraine
**ucraïnès** • *adj* Ukrainian
**ucraïnesa** • *adj* Ukrainian
**udol** • *n* howl
**udolar** • *v* bay, howl
**Uganda** • *n* Uganda
**ull** • *n* eye

**ullada** • *n* glance, look
**ulleres** • *n* circle, spectacles
**últimament** • *adv* recently
**ultimàtum** • *n* ultimatum
**ultramar** • *adj* overseas
**ultramarins** • *n* grocery
**ultratge** • *n* outrage
**un** • *num* an, one • *pron* one
**una** • *num* an
**unça** • *n* ounce
**ungla** • *n* fingernail, nail
**únic** • *adj* alone, one, only, unique
**únicament** • *adv* only
**unificació** • *n* unification
**unificar** • *v* unify
**uniforme** • *adj* level, uniform
**unió** • *n* join, union
**unir** • *v* unite
**unitat** • *n* unit, unity
**univers** • *n* universe ~itat • *n* university
**universitari** • *n* student
**Urà** • *n* Uranus
**urbà** • *adj* urban
**urgència** • *n* emergency, urgency
**urgent** • *adj* urgent ~ment • *adv* urgently
**urpa** • *n* claw
**Uruguai** • *n* Uruguay
**uruguaià** • *adj* Uruguayan
**uruguaiana** • *n* Uruguayan
**ús** • *n* use
**usar** • *v* use
**usual** • *adj* usual
**usuari** • *n* user
**úter** • *n* womb
**útil** • *adj* helpful, useful
**utilitat** • *adj* utility
**utilitzar** • *v* use

# V

**va** • *adj* windy
**vaca** • *n* cow
**vacances** • *n* holiday
**vaccí** • *n* vaccine
**vaccinar** • *v* vaccinate
**vacuna** • *n* vaccine
**vacunació** • *n* vaccination
**vacunar** • *v* vaccinate
**vaga** • *n* strike
**vagar** • *n* drift • *v* wander
**vagarejar** • *n* drift
**vagó** • *n* car, carriage
**vague** • *adj* vague
**vaixell** • *n* boat, ship, vessel
**vaixella** • *n* dish
**valdre** • *v* count
**valent** • *adj* brave, courageous
**vàlid** • *adj* valid
**validació** • *n* commit
**validesa** • *n* validity
**validitat** • *n* validity
**vall** • *n* valley
**valor** • *n* courage, value, worth
**valuós** • *adj* valuable
**vamba** • *n* sneaker
**vano** • *n* fan
**vapor** • *n* steam
**variable** • *adj* variable
**variació** • *n* variation
**varietat** • *n* breed, sort, variety
**varis** • *adj* various
**Varsòvia** • *n* Warsaw
**vas** • *n* glass
**vast** • *adj* vast
**vàter** • *n* toilet
**Vaticà** • *n* Vatican City

**vedat** ● *n* park
**vedell** ● *n* calf
**vedella** ● *n* beef
**vegada** ● *n* time
**vegetal** ● *adj* vegetable
**vehicle** ● *n* vehicle
**veí** ● *n* neighbour
**veixiga** ● *n* bladder
**vela** ● *n* sail
**vell** ● *adj* old
**veloç** ● *adj* fast, speedy **~ment**
　● *adv* fast
**velocitat** ● *n* speed
**vena** ● *n* vein
**vèncer** ● *v* defeat, mature, win
**venciment** ● *n* defeat
**venda** ● *n* sale
**vendre** ● *v* deal, sell
**veneçolà** ● *adj* Venezuelan
**veneçolana** ● *n* Venezuelan
**Veneçuela** ● *n* Venezuela
**venedor** ● *n* seller, vendor **~a** ●
　*n* vendor
**veneració** ● *n* worship
**venerar** ● *v* worship
**venir** ● *v* come
**venjança** ● *n* revenge
**vent** ● *n* wind
**ventall** ● *n* fan, range
**ventar** ● *v* fan
**ventilador** ● *n* fan
**ventós** ● *adj* windy
**ventre** ● *n* belly
**Venus** ● *n* Venus
**verb** ● *n* verb
**verbal** ● *adj* oral, verbal
**verd** ● *adj* blue, green
**verdaderament** ● *adv* fairly
**verdura** ● *n* vegetable
**veredicte** ● *n* award, judgment,
　verdict

**verga** ● *n* rod
**vergonya** ● *n* shame
**vergonyós** ● *adj* shy
**verí** ● *n* poison
**verificació** ● *n* verification
**verificar** ● *v* check
**verinós** ● *adj* poisonous, toxic
**veritable** ● *adj* true **~ment** ●
　*adv* truly
**veritat** ● *n* truth
**vermell** ● *adj* red
**vermellós** ● *adj* sandy
**vernís** ● *n* varnish
**verra** ● *n* sow
**vers** ● *prep* toward
**versat** ● *adj* proficient
**versàtil** ● *adj* versatile
**versatilitat** ● *n* versatility
**versió** ● *n* release, version
**vertical** ● *adj* vertical **~ment** ●
　*adv* vertically
**vertiginós** ● *adj* dizzy
**vespa** ● *n* wasp
**vesprada** ● *n* afternoon, night
**vespre** ● *n* evening, night
**vessar** ● *v* shed, spill
**vestir** ● *v* dress
**vestit** ● *n* dress, suit
**veta** ● *n* grain
**veterà** ● *n* veteran
**veterinari** ● *n* veterinarian
**vetllada** ● *n* night
**vetllar** ● *v* watch
**vetust** ● *adj* ancient
**veu** ● *n* voice
**veure** ● *v* see, view, witness
**vexar** ● *v* harass
**vi** ● *n* wine
**via** ● *prep* per ● *n* way
**viable** ● *adj* viable
**vianant** ● *n* pedestrian

V

viatge • *n* travel
viatger • *n* traveller
viatjar • *v* travel
víbria • *n* dragon
vici • *n* vice
víctima • *n* victim
victòria • *n* victory, win
victoriós • *adj* victorious
vida • *n* life
vidre • *n* glass
vidu • *n* widow, widower
Viena • *n* Vienna
Vietnam • *n* Vietnam
vietnamita • *adj* Vietnamese
vigent • *phr* in force
vigèsim • *adj* twentieth
vigilància • *n* surveillance
vigila|r • *v* watch ~nt • *adj*
   alert, vigilant
vil • *adj* base
vinagre • *n* vinegar
vinclar • *v* bow, link
vincle • *n* link
vinil • *n* vinyl
vint • *num* twenty
vintè • *adj* twentieth
vinya • *n* vineyard
vinyeta • *n* cartoon
viola • *n* viola
violació • *n* rape
viol|ar • *v* abuse, take ~ador •
   *n* rapist ~ent • *adj* violent
violència • *n* violence
violentament • *adv* violently
violí • *n* violin
violoncel • *n* cello
viril • *adj* manly
virtual • *adj* virtual ~ment • *adv*
   virtually
virtuós • *adj* virtuous
virtut • *n* virtue

virus • *n* virus
visat • *n* visa
visera • *n* peak
visibilitat • *n* visibility
visible • *adj* visible
visió • *n* vision
visita • *n* call, visit
visitar • *v* call, visit
visó • *n* mink
vista • *n* eyesight, view, vision
visual • *adj* visual
vital • *adj* vital ~itat • *n* vitality
vitamina • *n* vitamin
vitrina • *n* case
viu • *adj* alive, live, living
viure • *v* live
vivaç • *adj* lively, vivacious
vivenda • *n* housing
vivent • *adj* alive
vívid • *adj* vivid
vocabulari • *n* vocabulary
vocal • *adj* vocal
vol • *n* flight
vola|r • *v* fly ~dor • *adj* flying
   ~dora • *adj* flying ~nt • *n*
   steering wheel
volcà • *n* volcano
volcànic • *adj* volcanic
vòlei • *n* volleyball
voleibol • *n* volleyball
voler • *v* love, want
volta • *n* go, lap, round
voltar • *v* surround, wheel
voltor • *n* vulture
volum • *n* volume
voluntari • *adj* voluntary
voluntàriament • *adv*
   voluntarily
voluntat • *n* will
vomitar • *v* boot
vora • *n* border, edge, shore

**voral** • *n* shoulder
**vorejar** • *v* border
**vorera** • *n* shore, sidewalk
**vós** • *pron* you
**vosaltres** • *pron* you
**vostè** • *pron* you
**vostès** • *pron* you
**vot** • *n* voice, vote, vow
**votació** • *n* voting
**vota|r** • *v* cast, vote **~nt** • *n* voter
**vuit** • *n* eight
**vuitada** • *n* octave
**vuitanta** • *num* eighty
**vuitè** • *adj* eighth
**vuitena** • *num* eight
**vulgar** • *adj* base
**vulnerabilitat** • *n* vulnerability
**vulnerable** • *adj* vulnerable

**whisky** • *n* whiskey

**xafardejar** • *v* gossip
**xafarder** • *n* gossip
**xafarderia** • *n* gossip
**xai** • *n* lamb
**xampú** • *n* shampoo

**xantatge** • *n* blackmail
**xapa** • *n* badge
**xapar** • *v* plate
**xarop** • *n* syrup
**xarxa** • *n* Internet • *n* net, network, screen, web
**xat** • *n* chat
**xato** • *adj* flat
**xef** • *n* chef, cook
**xemeneia** • *n* chimney
**xenofòbia** • *n* xenophobia
**xerès** • *n* sherry
**xerrar** • *v* chat
**xic** • *n* boy
**xiclet** • *n* chewing gum
**xicot** • *n* boy, boyfriend
**xicota** • *n* girlfriend
**xifra** • *n* abstract, digit, figure, number, numeral
**Xile** • *n* Chile
**xilè** • *adj* Chilean
**xilena** • *n* Chilean
**xillar** • *v* call
**xilòfon** • *n* xylophone
**ximpanzé** • *n* chimpanzee
**ximple** • *adj* foolish, silly
**ximplet** • *adj* silly
**Xina** • *n* China
**xinès** • *adj* Chinese
**xinesa** • *n* Chinese
**xinesos** • *n* Chinese
**xinxa** • *n* bug
**Xipre** • *n* Cyprus
**xipriota** • *adj* Cypriot
**xiquet** • *n* boy
**xiqueta** • *n* girl
**xisclar** • *v* call, scream
**xiscle** • *n* call
**xiulada** • *n* whistle
**xiular** • *v* whistle
**xiulet** • *n* whistle

V
W
X

**xiulo** • *n* whistle
**xiuxiueig** • *n* whisper
**xiuxiuejar** • *v* whisper
**xoc** • *n* crash, shock
**xoca|r** • *v* hit, shock ~**nt** • *adj*
outrageous
**xocolata** • *adj* chocolate
**xocolatina** • *n* chocolate
**xoriguer** • *n* kestrel
**xuclar** • *v* suck
**xurma** • *n* mob
**xusma** • *n* mob
**xut** • *n* kick
**xutar** • *v* kick

**zambià** • *adj* Zambian
**zebra** • *n* zebra
**zel** • *n* zeal
**zero** • *n* love, zero
**Zimbabue** • *n* Zimbabwe
**zinc** • *n* zinc
**zombi** • *n* zombie
**zona** • *n* zone
**zoològic** • *n* zoo

X

Z

# Pronunciation

## Consonants

| IPA | Example | Equivalent |
|-----|---------|------------|
| b | bell | best |
| β | abans | a vest |
| d | drac | door |
| dz | tretze | pads |
| dʒ | mitjà | jeep |
| ð | cada | other |
| f | força | face |
| g | guant | get |
| ɣ | aigües | *like* get |
| k | cors | scan |
| l | laca | *American* look |
| ʎ | cella | billion |
| m | meu | mode |
| n | neu | need |
| ɲ | nyeu | onion |
| ŋ | sang | ring |
| p | por | span |
| r | ruc | *Scottish* rook |
| ɾ | mira | *American* ladder |
| s | set | sack |
| ʃ | caixa, Xíxona | fish |
| t | terra | stand |

| ts | potser | cats |
| tʃ | txec | cheap |
| v | hafni | of |
| z | zel | zebra |
| ʒ | joc, jo | rouge |

## Vowels

| IPA | Example | Equivalent |
|-----|---------|------------|
| a | sac | father |
| ɛ | set | pet |
| e | séc | face |
| ə | demà | alpha |
| i | sic | meet |
| ɔ | soc | off |
| o | sóc | story |
| u | suc | rule |

# Irregular English Verbs

| inf. | sp. | pp. | inf. | sp. | pp. |
|------|-----|-----|------|-----|-----|
| arise | arose | arisen | buy | bought | bought |
| awake | awoke | awoken | can | could | - |
| be | was | been | cast | cast | cast |
| bear | bore | borne | catch | caught | caught |
| beat | beat | beaten | choose | chose | chosen |
| become | became | become | cleave | cleft | cleft |
| beget | begot | begotten | come | came | come |
| begin | began | begun | cost | cost | cost |
| bend | bent | bent | creep | crept | crept |
| bet | bet | bet | crow | crowed | crew |
| bid | bade | bidden | cut | cut | cut |
| bide | bade | bided | deal | dealt | dealt |
| bind | bound | bound | dig | dug | dug |
| bite | bit | bitten | do | did | done |
| bleed | bled | bled | draw | drew | drawn |
| blow | blew | blown | dream | dreamt | dreamt |
| break | broke | broken | drink | drank | drunk |
| breed | bred | bred | drive | drove | driven |
| bring | brought | brought | dwell | dwelt | dwelt |
| build | built | built | eat | ate | eaten |
| burn | burnt | burnt | fall | fell | fallen |
| burst | burst | burst | feed | fed | fed |
| bust | bust | bust | feel | felt | felt |

| inf. | sp. | pp. | inf. | sp. | pp. |
|------|-----|-----|------|-----|-----|
| fight | fought | fought | mow | mowed | mown |
| find | found | found | pay | paid | paid |
| flee | fled | fled | pen | pent | pent |
| fling | flung | flung | plead | pled | pled |
| fly | flew | flown | prove | proved | proven |
| forbid | forbad | forbid | quit | quit | quit |
| forget | forgot | forgotten | read | read | read |
| forsake | forsook | forsaken | rid | rid | rid |
| freeze | froze | frozen | ride | rode | ridden |
| get | got | got | ring | rang | rung |
| give | gave | given | rise | rose | risen |
| go | went | gone | run | ran | run |
| grind | ground | ground | saw | sawed | sawn |
| grow | grew | grown | say | said | said |
| hang | hung | hung | see | saw | seen |
| have | had | had | seek | sought | sought |
| hear | heard | heard | sell | sold | sold |
| hide | hid | hidden | send | sent | sent |
| hit | hit | hit | set | set | set |
| hold | held | held | sew | sewed | sewn |
| hurt | hurt | hurt | shake | shook | shaken |
| keep | kept | kept | shall | should | – |
| kneel | knelt | knelt | shear | sheared | shorn |
| know | knew | known | shed | shed | shed |
| lay | laid | laid | shine | shone | shone |
| lead | led | led | shit | shit | shit |
| lean | leant | leant | shoe | shod | shod |
| leap | leapt | leapt | shoot | shot | shot |
| learn | learnt | learnt | show | showed | shown |
| leave | left | left | shred | shred | shred |
| lend | lent | lent | shrink | shrank | shrunk |
| let | let | let | shut | shut | shut |
| lie | lay | lain | sing | sang | sung |
| light | lit | lit | sink | sank | sunk |
| lose | lost | lost | sit | sat | sat |
| make | made | made | slay | slew | slain |
| may | might | – | sleep | slept | slept |
| mean | meant | meant | slide | slid | slid |
| meet | met | met | sling | slung | slung |
| melt | melted | molten | slink | slunk | slunk |

| inf. | sp. | pp. | inf. | sp. | pp. |
|------|-----|-----|------|-----|-----|
| slit | slit | slit | wed | wed | wed |
| smell | smelt | smelt | weep | wept | wept |
| smite | smote | smitten | wet | wet | wet |
| sow | sowed | sown | win | won | won |
| speak | spoke | spoken | wind | wound | wound |
| speed | sped | sped | wring | wrung | wrung |
| spell | spelt | spelt | write | wrote | written |
| spend | spent | spent | | | |
| spill | spilt | spilt | | | |
| spin | spun | spun | | | |
| spit | spat | spat | | | |
| split | split | split | | | |
| spoil | spoilt | spoilt | | | |
| spread | spread | spread | | | |
| spring | sprang | sprung | | | |
| stand | stood | stood | | | |
| steal | stole | stolen | | | |
| stick | stuck | stuck | | | |
| sting | stung | stung | | | |
| stink | stank | stunk | | | |
| stride | strode | stridden | | | |
| strike | struck | struck | | | |
| string | strung | strung | | | |
| strive | strove | striven | | | |
| swear | swore | sworn | | | |
| sweat | sweat | sweat | | | |
| sweep | swept | swept | | | |
| swell | swelled | swollen | | | |
| swim | swam | swum | | | |
| swing | swung | swung | | | |
| take | took | taken | | | |
| teach | taught | taught | | | |
| tear | tore | torn | | | |
| tell | told | told | | | |
| throw | threw | thrown | | | |
| thrust | thrust | thrust | | | |
| tread | trod | trodden | | | |
| wake | woke | woken | | | |
| wear | wore | worn | | | |
| weave | wove | woven | | | |